Bandits at Sea

Bandits at Sea

A Pirates Reader

EDITED BY

C. R. Pennell

New York University Press

NEW YORK AND LONDON

NEW YORK UNIVERSITY PRESS
New York and London

Library of Congress Cataloging-in-Publication Data
Bandits at sea : a pirates reader / edited by C. R. Pennell.
p. cm.
ISBN 0-8147-6678-1 (pbk. : alk. paper) —
ISBN 0-8147-6679-X (cloth : alk. paper)
1. Pirates. I. Pennell, C. R. II. Title.
G535 .B26 2001
910.4'5—dc21   00-012702

To Sarah and Sam

Contents

All illustrations appear as a group following p. 196

Acknowledgments

I would like to thank Wong Mun Wei for her help in proofreading some of the articles in this collection and for very many other things. I must also express my appreciation of the staff of the Inter-Library loans section of the Baillieu Library, University of Melbourne and in particular Mrs. Vija Pattison; without their help the task of checking some of the more obscure references would have been even more difficult than it was already. I am grateful to numerous students in my course on piracy at the University of Melbourne for making it quite clear which articles in the collection that was originally proposed should in fact be kept. David Starkey of the University of Hull provided a great many excellent suggestions. It was a pleasure to work with all the contributors; it is hard to imagine a more good-humored and helpful group of people. Niko Pfund of NYU Press was a very good motivator indeed. Finally I would like to thank my children, Sarah and Sam (in strict reverse alphabetic order), for their tolerance. Since I know they would like to have a book about pirates dedicated to them, this one is.

Bandits at Sea

Part I

Situating Piracy

Chapter 1

Introduction
Brought to Book: Reading about Pirates

C. R. Pennell

Not long ago, one of my children came home from her primary school with a library book about pirates. In it was a story about a Danish captain in the West Indies in the eighteenth century who raided ships under the pretense that he was a privateer equipped with letters of marque issued by the Danish king. The document was impressive to look at and no one could read Danish anyway. It eventually turned out that it was no more than a license to hunt wild pigs, and that the captain was not a privateer but a pirate.

I had not heard this story before and, hoping to find the source, I contacted a friend by e-mail, an expert on privateers. He replied:

> No, I haven't heard of the Danish letter of marque story. It is a pity that children's books focus on the irregularities of the privateering story—it's misleading. Children should, instead, be offered a detailed statistical analysis of privateers by port, by tonnage range, by number of guns carried, by prizes taken—I know someone who could supply Puffin with the text.

My daughter did not think much of this idea. But the point is a good one: the behavior of pirates is so dramatic in its content, apparently romantic in its action, and so photogenic in its possibilities that the temptation to ignore the one-two-three for the yo-ho-ho is very attractive. The flood of books on piracy and privateering is still flowing, mainly in the direction of *Treasure Island*, but some are a great deal better than others.

Treasure Island itself, first published in 1883, became the archetypical pirate story, and Long John Silver became the most notorious pirate hero. Stevenson's story may be what most English-speaking people think of when the subject of pirates is raised—and not just English speakers: it has been translated not only into all the major European languages but into many others too, Gujarati and Kordofanian, Vietnamese and Swahili among them. The Persian translation was published in 1986, some seven years after the Islamic revolution that brought Ayatollah Khomeini to power. Nevertheless, it is really quite an unusual pirate book. A great deal of pirate literature—and this is even more true of most pirate films—does not follow Stevenson's tradition, but guys it. From Barrie's Captain Hook through to the BBC's Captain Pugwash, fictional pirates have often been depicted as foolish, comic, and even incompetent. Or the stories have been retold as cliché-challenging accounts in which the pirates are small girls, or even grandmothers. The spoofs outnumber the spoofed.

But parody only works if the audience has an original to compare it with, and anyway Stevenson's book and its films have been much more popular than the many take-offs. It is, of course, remarkably well told, but it also provides a seemingly realistic and convincing account of pirates. It rings true, even if it is not. The one-legged cook was a common enough real-life figure, seamen did talk in a special and distinctive language, and there was considerable class conflict at sea. There was a real pirate named Israel Hands, too. Even some of the more exaggerated aspects of *Treasure Island* have some sort of historical ground. It may be that plank walking is hard to document, though that is in the nature of crime, but there is some evidence that it did happen, at least occasionally. Evidence for pirate cruelty abounds and is not particularly astonishing in the violent world of the seventeenth and eighteenth centuries.[1]

The cruelty of pirates is a common feature of many of the early factual or supposedly factual accounts of these criminals. Like the literature about other sorts of crimes, popular literature on piracy has a long history. It dates back to the books of Alexander Exquemelin, known as John Esquemeling in earlier English editions, and of Captain Johnson, sometimes identified as Daniel Defoe. The confusion of authorship symbolizes the importance of content over origin. The Dutch original of Exquemelin's *The Buccaneers of America, a True Account*, published in 1678, was translated first into German, then into Spanish, English, and French. Later, there were Italian and Russian versions. If the original book was occasionally tendentious (Exquemelin had no time for Harry Morgan), the translations were sometimes blatantly so, magnifying the role of one country's heroes over another's. Yet Exquemelin's book has been used over and over again as a sourcebook for writing about pirates. The English translation of 1684 has been reprinted many times, and has come to represent a sort of standard text of the work in English even though a more recent translation is far superior. Copyright has doubtless a lot to do with this.[2]

Captain Johnson's *General History of the Pirates*, which stands beside it as the other most important source on piracy, has an equally obscure origin. For many years it was believed that Daniel Defoe wrote it, and although that idea is now largely discredited, we are none the wiser about who Johnson was, nor about his purpose.[3] His text has been seen both as a diatribe against piracy and as a source for libertarians seeking heroes. Both Exquemelin's and Johnson's texts, for all their shortcomings as history, have provided so much of the evidence for studies of piracy that it is hard to shake ourselves free of their influence. In particular, Johnson's repeated descriptions of pirate self-government, of agreed rules freely arrived at, and of goods and dangers shared in common have made a powerful impression on those who want to see in the pirate life an example of primitive socialism and freedom. Just the same, his descriptions of careless pirate violence have fascinated and repelled readers.

There was, in reality, nothing attractive about pirate violence, except for sadists and voyeurs, and those who held pirates to be heroes skated quickly over this thin ice. Former pirates who were remaking themselves for a respectable audience and trying to join respectable society downplayed the violence of their peers. William Dampier, the only pirate known to have had his portrait painted in oils, used his autobiographical journal to portray himself as a heroic explorer and naturalist.[4]

Thus the common perception of seventeenth- and eighteenth-century pirates came to be rooted in a mixture of romanticization and (sometimes intentional) misrepresentation. By the time Barrie was writing, or Stevenson for that matter, the pirates were safely in the past and they could be seen as attractive figures. That is not possible or desirable with the pirates of our own time. They have not, of course, been romanticized. The reports of the International Maritime Bureau and of the International Maritime Organisation make it clear that while some pirates have been relatively limited in their use of violence, others have engaged in brutal behavior, and in the case of Thai pirates in the South China Sea, of mass rape and murder.[5] They are no one's heroes, except perhaps their own.

Academic historians are supposed to do more than merely restate published accounts, engage in polemics or romanticization, or pursue their own designs. Not all of them have consciously tried to do that, and no historian is exempt from hidden influences. Yet serious attempts to write about pirates from documentary and archival sources, and to examine piracy and privateering as political, social, and economic phenomena began around the beginning of the twentieth century. Stanley Lane-Poole's book, *The Barbary Corsairs*[6] appeared in 1890 and C. H. Haring's pioneering account, *The Buccaneers in the West Indies in the Seventeenth Century*, was published in 1910.[7]

Between the wars came encyclopaedia-like treatments such as those by Philip Gosse, *The History of Piracy* and *The Pirates Who's Who*.[8] Gosse straddled the difficult ground between scholarship and popular writing—his works of reference contained so few citations that details and ideas cannot be pursued[9]—and that line has been blurred ever since. A great deal of the writing that followed fell firmly on the popular side, much of it consisting of biographies of famous pirates and privateers: Morgan, and particularly Drake in English and Jean Bart in French. This was a rather nationalistic period: British authors wrote about English pirates and privateers, American authors concentrated on pirates and privateers who had operated out of what would become the United States, and French authors wrote about French privateers and the colonies of the French empire.

Attention was not entirely limited to the Western hemisphere. The North African corsairs received a good deal of attention, but largely from a European or, even more commonly an American, point of view. Of course, it has never been easy to write the pirates' side of the story, since they left very few records. The corsairing states *did* leave records, of course, but by and large European and American authors could not understand them because they were in Arabic, or worse still, in Ottoman Turkish. In any case, what interested European and American authors about North Africa was the fate of captives there, not the societies that captured them. Consequently American authors produced a good deal about the allegedly forgotten war with Tripoli in 1805, and British authors expounded on the fate of captives in Salé, on the Atlantic coast of Morocco and Algiers. They had a beguiling source in contemporary accounts of captivity that were (for obvious reasons) not very sympathetic toward North Africans.

After the Second World War, that perspective began to change. While European writers still relied on European documents they tried to use them to understand the North African perspective. In 1957 Sir Godfrey Fisher wrote a diplomatic history of British relations with Algiers, Tunis, and Tripoli. Although this still relied on British documents, it took more account of the North African states' objectives.[10] It was also rather dull, a plodding diplomatic and naval history. (One reason why David Hebb's much more recent book on English relations with Algiers and Salé is more readable is that it uses the British archives more imaginatively and refers to material based on indigenous sources.)[11] French scholarship, however, produced one of the most important books on the North African corsairs: Roger Coindreau's study of Salé in Morocco, published in 1948,[12] which used European sources with great care to describe the workings of this great corsairing center in its local context. He described how the corsairs were organized, how they attacked their victims, their ships, and their captains. Yet there is very little on the tumultuous events of seventeenth- and early eighteenth-century Morocco when the Salé corsairs were at their height. It would certainly have been hard for Coindreau to use local sources, because they skirt quickly round the subject of piracy. Salé became a very conservative and religious city once it had put its corsairing behind it, and its worthy chroniclers had no wish to raise memories of the less respectable aspects of their urban past.

During the 1970s, African and Asian nationalism inspired more historians in Europe and North America to seek a local voice to describe piracy. But many of them still had to rely on European sources because there was little alternative. Carl Trocki wrote about Malay sea raiding in the waters around nineteenth-century Singapore,[13] and James Warren wrote on the Sulu Sea around the Philippines. Both tried to give an "indigenous viewpoint."[14] Even in the case of the North African states where there is a large amount of archival material in Arabic and Turkish,[15] local sources were hardly used. Of the two best books on Algiers,[16] one did claim to use Turkish sources, but neither was footnoted, so it was hard to judge. The result was a mixed bag: Stephen Clissold's book, *The Barbary Slaves*, used European primary sources with some imagination[17] but Seton Dearden's book on the Qaramanli rulers of Libya was thoroughly Eurocentric in its approach. It was swiftly superseded by Kola Folayan's account of Tripoli under the last of the Qaramanli rulers. But being published in Nigeria, it was virtually unknown.[18]

Maltese archives were more plentiful and in 1970 Peter Earle made extensive use of them, and although he did not use North African sources, he did consult the secondary literature that had (most of it in French) and made the great advance of linking the two great enemy centers of corsairing into a single political, military, and (above all) economic system.[19] A few years later Clive Senior[20] took a similar approach that fitted river piracy on the Thames into a continuum that extended to the Caribbean buccaneers and English "renegades" in North Africa. Both Earle and Senior also amalgamated thematic description and analysis with a biographical approach to corsairs. Christopher Lloyd and Peter Kemp used the same methods in their synthesis of the history of the Caribbean pirates,[21] which appeared in 1960.

All these books represented an attempt to break away from straight biographies of pirates, an increasingly repetitive genre. Even the best of them, such as Dudley Pope's biography of Morgan,[22] did not stray far from the received wisdom and the published sources.[23] In 1981 Lloyd, writing alone, wrote an account of the English corsairs who operated out of North Africa.[24] By 1986 Robert Ritchie had brought the process full circle by using the career of the famous Captain Kidd as the starting point for a study of pirate society and the politics of privateering and suppression.[25] By now academic study of piracy was gaining a limited respectability. The British maritime historian John Bromley, who by the 1970s was in full tilt, wrote articles about privateering warfare and in particular about French corsairing,[26] and a conference on piracy was organized by the Commission Internationale d'Histoire Maritime whose papers were published in typescript in 1975.[27] Several themes were now emerging that would occupy historians of sea raiding over the next twenty years.

Pirate historians had already discovered economics. In 1953 Cyrus Kar-raker published *Piracy Was a Business* (in which he argued that pirates have their modern equivalent in racketeers)[28] and he was followed by a number of other economic historians of privateering and piracy. By the 1980s, privateer-ing economics was one of the main areas of attention. The leading exponents have been two British historians, Patrick Crowhurst who, like Bromley, has written extensively about French privateering[29] and David J. Starkey, who spe-cialized in privateering out of Devon ports.[30] An American historian, Carl Swanson, put the same economic emphasis into his analysis of colonial Amer-ican privateering,[31] and the Spanish historian Gonçal López Nadal wrote about Mallorcan corsairs in commercial terms.[32]

There was not much heroism, or heroics, to be found in economic analyses of piracy, but social and political history provided much more seductive mate-rial. In 1983 B. R. Burg published the provocatively entitled *Sodomy and the Pirate Tradition*,[33] which, not surprisingly, attracted a good deal of attention, not all of it complimentary. Burg was accused of projecting modern concepts backward in an anachronistic fashion. Nevertheless, the book went to a sec-ond edition, in which Burg was pleased to note that one reviewer had said that his book gave "a whole new meaning to the phrase 'Jolly Roger.'"[34] Around the same time, Marcus Rediker began to publish material on the social history of the Atlantic and Caribbean pirates.[35] He linked this to a radical political analysis, depicting piracy as part of the protest of workers against their condi-tions. Seamen, Rediker said, were "zealous abetters of liberty" whose "mili-tant resistance produced a major breakthrough in libertarian thought that would ultimately lead to revolution."[36] Pirates were part of this movement, exacting revenge on captains who mistreated their crews, and signaling their rebellion with their black flags depicting "King Death," a symbol that served many purposes. It was a defiance of danger, a threat to those they attacked, and a challenge to the respectable world with its respectable flags.[37]

The radical explanation of piracy was given added weight by one of the most prominent historians of the English Revolution, Christopher Hill, who linked the ideology of some of the Caribbean pirates with the radical ideolo-gies of the Ranters and other sectarians who had fled England for the West In-dies at the time of the Restoration:

> Former radicals had to adapt to a world in which their cause had been defeated, their ranks hopelessly thinned. The rough equality of pirate life may have been psychologically more congenial than the tensions and economic hazards of a slave-owning society, or the harsh discipline of a naval vessel.[38]

Hill went on to compare pirates with the social bandits described by Eric Hobs-bawm, only to reject a direct similarity and suggest that ideological pirates had more in common with the urban underworld where libertinist ideas found a hearing.

One case in particular, drawn from Johnson's *General History* and from trial records, seemed to confirm much of this socialist or libertarian scholarship. This was the exotic figure of Samuel Bellamy, the wreck of whose ship, the *Whydah*, has been found and is being excavated. Bellamy is famous, though, not for the contents of his wrecked ship, which throw considerable light on the everyday life of pirates, but for the rhetorically splendid rant with which Johnson credits him. Expressing his contempt for a merchant captain who refused to join his gang, Bellamy (according to Johnson) laid into Captain Beer with these words:

> damn ye, you are a sneaking Puppy, and so are all those who will submit to be governed by Laws which rich Men have made for their own Security, for the cowardly Whelps have not the courage otherwise to defend what they get by their Knavery; but damn ye altogether: damn them for a Pack of Crafty rascals, and you, who serve them, for a Parcel of hen-hearted Numskuls. They villify us, the Scoundrels do, when there is only this Difference, they Rob the Poor under the Cover of Law, forsooth, and we plunder the Rich under the Protection of our own Courage; had you not better make One of us, than sneak after the A———s of those Villains for Employment?
>
> Captain Beer told him that his Conscience would not allow him to break thro' the Laws of God and Man. You are a devilish Conscience Rascal d-n ye, reply'd Bellamy, I am a free Prince and I have as much Authority to make War on the whole World as he who has a hundred Sail of Ships at Sea, and an Army of 100,000 men in the Field; and this my Conscience tells me; but there is no arguing with such snivelling Puppies, who allow Superiors to kick them about the Deck at Pleasure; and pin their Faith upon a Pimp of a parson; a Squab, who neither practices not believes what he puts upon the chuckle-headed Fools he Preaches to.[39]

Here was an attractively radical voice, although it would be hard to imagine who had been able to record it, or had had time to do so at the time. Bellamy is a literary figure in Johnson, and while it would be wrong to deny the ideological content of some pirate thinking, both Hill and Marcus Rediker, who has great enthusiasm for it,[40] rather play down another of Hobsbawm's categories of bandits, the "avenger" as brute:

> bandits who not only practise terror and cruelty to an extent which cannot possibly be explained as mere backsliding, but whose terror actually forms part of their public image. They are heroes not in spite of the fear and horror their actions inspire, but in some ways because of them. They are not so much men who right wrongs, but avengers, and exerters of power; their appeal is not that of agents of justice, but of men who prove that even the poor and weak can be terrible.

These were the men Hobsbawm described as "public monsters."[41] This might almost be an echo of Johnson's epigraph for Edward Teach, Blackbeard:

> Here was an End of that courageous Brute, who might have pass'd in the World for a Heroe, had he been employ'd in a good Cause.[42]

That is not the epitaph of a freedom-loving Robin Hood.

Certainly some of these pirates are more difficult to portray as simple rebels against an unequal social order. Some were certainly violent sadists: Edward Low is one example. After he captured a ship, he sliced off its captain's ears and made him eat them, served with salt and pepper. Blackbeard is another. If Bellamy is the paradigm of the libertarian freedom-loving pirate, then Blackbeard is the archetype of the man of violence, an almost legendary drunk, the sort of man, Johnson says, who, laughing uproriously at the joke, fired a pistol into the knee of Israel Hands, his mate, and crippled him. And Teach's prostitution of his newly married wife to members of his crew is hard to explain in terms of primitive rebellion.

Yet the question still remains: are we to take these stories at face value or are we to see them as a sort of propaganda, either directed *at* the pirates, or serving their own ends: a victim might pause for thought before resisting a man with Teach's reputation. The origin of his nickname is obvious, but it was not just a physical feature, it was also a weapon of war. As Johnson describes it, his beard was

> black, which he suffered to grow of an extravagant length; as to Breadth, it came up to his Eyes; he was accustomed to twist it with Ribbons, in small Tails, after the Manner of our Ramilies Wiggs, and turn them about his Ears: In Time of Action, he wore a Sling over his Shoulders, with three Brace of Pistols, hanging in Holsters like Bandaliers; and stuck lighted Matches under his Hat, which appearing on either side of his Face, his Eyes naturally looking fierce and wild, made him altogether such a Figure that Imagination cannot form an idea of a Fury, to look more Frightful.[43]

Are we to accept as correct the explanation given by Woodes Rogers, a former pirate himself, who linked the extreme behavior of the bucanneers in Jamaica to their communal way of life?

> I must add concerning these Buccaneers that they live without Government; so that when they meet with Purchase, they immediately squandered it away, and when they got Mony and Liquor, they drank and gam'd till they spent it all; and during those Revels, there was no distinction between the Captain and the Crew: for the Officers having no Commission but what the Majority gave them, they were chang'd at every Caprice, which divided them, and occasion'd frequent Quarrels and Separations, so that they could do nothing considerable.[44]

Or was this special pleading? The drunkenness and the fecklessness are both part of the pirate image (and one that is given full rein in *Treasure Island*) and are the very things that respectable society found abhorrent and which romanticizers might find appealing. But then, early modern world seamen, pirates or not, were famous for their drunkenness and fecklessness. In any event it is always hard to disentangle disingenuousness from propaganda and either from historical reality.

At the root of these questions lay the basic historical problem of trying to understand a different society on its own terms, or at least on terms that were not those of the twentieth century; or, for that matter, those of developed Western societies.

In the 1980s and 1990s European-language authors also discovered Chinese pirates. People had written about Chinese piracy before, of course—notably Grace Fox's *British Admirals and Chinese Pirates*,[45] but they had focused on suppression, a European concern. Historians now turned to Chinese sources. Using Chinese materials, Ng Chin-Keong linked piracy with smuggling and rebellion in Amoy[46] in the late seventeenth and early eighteenth centuries. Dian Murray and Robert Antony in the United States worked on very similar themes in Chinese piracy a century or so later in time.[47]

But these new approaches were not used to deal with Mediterranean corsairs and Middle Eastern pirates. In the Gulf, Sultan al-Qasimi, the ruler of Sharjah, wrote about the allegations of piracy made by the British against his forebears, arguing that those allegations were really excuses to engage in imperialism.[48] He claimed that a piratical myth was made up in order to justify British hegemony in the Gulf, and the Qawasim inhabitants of Sharjah, whom the British called the main pirates in the region, did not in fact commit the crimes of which they were accused. Al-Qasimi based his work, originally a doctoral thesis at the University of Exeter, on documents from the Bombay archives of British India, copies of which he presented to Exeter University library.

It was not until the late 1990s that an important book on Gulf piracy, *The Blood Red Arab Flag* by Charles Davies, was published that made extensive use of local Arab historians and chroniclers as well as a more nuanced use of the papers at the India Office. Davies was not primarily concerned to acquit the Qawasim of the charge of piracy, although he does virtually do this by explaining that while they were not pirates, some of what they did was piracy. His aim was rather to situate Qasimi and other Gulf sea raiding in the context of regular warfare. This was directed not so much by Arabs against the British, as by supporters of the radical Islamic Wahhabi movement, the precursors of modern Saudi Arabia, against those they considered backsliding apostates. Since some of these apostates, particularly the Omanis, were commercial and political allies of the East India Company, the British tended to portray the Qawasim, sea-based allies of the Wahhabis, as pirates.[49] An author from the United Arab Emirates, Abd al-Wahhab Ahmad al-Rahman, in a book published around the same time took the argument a step further, suggesting that the sea raiding was a form of resistance to imperial pressure.

Although some work was done on Malta, much less was written on North Africa and Malta in the 1980s and 1990s, apart from Libya. There were some articles which extended the economic knowledge of corsairing,[50] and a good overview of politics of corsairing at Salé.[51] The most substantial work on Algiers was about the captives held there and the process of ransoming them[52] and was only really followed up in Spanish.[53] Sometimes these accounts were too oriented toward the mechanics, economics, and organization of piracy and corsairing, and the actual pirates themselves were relegated to the sidelines. However, publication or republication of the diaries of two European residents of Tripoli, Thomas Baker, the English consul, at the end of the seventeenth century and Miss Tully, the sister of the British consul, at the end of the eighteenth, shed some light on the corsairs that helped to remedy this lack.[54] Baker talks of the death of his "particular" friend "Cara Villy Rais . . . who died 4 dayes since of an Apoplexie, say some. But I am of ye opinion, a Surfeit (by taking too many drams of ye Bottle) did his business. And soe farewell to an honest, drunken fellow, both: to my own knowledge.[55] And he describes the arrival in Tripoli of a Mallorcan captain who was supposed to ransom a fellow countryman, but instead changed sides and became a Tripolitan corsair. As Baker put it, he "most infamously Renounced his Baptism, and turned Turk." Moreover, Baker reckoned he had always intended to do this. The value of such material is immense, because while Baker (and Miss Tully) doubtless labored under the misapprehensions and prejudices of their time, they were not consciously writing for effect in the way of a published author. Baker's references to the sometimes riotous goings on in Tripoli quite often bear a striking resemblance to the stories about Port Royal in Jamaica at the same time.

At the other end of the Mediterranean, Wendy Bracewell wrote a book on a topic of perennial interest, the uskoks of Senj,[56] maritime bandits of the Croatian (or Yugoslav) coast at the turn of the sixteenth and seventeenth centuries.[57] In an article that came out some years before her book, Bracewell had launched into the other big theme of the 1980s and 1990s: women pirates.[58] This was published in 1988 in a thoroughly obscure Yugoslavian literary journal, which accounts for its lack of notice. It raised themes such as the political attitudes behind depictions of pirate women, and the importance of women as part of an overall pirate and raiding economy that have dominated recent work on women pirates. Dian Murray had presented the same issues a few years earlier in an article on the Chinese woman pirate Cheng I Sao

("Madam Cheng"),[59] and she contributed a chapter on Cheng I Sao to a commercially successful collection edited by Jo Stanley in 1995.[60] Both Murray and Bracewell linked women pirates with the everyday role of women in coastal and raiding communities. The women organized raids and negotiated and went to sea because their communities lived on the sea and they were accustomed to it. Even in European, or at least in English, ships, women went to sea more frequently than was once acknowledged.[61]

Stanley hoped in her book to reverse the way in which women in general and women pirates in particular were "written out" of maritime history.[62] She had a specifically political intention and while she acknowledged the more general factors that Murray and Bracewell made plain, her collection in the end more closely resembled the old-fashioned work on pirate women. Because it had to focus on individuals, it was highly personalized and dealt with pirate queens like Artemisia, Lady Killigrew, and Alfhild the Dane. There was also a measured chapter by Anne Chambers on Grace O'Malley, the Irish pirate who took on Queen Elizabeth I. Others were more workaday figures like Mary Read and Anne Bonny, everyone's favorite women pirates, largely because their stories are so accessible from Johnson's *General History*. Stanley was rightly skeptical about the accuracy of Johnson's account, and tried to analyze it as a literary and political representation in order to seek a wider explanation.

By the middle of the 1990s, then, writing on the history of sea raiding was focused on three main themes: the economics of privateering, the ideology and political significance of piracy, and the importance of women pirates. But that did not exhaust the interest of writers in piracy. Piracy also retained an immediate relevance: piracy still continued in the South China Sea and in the Straits of Malacca. This became a matter of international diplomacy.[63] In the Gulf of Siam women on refugee boats leaving Vietnam were regularly raped by Thai pirates. The men were often killed. Roger Villar's account, *Piracy Today*, paid more attention to the attacks on merchant ships and on European yachts.[64] But the boat people were the subject of a book edited by Eric Ellen, the director of the International Maritime Bureau, an organization based in London that concerns itself with marine crime, particularly piracy.[65]

Yet the romanticism continued, and there was a resurgent popular interest in piracy. The Internet helped, as did the efforts of naval reenactors, particularly in the United States. The public imagination was further stimulated by the discovery of the wreck of the *Whydah*, Samuel Bellamy's pirate ship that had sunk off Cape Cod in the United States in 1717. A team which includes Ken Kinkor and is led by a professional salvor, Barry Clifford, located the wreck in 1984 and began a slow maritime excavation of the site, which was still continuing when this book went to press. In 1997 another project, off the North Carolina coast, began to investigate the possible wreck site of a second famous pirate vessel, the *Queen Anne's Revenge,* the flagship of Edward Teach, or "Blackbeard."

There was also an extraordinarily successful exhibition on pirates at the National Maritime Museum in Britain; this later did an international tour. David Cordingly, who was largely responsible for organizing the exhibition, went on to write a full-length book about piracy which quickly became a standard work, although it is confined to the Caribbean and Atlantic and leaves out Mediterranean corsairing and Chinese piracy almost completely. Although it too paid little attention to the economics of piracy, it succeeded because it was well written and attractive, and made a serious attempt to disentangle the various myths.[66]

Cordingly went on to edit one of the many highly illustrated books that came out in the late 1990s. Its title, *Pirates: Terror on the High Seas from the Caribbean to the South China Sea,* and coffee-table format suggested that this was a potboiler. Cordingly is a respected historian of maritime art and although the book was written in middlebrow, nonacademic English, and avoided economics, the authors were experts in their fields—Marcus Rediker, Dian Murray, Eric Ellen of the International Maritime Bureau, and others. The same names crop up frequently in writing about pirates because such a small pool of authors work on the subject. Cordingly's article in this book—on pirate maps and pirate explorers—pointing to the contribution of pirates and privateers, considerably enhanced our knowledge of the history of navigation and exploration. This was illustrated by the republication of the sailing guide to the Mediterranean drawn up by Piri Reis, the sixteenth-century Ottoman pirate-turned-privateer-turned-admiral. It was printed in a splendid full-color reproduction of the Ottoman Turkish original and its maps, along with a modern Turkish and English translation and, for some odd reason, a transliteration of the Ottoman Turkish.[67] Interestingly, though, the original from which the reproduction was taken was one of the many sumptuous, highly decorated versions, suitable for presentation to rich laymen ashore, rather than one of the far rougher copies, with many orthographic mistakes, that were clearly made for use by real seamen.[68] Neither modern nor seventeenth-century Turks wanted to show their cultural hero as a rough man of the sea.

Another consequence of growing public demand was the reissue, yet again, of some of the classics of pirate literature. Two of Gosse's books, *The Pirates' Who's Who* and *The History of Piracy,* Exquemelin's *The Buccaneers of America,* and Johnson's *General History* were all reissued in the late 1990s. Some less well-known accounts were republished too, among them Aaron Smith's *The Atrocities of the Pirates,* which is an autobiographical account of his capture of Cuba, his forced service in a pirate ship, and his subsequent trial for piracy in Britain. The book first appeared in London in 1824, and was republished by the famous Golden Cockerel Press in London in 1929. There was clearly a market for this material: a selection of captive narratives was also published with extracts of accounts covering China and Tunisia, but concentrating on the victims of Atlantic piracy. The balance was restored to some extent by a similar anthology of captivity accounts from North Africa,[69] which had a more deliberately academic approach.

Some of the older academic accounts were reissued too: Coindreau's book on the Salé pirates was republished in Morocco, and Henry Ormerod's famous *Piracy in the Ancient World*, which was first published in 1924. Ormerod is still immensely valuable because of its concern with the geographical conditions in which piracy flourished in the Mediterranean, and the economic and social effects of piracy on victim populations, particularly the abandonment of the coast for fear of pirates. But the scope for comparison that Ormerod offers with other manifestations of piracy is even more suggestive: he describes pirates sharing out the proceeds of their raiding in ways that closely resemble the practices of pirates in the Caribbean and in the supposedly protoanarchist pirate republic in Madagascar in the eighteenth century.[70] Could it be that this practice of sharing was a matter of practical organization among pirates, rather than a specifically ideological activity?

Much recent academic discussion of piracy carries on the tradition of individual case studies. Manuel Ocaña Torres wrote a book in Spanish about Spanish corsairing in the Strait of Gibraltar in the eighteenth century, centered on economic organization. But many of these studies appeared in articles, either in journals or collections such as that edited by David J. Starkey and others from papers given at a conference in Holland in 1991. Starkey's book was intended to provide a basis from which to make comparisons between piracy and privateering in different parts of the world. Not surprisingly it found that there was more in common between systems of privateering than between manifestations of piracy. The first was an activity sanctioned by government, while piracy was a more individualistic enterprise, and one that—as Starkey points out in his introduction—generated fewer documents because it was illegal. Nine out of the fourteen articles are concerned with privateering, with a pronounced emphasis on organizational factors—recruitment, finance, economics—and the authors are largely concerned with northern Europe. Only a few concern piracy as such: three of them by contributors to this present collection, *Bandits at Sea*. John Anderson carried forward his general article on the economics of piracy to look at South-East Asia and China, Dian Murray turned her attention to social and economic conditions surrounding piracy in Chinese waters, and Marcus Rediker expanded on his and Christopher Hill's ideas about the utopian aspects of piracy. Another collection, largely in French Spanish and Catalan, did focus on the Mediterranean, but once again mainly on the Christian shore, and equally, largely on state-sponsored and legalized raiding.[71] Even so, as its editor Gonçal López Nadal points out in *Bandits at Sea,* the boundaries between the two were hard to trace.

Not all the apparently academic work was really worthy of the name. Many writers on piracy were so jingoistic about their subject (or about the prospect of making a splash) that they abandoned caution and their critical faculties. Dian Murray's article in this collection points to one example of this phenomenon, but there were plenty of others. In the rush to publish and republish, the mistakes and carelessness of previous generations of writers were reproduced. This is the source of yet another tension between the pirate as a historical figure and the pirate as a literary romance.

One bizarre example of this is the case of Benito de Soto, a celebrated pirate who was hanged in Gibraltar, while his crew were hanged in Spain in January 1830. Their ship was originally a Brazilian slaver, *Defensor de Pedro*, that sailed from Rio de Janeiro in November 1827. The crew mutinied on the west coast of Africa and in 1828 plundered an East Indiaman, the *Morning Star,* whose captain was Thomas Gibbs. According to Francis Bradlee in his book on West Indian piracy published in 1923,[72] the name of the *Morning Star's* captain was Sauley, and the attack took place in 1832. As he accompanies his account with a picture of the *Morning Star* sinking, which did not happen, and bloodcurdling talk of "awful savagery," Bradlee is hardly a reliable source. The following year, Philip Gosse's *Pirates' Who's Who* gave the same date of 1832, and stated that de Soto and his mates shipped out of "Buenos Ayres" and that de Soto was sent to Spain to be hanged. Gosse's *History of Piracy*, published in 1932, gets the date of departure and the date of the attack on the *Morning Star* correct, omits the date of the pirates' execution, but implies that de Soto was hanged in Gibraltar. The repetition of errors has continued until today. A 1995 reference book on piracy, Jan Rogozinski's *Dictionary of Pirates*, described de Soto's ship as "an Argentinean [*sic*] slaver" that took the *Morning Star* in 1832.[73] Rogozinski's book showed every sign of being written in haste, had an unreliable bibliography, did not always cite sources for the entries, and was littered with mistakes.

Another motivation for misleading information was agitprop: a curious book by three German anarchists about women pirates seems to have been clearly designed as a situationist challenge. It was bound in a pink cover with an unattributed picture of a bare-breasted woman in a classical pose and, superimposed in the top left-hand corner, a pirate flag. No flagpole could be seen: the Jolly Roger simply fluttered provocatively and unsupported over the woman's head. The contents were in much the same mold: they included a number of recipes and a provocative chapter asserting that Bartholomew Roberts may have been a woman. Having raised the possibility, the authors then referred to Roberts throughout as "she," basing their argument on a picture of Roberts with "thigh muscles like Martina Navratilova," on Roberts's refusal to drink alcohol, curse, or smoke, on Roberts's partiality to tea and fruit juice, refined language, gaudy clothes, and dislike of women aboard ship. "Black Barty was also very open and creative with respect to the visual arts"— the visual arts in question being the design of a succession of pirate flags:

> The skull with grappling knife was followed by a creation with the form of Bartholomew Roberts herself, holding a flaming sword in one hand and an hourglass in the other standing on a skull between each foot.[74]

This infuriated many readers: the huffing and puffing on Internet maritime history groups was echoed by some of my own students who were insulted (or said they were) by what they saw as "bad history." This was surely the authors' intention. Their stated purpose was to challenge male-dominated academic assumptions, and what better way to do so than by provoking the reader with unprovable assertions? After all, a good deal of male-oriented writing about pirates is just as ill-founded. The book presented the reader with a spectacle that shook his (or her) grasp of reality.

Piracy is attractive to anarchists anyway, but not all of them make the material itself part of the challenge to respectable society. Others have developed Hill's and Rediker's idea that many Caribbean pirates were seeking an ideological refuge. One, Peter Lamborn Wilson, has applied it to the "renegades" in North Africa, and particularly in Salé. Wilson is an anarchist with some reputation as a student of Sufism, and of antiauthoritarian and heterodox forms of Islam. Morocco in the first half of the seventeenth century was politically fragmented and abounding in the sort of debates over religion and rebellion that would exercise English rebels later in the century. Wilson did not really prove much beyond a coincidence in timing: there was no coherent body of evidence to show that the Englishmen in Salé studied Islam or Sufism. But his book raised issues about the Salé corsairs that break out of the Eurocentric, conservative stereotypes about slaves and renegades, Muslim enemies, and Christian heroes.[75]

Amidst this cacophony of diverse, often strident, and sometimes ill-informed voices, we need a guide, or at least a starting point. That is what this collection is designed to provide. Most of the articles included here have been published before, but in scattered, and sometimes very obscure forms. Yet their topics represent some of the main themes in writing about piracy today.

The collection falls logically into two parts. The first is conceptual: how are pirates to be identified and described? This is an important task not only for historians: it exercized lawyers and governors in the sixteenth, seventeenth, and eighteenth centuries. When states were poorer and their reach less sure than today, military activity had to pay for itself. Without a distinction between legitimate and illegitimate raiding, it was impossible to impose a secure exercise of state authority and any sort of control over illegal activity. But what was often at stake was the superiority of one group of plunderers over another, and the claim to legitimate authority was often a legitimization of force. Anne Pérotin-Dumon's article opens with one of the most famous quotations about piracy, from St. Augustine's *City of God*, in which the pirate tells the emperor that only a difference of power separates the governor from the thief.

> It was a witty and a truthful rejoinder which was given by a captured pirate to Alexander the Great. The king[76] asked the fellow, What is your idea, in infesting the sea? And the pirate answered with uninhibited insolence. "The same as yours, in infesting the world! But because I do this with a tiny craft, I am called a pirate: because you have a mighty navy, you are called an emperor."

That, of course, is the thrust of Samuel Bellamy's famous rant, but it is a concept that crossed cultures. In the second half of the seventeenth century a Turkish corsair captain boasted that he had no wish to become a government commander: "To become a Beg or a Pasha would mean nothing to me; I too, like yourselves, am a corsair!"[77]

Thus, any attempt to understand piracy has to balance the tension between the government and the individual, and this at a time—in the sixteenth, seventeenth, and eighteenth centuries—when the nature of the state was changing. Pérotin-Dumon's article is centered on that tension and its political meaning and consequences. This political question of definition had legal consequences, among others: the tension was resolved in law and regulation. David J. Starkey's first article is an examination of the ways in which the early British state attempted to set the dividing lines between legitimate and illegitimate raiding.

The tension between the early modern state and the early modern pirate was not only a matter of politics, but also of economics; not just power, but also money. The boundary lines between them are very blurred: Gonçal López Nadal's article explores the margins between legality and illegality, and between warfare and regular trade, and situates sea raiding in a borderland, along with smuggling, between regular trade and illicit behavior. The economics of privateering has been examined often enough, but in the absence of pirates' account books—and we are unlikely to get many of those—the economics of piracy is more obscure. David Starkey's second article outlines the main considerations. John Anderson's chapter looks at the other side of the question: the costs of piracy and privateering to the victims, to trade, and so to the wealth of the organized state.

The second part of the book consists of chapters that pick up on some of these themes and develop them in particular case studies. My own (Richard Pennell's) article on northern Morocco situates piracy geographically in a region of poor resources, weak government, and ample opportunity. Ken Kinkor's previously unpublished paper examines the nature of pirate communities and how they included black men, a group that was excluded from most legal communities at the time. Some of the other papers explore these questions as well, particularly Dian Murray's on Cheng I Sao, Wendy Bracewell's on the Uskoks of Senj, and John Appleby's on Ireland. Since space was limited, these chapters also develop other concerns that run through recent work on the history of piracy, particularly the social organization of pirates—a concern both of B. R. Burg and of Marcus Rediker's article on the "Seaman as Pirate"—and the question of gender and sexuality.

The search for women pirates has tended to produce some of the most inflated and purple prose of all writing about piracy. Dian Murray's article on Cheng I Sao, Marcus Rediker's on the perennial favorites, Bonny and Read, and Wendy Bracewell's on the women Uskoks are, in contrast, cool-headed attempts to place these accounts of women pirates in their historical and historiographical contexts. The historical debate has sometimes seen sharp disagreements, notably over Burg's book on the homosexual activities of pirates. Dian Murray, in her article on homosexuality among Chinese pirates, is clear about her dissent, but as the section of Burg's book that is reproduced here will show, his account—and hers—go far beyond the problems of sexuality to questions of the nature of community in out-groups, and relations between individuals where those cannot be regulated by law. Once again, one essay stands in for many themes.

There is a virtue in necessity, too: the very fact that one essay *can* cover so much ground is an indication of the range that the study of piracy includes. These essays show some of that range: the individual against the state, men and women against the sea, men and women's relations with each other, and the gain and loss of wealth. These are powerful themes, and romantic ones. It is undeniable that one of the attractions of piracy is that romantic quality and the need in a conformist world to find heroes or heroines. To recognize this one does not have to go quite as far as one of my more starry-eyed students, who wrote in her take-home exam:

> They drank rum every night and played on the ocean all day. Even though the profession had a high mortality, it would have been worth living for a while, just for the adventure.

NOTES

1. See David Cordingly, *Life among the Pirates: The Romance and the Reality* (London: Little, Brown, 1995).

2. A. O. Exquemelin, *Bucaniers of America, or, A true account of the most remarkable assaults committed of late years upon the coasts of the West-Indies, by bucaniers of Jamaica and Tortuga, both English and French. Wherein are contained more especially, the unparrallel'd exploits of Sir Henry Morgan, our English Jamaican hero, who sack'd Puerto Velo, burnt Panama, &c., Written originally in Dutch, by John Esquemeling, one of the bucaniers who was present at those tragedies; and thence translated into Spanish, by Alonso de Bonne-Maison ... Now faithfully rendered into English* (London: Printed for William Crooke, 1684). An edition of this version was published in 1924. A. O. Exquemelin, *The Buccaneers of America: A True Account of the Most Remarkable Assaults*, rev. and ed. William Swan Stallybrass (London: Routledge and New York: Dutton, 1924). It has been through several reprints, for example, New York: Dorset Press, 1987 and Glorieta, New Mexico: Rio Grande Press, 1992. These keep the same page numbering and have been used for quotations in this collection, except where noted. The far superior Penguin edition—A. O. Exquemelin, *The Buccaneers of America*, trans. Alexis Brown (Harmondsworth: Penguin, 1969)—has been reissued (London: Folio Society, 1972).

3. Captain Charles Johnson, *A General History of the Robberies and Murders of the Most Notorious Pyrates and also their Policies, Discipline and Government from their first Rise and Settlement in the Island of Providence, in 1717, to the Present Year, 1724, with the Remarkable Actions and Adventures of the two Female Pyrates, Mary Read and Anne Bonny, to which is Prefix'd an Account of the famous Captain Avery and his Companions; with the Manner of his Death in England*, ed. Manuel Schornhorn (London: Dent, 1972). Schornhorn accepts the attribution to Daniel Defoe, and he is given as the author, but otherwise this is the most scholarly edition. Defoe's authorship was challenged by P. N. Furbank and W. R. Owens, *The Canonisation of Daniel Defoe* (New Haven: Yale University Press, 1988), and their criticisms of the ascription are widely accepted.

4. Dampier's autobiographical journal has recently been reissued in a new edition: *A New Voyage Round the World: The Journal of an English Buccaneer*, ed. Mark Beken (London: Hummingbird, 1998). The most recent life of Dampier is by Anton Gill, *The Devil's Mariner: A Life of William Dampier, Pirate and Explorer, 1651–1715* (London: Michael Joseph, 1997).

5. For a representative literature on modern piracy in Southeast Asia, see Robert C. Beckman, Carl Grundy-Warr, and Vivian Forbes, *Acts of Piracy in the Malacca and Singapore Straits*, ed. Clive Schofield, vol. 1, 4, *International Boundaries Research Unit, Maritime Briefing* (Durham: University of Durham International Boundaries Research Unit, 1994); Eric Ellen, ed., *Piracy at Sea* (Paris: International Chamber of Commerce, 1989), and especially the article by Pascal Boulanger, "The Gulf of Thailand," idem, 83–96.

6. Stanley Lane-Poole, *The Barbary Corsairs* (London: T. Fisher Unwin, 1890); American edition: *The Story of the Barbary Corsairs* (New York: C. P. Putnams's Sons, 1890).

7. C. H. Haring, *The Buccaneers in the West Indies in the Seventeenth Century* (London: Methuen, 1910). The American edition (New York: E. P. Dutton, 1910) was reprinted (Hamden, Conn.: Archon Books, 1966).

8. There have been many editions of Gosse's works since the first editions in the 1920s and 1930s: Philip Gosse, *The Pirates' Who's Who* (London: Dulau and Co., 1924) and *The History of Piracy* (London: Longmans Green, 1932).

9. This paragraph is based on Larry Schweikart and B. R. Burg, "Stand by to Repel Historians: Modern Scholarship and Caribbean Pirates, 1650–1725," *Historian* 46, no. 2 (1984): 219–234.

10. Sir Godfrey Fisher, *Barbary Legend: War, Trade, and Piracy in North Africa, 1415–1830* (Westport, Conn.: Greenwood Press, 1974).

11. David Delison Hebb, *Piracy and the English Government, 1616–1642* (Aldershot: Scolar Press, 1994).

12. Roger Coindreau, *Les Corsaires de Salé* (Paris: Société d'éditions géographiques, maritimes et coloniales, 1948).

13. Carl Trocki, *Prince of Pirates, the Temenggongs and the Development of Johor and Singapore 1784–1885* (Singapore: Singapore University Press, 1979).

14. James F. Warren, *The Sulu Zone, 1768–1898: The Dynamics of External Trade, Slavery and Ethnicity in the Transformation of a Southeast Asian Maritime State* (Singapore: Singapore University Press, 1981).

15. Abdeljelil Temimi, *Sommaire des Registres Arabes et Turcs d'Alger, Publications de la Revue d'Histoire Maghrèbine no 2* (Tunis: Revue d'Histoire Maghrèbine, 1979).

16. William Spencer, *Algiers in the Age of the Corsairs* (Norman, Okla.: University of Oklahoma Press, 1976); John B. Wolf, *The Barbary Coast: Algiers under the Turks 1500–1830* (New York: W. W. Norton, 1979).

17. Stephen Clissold, *The Barbary Slaves* (London: Paul Elek, 1977).

18. Kola Folayan, *Tripoli during the Reign of Yusuf Pasha Qaramanli* (Ile-Ife: University of Ife Press, 1979).

19. Peter Earle, *Corsairs of Malta and Barbary* (London: Sidgwick and Jackson, 1970).

20. C. M. Senior, *A Nation of Pirates: English Piracy in Its Heyday* (Newton Abbot: David and Charles, 1976).

21. Peter Kemp and Christopher Lloyd, *The Brethren of the Coast: The British and French Buccaneers in the South Seas* (London: Heinemann, 1960).

22. Dudley Pope, *Harry Morgan's Way: The Biography of Sir Henry Morgan, 1635–1684* (London: Secker and Warburg, 1977). Published in the United States as *The Buccaneer King: The Biography of the Notorious Sir Henry Morgan, 1635–1688* (New York: Dodd Mead, 1978).

23. Schweikart and Burg, "Stand by," 226.

24. Christopher Lloyd, *English Corsairs on the Barbary Coast* (London: Collins, 1981).

25. Robert C. Ritchie, *Captain Kidd and the War against the Pirates* (Cambridge, Mass.: Harvard University Press, 1986).

26. A collection of his articles was published as J. S. Bromley, *Corsairs and Navies, 1660–1760* (London: Hambledon Press, 1987).

27. Michel Mollat, ed., *Course et piraterie: Études presentées à la Commission*

Internationale d'Histoire Maritime à l'occasion de son XVè colloque international pendant le XIVè Congrès International des Sciences Historiques (San Francisco, août 1975), 3 vols. (Paris: Institut de Recherche et d'Histoire des Textes, Centre National de la Recherche Scientifique, 1975).

28. Cyrus Harreld Karraker, *Piracy Was a Business* (Rindge, N.H.: R. R. Smith, 1953).

29. Patrick Crowhurst, *The French War on Trade: Privateering, 1793–1815* (Aldershot: Scolar Press, 1989); Patrick Crowhurst, "Profitability in French Privateering 1793–1815," *Business History* 24 (1982): 48–60.

30. David J. Starkey, *British Privateering Enterprise in the Eighteenth Century* (Exeter: University of Exeter Press, 1990).

31. Carl E. Swanson, *Predators and Prizes: American Privateering and Imperial Warfare, 1739–1748* (Columbia, S.C.: University of South Carolina Press, 1991).

32. Gonçal López Nadal, *El corsarisme mallorqui a la Mediterránea occidental 1652–1698: Un comerç forçat* (Barcelona: Conselleria d'Educació i Cultura de les Balears, 1986).

33. B. R. Burg, *Sodomy and the Pirate Tradition: English Sea Rovers in the Seventeenth Century Caribbean* (New York: New York University Press, 1983).

34. B. R. Burg, *Sodomy and the Pirate Tradition: English Sea Rovers in the Seventeenth Century Caribbean*, 2d ed. (New York: New York University Press, 1995), xvii.

35. Marcus Rediker, "'Under the Banner of King Death': The Social World of Anglo-American Pirates 1716–1726," *William and Mary Quarterly* 38 (1981): 203–227; Marcus Rediker, *Between the Devil and the Deep Blue Sea: Merchant Seamen, Pirates and the Anglo American Maritime World 1700–1750* (Cambridge: Cambridge University Press, 1987).

36. Peter Linebaugh and Marcus Redicker, "The Many Headed Hydra: The Atlantic Working Class in the Seventeenth and Eighteenth Centuries," in *Jack Tar in History: Essays in the History of Maritime Life and Power*, ed. Colin Howell and Richard Twomey (Fredericton: Acadiensis Press, 1991), 11–36.

37. Rediker, *Between the Devil*, 254–287.

38. Christopher Hill, "Radical Pirates?" in *The Collected Essays of Christopher Hill* (Brighton, Sussex: Harvester Press, 1985), 26.

39. Johnson, *General History*, 587.

40. Rediker, *Between the Devil*, 269.

41. E. J. Hobsbawm, *Bandits* (London: Weidenfeld and Nicolson, 1969), 8.

42. Johnson, *General History*, 82.

43. Johnson, *General History*, 84.

44. Quoted in Burg, *Sodomy*, 156.

45. Grace Fox, *British Admirals and Chinese Pirates 1832–1869* (London: Paul, Trench, Trubner, 1940).

46. Ng Chin-Keong, *Trade and Society: The Amoy Network on the China Coast, 1683–1735* (Singapore: Singapore University Press, 1983).

47. Dian Murray, "Mid-ch'ing Piracy: An Analysis of Organizational Attributes," *Ching-shih wen-ti* 4, no. 8 (1982): 1–28; Robert J. Antony, "Aspects of the Socio-Po-

litical Culture of South China's Water World, 1740–1840," *Great Circle* 15, no. 2 (1993): 75–90; Robert J. Antony, "The Problem of Banditry and Banditry Suppression in Kwangtung South China, 1780–1840," *Criminal Justice History* 11 (1990): 31–53.

48. Sultan ibn Muhammad al-Qasimi, *The Myth of Arab Piracy in the Gulf* (London: Croom Helm, 1986).

49. Charles E. Davies, *The Blood Red Arab Flag: An Investigation into Qasimi Piracy 1797–1820* (Exeter: University of Exeter Press, 1997).

50. Michel Fontenay, "Los fenómenos corsarios el la 'periferazión' del Mediterráneo en el siglo XVII," *Areas (Murcia)* (1984): 116–121; Michel Fontenay, "La place de la course dans l'économie portuaire: l'exemple de Malte et des ports barbaresques," *Annales*, no. 6 (1988): 1321–1347; C. R. Pennell, "Tripoli in the Late Seventeenth Century: The economics of corsairing in a 'sterill country,'" *Libyan Studies* 16 (1985): 101–112.

51. Jerome Bookin-Weiner, "Corsairing in the Economy and Politics of North Africa," in *North Africa: Nation, State, and Region*, ed. George Joffé (London: Routledge, 1993), 3–33.

52. Ellen G. Friedman, *Spanish Captives in North Africa in the Early Modern Age* (Madison, Wis.: University of Wisconsin Press, 1983).

53. Emilio Sola, *Cervantes y la Berbería: Cervantes, mundo-turco-berberisco y servicios secretos en la época de Felipe II* (Madrid: Fondo de Cultura Económica, 1996).

54. Thomas Baker, *Piracy and Diplomacy in Seventeenth-Century North Africa: The Journal of Thomas Baker, English Consul in Tripoli, 1677–1685*, ed. C. R. Pennell (London: Associated University Presses, 1989); Miss Tully, *Narrative of A Ten Years' Residence At Tripoli in Africa: From the Possession of the Family of the Late Richard Tully, Esq., the British Consul: Comprising Authentic Memoirs and Anecdotes of the Reigning Bashaw, His Family, and Other Persons of Distinction: Also, An Account of the Domestic Manners of the Moors, Arabs, and Turks*, 2d ed. (London: Darf, 1983).

55. Baker, *Piracy and Diplomacy*, 114.

56. Catherine Wendy Bracewell, *The Uskoks of Senj: Piracy, Banditry, and Holy War in the Sixteenth-Century Adriatic* (Ithaca: Cornell University Press, 1992).

57. Previous work included G. E Rothenberg, "Venice and the Uskoks of Senj 1537–1618," *Journal of Modern History* 33 (1961): 148–156; P. Longworth, "The Senj Uskoks Reconsidered," *Slavonic and East European Review* 57, no. 3 (1979): 348–368.

58. Wendy Bracewell, "Women among the Uskoks: Literary Images and Reality," in this collection.

59. Dian Murray, "One Woman's Rise to Power: Cheng I's Wife and the Pirates," in *Women in China: Current Directions in Historical Scholarship*, ed. Richard W. Guisso and Stanley Johannesen (Youngstown, N.Y.: Philo Press, 1981), 147–162.

60. Dian Murray, "Cheng I Sao in Fact and Fiction," in this collection.

61. Suzanne J. Stark, *Female Tars: Women Aboard Ship in the Age of Sail* (Annapolis: Naval Institute Press, 1996).

62. Jo Stanley, ed., *Bold in Her Breeches: Women Pirates across the Ages* (London: HarperCollins, 1995), xvii.

63. Beckman, Grundy-Warr, and Forbes, *Acts of Piracy in the Malacca and Singapore Straits.*

64. Captain Roger Villar, *Piracy Today: Robbery and Violence at Sea since 1980* (London: Conway Maritime Press, 1985).

65. Ellen, *Piracy at Sea.*

66. David Cordingly, *Life among the Pirates: The Romance and the Reality* (London: Little, Brown, 1995).

67. Muhiddin Piri Reis, *Kitab-ı Bahriye*, trans. Vahit Çabuk, 4 vols. (Istanbul: Historical Research Foundation, 1988).

68. Svatopluk Soucek, "Tunisia in 'Kitab-ı Bahriye' by Piri Reis." Ph.D. dissertation, Columbia University, 1970, 39–48.

69. Paul Baepler, ed., *White Slaves, African Masters: An Anthology of American Barbary Captivity Narratives* (Chicago: University of Chicago Press, 1999).

70. Henry A. Ormerod, *Piracy in the Ancient World: An Essay in Mediterranean History* (Liverpool: Liverpool University Press, 1924), 157; Baltimore: Johns Hopkins University Press, 1997.

71. Gonçal López Nadal, ed., *El Comerç Alternatiu: Corsarisme i contraban (ss.xv–xviii)* (Palma de Mallorca: Conselleria de Cultura, Educació i Esports, Govern Balear, 1990).

72. Francis B. C. Bradlee, *Piracy in the West Indies and Its Suppression*, 2d ed., *American Maritime History* (Salem, Mass.: Essex Institute, 1923, reprint New York: Library Editions, 1970).

73. Jan Rogozinski, *Pirates* (New York: Facts on File, 1995), 324.

74. Ulrike Klausman, Marion Meinzerin, and Gabriel Kuhn, eds., *Women Pirates and the Politics of the Jolly Roger* (Montreal: Black Rose Books, 1997), 185.

75. Peter Lamborn Wilson, *Pirate Utopias: Moorish Corsairs and European Renegades* (New York: Autonomedia, 1996).

76. St. Augustine, *The City of God*, trans. Henry Bettenson (Harmondsworth: Penguin, 1972), book 4, chapter 4.

77. Henry Kahane, Renée Kahane, and Andreas Tietze, *The Lingua Franca in the Levant: Turkish Nautical Terms of Italian and Greek Origin* (Istanbul: ABC, 1988), 195.

Chapter 2

The Pirate and the Emperor
Power and the Law on the Seas, 1450–1850

Anne Pérotin-Dumon

> For elegant and excellent was the pirate's answer to
> the great Macedonian Alexander, who had taken
> him: the king asking him how he durst molest the
> seas so, he replied with a free spirit, "How darest
> thou molest the whole world? But because I do with
> a little ship only, I am called a thief: thou doing it
> with a great navy, art called an emperor."
> —St. Augustine, *The City of God,*
> book 4, chapter 4

I

There is a description of piracy that spans the ages: illegal and armed aggression at points of maritime traffic that are important but under weak political control. The aggression is committed by the marginal who seek to appropriate the wealth of the more affluent, or by newcomers desiring to force their way into preexisting trade routes.[1] This elementary description tells us about plundering and illegality; it tells us about immediate causes and motivations. But it leaves out the questions of what law is invoked against the pirate, and behind the law, of what power is involved in this maritime confrontation over matters of trade.

In the rise of merchant empires at the beginning of the modern era, what is called piracy is also easily recognizable. From sea to sea and age to age, we observe the same phenomena appearing—at once picturesque, violent, and sordid. From the Barbary coast to the Rio de la Plata, from Madagascar to the Chinese coast of Fukien, we could sketch a sort of sociology of piracy: by examining where pirates were based (retreats lodged in sheltered but deserted bays or on islands all along the coasts near frequented routes); by describing their behaviors in a single-sex society (verbal exaggeration, eccentricity in clothing, and infantilism); and finally by analyzing pirates' methods (raiding along the coasts or intercepting ships, living in complicity with the local inhabitants or exercising tyranny over them, and so forth). Similarities exist also in how different authorities reacted, even down to the very expressions they used for their policies against pirates: to "cleanse the sea" and then to grant pardon, whether it was in the Low Countries, whose North Sea fishing fleets suffered the assaults of Norman and Scottish pirates during the sixteenth century, or the Ching dynasty facing a confederation uniting several thousand pirates along its southern coasts at the beginning of the nineteenth century.[2] These commonalities suggest collective patterns that, with the question of the damage done to commerce, have been the main subjects of work on piracy and its repression in the age of European expansion.

This chapter considers the other issue raised by piracy, one that has received little attention (and that with erroneous premises): the political significance of piracy and its repression. To understand piracy in the era of Europe's overseas commercial expansion, we must begin by considering the choices and conflicts that arose around control of the seas and trading routes: whether to aim for monopoly over Atlantic routes, as in the Iberian, and later English and French, cases, or to work to keep them free and open, as in the Dutch case; whether to suppress Europeans who rebelled against this control or to eliminate non-European rival trading networks. These were all political decisions and policies expressing state power. The political will and policies that created merchant empires at the same time produced the piracy of that age. The common view that pirates existed "where commerce is active" is incomplete because it fails to consider the crucial political factor. Active commerce is indeed a necessary precondition for piracy, but it is not a sufficient one. Rather, the history of piracy in this period shows that it arises above all from change in the political realm—either the will of a state to establish commercial hegemony over an area where it had previously been weak or nonexistent, or from the conflict between two political entities, one an established trading power and the other a newcomer. The prize of piracy is economic, but as a historic phenomenon, the dynamic that creates it is political.

Most of the literature on this "imperial" piracy has retained a legalistic approach. It has considered what laws were used against pirates; it has assessed the wrongs done according to these laws. It has not inquired into what authority made the laws in the first place, and has failed therefore to identify what power was at stake in such maritime confrontations over trade. Moreover, a legalistic approach runs into the fact that there is not, and never has been, an authoritative definition of piracy in international law. The historiographical limitations of our topic and ambiguities around the notion of piracy in law and politics are analyzed in the second section of this essay.

In the third, fourth, and fifth sections of this chapter I deal successively with three episodes of piracy related to the rise of European merchant empires. The third section treats the first of these (1520–1650), when Iberians declared pirates other Western Europeans with whom they came into conflict in regions where they had asserted initial imperial dominion. This piracy was especially characteristic of the Atlantic routes to America, where the Iberian trade had not needed to supplant an indigenous trade but quickly experienced competition from other European merchants who organized trading voyages to America. French and later English "pirates" were, as the Greek word suggests, adventurers who wandered the seas in contempt of sixteenth-century Spanish monopolies that refused them license to trade beyond the Canary Islands. They are of special interest because of their role in expanding and intensifying European seaborne trade beyond the Iberian domain.

The second episode of piracy, analyzed in the fourth section, hit territorially based merchant empires that excluded foreigners. This piracy can be seen in two subepisodes. The first of these (1660–1720) concerns the well-known cases of France and England. During this period, in which they established their own trading and colonial power, they outlawed cosmopolitan gangs of freebooters that challenged their new commercial regulations and drove away the Dutch, whose entrepôt-based empire in the Atlantic was premised upon free trade.[3] French and English courts of admiralty tried their own nationals as pirates. This suppression of piracy within national frameworks is important as an indicator of new state power; in particular the array of policies used to subdue pirates—including punishment or pardon, regulation or toleration—shows the concrete limits within which a state was able to assert itself.

In the second subepisode (1714–50), pirates resurface to challenge established commercial hegemonies. The fourth section of this chapter also deals with this case, when smugglers resisted Spanish efforts to reimpose their claims over trade routes and networks. This outbreak of piracy is worthy of attention because it reflects the vicissitudes in control of large-scale commerce by merchant empires, not simply according to their laws on the matter, but rather to their political strength or weakness. Here historians have often failed to differentiate simple contraband from piracy. What created the shift from the former to the latter was the effort of a state power to control trading routes. Where previously a weak or tolerant state had tolerated smugglers, now their resistance made them pirates.

A third type of piracy can be seen in the conflicts between Europeans and non-Europeans from 1500 on. These encounters, analyzed in the fifth section of this chapter, were particularly prominent in the Indian Ocean, where the

European newcomers met an armed resistance to their prohibitions from the established indigenous traders. The sixteenth-century Portuguese, for example, seeking to impose a monopoly over the pepper trade in India, treated the people of Malabar as pirates.

Even circumscribed into these three broad episodes, the field of the phenomenon remains vast. It would be wonderful to accomplish what Samuel Johnson proposes in the opening verses of "The Vanity of Human Wishes":

> Let observation with extensive view
> Survey mankind from China to Peru;
> Remark each anxious toil, each eager strife
> And watch the busy scenes of crouded [*sic*] life.

Reality, however, requires a compromise between breadth and precision. My focus here will be the Atlantic route to the East Indies and the Caribbean, regions that were hotbeds of world piracy between 1520 and 1820. The questions that most clearly emerged from this Atlantic piracy are then addressed comparatively in other specific situations where pirates and growing merchant empires faced off on other seas.

II

Most of what has been written on piracy is part of the body of work done on the naval and commercial expansion of Europe linked to the formation of modern states. Because of a nationalistic bias in the literature of the time, the studies done of sixteenth- and seventeenth-century European piracy failed to inquire into its political significance. They assumed the legitimacy of European states rather than considering how those states were formed and then established legitimacy over pirates as parts of the historical process to be studied. This literature focuses on English pirates and Dutch sea rovers more as national heroes against Catholic Hapsburgs than as instruments to the achievement of English and Dutch state power. Later, when France and England hung their most notorious freebooters, the legal apparatus for doing this is studied, not its political roots. As Kenneth Andrews has noted, this approach has obscured the international dimension of Caribbean piracy.[4]

The historiography of piracy, which flourished particularly between 1880 and 1940, was contemporary with the second wave of European expansionism, after a victory over indigenous piracy that was considered definitive.[5] It was influenced by the belief that the progress of "civilization" was served by commercial expansion. This framed an interpretation of piracy along cultural lines, distinguishing indigenous piracy from Western civilization. The suppression of non-European piracy became the equivalent on the sea of the "civilizing mission" in French colonial territories (even for the English, who sought, in contrast to the French, to maintain local indigenous institutions). Only the era of decolonization made it possible to begin to approach the history of piracy critically, at the same time as the history of European expansion was being revised. In the decade of the 1960s, the work of Nicholas Tarling on British imperialism in Malaysia, with its maritime implications, illuminated the colonialist premises that had caused non-European rivals to be designated as pirates.[6]

The older historiography of European piracy tied to the rise of merchant empires is marked in other ways by the frame of reference of nineteenth-century expansion. What was a novelty of the time—powerful states endowed with naval forces that kept the great oceanic routes open—was projected onto the past. This led to an anachronistic conception of the power of the state in the naval realm, and of the relationship between war and commerce in the sixteenth and seventeenth centuries. The meaning of piracy at the beginning of the modern era came to be implicitly assessed against these notions of an all-powerful state, of a public sector quite distinct from the private sector, and of a navy serving the glory of the nation by suppressing pirates.

Nation-states in the process of formation were capable of none of this, especially because these states were engaged in expensive wars among themselves. With the means of the time, they were incapable of sending strong fleets frequently enough to control seas far away from their European bases. It was not until the nineteenth century that first England, and then the United States, strove to apply the doctrine of total mastery of the seas, justifying vast naval forces.

One must also note the subtle but enduring error of perspective that consists in treating war and commerce as if they had always been incompatible. In sixteenth-century Europe, war and commerce went together, like mathematics and astrology, or physics and alchemy. For a long time, only those prepared to defend themselves could undertake any long-distance voyage. If they were also ready to go over to the attack, they were suited to a form of trade that could require the use of force, or the threat to do so, at any point. When Northern European pirates entered the Mediterranean and targeted the Venetians in the late sixteenth and early seventeenth centuries, Alberto Tenenti observes that their combination of commercial and aggressive operations was new to the region.[7] Northern European merchant empires initially arose in close association with both war and commerce; when the two elements were combined in a predatory and aggressive trade, it was piracy. And commerce was equally nourished when the cargo sold in home ports had been seized rather than bought.

Violence, then, was not a trait of piracy but more broadly of the commerce of that age. Commercial profits were linked pragmatically to considerations of war and aggression, though at the same time the state could be expected to put protective formations in place, like convoys that became a regular practice in the seventeenth century. The Dutch theoreticians Grotius and De la Court who, already in the seventeenth century, insisted that war was harmful to commerce and put their hopes in free trade rather than control of the seas, were exceptions. Similarly, merchants were more likely to arm their vessels than, like those of the Low Countries or Japan, to opt to purchase a safe-conduct.[8]

Let us examine now the question of the legal authority by which police power and justice pursued pirates. In the age that concerns us piracy was rarely limited to the simple case of a state with the right to use force against a few isolated wrongdoers captured near its coasts. More often the crime occurred far from territorial water (or, before this notion existed, far from the coasts) and belonged to the international domain. Whether national or international, piracy was the object of numerous codes and legal treaties, especially from the time when European states began to authorize and regulate attacks on the sea in the form of privateering wars. But crimes of piracy were always handled within a national legal framework. Although they belonged more properly to the domain of international law, they were brought before national admiralty courts or commercial jurisdictions.[9]

The difficulties that have historically surrounded the international crime of piracy in maritime law are no different in essence from those encountered by twentieth-century jurists. Piracy raises the question of what sort of power and order can ever be enforced on the sea, an area not settled by human societies and therefore not carved into political units. The sea falls de facto into the international domain; it lies in between nations. But judicial institutions belong to land communities; consequently, they lack legal authority to judge crimes occurring on the sea. Even in our day, international law has not progressed very far; the notion of an overall legal imperative by which all are bound remains in its infancy.[10] Its application is limited by numerous obstacles, like the fact that it requires the voluntary cooperation of states that in practice refuse to submit to international law (for example, the outlawing of war) because they perceive it as an infringement on their national sovereignty.

Since antiquity, there has been a consensus that the pirate should be considered as *hostis humani generis* and his offense an attack on the law of nations. But this general opinion has not been concretized as a tool of law; a proper "law of nations" never existed. Humanity is not a wielder of law—only states are—and there is no international tribunal of a supranational entity with coercive authority at its disposal to try the offenders. Among the matters under study by the Commission of International Law (appointed by the UN General

Assembly), there is a proposed code of crimes against the peace and security of humanity that is supposed to deal with piracy. So far, it appears that the conclusion of experts who discussed this at the time of the League of Nations remains valid: there is no authoritative definition of international piracy.[11]

The lack of a legal definition for international piracy shows in the relativity that has always characterized the identity of the pirate (consequently, the terms employed in this chapter—pirate, privateer, corsair, freebooter, and so forth—are used not in reference to ideal categories but following our sources). Consider the case of Jean Florin, one of the Norman captains who ventured to attack the Spanish monopoly over the wealth of the Indies. As early as 1523, lying in wait between the Canary Islands and the Azores, Captain Florin captured two vessels returning from Mexico. In the eyes of the Spanish, this man was a pirate if ever there was one. But in Normandy in the church of Villequier, of which he was the lord, beautiful stained glass windows recount this local hero's capture of Montezuma's treasure. In Malaysia around 1830, the sailor whom the officials of the English trading company called a "ruffianly pirate," was a hero to local Malay merchants. The same relativity has affected judgments on the repression of piracy. At the very end of the seventeenth century, Bellomont was appointed governor of the colony of New York, with a mission to put an end to the activity of pirates along the coast. Referring to differing opinions that were expressed on the way he carried out his charge, the governor wrote: "They say I have ruined the town by hindering the privateers (for so they called the pirates)."

However, the epigraph at the beginning of this chapter about the pirate and the emperor (an anecdote borrowed by St. Augustine from an ancient writer) makes clear that the dispute about whether someone should be called a pirate or not is really about who has the power.[12] In the twentieth century, the anticolonial wars exhibited a similar dynamic of "pirate and emperor," translated into disputes over recognition or illegality. In the 1930s the Nicaraguan patriot Augusto Sandino was a bandit in the eyes of the North Americans, and in the 1940s the German authorities of occupied France viewed as terrorists the *résistants* loyal to *France libre*.

The parallels with native or Creole resistance against European conquest or dominance are legion throughout the era of European expansion. On the Malabar coast of India in the sixteenth century, the Kunjalis were the main adversaries of the Portuguese, who treated them as *cossarios;* for the Zamorin princes of Calicut, the Kunjalis were their naval force and were patriots *avant la lettre*. During the wars of Spanish American independence between 1810 and 1830, when there were important actions at sea, royalists long insisted on labeling the *corsarios insurgentes* simply as pirates. These examples illustrate another political dimension of piracy to which I will later return: A dynamics of power is at play between an established power of superior strength and a newcomer of lesser, lacking recognition, that challenges it.

Confrontations at sea were both an important instrument of state power and of a measure of the degree to which state authority was actually established. Gaston Zeller some time ago noted that the development of nationalism in the sixteenth century started with the conquest of the seas and was most often exerted in the economic domain in the form of protectionist and exclusionist commercial legislation.[13] Western European state-building and commercial expansion were parallel developments that fed upon each other; hence the influence of politics in defining piracy at the time and, conversely, the role of piracy in the nation-building process.

The sixteenth and seventeenth centuries witnessed an extraordinary debate over the state's lawmaking power and the political foundations of law, over the questions of warfare and violence. This was the time when a Francisco de Vitoria could claim that the Hapsburg monarchy's right to conquest ended where the natural rights of Amerindian societies began; when a Montaigne could write that "laws maintain their credit not because they are just, but because they are laws. This is the mystical basis of their authority; they have no other, and this serves them well."[14] That Augustine's anecdote about a confrontation between Alexander the Great and a pirate provided the setting for a reflection on the foundations of political power perhaps reveals the unique relationship between politics and the sea that then existed.[15]

Jurists like Bodin and Suárez, Grotius and Pufendorf were indeed dumbfounded by the conflicts brought on by the rise of states and their commercial expansion. Confronted by the powerlessness of diplomacy to resolve problems caused by the arrival of European newcomers in so many lands and on so many seas, they sought to regulate relations in a world composed of new states. A few even believed with Grotius that the sea should be open and long-distance trade free of all conflict. The propositions of many remained utopian: As mentioned, it is within a national framework that laws dealing with international matters were elaborated, among them those on navigation and trade that dealt with piracy. Different laws supported differing policies: either, as in the case of English and French monarchies after the Iberians, to control trading routes and monopolies; or, as in the case of the Dutch Republic, to keep trade open and free— save in regions where the Dutch themselves claimed a monopoly. Both types of policies, however, involved the power of a state.

The fact that public authorities decided on matters of navigation and trade ultimately sealed the fate of pirates, even when, as in the Dutch case, the state opted for freedom of trade and the seas. When the Dutch economist De la Court included the assertion that "seas must be kept free and open" among his general maxims for the welfare of humankind, it was, he said explicitly, in the interests of the Hollanders, who "are the great, and indeed only carriers of goods throughout the world; catching herring, haddock, cod and whale, making many sorts of merchandize [*sic*] for foreign parts."[16] De la Court called for a fleet that would serve only to protect Holland merchantmen from Flemish or English rovers and robbers.

In fact, however, privateering as an activity required immediate material rewards for those who carried it out; Dutch privateers, their compatriot observed, tended not to defend their own merchant fleet but to attack the enemies' ships and to take prizes, a modus operandi that fell short of clearing the sea from *hostis humani generis*.[17]

III

A captain of Honfleur, Gonneville, left in 1503 to trade with the Indians along the coast of Brazil; he carried a cargo of knives, mirrors, and other "trinkets of Rouen." The hides, bird feathers, and dyewood that he brought back were lost in the storm encountered on the home journey of the ship *l'Espoir*. But the "relation" of his voyage was preserved, and begins thus:

> Trafficking in Lisbon, Gonneville and the honorable men Jean l'Anglois and Pierre le Carpentier, having seen the beautiful riches of spice and other rarities coming into this city on the Portuguese ships going to the East Indies, discovered several years ago, made a pact together to send a ship there, after making a thorough enquiry of several who had made such a voyage, and having hired at high wages two Portuguese who had come back from there . . . in order to help them with their knowledge on the route to the Indies.[18]

In a few lines, the captain from Honfleur described the careers of thousands of his kind, from 1500 until around 1700, whose activities were carried on with the sponsorship of the merchants of French and English ports: learning in the principal Iberian commercial centers of the existence of new resources, going in search of them oneself, bypassing the Iberian intermediary, finding a pilot who knew the route to these riches, and leaving, finally, on a venture with one's cargo of trumpery wares. These men were convinced that, in spite of Iberian claims, the sea and the riches of "Peru" or "Brazil," unlike those of the Mediterranean and the Indian Ocean, were free and open to their enterprises. The Dutch—who persisted in these views (and acted on them) later than other Northern Europeans—coined an appropriate name for themselves and others of their kind: *vribuiter* or freebooter.

Such pirates, explorers, and traders prepared the way for regular maritime connections across the Atlantic and for the rise of new merchant empires following those of the Iberians. From Newfoundland to Brazil, their innumerable "trafficks, trades and barters" of manufactured goods and trumpery wares for exotic products constituted the main form of exchange between the Old World and the New (with ecological consequences that in our own times are receiving increasing attention). As Spain succeeded in keeping the hands of pirates off its principal Atlantic sea lanes and mainland American empire, petty exchanges concentrated on the margins. On North American and Brazilian coasts and in the Caribbean region, this petty commerce brought new societies into being initially based on plunder and smuggling. Atlantic and American piracy expanded to an intercontinental scale established exchanges between Northern and Southern Europe, fish and forest products for sugar and dye products. According to the distinction proposed by Robert López between the "inner" and "outer" areas of large-scale commerce, the Atlantic and the Caribbean were still an "outer area" for those pirate explorers, but their actions nonetheless foretold the creation of a new "inner area," with regular routes and with predictable costs and profits.[19]

The role pirates could play as adventurous merchants and explorers for new routes and commercial goods, in defiance of empires, may be seen in East Asia, where they challenged the Ming. The *wakō* (or *wokou* for the Chinese, meaning "Japanese bandits") started spreading along the Korean and then Chinese coasts at the end of the thirteenth century. Their plundering marked the beginning of a remarkable Japanese expansion toward mainland Asia that would lead them on to Java and Manila.[20] Later, seeking to escape the constrictive policy of the Ming empire that banned trade with foreigners, Hokkien merchants, studied by Wang Gungwu, left the coasts of China to settle overseas, some of them in Manila like their Japanese counterparts. Between the fourteenth and eighteenth centuries, they formed prosperous communities that defied the agrarian-bureaucratic orientation of the Chinese Empire.[21] Ironically, European intruders would rely on these Chinese and Japanese overseas merchant communities to establish themselves commercially on the margins of the Chinese and Japanese trading systems.

In the second half of the sixteenth century, the English followed French incursions into Iberian America. The first "privateering voyage" of John Hawkins in 1562 is well documented.[22] Through his long-term correspondents in the Canary Islands, the Englishman learned of the Guinea trade and of sugar in the Spanish Greater Antilles: Slaves instead of knives and mirrors and sugar rather than feathers and shells were the basis for a potentially much more substantial venture. After bribing a Spanish pilot, Hawkins sailed for the West African coast, where he was able to buy three hundred slaves "partly by the sword, partly by other means." The slaves he sold at Hispaniola, in exchange for sugar as well as hides, ginger, gold, and pearls. As he had hoped,

Hawkins obtained a trading license from local officials, after a sufficient show of force to provide the excuse they would need to explain, in reporting to the king, why they had been constrained to admit a foreign vessel.

Voyages like this were more or less repeated for half a century (1560s to 1630s) by other intruders. Once the facade of hostility had been displayed, the Spanish governor could close his eyes and allow inhabitants to trade with the English, bringing them wares they needed anyway because they were rarely visited by their national merchants. Sometimes a fort would threaten to shell the English ship, forcing it to retreat to an undefended (and thus more hospitable) site nearby. There, business could be conducted peacefully at night with inhabitants who came down from the capital. Sometimes French and English corsairs carried out joint operations, and the display of superior forces would persuade local officials to grant them a trading license. Simply by being continuously present and by scaring other ships off, English pirates managed to force locals to trade with them. "Coming or going, we always have a corsair in sight. . . . If this continues . . . they will compel us to do business with them rather than with Spain," complained a Spanish official from Hispaniola in 1595.[23]

After a trip of several months, a pirate was anxious to get rid of his cargo (if, for example, as in the case of Hawkins, some slaves had fallen ill), and it was necessary to force the exchange and make use of cannon against the colonists. This kind of exchange Spaniards would also accept, but "whether by consent, or by compulsion, I can't say," as one pirate boasted of this method in *The History of the Pyrates*, sometimes attributed to Defoe.[24] At times, even under those conditions no exchange would be possible, but pirates would still need return merchandise or simply fresh provisions and water. This could lead them then to loot the churches, official buildings, and private houses of Spanish American towns, though pirates were often content to attack unprotected settlements along the coasts, sugar mills, and cattle farms.

Before there were North European pirates, the first Castilian entrepreneurs operating in America had also sometimes been traders and sometimes raiders. The two words "raiding" and "trading" appear over and over in the literature to describe these two modes of operation.[25] Whether pirates chose one mode or the other depended on a variety of circumstances, such as whether or not one was familiar with potential local partners, far from or close to one's base, at the beginning or the end of one's venture, and so forth. What mattered was to be ready for either option. When the Dutch West Indies Company was founded in 1621 as a joint-stock freebooting venture to compete with the Spanish trade, it set for itself the dual objectives of commerce and privateering raids. The freebooter admiral Piet Heyn quickly made his presence felt in the Greater Antilles and on the Spanish Main; he captured the Mexican fleet at Matanzas Bay, in Cuba, in 1627.

The mixture of seduction, distrust, and violence visible in the dealings of pirates with Spanish officials and colonists was a common combination in early encounters between people of mutually exclusive cultures. The emergent nationalism of the time was often defined by cultural differences. When all was said and done, the pirate was the "other." He was a problem because he was culturally different. The Spanish Crown reacted with hostility when non-Spaniards tried to create free zones in the east of Cuba and in the northwest of Hispaniola at the beginning of the seventeenth century. The presence of the "other" was as much a cause of annoyance as the losses represented by those *rescates*, or illicit transactions with foreigners. The "age of great piracy" is also that of Reformation: cultural differences came to crystallize around confessional ones. For Catholic Spaniards, contacts with "Huguenots" and "Lutherans" were unacceptable and had to be furtive.[26] As the American trade was increasingly threatened by the intrusions of non-Spaniards in the second half of the sixteenth century, the Inquisition expanded to the New World. Its role would often be essential in the pursuit of intrusive traders like Hawkins.

Lacking precise estimates of the damage that pirates inflicted on trade in European waters prior to 1500, there has been a tendency to consider as unprecedented the piracy that accompanied overseas expansion. A brief glance at the past makes one skeptical, however, about whether it is possible to speak of increasing insecurity on the sea.[27] There are the several thousand letters of the fourteenth and fifteenth centuries preserved in the Archives of Aries (in Provence), which document how the city was then part of a typically Mediterranean network of information and on the alert against Catalan, Saracen (Moorish), Pisan, and Genoese pirates. Before 1500, there were Breton, Norman, Welsh, and Cornish pirates who threatened regular traffic between the main English and French ports, kidnapping travelers and holding them for ransom, just as Barbary pirates would continue to do for centuries in the Mediterranean. In ports that lacked the rich export merchandise of Bordeaux or Plymouth, men could just as easily be pirates as carriers, or both, as were the Bretons.

Writing on the export of French wines to England, Russell Menard notes that the problem of insecurity was of long standing: As reflected in the cost of transportation, troubles began at the time of the Hundred Years' War and continued intermittently through the sixteenth century, when France and England were too weak to police their seas.[28] Trading and raiding were already alternatively practiced in the Atlantic and the Channel, but in the sixteenth century the patterns of European piracy spread like a turbulent climatic front. Shortly after 1500, the front of this tornado was already at the Azores and the Canary Islands, a third of the way toward America; by the middle of the sixteenth century, it had reached the Greater Antilles. A century later, European pirates had touched the coasts of North Africa, where they occasionally allied with native pirates. By the end of the seventeenth century, European pirates were at Madagascar and southern Africa; and then they reached India, operating from the south of Bombay, the Malabar coast, and as far as the Bay of Bengal.

In *The Military Revolution*, Geoffrey Parker describes the developments that were a prerequisite for this Western hegemony: the great progress in the domain of armament and strategy made by Europeans on both sea and land at the beginning of the modern era.[29] When the freebooter Captain Fleury sailed from Dieppe in 1618 to carry on trade with the "continent of Peru," he had not left Norman waters before he was busy fighting with Dutch, Breton, and English ships. We are fortunate to have an extremely evocative account of his two-year expedition, which took the Frenchman to Cape Verde, Brazil, the Caribbean, Central America, and Florida.[30] After describing the Indian communities that received the freebooters, saving them from exhaustion and starvation, the anonymous narrator enthusiastically refers to "rounds of cannon, catapults and muskets" fired by Fleury's men and the prizes they took of "powder, leads and guns." A few decades later, in 1642, Captain William Jackson sailed from London to raid on the Spanish Main. He enlisted almost a thousand men between the islands of Barbados and St. Christopher (today St. Kitts). "Commanders, and officers spent their time in exercising their souldiers [*sic*] to make them more ready and expert on all occasions." The English corsair proudly listed his stock of "Muskitts, Carbines, Fire-locks, Halfe-pikes, Swords, Cutlases & yᵉ like offentius weapons."[31] Thus, an old phenomenon, the long-term insecurity of the seas, was aggravated by a new development, the improvements in naval gunnery that gave the advantage to aggressive merchants. Violence could spread more easily because European navigation had brought previously separate trading zones into contact with one another.

While the front of European piracy reached shores ever more distant, Japanese *wakō* pirates and their Chinese accomplices were breaking into the defenses of a declining Ming empire. In the Indian Ocean between 1650 and 1750, Mughal forces were held in check on the Malabar coast by a force of their own former corsairs. What we have here are the signs of a changing political dynamic, of new powers seeking to gain control of large-scale commerce and of new commercial hegemonies being established. "Whether it was at the beginning, the middle, or the end [of the seventeenth] century," wrote Louis Dermigny, "pirates developed everywhere on the flanks of massive mainland empires in crisis or decline: the Spanish empire, the Mughal empire and the Chinese empire."[32]

Fernand Braudel, among others, has brought to light the function piracy played culturally as well as economically.[33] Running through a multitude of examples with an encyclopedic faith less in evidence today, the historian of the Mediterranean rightly perceived that armed trade was just as important as peaceful trade, and that both of these vast movements of exchange promoted conflict as well as contact between cultures. With particular insight, Braudel explained the spread of aggression to the seas as an encounter between different kinds of merchant states, those in the process of formation and expansion and those losing momentum and influence. Thus, in Braudel's terms, the assaults of Northern European pirates on Spanish and Venetian commerce at the beginning of the seventeenth century were "the sign of a recent arrival." Venetian regular forces and Spanish Caribbean squadrons, as the instruments of established commercial powers, treated the newcomers—the French, English, and Dutch who challenged them—as pirates. In practice, however, the forces of both powers displayed lethargy and defeatism toward the intruders; they remained in port or gave themselves up without battle.[34] It is as if they were vaguely aware that the dynamic of change was no longer on their side (while also knowing that galleys and galleons do not easily fight pirate ships).

The Europeans denounced indigenous piracy, but Braudel's remark is equally apt for this phenomenon, that it was the "sign of a recent arrival." The process was the same—attacks on established merchant powers by outside competitors—but the main actors exchanged dramatis personae. In the Indian Ocean, the newcomers were the ones to accuse the long-term occupants of piracy. Thus, in the Indian Ocean the Portuguese claimed a commercial monopoly and treated as pirates the Malabar sailors who resisted them along the southern coasts of India, which they defended for the Mughal emperor. In the Mediterranean the established Venetian and Spanish traders were the ones to bar North European competitors from their monopoly and treat them as pirates. Whether they were pirates or not, the intruders from Northern Europe challenging old Mediterranean powers and the Asiatic merchant communities resisting the intrusion of Europeans represented two sides of the same coin. By insisting on their hegemonic pretensions, the Spaniards in the Mediterranean and the Portuguese in Asia were both attempting to compensate for their lack of effective control, a point to which I return later. The second imperialist push of Europe in the nineteenth century would reproduce situations in which non-European merchants were pursued as pirates by Europeans, now backed by better naval forces. So it happened with the Qawasim, seafarers from a commercial emirate that stubbornly refused to cede to the English control over the entry to the gulf in the course of the nineteenth century.[35]

When situations of piracy reveal that shifts in power are occurring and new hegemonies are being established, what starts as a dispute over trade may ultimately become one over political control. A case in point is the Mappila merchant community in sixteenth-century Calicut, studied by Geneviève Bouchon. Unlike other Muslim merchant communities that dominated long-distance trade in Calicut, the Mappila were native and specialized in the South Indian coastal trade and the Java trade. The arrival of the Portuguese caused the departure of the Arabs at the beginning of the sixteenth century. In a context of war brought about by Portuguese intrusion, Mappila power rose in Calicut. They started fitting out their privateers, who regardless of official conflicts, would, throughout the century, relentlessly attack Portuguese spice trade circuits. Such piracy had a clear political outcome: the Mappila came to dominate Calicut and for a time threw off the yoke of the Zamorin.[36]

The Malay seafarers resisting the English who were in the process of replacing the Dutch domination in the 1830s and 1840s offer another example. Before the coming of the English, it was customary for maritime adventurers progressively to extend their commercial control over an area from which over time they would dislodge the previous political power. During the time Malay sultanates were created, piracy provided the basic mechanism for shifts in political control. Between the fifteenth and the eighteenth centuries, these sultanates, as studied by Denys Lombard, displayed an astonishing similarity to their Dutch foes: they, too, were maritime states centered around port cities and their merchant elites.[37] European intrusion and naval control interrupted this dynamic of state building. Pirates were now condemned to remain pirates instead of evolving toward the creation of a maritime state. "If this has been called piracy," writes Tarling, "it was also an aspect of the political dynamics of this part of the world."[38]

IV

Turning to English and French piracy in the seventeenth century, we leave the global stage to consider markedly national episodes that would be remembered as the "suppression of piracy." The excesses of a last generation of pirates, those who were gradually outlawed, have with reason inspired much romantic fiction.[39] Life had become extremely difficult for the last freebooters; nothing could be taken for granted any more. "My commission is large and I made it myself," proclaimed Captain Bellamy in *The History of the Pyrates*. "I am a free prince and I have much authority to make war on the whole world," says a couplet of the ballad of Captain Avery. As they faced growing hostility, pirates dispersed, carrying their enterprise to its greatest geographic extension at the beginning of the eighteenth century, as already noted. Fleeing a Caribbean that was becoming less hospitable, they made for the coasts of North America, Africa, and the Indian Ocean.

Near the end of the eighteenth century, pirates were depicted as a social plague in a new literature, especially in English, with titles such as *Piracy Destroy'd or, A short discourse shewing the rise, growth and causes of piracy of late; with a sure method how to put a steady stop to that growing evil.*[40] "The pirate," wrote Daniel Defoe in this spirit, "destroys all government and all order, by breaking all those ties and bonds that unite people in a civil society under any government." The pirate is barbarous and antisocial, and must therefore be destroyed. One finds here the ancient accusation against the pirate as *hostis humani generis*. The practices of such folk were, of course, delinquent and violent, but they had long been so. The appearance of this negative campaign against them in public opinion was not accidental. It coincided with the launching of a new commercial policy by the state, which was directed against French and English pirates' naval and judiciary "campaigns" (the word is in itself a clear indication of state action) that would be sustained over several decades.

Individual operations of "gentlemen of fortune" were ridiculed as archaic and unresponsive to the laws of the market, which required information, provisions, investments, and so forth. "He could have made a great profit on indigo, but he wanted nothing but gold, silver or jewels," noted the Jesuit missionary and historian Charlevoix, writing of l'Olonnais. The "freebooter admiral," whose forces from Tortuga Island began to abandon him after a defeat in Puerto Rico in 1669, did not understand that the future was in the plantation economy.[41] For the governor of the Isle of Bourbon (today Réunion), the *forbans* of Madagascar whom it was his responsibility to repress were equally *passés*. They possessed diamonds in the rough, but to no use, because they had not "a penny's worth of capital."[42]

The author of *The History of the Pyrates* superbly recast an earlier narrative, *The Successful Pirate Charles Johnson (1713)*. One revealing change that he introduced is that pirates are no longer successful. His novel is the account of commercial ventures that failed because they were itinerant and improvised—not only illegal but carried out "like a lottery." Facing repression by the merchant empires, fugitives from the Caribbean almost succeeded in establishing a trading circuit to supply New York with slaves, parallel to the Royal African Company, and they made of their Malagasy hideaways an entrepôt dealing in goods between Europe, Asia, and America, in contempt of the East India Company. Baldridge, a Madagascar pirate of Anglo-Saxon stock, in 1691 received an order for two hundred slaves from a New York merchant specializing in the slave trade; Baldridge, however, turned out to be incapable of furnishing more than thirty-four.[43] His failure illustrates the fact that it was becoming increasingly difficult to maintain independent trade circuits parallel to those controlled by a mercantilist state; pirates were turning into mere parasites.

Islands that had begun as cosmopolitan rendezvous for pirates (who counted Flemish, Germans, Portuguese, and Maltese in their ranks) were now turned into export colonies exclusively linked to metropolitan merchants. The pirates failed to understand the change and clung to free trade and outmoded depredation. They tended to sell their prizes and spend their profits elsewhere than on their island, contributing to a national trade deficit. In a report of 1685, colonial authorities of the French island of Martinique observed that pirates "go to buy their weapons, nautical equipment and munitions in Jamaica, where they bring absolutely all the money they make, which considerably prejudices the colony."[44] Or they brought back booty that was unmarketable. Because piracy depended on rumors telling of the success of this or that venture, accumulating disappointments led to a thinning of the ranks. The last outlaw holdouts could only declare a paranoid war against the human race.

To these Don Quixotes of piracy, Defoe contrasts the merchant of the future:

> Every new voyage the merchant contrives is a project, and ships are sent from port to port, as markets and merchandizes [*sic*] differ, by the help of strange and universal intelligence; wherein some are so exquisite, so swift, and so exact, that a merchant sitting at home in his counting-house, at once converses with all parts of the known world. This and travel, makes a truebred merchant the most intelligent man in the world, and consequently the most capable, when urged by necessity, to contrive new ways to live.[45]

Heralded by such outstanding pamphleteers as Defoe, a whole new era was under way: large-scale commerce and colonies had become national objectives for France and England. The state assumed control of long-distance seaborne trade and of overseas settlements where agricultural export commodities were now being produced. In England a new class of merchants arose who had made their wealth in the West Indian trade, that is, outside the framework of chartered commercial companies. With influence in political circles, these merchants oriented the trade policy of the state toward excluding foreigners and retaining for themselves the monopoly of provisioning and marketing in the colonies.[46] The state now financed embryonic national fleets to protect convoys of merchant ships and attack the enemy at sea.

There was a general trend in Western European countries in the course of the seventeenth century: Merchants laid down their weapons and accepted that the state would protect their business in exchange for regulating and taxing it.[47] There would have been no "suppression of piracy" without this change in relationship between merchant and state. Freelancers who would not, or could not, adapt themselves to the new commercial age would be declared pirates. As trade carried by caravan merchants was displaced to the profit of transoceanic commerce in the course of the seventeenth century, so were small ventures of merchant captains forced out by the merchant houses allied to a mercantilist state that were to make the eighteenth century the golden age of Atlantic trade.

The actual policy put into effect at the end of the seventeenth century had a more modest goal than the "destruction of piracy" advertised: It was, as worded in the Jamaican Act of 1683, "the restraining and punishing of privateers and pirates." As mentioned earlier, the more ambitious tactics of protecting ships through convoys and cleaning out the freebooters' retreats could only be realized with much difficulty over an extended period of time. What appears to have been more effective in practice was attracting merchants into the commercial orbit of the state. In order to work, the measures and privileges described above had to make commerce more profitable and safer with rather than without the tutelage of the state. Further, the state had to encourage the formation of political blocs that were hostile to pirates and had an interest in their repression.

The recent study by Robert Ritchie, *Captain Kidd and the War against the Pirates,* shows that punishment and repression were effective because the powerful East India Company succeeded in making Kidd a political issue in the conflict between Whig and Tory factions, and because the Tories had a stake in the operation of repression against pirates.[48] Unlike many superficial accounts of Kidd's adventures, Ritchie sheds new light on the subject because he analyzes the political circles involved in the case in England and in the colonies, whose influence led to the pirate's execution in 1701.

Few pirates, however, were, like Kidd, sent back to the metropolis. Repressing them was left in the hands of local authorities where they were operating. There, *raison d'état* alone was not enough; local public opinion and local considerations had to be taken into account. One is reminded of the way local authorities have dealt in the twentieth century with guerrillas in the Philippines or in Colombia. The law authorized an arsenal of pardons and rewards, amnesties and punishments; implementing it successfully required dextrous use of both positive and negative instruments. In 1720 the governor of the Isle of Bourbon received an order from Versailles to obtain the surrender of French elements among the pirates' nest of Madagascar.[49] When the hostility they encountered from native Malagasy appeared to make the pirates receptive to the king's request, the governor offered them amnesty. With the consent of Bourbon colonists, repentant *forbans* who had made the trip from Madagascar were received, at first on a trial basis. On condition that they burn their fleet and deliver their treasure to the authorities, the *nouveaux* habitants were divided among different parishes; they were married off, and given pensions and land grants. Those found undesirable were allowed to return to Europe. It was not long, however, before Labuse—their leader—and a few recalcitrants took to the sea again, soon to be captured and hung. This news was widely publicized to emphasize the efficiency of royal justice against piracy.

Beyond repressing pirates, however, remained the task of implementing the exclusive commerce in the colonies themselves. This proved arduous in part because the new arrangements were less beneficial to colonists than to metropolitan merchants. Both the Navigation Acts as well as Colbert's edicts caused riots in the colonies, at about the same time as fiscal measures caused a revolt in French Brittany. Although the latter was severely crushed, freebooters in Saint-Domingue (today Haiti) received surprising clemency. The reason for this milder reaction in the colony, Charles Frostin wrote, was that "reprisals could strangle a young economy."[50] The governor had to keep a balance between local and metropolitan interests, a point that I examine below.

The official correspondence of French and English colonial authorities reveals that they faced the same dilemma with freebooters at the end of the seventeenth and beginning of the eighteenth centuries: If repression were too severe, it would only encourage freebooters to try their chances elsewhere, thus depriving the island of hands badly needed for both the economy and defense. Jamaican officials feared that disgruntled freebooters would swell the ranks of others on the island of Tortuga or Curaçao, while at the same time the governor of Saint-Domingue imagined that they might already be sailing for Jamaica. For both the French and English, an incipient public sector experienced the limitations of state economic intervention and risked undermining prosperity by encouraging evasion.[51]

Being so close to the riches of the Spanish Main, Jamaica and Saint Domingue would harbor incorrigible *forbans* for several generations. And colonial officials themselves were not completely prepared to give up the freebooter economy of free trade for that of the plantations. Governor Modyford, of Jamaica, was one of these figures incurably attached to the old ways. In March 1665 he offered a grim picture of an island deserted by freebooters: defense forces reduced to one-fifth of what they had been, merchants leaving Port Royal or withdrawing credit, and so forth. When rumors of war against the Spanish arose, Modyford seized upon them to grant letters of marque—in other words, to return to the golden age of freebooter commerce. He described how this transformed the despairing mood of the island: "Your Lordship cannot imagine what an universal change there was on the faces of men and things, ships repairing, great resort of workmen and laborers, many returning, many debtors released out of prison and the ships from the Curaçao voyage . . . brought in and fitted out again, so that the regimental forces at Port Royal are near 400."[52]

The *guerre de course* of the seventeenth and eighteenth centuries played an ever-increasing role in international conflicts; colonial authorities used privateers to supplement the chronically short regular forces sent from Europe. As Modyford made clear, freebooters were encouraged to "render their bravery useful to the prince." Enlisting in wartime, they could raid and take prizes under conditions that were now codified: Licenses were issued for a given length of time, action was limited to the official period of conflict, rules were established to divide the booty after the state got its percentage, and so forth. To remain within their chosen vocation, many freebooters submitted themselves to colonial authorities. The new framework allowed what proved to be the largest of all freebooting operations in the second half of the seventeenth century: the sack of Panama by the English pirate Morgan in 1670, and the raid on Cartagena during the War of the League of Augsburg (King William's War) in 1697, a joint operation of freebooters commanded by the governor of Saint-Domingue, Du Casse, with a fleet sent from France under Pointis, a naval officer.

Numerous complaints were raised, however, against freebooters: They were undisciplined under command, mediocre in military performance, and insatiable on payday. But they had to be taken as they were, remarked Exquemelin, who wrote perhaps the most famous buccaneer's memoirs of the seventeenth century, "for they are so accustomed to the buccaneering life [that] it is impossible for them to give it up."[53] One had no choice but to allow them to mount operations of plunder, even though their strategic value was doubtful. At any rate, this way of dealing with pirates had proved more successful than encouraging them to become planters, and the level of disorder on the seas had undoubtedly been reduced.

Although arming and enlisting freebooters under the legal cover of privateering war did curb piracy, it did not eradicate it. Corsairs could not be easily demobilized after peace was concluded. In the words of *The History of the Pyrates*, "privateers are a nursery for pyrates against a peace." The years following the wars of the League of Augsburg (1689–97) and of the Spanish Succession (Queen Anne's War, 1702–13) witnessed a new growth of piracy. More broadly, privateering wars prolonged the functional association between war and commerce. Indeed, during the wars of American independence, attacking the commerce of the metropolis—for North American and Spanish American colonists lacking regular navies—remained the preferred way to make war at sea.

Things began to change in the nineteenth century. Now, the idea was that "civilized nations" should not allow private individuals to wage wars, and that trade should not be a military target. Napoléon (whose insight was informed by the existing English mastery of the seas) is said to have remarked:

> A time may come . . . when the great belligerent powers may carry on warlike operations against each other, without the confiscation of merchant ships, or treating their crews as legitimate prisoners of war; and commerce would then be carried on, at sea, as it is carried on by land, in the midst of the battles fought by their armies.[54]

In order fully to extinguish European piracy (and the American piracy that derived from it), it was thus necessary both to abandon commercial exclusivism in favor of free commerce and to replace privateers by regular navies. At the Paris peace conference ending the Crimean War in 1856, privateering was "abolished." The British delegate thought that "our state of civilization and humanity required that an end should be put to the system which no longer belongs to our time." Although the decision (which was not ratified by the United States, Mexico, and Spain) closed off about two centuries of established privateering, or *guerre de course*, between "civilized" nations of the Western world, at the same time it legitimated the campaigns the same nations would undertake against indigenous "pirates" in the second push of imperialism that was under way. Once again, as mentioned at the beginning of this chapter, non-European commercial competitors would be eliminated under the accusation of piracy.

V

If one considers how seventeenth- and eighteenth-century European monopolies functioned in various trading regions of the world, their weakness at the local level is striking. Ports that had direct, exclusive relations with European metropolises formed a very loose network of control. Only the main ones were fortified, and these were often paired with smugglers' retreats, like Baru near Cartagena or El Garote near Portobello. Secondary ports, for example in the French or Spanish Caribbean, had practically no direct relationship with metropolitan ports but were linked by coasting trade to the main ones feeding transatlantic commerce. Contraband had to make up for the chronic undersupply and exorbitant prices imposed by chartered commercial companies and state-controlled trade circuits. As early as 1619, Governor Nathaniel Butler of Bermuda laid out the situation candidly. Within a month after the only ship sent that year by the company had departed, colonists began to lament. Butler was forced to authorize trade with "a Dutch gentleman from Middleborough" who had timely offerings of "victuals, courne, shoues [*sic*], shirts and the like."

> Noble Sir, it is noe small advantage that a very mean conceit hath over the perfectest judgement in the world, when the one worcks upon the ground of experience, this other from a discourse of reasonable apprehension only. Being therefore thus advantaged, let me tell you that ther is not a securer nor speedier waye to firm this plantation and to refine it from the miscarriages that maye betide it by accidental meanes [referring to hurricanes] than the discreet admittance and kind wellcome of such as shall warrantably passe in course this waye.[55]

Contraband used cabotage routes along with monopoly trade. Foreign schooners sailed to French or Spanish colonies, bringing cargo to and from large vessels bound for Europe that operated from their neutral entrepôts, like the Dutch islands of St. Eustatius and Curaçao or from New England ports. Coasting trade and smuggling existed in a symbiotic relationship; exclusive trade and the one with foreign entrepôts de facto coexisted at the local level.[56]

Smuggling between islands was particularly important in wartime, when legal transatlantic trade with the metropolis was interrupted. Frequent wars between European merchant states were a principal factor in keeping monopolistic barriers permeable at the local level.

European commercial monopolies functioned differently in Asia, but they were equally weak at the local level. Recent scholarship, such as that of Denys Lombard and Michael Pearson, has corrected previous exaggerated assumptions about European control over Asiatic trade and shown how preexisting networks of merchant communities from the Near East and East Africa to India and the Chinese Sea remained powerful and resisted European intrusion.[57] The permeability of the Portuguese monopoly over the Malabar pepper trade is a well-documented example.[58] Pilferage of part of the pepper production (sometimes the best quality) as well as armed resistance to Portuguese pretensions, particularly by the Zamorins of Calicut, never stopped. The Portuguese had no control over areas where the pepper was grown; they could only impose contracts on suppliers at low price and sell Portuguese passes to carriers to the main port. In K. N. Chaudhuri's phrase, the Portuguese had "to strike a compromise" with non-European merchants and carriers whose local channels of supply continued to function beyond Portuguese control. As in the case of the Java and Malaysia spice trade, smuggling and legal trade were imbricated.

In every case, the acceptance of a monopoly over the main routes required a state's tolerance of smuggling outside them. To maintain a certain equilibrium between the official exclusive circuits and informal smuggler trade was an important task for colonial administrators. In American colonies, they did this by protecting the functioning of transatlantic trade for the metropolis, while regularly permitting the importation of foreign products under the pretext of scarcity caused by a war or a hurricane. Officials even encouraged their own subjects to engage in smuggling if it produced a greater benefit than loss for the economy of a colony as a whole, as was the case for the French Caribbean with Spaniards who paid in silver. Such a strategy might even meet with royal approval: There were companies chartered for contraband, like the Portuguese Companhia do Graõ-Para e Maranhaõ, which carried commerce between Brazil and the Spanish American province of Quito, via the Amazon and the Mato Grosso.[59] There are even examples of colonial authorities who had to arbitrate between the interests of a contraband company and those of freelance smugglers, as in the case of the South Sea Company and private smugglers of Jamaica, both interested in cutting into Spanish Caribbean trade.

For local authorities, the key was keeping complicity between royal officials and foreign merchants within acceptable limits. "To understand service in hot climate," to use the euphemism of an English governor, was to know how to harmonize legal and illegal trading interests: on the one hand, metropolitan merchant houses and transatlantic exclusive trade; on the other hand, local merchants involved with foreigners. Sent on mission throughout Spanish America in the middle of the eighteenth century, Spanish officials Jorge Juan and Antonio de Ulloa emphasized the laxity of appointed authorities, who camouflaged their excesses with similar euphemisms. On the situation in Guayaquil, the main port in the province of Quito and center of Pacific smuggling for the viceroyalty of Peru, they noted: "In those areas, acquiescing to or patronizing smugglers is generally labelled 'to live and let live'; officials who allow the trade to go on in return for payment of a bribe for each fardo are called men of good will who will harm no one."[60] This chronic fragility of European trade monopolies was never more obvious than when piracy periodically resurfaced, when a policy of control called previous tolerance into question. Suddenly the equilibrium between exclusion and permeability would be shattered because one of the two sides had gone too far: Either a state had imposed an exorbitant control that killed illegal but necessary alternatives; or contraband had developed into a full-fledged countersystem that evidently threatened official trade.

The policy of the Ming dynasty, between the fourteenth and the seventeenth centuries, exemplifies an exorbitant state control that led to a resurgence of piracy, when it sought repeatedly to impose strict control over international trade.[61] This policy threatened the activities of Japanese merchants (the *wakō* mentioned above) who had penetrated the Chinese coasts, along with their Chinese partners. A well-known episode of this struggle took place in the second part of the sixteenth century: for twenty years, there was a rash of kidnappings, raids, and plunderings from the coast of Cheking in the north to Fukien in the south. These were Japanese raids of defense against a ruinous state policy of a declining imperial power. Ming emperors proved incapable of deploying the measures of control and defense that their policy would have required. To reestablish their sway, they had to use both the carrot and the stick (as would the French and English in their campaigns against pirates a century later), reinforcing the presence of the state on the coasts while loosening the ban on Chinese trade with foreigners.

The Caribbean provides an example of how state power, reacting to full-blown contraband, could trigger a cycle of piracy. Acting on the warranties of the Treaty of Utrecht (1713), Spain began to organize a better resistance against companies of smugglers that had routinely cut into its colonial trade with impunity.[62] It established naval patrols and mobilized corsairs for Puerto Rico and for Venezuela against English smugglers from Jamaica and Dutch ones from Curaçao; and, for the Pacific coast of South America, against Spanish smugglers who, with French and English accomplices, maintained a trade network parallel to the legal one between Lima and Panama. Although it was a time of peace, Spanish pursuit of the smugglers was conducted on a true war footing, "como si hubiese guerra viva." In turn, those whose smuggling had been disturbed resisted with arms and resorted to "forced exchange." In imposing its interests by force, Spain induced the smugglers to return to piracy; confronting them in this form, it had some success in curbing the large-scale contraband that had plagued official trade.

Thus, ironically, the hegemonic nature of some merchant empires did much to keep piracy alive. As long as monopolies went along with commercial wars, piracy simply fluctuated according to the degree of a state's authority at sea. It was the linkage between trade, war, and hegemonic policies that engendered a cycle in which smuggling and piracy alternated. Enlisting European pirates into a *guerre de course* did keep them under control. To eliminate piracy as a phenomenon, however, trade monopoly had to be given up altogether. This was a policy toward which England, France, and Spain only gradually moved till the second half of the eighteenth century.

The episodes of world-scale piracy that I have examined in the sixteenth and seventeenth centuries are indicative of important shifts in world powers that took place then. Piracy was identified with ventures that opened up new trading areas and broke into old established circuits. It emerged more specifically as a response to territorially based merchant empires with hegemonic commercial policies—first Spain and Portugal, then England and France—as opposed to "entrepôt-based empires" such as that of the Dutch in the Atlantic. There are clear parallels between European patterns surrounding piracy in this period and those in Asiatic trade: Spanish hegemonic policy recalled that of the Ming engaged in pursuing pirates; French and English freebooters resembled the sixteenth-century Japanese *wak_* in opening spheres to new trading powers; and Dutch port cities and merchant political elites had similarities to those of Malay sultanates. Behind variations in forms of piracy were differences in the political economy of various merchant empires.

NOTES

1. Roger Villar, *Piracy Today: Robbery and Violence at Sea since 1980* (London: Conway Maritime Press, 1985).

2. James D. Tracy, "Herring Wars: The Habsburg Netherlands and the Struggle for

Control of the North Sea, ca. 1520–1560," *Sixteenth Century Journal* 24, no. 2 (1993): 249–72. CSPCS and CSPAWI; Dian H. Murray, *Pirates of the South China Coast, 1790–1810* (Stanford: Stanford University Press, 1987).

3. Jonathan I. Israel, *Empires and Entrepots: The Dutch, the Spanish Monarchy, and the Jews, 1585–1713* (London: Hambledon Press, 1990), after Peter W. Klein, *De Trippen ill tie 17e eeuw: een studie over het ondernemersgedrag op de Hollandse stapelmarkt* (Assen: Van Gorcum, 1965).

4. Kenneth R. Andrews, "The English in the Caribbean, 1560–1620," in *The Westward Enterprise: English Activities in Ireland, the Atlantic and America, 1480–1650*, ed. Kenneth R. Andrews, N. P. Canny, and P. E. H. Hair (Detroit: Wayne State University Press, 1979), 103–23, reference here to 104.

5. Several examples will illustrate how a Eurocentric interpretation of piracy developed following its "suppression" by regular naval forces in the nineteenth century. About Caribbean piracy till the 1820s, in the aftermath of the wars of Spanish American independence, Francis B. C. Bradlee wrote a hundred years later: "Revolutionary governments are, at best, generally attended by acts of violence, but when undertaken by the ignorant and depraved People of the South American colonies, it . . . led to rapine and piracy." Francis B. C. Bradlee, *Piracy in the West Indies and Its Suppression*, 2d ed., American Maritime History (Salem, Mass.: Essex Institute, 1923), 1. For Admiral Jurien de la Gravière, the conquest of Algiers in 1830 was the ultimate triumph of a *Gallia victrix* that "avenges Christendom." Jurien de la Gravière, *Les corsaires barbaresques et la marine de Soliman le Grand* (Paris: E. Plon, 1887), last chapter. This judgment was also echoed by the English historian Stanley Lane-Poole: "For more than three centuries, the trading nations of Europe were suffered to pursue their commerce or forced to abandon their gains at the bidding of pirates. Nothing but the creation of the large standing navies crippled them. Nothing less than the conquest of their too convenient coasts could have suppressed them." Stanley Lane-Poole, *The Story of the Barbary Corsairs* (New York: C. P. Putnams's Sons, 1890), 3.

6. Nicholas Tarling, *Piracy and Politics in the Malay World: A Study in British Imperialism in Nineteenth-Century South-East Asia* (Melbourne: Cheshire, 1963).

7. Alberto Tenenti, *Naufrages, corsaires et assurances maritimes à Venise, 1592–1609* (Paris: S.E.V.P.E.N., 1959), 39–40.

8. Tracy, "Herring Wars."

9. In studying naval wars, even the best historians have succumbed to the temptation to take the letter of these laws and their jurisprudence at face value. See Richard Pares, *Colonial Blockade and Neutral Rights, 1739–1763* (Oxford: Clarendon Press, 1938; reprint, Philadelphia: Porcupine Press, 1975).

10. Monique Chemillier-Gendreau, "Fragilité et carence du système juridique mondial: L'état souverain aurait-il peur du droit international?" *Le Monde Diplomatique*, May 1989, 24–25.

11. Barry Hart Dubner, *The Law of International Sea Piracy* (The Hague: M. Nijhoff, 1980), 41–55.

12. On echoes of the pirate's response in popular English satire in the early eighteenth century, emphasizing the relativity of the claims made by empires, see J. H.

Baer, "The Complicated Plot of Piracy," *Eighteenth Century: Theory and Interpretation* 23, no. 1 (1982): 3–26.

13. Gaston Zeller, *Histoire des relations commerciales*, vol. 2, *Les temps modernes de Christophe Colomb à Cromwell* (Paris: Presses Universitaires de France, 1953).

14. Michel de Montaigne, *Essais (1580–1595)*, trans. George R. Ives (New York: Heritage Press, 1946), book 3, chapter 13, 1464.

15. Baer, "Complicated Plot."

16. Pieter de la Court, *Political Maxims of the Republic of Holland*, translation of *Het interest vim Holland, ofte grond van Hollands welwaren* Amsterdam, 1662 ed. (New York: Arno Press, 1972), 48.

17. Ibid., part 2, chapter 1, "The Necessity of Clearing the Seas from Pirates," passim.

18. Published in Charles-André Julien, ed., *Les Français en Amérique pendant la première moitié du XVIè siècle* (Paris: Presses Universitaires de France, 1946), 26.

19. Russell R. Menard, "Transport Costs and Long-Range Trade, 1300–1800: Was There a European 'Transport Revolution' in the Early Modern Era?" in *The Political Economy of Merchant Empires*, ed. James D. Tracy (Cambridge: Cambridge University Press, 1991), 228–276, reference here to note 11.

20. Paul Akamatsu, "Le décollage des grands marchands japonais au 17è siècle," in *Marchands et hommes d'affaires asiatiques dans l'Océan Indien et la Mer de Chine 13è–20è siècles*, ed. Denys Lombard and Jean Aubin (Paris: Editions de l'Ecole des Hautes Etudes en Sciences Sociales, 1988), 129–145, reference here to 128–129.

21. Wang Gungwu, "Merchants without Empire: The Hokkien Sojourning Communities," in *The Rise of Merchant Empires: Trade in the Early Modern World, 1350–1750*, ed. James D. Tracy (New York: Cambridge University Press, 1990), 400–421.

22. Clements R. Markham, ed., *The Hawkins Voyages during the Reigns of Henry VIII, Queen Elizabeth, and James I* (London: Hakluyt Society, 1878). English and Spanish sources referring to English privateering voyages have been published by Irene A. Wright, ed., *Spanish Documents concerning English Voyages to the Caribbean*, 1967 Kraus reprint edition (London: Hakluyt Society, 1929); and Irene A. Wright, ed., *Documents concerning English Voyages to the Spanish Main*, 1967 Kraus reprint edition (London: Hakluyt Society, 1932); and Kenneth R. Andrews, ed., *English Privateering Voyages to the West Indies, 1588–1595* (Cambridge: Hakluyt Society, 1959). Andrews has studied English piracy extensively in *The Spanish Caribbean: Trade and Plunder, 1530–1630* (New Haven: Yale University Press, 1978); *Trade, Plunder, and Settlement: Maritime Enterprise and the Genesis of the British Empire* (New York: Cambridge University Press, 1984); and Andrews, "The English in the Caribbean." Spanish treatments include Antonio Rumeu de Armas, *Los viajes de John Hawkins a América, 1562–1595* (Seville: Escuela de Estudios Hispano-Americanos, 1947); and Antonio Rumeu de Armas, *Piraterías y ataques navales contra las Islas Canarias*, 5 vols. (Madrid: Instituto Jerónimo Zurita, 1947–50), republished in 1991 as *Canarias y el Atlántico: Piraterías y ataques navales* (Santa Cruz de Tenerife: Viceconsejería de Cultura y Deportes) as a fascimile edition.

23. Quoted in Andrews, "The English in the Caribbean," 119–120.

24. Captain Charles Johnson, *A General History of the Robberies and Murders of the Most Notorious Pyrates and also their Policies, Discipline and Government from their first Rise and Settlement in the Island of Providence, in 1717, to the Present Year, 1724, with the Remarkable Actions and Adventures of the two Female Pyrates, Mary Read and Anne Bonny, to which is Prefix'd an Account of the famous Captain Avery and his Companions; with the Manner of his Death in England*, ed. Manuel Schornhorn (London: Dent, 1972).

25. John H. Elliot, "The Spanish Conquest and Settlement of America," in *Cambridge History of Latin America*, ed. Leslie Bethell (Cambridge: Cambridge University Press, 1984), 149–206, reference here to 156; Paul E. Hoffrnan, *The Spanish Crown and the Defense of the Caribbean, 1535–1585: Precedent, Patrimonialism, and Royal Parsimony* (Baton Rouge: Louisiana State University Press, 1980); Andrews, *The Spanish Caribbean* and *Trade and Plunder*.

26. Arturo Morales Carrión, *Puerto Rico and the Non-Hispanic Caribbean: A Study in the Decline of Spanish Exclusivism* (Rio Piedras: University of Puerto Rico Press, 1952); and Rumeu de Armas, *Piraterías*.

27. For European piracy before the European expansion, see Michel Mollat, *Le commerce normand à la fin du Moyen-Age* (Paris: E. Plon, 1952); and D. Mathew, "The Cornish and Welsh Pirates in the Reign of Elizabeth," *English Historical Review* 39 (1924): 337–348. On piracy in the coastal towns of Provence, see Philippe Rigaud, "Letras de la Costiera: La Provence et la guerre de course, XV–XVIes siècles," unpublished ms.

28. Menard, "Transport Costs," note 45.

29. Geoffrey Parker, *The Military Revolution: Military Innovation and the Rise of the West, 1500–1800* (New York: Cambridge University Press, 1988).

30. J-P. Moreau, ed., *Un flibustier français dans la mer des Antilles en 1618* (Clamart, France: Ed. J-P. Moreau, 1987).

31. William Jackson, "A Briefe Journall or a Succinct and True Relation of the Most Remarkable Passages Observed in that Voyage undertaken by Captaine William Jackson to the Westerne Indies or Continent of America. Anno Domini 1642," in *Camden Miscellany* 34 (Third Series) (London: Royal Historical Society, 1924), 2–3.

32. Louis Dermigny, *La Chine et l'Occident: Le commerce à Canton au XVIIIe siècle, 1719–1833* (Paris: S.E.V.P.E.N., 1964). See in particular the chapter entitled "Piraterie et conjoncture," 92–103.

33. Fernand Braudel, *The Mediterranean and the Mediterranean World in the Age of Philip II*, trans. Siân Reynolds, 2 vols. (London: Collins, 1972–73), 2:865–891.

34. Alberto Tenenti, *Piracy and the Decline of Venice 1580–1615*, trans. Janet and Brian Pullan (Berkeley: University of California Press, 1967); Enriqueta Vila Vilar, *Historia de Puerto Rico 1600–1650* (Seville: Escuela de Estudios Hispano-Americanos, 1974).

35. Sultan ibn Muhammad al-Qasimi, *The Myth of Arab Piracy in the Gulf* (London: Croom Helm, 1986).

36. Geneviève Bouchon, "Un microcosme: Calicut au 16e siècle," in *Marchands et*

hommes d'affaires asiatiques dans l'Océan Indien et la Mer de Chine 13è–20è siècles, ed. Denys Lombard and Jean Aubin (Paris: Editions de l'Ecole des Hautes Etudes en Sciences Sociales, 1988), 49–57, reference here to 55–56.

37. Denys Lombard, "Le sultanat malais comme modèle socio-économique," in *Marchands et hommes d'affaires asiatiques dans l'Océan Indien et la Mer de Chine 13è–20è siècles,* ed. Denys Lombard and Jean Aubin (Paris: Editions de l'Ecole des Hautes Etudes en Sciences Sociales, 1988), 117–124.

38. Tarling, *Piracy and Politics,* 4.

39. Scholars like C. H. Haring, *The Buccaneers in the West Indies in the XVIIth Century* (New York: E. P. Dutton, 1910; reprint, Hamden, Conn.: Archon Books, 1966), I. A. Wright, and later K. R. Andrews (see note 22) have been exceptions in the literature on sixteenth- and seventeenth-century European pirates, which remains nationalistic and largely anecdotal because it is strictly based on pirates' narratives. The best-known of these narratives include Alexander Olivier Exquemelin, *De Americaensche zee-roovers* (Amsterdam, 1678), a best-seller in its time that was adapted in English under the title *The Buccaneers and Marooners of America: Being an Account of the Famous Adventures and Daring Deeds of Certain Notorious Freebooters of the Spanish Main* (1684); *The Life and Adventures of Capt. John Avery (1709?), The Successful Pirate Charles Johnson (1713),* ed. Joel H. Baer (Los Angeles: Augustan Reprint Society, Williams Andrews Clark Memorial Library, University of California, 1980). *The Successful Pirate* was reworked in the *General History of the Pyrates,* published in 1724 (see note 24). A recent innovative approach has been in labor history: Marcus Rediker, *Between the Devil and the Deep Blue Sea: Merchant Seamen, Pirates and the Anglo American Maritime Worlds 1700–1726* (Cambridge: Cambridge University Press, 1987), and by the same author, "The Anglo-American Seaman as Collective Worker, 1700–1750," in *Work and Labor in Early America,* ed. Stephen Innes (Chapel Hill: University of North Carolina Press, 1988). Another insightful study of pirates in political history is Robert C. Ritchie, *Captain Kidd and the War against the Pirates* (Cambridge, Mass.: Harvard University Press, 1986) and, by the same author, *Pirates: Myths and Realities,* James Ford Bell Lectures no. 23 (St. Paul: Associates of the James Ford Bell Library, University of Minnesota, 1986).

40. *Piracy destroy'd: or, a short discourse shewing the rise, growth and causes of piracy of late; . . . In a letter from an officer of an East-India ship . . . to the deputy governour of the East-India-Company, London* (London: Printed and sold by John Nutt, 1701). There is a microfilm copy of this book in *The Eighteenth Century* (Woodbridge, Conn.: Research Publications, 1985; reel 1132, no. 34).

41. Pierre-François-Xavier de Charlevoix, *Histoire de l'Isle espagnole ou de S. Domingue. Ecrite particulierement sur des memoires manuscrits du p. Jean-Baptiste Le Pers, jesuite, missionaire à Saint Domingue, & sur les pieces originales, qui se conservent au Dépôt de la marine,* 2 vols. (Paris: F. Barois, 1730–31), 2:73.

42. Albert Lougnon, *L'île Bourbon pendant la Régence; Desforges-Boucher, les débuts du café* (Nérac, France: Couderc, 1956), 244, note 10.

43. Jacob Judd, "Frederick Philippe and the Madagascar Trade," *New York Historical Society Quarterly* 55 (1971): 354–374.

44. National Archives, France, Series Colonies C 8A/4, 67–85, Governor Bégon and Intendant Saint-Laurens of Martinique, January 25, 1685.

45. Daniel Defoe, *An Essay Upon Several Projects: Or, Effectual Ways for Advancing the Interests of the Nation* (London, 1697), quoted in Thomas L. Haskell, "Capitalism and the Origins of the Humanitarian Sensibility, Part II," *American Historical Review* 90, no. 3 (1985): 547–566, 588.

46. Robert Brenner, "The Social Basis of English Commercial Expansion, 1550–1650," *Economic History Review* 32 (1972): 361–384.

47. This general trend is explored by several of the articles in James D. Tracy, ed., *The Political Economy of Merchant Empires* (Cambridge: Cambridge University Press, 1991). By accepting the protection sold by modern states, merchants returned to a formula that had been used for centuries in the Mediterranean. See Frederic C. Lane, "The Economic Meaning of War and Protection," in *Venice and History: The Collected Papers of Frederic C. Lane* (Baltimore: Johns Hopkins University Press, 1966), 383–398.

48. See note 39 above.

49. Lougnon, *L'île Bourbon*. On the last Madagascar pirates in 1710–17, Lougnon writes: "A bout de souffle, très pauvres, ils soupiraient après l'amnistie" (164–165).

50. Charles Frostin, *Les révoltes blanches de Saint-Domingue aux XVIIè et XVIIIè siècles (Haïti avant 1789)* (Paris: L'Ecole, 1975), 111. On mercantilism calling for smuggling and piracy, see also Shirley Carter Hughson, *The Carolina Pirates and Colonial Commerce, 1670–1740*, Johns Hopkins University Studies in Historical and Political Science, ser. no. 5–7 (Baltimore: Johns Hopkins University, 1894).

51. See C.S.P.C.S. and political and administrative correspondence from the French Caribbean islands, Paris, National Archives Col. Ser., C7A, 8A, and 9A.

52. C.S.P.C.S., America and West Indies (1661–1668), 406. Governor Modyford, August 21, 1666. To justify the fact that he was giving freebooters arms instead of disarming them, Modyford displayed the same logic as those who today oppose reduction in armaments because it would put them in an inferior position toward an enemy who is not going to disarm: "Had it not been for that reasonable action, I could not have kept my place against the French buccaneers."

53. Exquemelin, *The Buccaneers and Marooners*, 225.

54. Charles Jean Tristan Montholon, Marquis de, *History of the Captivity of Napoleon at St. Helena*, 4 vols. (London: H. Colburn, 1846–47), 2:288.

55. Vernon A. Ives, ed., *The Rich Papers: Letters from Bermuda, 1615–1646: Eyewitness Accounts Sent by the Early Colonists to Sir Nathaniel Rich* (Toronto: University of Toronto Press, 1984), 179–180.

56. Anne Pérotin-Dumon, "The Informal Sector of Atlantic Trade: Cabotage and Contraband in the Port of Guadeloupe (1650–1800)," in *Atlantic Port Cities: Economy, Culture, and Society in the Atlantic World*, ed. Franklin W. Knight and Peggy K. Liss (Knoxville: University of Tennessee Press, 1990), 58–86.

57. Denys Lombard, "Y a-t-il une continuité des réseaux marchands asiatiques," in *Marchands et hommes d'affaires asiatiques*, ed. Denys Lombard and Jean Aubin, 11–17; Michael N. Pearson, *The Portuguese in India, New Cambridge History of India* (New York: Cambridge University Press, 1987), passim.

On the local weakness of European monopolies in Asia, see also K. N. Chaudhuri, *Trade and Civilization in the Indian Ocean: An Economic History from the Rise of Islam to 1750* (New York: Cambridge University Press, 1985), 72–73; Niels Steensgaard, *The Asian Trade Revolution of the Seventeenth Century: The East India Companies and the Decline of the Caravan Trade* (Chicago: Chicago University Press, 1974); M. N. Pearson, *Merchants and Rulers in Gujarat: The Response to the Portuguese in Sixteenth-Century Western India* (Berkeley: University of California Press, 1976); and the following articles from Leonard Blussé and Femme Gaastra, eds., *Companies and Trade: Essays on Overseas Trading Companies during the Ancien Regime* (Leiden: Leiden University Press, 1981): Pierre H. Boulle, "French Mercantilism, Commercial Companies, and Colonial Profitability," 97–117; Pieter Emmer, "The West India Company, 1621–1791: Dutch or Atlantic," 71–95; Denys Lombard, "Questions on the Contact between European Companies and Asian Societies," 179–187; Om Prakash, "European Trade and South Asian Economies: Some Regional Contrasts, 1600–1800," 189–205.

58. Michael N. Pearson, "Corruption and Corsairs in Sixteenth-Century Western India: A Functional Analysis," in *The Age of Partnership: Europeans in Asia before Dominion*, ed. Blair B. King and M. N. Pearson (Honolulu: University Press of Hawaii, 1979), 15–41; Pearson, *Portuguese in India*, 44–51.

59. Dauril Alden, "Late Colonial Brazil, 1750–1808," in *Cambridge History of Latin America*, ed. Leslie Bethell (Cambridge: Cambridge University Press, 1984), 2:149–206.

60. Jorge Juan and Antonio de Ulloa, *Discourse and Political Reflections on the Kingdom of Peru, Their Government, Special Regimen of their Inhabitants, and Abuses which have been Introduced into One and Another, with Special Information on Why They Grew up and Some Means to Avoid Them*, trans. John J. TePaske and Besse A. Clement (Norman: University of Oklahoma Press, 1978), 50.

61. Wang, "Hokkien Sojourning Communities"; Kwan-wai So, *Japanese Piracy in Ming China during the Sixteenth Century* (East Lansing: Michigan State University Press, 1975); Ray Huang, *A Year of No Significance: The Ming Dynasty in Decline* (New Haven: Yale University Press, 1981).

62. Pares, *Colonial Blockade;* Vicente De Amezaga Aresti, *Vicente Antonio de Icuza, comandante de corsarios* (Caracas: Comisión nacional del Cuatricentenario de Caracas, 1966); Fernando Serrano Mangas, "Contrabando en las costas y corrupción administrativa en el comercio de indias, 1700–1760," *Revista del Archivo Nacional* (Ecuador) 5 (1985): 53–63; J. C. M. Ogelsby, "Spain's Havana Squadron and the Preservation of the Balance of Power in the Caribbean, 1740–1748," *Hispanic American Historical Review* 49 (1969): 473–488; Angel López Cantos, *Historia de Puerto Rico, 1650–1700* (Seville: Escuela de Estudios Hispano-Americanos, 1975).

Chapter 3

The Geography of Piracy
Northern Morocco in the Mid-Nineteenth Century

C. R. Pennell

In the first decades of the nineteenth century, the Strait of Gibraltar was, as always, a disorderly place. Sea raiding had been going on in this region for centuries: corsairs in deep-water ships, licensed by the governments to attack commercial shipping, with religion as the excuse. Now ships were licensed for a secular political cause: privateers flying the flags of the newly independent South American states raided the shipping of their former Spanish overlords (and almost anyone else's shipping as well). That lasted until the early 1830s, by which time the French occupation of Algiers and the Moroccan Sultan's effective abandonment of corsairing had put an end to state-sponsored sea raiding in the Mediterranean. Then, for the next twenty-five years, another sort of raiding forced itself on international attention: that done by Moroccan fishermen, using rowing boats, and based in tiny coves along the western coastline of the Guelaya peninsula, which juts out into the Mediterranean at the far western end of Morocco. These men held no commissions or licenses from the Sultan who thought of them as criminals and rebels.

Although its traces can only be found in the archives after it became a major political and diplomatic issue,[1] there was almost certainly a long history of small-boat raiding in the region.[2] Fernand Braudel described two sorts of sea raiding in the sixteenth-century Mediterranean. On the one hand there was the privateering of big ships operating from Muslim cities like Salé and Rabat, Algiers, Tunis or Tripoli, or by Christian captains from Malta, France, Tuscany, and so on. This sort of privateering was an ancient form of war with its own rules which were recognized by all sides.[3] At least in theory, it was justified in terms of religion. On the other hand were the small-scale brigands, "minor carnivores," as Braudel called them,[4] who raided shipping without regard to any law, and without any ideological or religious motive. All ships, Christian or Muslim, were equally fair game.[5]

Both corsairs in big ships and sea bandits in small ones had economic motivations for their raiding. Corsairing in Algiers provided income for the state.[6] Similarly, the rulers of seventeenth- and eighteenth-century Tripoli, a rich variety of outsiders (Turks, Europeans, and ethnically mixed Turks and Arabs) turned to the sea for wealth. They left the hinterland of the city to the Arab and Berber tribes who lived with some difficulty in an arid environment on nomadic herding and harvesting, oasis agriculture, and cross-desert trade.[7] Much more comparable with the rowing-boat pirates of the Guelaya peninsula, however, were the individual sea brigands whom Braudel describes in other parts of the Mediterranean, inhabiting harsh and difficult regions, and unconstrained by governments which did not control the peripheral regions of their states.

Sea raiders in both big and small ships had another thing in common. They were most active where the maritime environment gave them most opportunity. Narrow straits which funneled shipping into places where ambush was easy, and escape less chancy, called the pirates into certain areas.[8] Big carnivores or small found their bases in places where they were protected from retaliation.

Thus in the sixteenth century, as in Greek and Roman times,[9] a combination of broad environmental factors pushed some inhabitants of the Mediterranean shores into sea raiding. Their poverty provided them with motivation, the maritime geography of the region gave them their opportunity, and influenced their tactics and their choice of targets. Patterns of political control and rivalry encouraged their raiding.

These interlocking factors, impulses, and choices were also at work among the Moroccans of the Guelaya peninsula in the early nineteenth century. Their harsh surroundings, the environmental and economic poverty of the region, and its peculiar political geography, linked together so that some Guelayis chose to turn to sea raiding. This article will examine the articulation of these various factors, and how Moroccan fishermen in rowing boats caught the attention of great European powers, and became a matter of international concern. Their hunting ground, after all, was a great international waterway.

The Political and Physical Frontier in the Strait

The Strait of Gibraltar is either a barrier between Morocco and Spain or a link. At different times one or the other function has been more important. When Muslim states occupied both sides of the Strait, ports on the African shore joined Spain, Morocco, and Algeria with the trade routes across the Sahara.

In the twelfth century, Ceuta, at the entrance to the Mediterranean, had been turned into a great trading place by Italian commerce. Other ports included Tangier to the west and, to the east, several small harbors on a rocky, cliff-lined coast dotted with coves. Badis was a bustling port in the thirteenth and fourteenth centuries,[10] as were al-Muzimma in Alhucemas Bay,[11] and Ghassassa on the western side of the Guelaya peninsula.[12] Melilla, on the other side of the peninsula, had been a port since Carthaginian times.

The lively maritime commerce of the medieval Rif stagnated after the *Reconquista* of Islamic Spain by the Christian states. When the Portuguese took the war onto North African soil by occupying Ceuta in 1415, they began to undermine Morocco's Mediterranean commerce. The Spanish occupation of Melilla (1497), Ghassassa (briefly in 1506), Badis (briefly in 1508 and permanently in 1564), and finally an islet in Alhucemas Bay (1673), completed the process.[13] The enclaves and islands first became "*fronteras*," marcher castles on the Islamic frontier, and then a combination of military garrisons and penal colonies.

Commerce virtually disappeared from Morocco's Mediterranean coast, and the economic orientation of the country shifted to the Atlantic coast. With Spanish forts blocking every good anchorage, the Strait became a barrier rather than a link. The Rif mountains declined into a backwater and political and economic systems developed there which were locally organized and resulted from local conditions. This was a poor, frontier society in which smuggling, raiding, and piracy had major roles.

A Permeable Frontier

There never was a clean division between the "Christian" north coast and the "Muslim" south. People moved backward and forward with scant regard for the political authorities, and sometimes in open opposition to them.

The Spanish penal settlement of Melilla was so unpleasant that many of the prisoners, and some of their guards, escaped to the *campo moro*, where some became Muslims and settled down, though others were killed or enslaved. Less frequently, Rifis became Spaniards.[14] State officials and governments played little part in this, although the Spanish authorities maintained a network of political contacts in the hinterland: spies and go-betweens in ransom negotiations.

In fact, traders were much more important, although Moroccan sultans regularly forbade trade with the Spanish, on the grounds that it was trading with the enemies of Islam. Several times in the eighteenth and early nineteenth centuries, the sultans besieged the Spanish *presidios* and did their best to break commercial relations between the Spanish and the local population. In 1812

Sultan Sulayman sent a military expedition to the Guelaya to punish the people for selling corn to the Spanish.[15] In the usual style of such expeditions, it laid about it, burning villages, pillaging and devastating fields. But another expedition had to be sent in 1813.[16] This was episodic reprisal, not control.

Trading continued regardless of the Sultan's wishes. Sometimes formal arrangements were made between the Spanish and local tribes,[17] otherwise individuals brought goods to market.[18] There was plenty of outright smuggling, by Spaniards and Rifis alike. A favorite item in the 1840s was leeches, a farmed monopoly of the Moroccan state. These were smuggled out in huge numbers, having been purchased through intermediaries in the Spanish fort at Peñon de Vélez. In 1847, Moroccan port officials in Tangier found 24,000 contraband leeches on board a small Spanish *falucha*.[19]

At the same time, the Spanish in the *presidios* and the inhabitants of the surrounding countryside carried on an intermittent but endemic war. The episodic raiding and counterraiding was a mixture of entrepreneurship, reprisals, religious rivalry, and bravado. Sometimes the war was carried on offshore when Rifis would surround small Spanish boats at sea. The Spanish did much the same sort of thing in return.[20]

There was also a more permanent, organized opposition. Facing the *presidio* at Badis was a Moroccan fort which was usually under the direct control of the government. In the 1840s and 1850s the Sultan sent regular orders for the rotation of troops there.[21] Further east such efforts were locally organized. On the beach at Alhucemas, the Burj al-Mujahidin (Fort of the Fighters of *Jihad*) was permanently manned by contingents drawn from among the local people, and from time to time they exchanged shots with the Spanish island.[22] At Melilla, the local contingents were sometimes supplied with guns by the central government but they were not controlled by the Sultan.[23]

Moroccan sultans had so little control over the Guelaya peninsula that the 1799 treaty between Morocco and Spain specifically excluded the Rif coast from the promises of Moroccan friendship for Spain, because the Sultan could not prevent the local people from attacking the Spanish.[24] In 1844 the Sultan described the Rifis to the British Consul-General "not so much as common subjects, but as savage bandits, who are outside the domain of the law and are not at present subject to its authority."[25]

This remark was not just a diplomatic palliative. In 1841, the Sultan told the governor of Tetuan to arrest anyone from the Guelaya tribe of Banu Shikar because they were inveterate smugglers and their profits went toward financing their rebelliousness. In 1850, he gave the same instruction about the Buquyya tribe near Badis.[26] In short, the Guelayis were troublemakers, bandits, and smugglers. That behavior was to a large extent influenced by the very difficult environment in which they lived.

Sea Raiding and the Environment

The Guelaya peninsula is ungrateful land to farm. In 1854, the French consul Charles Jagerschmidt described the main pirate village:

> The village of Azanen . . . is extremely poor. The main resource of the inhabitants is fishing; they are a miserable people, generally lazy and only cultivate the land to the extent that they need to; some undertake a bit of commerce in wood or salt, which abounds in the country.[27]

Not all the Guelaya peninsula was as bleak as this, but nowhere was it very rich. On average, the area gets less than 600 mm of rain a year, and less than 400 mm inland. When it does rain, water mostly runs off the hard igneous and arenaceous rocks of the peninsula. The mountains are denuded of trees, and have been for some centuries. Deep gullies in the bare slopes, cut by torrents which flow during the winter rains, are typical of the environmental degradation of the Rif as a whole.

This degradation originated in the still rather obscure environmental history of the Rif. A high population led to intensive clearing of the hillsides, erosion, and gullying of mountain slopes which had once been thickly wooded. Deforestation probably began in the late seventeenth century: parts of the central Rif, which today are denuded of trees, were described as being thickly wooded in the mid-seventeenth century.[28] The Rifis coped with these difficult conditions by emigrating to more prosperous parts of Morocco, and from the 1850s onward to French Algeria, where they were employed in the winter, returning in the summer for the harvest. Banditry and smuggling were other outlets.[29]

The Guelaya peninsula shared these traits. The total population in the early nineteenth century is unknown but people from the area considered it very high. The Guelayi cook of the British Consul-General in Tangier, Edward Drummond-Hay, told him in 1832 that the Guelaya could "send forth 40,000 armed men," which Drummond-Hay thought an exaggeration.[30] Alternatives to agriculture were few: mining soapstone, and a local gunsmithing industry whose products had a higher reputation than those of the big city of Tetuan.[31]

Cultivation was confined to gardens in the valleys, such as those around the shrine of Sidi Misa'ud, where a small creek almost joins the sea: it is cut off from the Mediterranean by a shingle bank between six and ten feet wide. The ruins of the medieval port of Ghassassa are on the top of a hill on the northern bank. Further south, there is more cultivation behind the beach at Azanen. Captain H. W. Giffard of the British navy described this area in 1852:

> The land all about was highly cultivated and over great extent, of moderate height but undulating and intersected with some gullies and ravines, no bush cover and no large hills within 4 or 5 miles, several villages about two miles from

the shore, and numerous detached houses. Rounding the promontory we observed a few horses, mules, donkeys, much cattle, flocks of sheep and goats, and a deep open bay called Zera with six boats at the bottom, near which, a rivulet with steep and high banks in places, runs into the sea, on the right of the Bay the land again became high and mountainous close to the sea, it was a sandy rise with very low bush and back near the village we saw olive trees; numerous armed parties watched us, and it has all the appearance of a very populous and flourishing district.[32]

Such fecundity was hard-won. When John Drummond-Hay, the British Consul-General in Tangier, cruised up the Guelaya coast with some naval officers in the spring of 1856, he recorded that:

> We were surprised to observe the care and industry, shown by these wild people in the cultivation of the soil. Every patch of arable ground, appeared to have been taken advantage of and we observed that terraces, were frequently built on the sandy slopes to prevent the soil being carried away by the heavy rains.[33]

The mainstay of the local population was fishing. The Rif coast is rich in fish because cool currents flow into the Mediterranean from the Atlantic and provide a rich supply of plankton.[34] Drummond-Hay reckoned that he must have seen "upwards of forty or fifty boats" in his trip along the Rif coast, eight or nine large ones near Azanen; Giffard saw isolated boats in other places and six or seven near Azanen. These were big boats, rowed by as many as sixteen oars, and able to carry more than thirty men,[35] so that they could also be used for trade.

Since little enough was produced locally, the coasting trade was a lifeline, linking Tetuan to the west and Algeria to the east of the Rif. It is impossible to know how big it was, nor the extent to which it was affected by the French occupation of Algiers and Oran, but in the 1850s it was thriving, encouraged by the French conquerors of Algeria, both for political and for economic reasons.[36] Some Rifis, especially Guelayis, migrated to western Algeria to find employment,[37] while others engaged in the coasting trade.

Economic Incentives to Piracy

This coastal trade was threatened by the Spanish who were strategically situated to stop it. Rifi boats trading between Tetuan and Algeria had to pass in front of three *presidios* (four after the Spanish occupied the Chafarinas Islands in 1849). The Spanish attacked them.

In October 1832, a lateen-sailed craft on its way from Algeria to Tetuan with a cargo of wool, salted ox skins, dry goatskins, wax, ticking, striped wool cloth, matting, and foodstuffs, was stopped at Melilla. The Algerian owner called this aggression, although the Spanish military justified it as a retaliation for "the outrage those people inflicted on the Spanish flag." The same excuse was given for capturing a boat belonging to the Banu Sicar tribe in Guelaya in 1832. In October 1834 two small boats from the Banu Sa'id tribe were captured when, the Governor of Melilla claimed, they attacked the Spanish coast guard—an unlikely scenario. The Banu Sa'id did not usually attack the Spanish and the boats had women and a child aboard.[38]

This war on Moroccan trade was stepped up after the appointment as governor of Melilla of Colonel Manuel Buceta in 1854. The boat bringing him to his new command was attacked by three Rifi boats, which were driven off. The experience determined Buceta, a very bellicose man, to break the siege of Melilla. In 1855 he led a big raid out of the city, but lost many men when the troops got beyond the range of covering fire from Melilla.[39] Then Buceta began a commercial war against Moroccan shipping. The navy ministry described this as a war on smugglers, but European and Moroccan "smugglers" were treated in quite different ways. Under standing instructions, European smugglers were taken to Malaga and dealt with by the customs authorities; Moroccan vessels were treated as prizes taken in war.[40]

The campaign was vigorously pursued. In August 1856 Buceta boasted that in twenty-one months, forty-four Moroccan ships had been seized and confiscated, leading to "the complete paralysation of the coastal trade which they used to carry on with Tetuan and Algeria." He considered this a great success, because it forced the local leaders to promise to prevent any more attacks on Spanish ships and to return the crew and boats they had captured.[41]

Did Spanish raiding of Rifi ships cause or result from the rise in Rifi piracy? Undoubtedly, attacks on Spanish ships did increase in the 1850s—and tailed off after 1856—but not all the victims were Spanish. Some were British and, in one case, French, with whom the Rifis had no specific quarrel. Even the French consul, Jagerschmidt, who disliked the British, knew that the Guelayis distinguished between attacks on British and on Spanish vessels:

> They openly admit that the robberies they commit on British ships are acts of piracy. . . . But they absolutely reject the term pirates when applied to their attacks on Spanish shipping. They attack the Spanish openly, under the very guns of Melilla, and declare that when they act in this way they are acting in accordance with the rights of war.[42]

Moreover, the pirates, who were all Guelayis, were not those at the sharp end of Buceta's policy of interdicting trade. Most of the victims came from the Banu Sa'id, further west and an important center of coastal trade with Tetuan and Algeria. The Banu Sa'id were not pirates: they had fewer opportunities for piracy, since few European ships approached their beaches, and they were under the influence of a local religious leader, Sidi Muhammad al-Hadary who opposed piracy.

Al-Hadary's personal reputation for holiness, grounded partly on good works, was put at the service of the British and French consuls in Tangier, and eventually the Spanish military authorities in Melilla, to recover their crews and put a stop to piracy.[43] According to him this was motivated by religious principle: he even rescued Spanish seamen although the Spanish were detested by most Rifis. Yet al-Hadary was also a major participant in the coastal trade on his own account: he had several boats trading with Algeria and Tetuan. Despite the assistance he had given the Spanish in rescuing their seamen he was just as subject to attacks on his boats, so it was in his interest to reduce the possibility of conflict.[44]

In any event, the attacks on his, and other Sa'idi, boats took place sometime after Guelayi attacks on Spanish shipping had stopped, although al-Hadary believed they might provide an excuse for the raiding to start again, and worried that reprisals might spiral out of control.[45]

The Geographical Backdrop to Piracy

If the Guelayis were not the main victims of Spanish raiding, it is likely that other factors were also involved. That one Guelayi tribe, the Banu Bu Gafar, was responsible for nearly all the attacks suggests what those other factors might be. All accounts of the incidents show that these were opportunistic pirates and it was the physical geography of the region that gave the Banu Bu Gafar their chance. The same currents that brought fish to the coast of the Rif brought European ships as well, and the same rocky coastline that made cultivation so difficult, hid them from reprisal.

In 1863 the *Nautical Magazine* warned captains of the danger of being becalmed between Peñon de Vélez and Alhucemas:

> In summer, calms are frequent on the Riff coast, and if there is any wind on the coast it is generally light from the East or S.E., even while in the offing a fresh levanter may be blowing. Sometimes a N.E. sea will be running on the coast, which contributes to set vessels down upon it that may be becalmed in this barbarous neighbourhood. . . . The general current on penetrating into the Mediterranean splits more in proportion the further it is from the Strait, inclining to the S.E. on the African coast; as in other parts light winds and calms prevail, hence vessels beating to the eastward in mid channel should be cautious in their southern boards until they get on the coast of Algiers. They should remember that it is easy to get becalmed even at twenty to thirty miles from the Morocco coast, and

be drawn by the current towards Cape Tres Forcas, where they will be exposed
to the pirates.[46]

Natural forces combined to strand hapless merchant ships right in front of
beaches where there were a large number of sea-going rowing boats owned by
people who were poor. And nature protected the Gafaris from reprisals.

The fishing boats operated out of small coves backed by high cliffs and
rocky terrain, with narrow gullies leading up into the interior. It was a natural
defensive position. In October 1851 Lieutenant Ashmore Powell of the British
Royal Navy mounted a cutting-out expedition to punish the Gafaris for their
attack on the *Violet*, and met with fierce resistance:

> The sides of the creek which were nearly precipitous were lined with pirates
> under cover, with their long guns appearing over the rocks.[47]

Four months later, he and Captain Henry Giffard surveyed the coast to find
suitable sites for a landing:

> From this the coast westward is high, rocky and precipitous, without cultivation
> for full three miles, when a little [illegible] is observable up a narrow ravine with
> a small sandy beach to the sea, three quarters of a mile from this is the pirates
> creek, which Commander Powell attacked but could not land, we observed one
> boat, but there might be many more concealed, the natives collected in numbers
> on the rocks commanding it, as if it was a place they wished to defend, round the
> southern point of this creek was another sandy beach which led to a narrow val-
> ley opening with larger dimensions as it ascended amongst the hills, where it was
> highly and richly cultivated, with terraced gardens &ca and over a large extent
> of ground, here was a village and numerous detached houses, it would be diffi-
> cult of attack without a large force.[48]

The high cliffs made excellent lookouts to observe passing ships, spot suitable
victims, and to be forewarned about any reprisals. If an attack was threatened,
their boats were easy to hide, either by burying them in the sand, or by pulling
them up into caves and ravines.[49] Drummond-Hay's Guelayi cook told him
about a vast cave at Marsa Ifri, "so large that fishing boats shelter in it." In the
1940s, it was still remembered as a place where pirates used to hide their boats.[50]

The caves and coves also served as places to dispose of the booty. Powell
came across a busy scene:

> On the 18th at 2 P.M. I made out a vessel stranded at the bottom of a deep Bay
> four miles to the westward of Tres Forcas. Some casks were on the Beach, and a
> number of men were plundering the vessel. . . . under cover of the guns I pro-
> ceeded in the cutter and gig to reconnoitre. At the bottom of the Bay we found
> the vessel bilged and partly hauled up a narrow creek which terminated in a
> gully in the mountain. In this creek two large piratical boats were hauled up, and

the beach was strewed with large masts, yards and equipments of vessels that had been plundered.

All this made it very difficult to take revenge on the pirates. Powell found it easy enough to shell one of the creeks, but in another bay things were more difficult:

> The Janus was anchored in a position to command the Beach, although the piratical boats being sheltered behind some sandhills we were unable to destroy them with our guns.

His landing party was fiercely resisted by Rifis firing down from cover behind rocks. Despite covering fire from *Janus*, ten men were wounded in the engagement, many dangerously, including Powell.[51]

These difficulties deterred the French from a naval reprisal after the *Jeune Dieppois* was captured in 1856. The Minister for War explained to the Governor of Algeria that the mountains along the Rif coast resembled those of Grande Kabylie in Algeria, where the French army was having much trouble at the time. A naval bombardment would be pointless, because there was no port on the coast, and no real villages to burn. The wall of cliffs made any landing to burn the crops far too dangerous. Only a combined operation with the British in Gibraltar and the Spanish in Melilla, and a deep thrust from the French from Algeria might work, but this posed other political problems. The Spanish might use the opportunity to extend their *presidios* or the British to occupy territory permanently, which would have severe repercussions on French power in Algeria.[52] Such geostrategic problems stymied European action.

The Political Geography of Suppression and Invasion

One of the contributing factors to Guelayi piracy was the loose nature of the Moroccan government's control of the region. So, when the political geography of the region was changed, piracy was ended, for the moment. Under diplomatic pressure from the British the Moroccan government decided to take control of the Rif. In late 1855 an extremely tough and able commander, Muhammad bin 'Abd al-Malik bin Abu, took eight thousand troops into the eastern Rif, imposed heavy fines, and demanded punitive taxes. In the settlements of the Banu Bu Gafar he burned boats, destroyed villages, confiscated cattle, and took hostages against future good behavior.[53]

At first this "success" rebounded against the Moroccan government. In August 1856 the French Consul-General claimed that now that bin Abu had collected taxes, the Sultan could no longer claim that the Rif was beyond his control. Therefore he was responsible for the piratical attacks of its inhabitants and should pay an indemnity of 35,000 francs for the loss of the *Jeune Diep-pois*. Independently, the British Consul-General demanded compensation for British ships that had been captured.[54] In May 1856, after another British ship had been taken, bin Abu was sent back to the Rif with the Sultan's instructions to stay there until he had forced the Guelayis to pay reparations. He did so in no uncertain terms, by levying heavy fines and imposing heavy taxes.[55]

When bin Abu came back, both the French and British indemnities were paid, and both European governments expressed the hope that the Sultan would remain in control of the area.[56] To the extent that attacks on shipping now stopped, even on Spanish boats, this was what happened. Drummond-Hay tried to go one stage further. He was able to persuade the Sultan of the need to build a new walled town on the coast. He said that this would strengthen the government's presence in the Rif, that customhouses would provide revenue, and the Rifis would be diverted into a legal trade away from smuggling into Algeria.[57] He could not persuade the Sultan to find the money to put these plans into effect, and the political and economic orientation of the Rif was not permanently altered as he had hoped. Consequently, when government control over the Rif broke down again in the late nineteenth century, piracy reappeared—although this time it was centered slightly further to the west, in the Alhucemas region.[58]

Conclusion

The reappearance of piracy in the Rif at the end of the nineteenth century, while not the subject of this article, indicates that piracy was not simply "caused" by one or more permanent factors. It was a response to specific circumstances, which were themselves influenced by geographical considerations. Environmental degradation had impoverished a region of high population. A traditional religious and ideological enemy physically occupied parts of the coast, throttling the economy and shattering local people's trade along the coast; it also made it far too difficult and expensive for the Moroccan government to maintain detailed control.

The political and economic circumstances of the region provided motives for piracy, but other parts of the coast suffered equally badly—the Banu Sa'id for instance. But they lacked the opportunities provided by convenient currents, handy beaches, and deep cave refuges which could be easily defended. Conjunctural factors interlocked with these more permanent ones. Changing patterns of political control and the aggressiveness with which both the Moroccan government and the Spanish in the *presidios* asserted control of the coast made piracy more or less attractive or possible. An interplay between political and economic structures on the one hand, and the physical geography of the region on the other, influenced the Guelayis in their choice of being fishermen or bandits.

NOTES

1. C. R. Pennell, "Dealing with Pirates: British French and Moroccans 1834–1856," *Journal of Imperial and Commonwealth History* 21 (1994): 54–83.

2. Fernand Braudel, *The Mediterranean and the Mediterranean World in the Age of Philip II*, trans. Sian Reynolds, 2 vols. (London: Collins, 1972–73), 744, points out how long piracy and banditry had existed in the Mediterranean.

3. Ibid., 880–887.

4. Ibid., 871.

5. Ibid., 867, 877–878.

6. Ibid., 880–887.

7. C. R. Pennell, "Tripoli in the Late Seventeenth Century: The Economics of Corsairing in a 'Sterill Country,'" *Libyan Studies* 16 (1985); K. S. McLachlan, "Tripoli and Tripolitania: Conflict and Cohesion during the Period of the Barbary Corsairs," *Transactions of the Institute of British Geographers* 3 (1978): 285–294.

8. Braudel, *Mediterranean*, 130, 887.

9. Ibid., 866; Henry A. Ormerod, *Piracy in the Ancient World: An Essay in Mediterranean History* (Liverpool: Liverpool University Press, 1924).

10. Fouad Zaïm, *Le Maroc et son espace méditerranéen* (Rabat: Confluences, 1990), 32; David M. Hart, *The Aith Waryaghar of the Moroccan Rif: An Ethnography and History* (Tucson: University of Arizona Press, 1976), 348.

11. Zaïm, *Espace*, 32.

12. Ibid., 35–36.

13. Ibid., 73–74.

14. Henk Driessen, *On the Spanish-Moroccan Frontier: A Study in Ritual, Power and Ethnicity* (Oxford: Berg, 1992), 24–29; Braudel, *Mediterranean*, 861.

15. Zaïm, *Espace*, 114.

16. Abu al-'Abbas Ahmad bin Khalid al-Nasiri, *Kitab al-istiqsa l-akhbar duwwal al-Magrib al-Aqsa*, 9 vols. (Rabat: Dar al-Kitab, 1956), 9: 127–128.

17. Zaïm, *Espace*, 112.

18. Driessen, *Frontier*, 33.

19. Spain, Archivo Histórico Nacional (hereafter AHN), Estado 5825, note by Beramendí, Spanish Consul-General, Tangier, 26 March 1847.

20. Driessen, *Frontier*, 21–23.

21. E.g., the following letters from Mawlay 'Abd al-Rahman to Busilham b. 'Ali in Archives du Palais Royale, Rabat, Morocco (hereafter MAPR), 5/5–8, 22 Shawwal 1256/17 December 1840; 5/5–26, 4 Shawwal 1260/17 October 1844; 5/14–21, 23 Safar 1265/18 January 1849; 5/14–38, 3 Muharram 1266/19 November 1849; 5/15–17, 3 Muharram 1267/8 November 1850.

22. Hart, *Aith Waryaghar*, 360.

23. MAPR 6/5–33, Mawlay 'Abd al-Rahman to Muhammad 'Ash'ash, 13 Jumada II 1258/22 July 1842 concerning the supply of a gun to the fort in the Guelaya.

24. Clive Parry, ed., *The Consolidated Treaty Series*, 231 vols. (Dobbs Ferry, N.Y.: Oceana Publications, 1969–1981), 54: 413–428.

25. Ibid., 97: 326–331.

26. MAPR 9/4–35 Mawlay 'Abd al-Rahman to Muhammad 'Ash'ash, 16 Sha'ban 1257/3 October 18412; 4/4–10 Mawlay 'Abd al-Rahman to 'Abd al-Qadir 'Ash'ash, 1 Muharram 1267/6 November 1850.

27. Archives du Ministère des Affaires Etrangères, Quai d'Orsay, Paris, France (hereafter MAEF), Correspondance Politique Maroc 27, Jagerschmidt to [Ministre des Affaires Etrangères], Tangier, 10 August 1854.

28. John Robert McNeill, *The Mountains of the Mediterranean World: An Environmental History* (Cambridge: Cambridge University Press, 1992), 99–101.

29. McNeill, *Mountains,* 117–119, 123–124.

30. Bodleian Library, Oxford, Britain, MS Eng Hist E354, Commonplace book of E. W. A. Drummond-Hay, 141; MS Eng Hist E355, Memoranda of African Geography, 13.

31. Bodleian Library, MS Eng Hist E355, 13; MS Eng Hist E354, 168.

32. PRO FO99/69, 113–124 Captain H. W. Giffard [R.N.] to [Parker] HMS Dragon, Gibraltar, 23 January 1852, Copy.

33. PRO FO99/74, 24–42, "Copy of Mr Drummond Hay's Diary during his cruize to the Reef coast on board H.M.S. Miranda."

34. McNeill, *Mountains,* 125.

35. PRO FO99/74, 24–42, "Copy of Mr Drummond Hay's Diary during his cruize to the Reef coast on board H.M.S. Miranda"; FO99/69, 113–124 Giffard to [Parker] HMS Dragon, Gibraltar, 23 January 1852, Copy; FO174/41, Gulieglmo Colombino to Sardinian Consul General in Tangier, Tlemasaman [*sic*], 22 July 1834.

36. C. R. Pennell, "The Maritime Trade on the Northern Morocco Coast in the Early Nineteenth Century," *Morocco*, (n.s.), 1 (1996): 85–96.

37. McNeill, *Mountains,* 212–222.

38. AHN, Madrid, Estado 5825, "Expediente Cárabos morunos" José Rico to [Primer Secretario del Despacho de Estado], Tangier, 27 November 1832, no. 274; Javier Abadui [Capitán-General de Granada] to [Primer Secretario del Despacho de Estado], Granada, 20 January 1833; Rico to Zea Bermúdez, Tangier, 9 April 1833, no. 299; minute, 17 April 1833; Estado 5825, "Expediente 1834" Minute 1 Secretaría de Estado, Madrid, 26 January 1835; Estado 5825, "Expediente 1835" Beramendí to Martínez de la Rosa, Tangier, 4 January 1835, no. 409; Estado 8364, Beramendí to [Martínez de la Rosa], Tangier, 20 July 1836, no. 548 and Tangier, 23 June 1835, no. 457.

39. MAEF ADP Maroc 3 1853–1866, "Pillage du Jeune Dieppois," C. De Bouzel to [Ministre des Affaires Etrangères], Malaga, 16 July 1855.

40. Archivo General de la Marina "Alvaro Bazán," El Viso del Marqués, Spain, Guardacostas Asuntos Particulares 1856 legajo 1201, Minute of Juan Salomón, 10 January 1856.

41. Archives de l'Ancien Gouvernement de l'Algérie, Aix-en-Provence, France (hereafter, Aix, Gouvernement de l'Algérie), 30H26 Dossier 1, Zugasti (Spanish Consul-General in Algiers) to Governor of Algiers (trans A. Hanoteaux), Algiers, 9 September 1856, no. 128.

42. MAEF Correspondance Politique Maroc 25, 184, Jagerschmidt to de Turgot, Tangier, 7 June 1852.

43. C. R. Pennell, "John Drummond-Hay: Tangier as the Centre of a Spider's web," in *Tanger 1800–1956, Contribution à l'histoire récente du Maroc*, ed. A. Bendaoud and M. Maniar (Rabat: Editions Arabo-Africaines, 1991), 107–134.

44. Pennell, "Maritime Trade."

45. PRO FO174/135, 141, al-Hadary to Wazir Sifar, 10 Safar 1275/28 September 1858 (translation).

46. "The Western Division of the Mediterranean—Navigation Passages from West to East," *Nautical Magazine* 32 (1863): 460–461.

47. PRO FO174/56, copy of letter from Lieut. Powell [commander of Janus] to Sir William Parker [V-Admiral commanding Mediterranean Fleet], Tangier, 22 October 1851.

48. PRO FO99/69, 113–124, Captain H. W. Giffard to "The Admiral in the Mediterranean" [Parker] HMS Dragon, Gibraltar, 23 January 1852, Copy.

49. PRO FO99/81, 67–78, Drummond-Hay to Hammond, Tangier, 11 August 1856.

50. Bodleian Library MS Eng Hist E354, 141 and 163; Rafael Fernández de Castro y Pedrera, *Historia y exploración de las ruinas de Cazaza, villa del antiguo reino de Fez, emplazada en la costa occidental de la península de Tres Forcas* (Tetuan: Instituto Generalissimo Franco, 1943), 4, and photographs 1, 2, and 3.

51. PRO FO174/56, copy of letter from Lieut. Powell [commander of Janus] to Sir William Parker, [V-Admiral commanding Mediterranean Fleet], Tangier, 22 October 1851.

52. MAEF ADP Maroc 3 1853–1866, Dossier "Pillage du Jeune Dieppois" Vaillant to [Governor General of Algeria], Paris, 22 August 1856.

53. Archives du Ministère des Affaires Etrangères, Nantes, France, Tanger (hereafter ADN), Anciens Fonds, 115–a 15/2, "Correspondance de l'Agence Consulaire de Tétouan 1849–1844," bundle for 1855, Nahon to Fr Chargé in Tangier, Tetuan, 29 November 1855.

54. PRO FO174/134, 35–37, John Drummond-Hay to al-Khatib, 29 May 1856 (translation).

55. PRO FO99/81, 20–25, Drummond-Hay to Clarendon, Tangier, 13 July 1856; ADN, Tanger AF 115 A-15/3, "Correspondance de l'Agence Consulaire de Tétouan 1856," Nahon to Castellon, Tetuan, 11 November 1856.

56. Aix, Gouvernement de l'Algérie, 30H26 Dossier 5 [Walewski] to Vaillant [Min of War], Paris, 8 October 1856.

57. PRO FO174/134, 257, John Drummond-Hay to al-Khatib [Tangier], 18 April 1857, "Secret."

58. Hart, *Aith Waryaghar*, 355.

Chapter 4

The Origins and Regulation of Eighteenth-Century British Privateering

David J. Starkey

The term "privateering" embraced a variety of activities common in the maritime wars of the eighteenth century. Principally it related to the privately owned vessels licensed by the state to set out with the specific intention of seizing enemy property on the high seas. In Britain these private men-of-war ranged in size and ambition from the tiny "cockleshells" of the Channel Islands which harassed French coastal traffic in the adjacent waters, to the ocean-going squadrons fitted out in London and Bristol to cruise more distantly in search of Spanish register ships and French East Indiamen. Also within the "privateering" compass lay the armed merchantmen, vessels primarily concerned with trade but equipped with commissions to take advantage of a chance meeting with a potential prize. Indeed, some enterprises combined predatory and commercial aims, a private man-of-war perhaps abandoning a barren cruise to take in a cargo, or an armed trader indulging in commerce raiding on the return leg of a voyage. Such varied activities shared much common ground, of course: their main purpose was to earn profits for the individuals concerned in the venture; their means were often violent, involving the forced appropriation of foreign ships and property; and their legitimacy was undoubted, these acts of private maritime warfare being formally sanctioned by the state.

While their aims and means had close affinities with those of pirates, privateers were also closely related to state navies since their authority was valid only in wartime and against enemy property. Thus, privateers inevitably carried the taint of piracy despite their potential utility to the state in an age when destruction of enemy commerce was afforded a high strategic priority. This paper examines the peculiar, slightly paradoxical, status of privateering in eighteenth-century warfare by focusing on the evolution of the phenomenon and on the regulatory measures adopted by the state to maximize its efficiency as a tool of war. Such an examination is intended to throw some light on the nature of British privateering enterprise in the wars of the eighteenth century.[1]

Origins

Although the phrase "private man-of-war" was not coined until 1646 and the term "privateer" dates back only to 1664,[2] it is clear that forms of privateering had been practiced much earlier. The activity, in fact, developed from a number of sources which can be traced back to medieval times. Certainly its roots lie in the ancient custom of reprisal. This was a means by which an individual could redress, by force if necessary, a proven grievance against a foreign subject. It was a measure of last resort, for the wronged party could only petition his sovereign for "letters of marque, and reprisal" once all efforts to obtain satisfaction using the legal processes of the foreign state had failed. Once granted, the "letters of reprisal" empowered the petitioner to recover the amount of his loss from any of the transgressor's compatriots, with any surplus accountable to his own sovereign. Such a device made possible minor acts of war without breaking the general peace but it was open to abuse as it led to the proliferation of counter-reprisals. Nevertheless, reprisals were sought and granted throughout the Middle Ages; in England, the procedure was regulated by statute in the early fifteenth century, while in France requests for grants of reprisal were judged in Parlement.[3]

From this concept of the redress of individual loss by reprisal in peacetime there evolved the notion of "general" reprisals against an enemy nation in wartime. Nations could justify acts of war as retaliatory measures against an aggressor, and therefore reprisals against the subjects of the offending nation were permissible. In July 1739, for instance, general reprisals were granted against Spanish commerce in retaliation for the depredations purportedly committed by the Spanish *guarda-costas* in the Caribbean, while in December 1780 the reluctance of the United Provinces to respond to a series of published British grievances provoked the authorization of general reprisals against Dutch trade and shipping. Moreover, the terminology of medieval reprisals survived and was still applied to the "general" reprisals of the later era. Thus, the terms "letter of marque,"[4] "letters of marque and reprisal," and "letters of reprisal" were used to describe the licenses granted to privateers from the mid-sixteenth century, though this usage was inappropriate in the strictest sense, as the rights implied by such grants were only applicable in peacetime.[5]

Another origin of privateering is to be found in the use of private ships by the state for purposes of war in the days when royal navies were nonexistent or inadequate. In England, the Norman kings depended upon the coast towns, particularly the Cinque Ports, to mobilize a set number of ships during an emergency, occasionally, as in 1242, ordering all the vessels of the Channel ports to commit every possible injury upon the enemy at sea.[6] In the fourteenth and fifteenth centuries there were several instances of "putting out to contract the keeping of the seas,"[7] while Henry VIII made use of a large number of hired merchant ships to augment his fledgling navy in the French wars of the 1540s. It was therefore customary for the state to hire or impress privately owned vessels, authorizing them, by virtue of "commissions," to act as ships of war. Though the growth of navies in the seventeenth century meant that the state became less reliant on the merchant service, the capacity to commission merchant vessels was retained and on occasion it was invoked to authorize acts of private maritime warfare. For example, in the American Revolutionary War, when it was theoretically impossible to grant reprisals against the rebellious North American colonists, who were still subjects of His Britannic Majesty, commissions were issued to authorize the seizure of goods carried in contravention of the 1775 Prohibition of Trade Act.[8]

If the letter of marque and the privateer commission derived from separate origins, the difference in the application of their respective powers was purely technical by the eighteenth century. Indeed, it was the Admiralty's practice to address "the commanders of such merchant ships and vessels as may have letters of marque, or commissions, for private men-of-war."[9] This terminological elasticity was stretched still further by the application of the term "letter of marque" to a particular form of eighteenth-century privateering vessel, the armed merchantman, as well as to the document she carried. This strain of "privateering" derived from a third origin of the activity, and again it can be traced back over the centuries.

Trading vessels had long since carried arms to protect themselves against assailants, particularly in the more distant trades to Africa, the West Indies, and Asia. In such dangerous areas they might be called upon to use their weapons and a successful action against a pirate or enemy ship might result in its capture. However, it became a principle of maritime law that a captor without a commission had no legal title to his prize, which was usually condemned as a "droit and perquisite" of the Admiralty. Therefore, to reap the rewards of such an encounter, or to profit from a meeting with a weak or incapacitated enemy vessel, owners of these armed traders began to take out commissions for their vessels in wartime. Thus, by the eighteenth century, the privateering forces of belligerent powers included a number of merchant vessels, armed primarily to deter aggressors, but licensed to take prizes should the opportunity afford itself in the course of a commercial voyage.

In broad terms, two separate types of privateering activity had developed from these origins by 1700. In the first place, the commissioned merchantman, or "letter of marque" as she became known, clearly evolved from the customary need to arm vessels engaged in long-distance trades. The "letter of marque" carried a cargo, and its safe delivery was the captain's main priority. To this end he might delay his departure until the sailing of a convoy, or he might seek the company of a British man-of-war or privateer in potentially dangerous waters, or he might gamble and sail independently, taking care to avoid areas where enemy men-of-war or *corsaires* were known to cruise.[10] Either way, captains of commissioned trading vessels were usually under orders to make prize of enemy property if the opportunity arose. Such a capture might add greatly to the profit of a commercial venture and the captain and his crew would also benefit from the distribution of prize money on top of their basic wages. Amongst the commissioned merchantmen were the vessels owned or hired by the great chartered companies. The Royal Africa Company, the Hudson's Bay Company, and, most significantly, the East India Company, all took out letters of marque for their vessels during wartime. As with other armed traders, the licenses carried by these ships added a predatory dimension to their regular trading voyages.

The second type of privateer, the private man-of-war, was a descendant of the private reprisal vessels and the merchant fighting ships of the medieval and early modern age. These were the privateers proper, the additional forces that formed "an effective constituent of England's naval power."[11] Some were purpose-built, though the majority were merchantmen converted for the task of commerce destruction. Naval vessels were occasionally bought and fitted out as private men-of-war; in February 1745, for instance, a group of Bristol merchants purchased H.M.S. *Hastings* and adapted her for privateering.[12] Prize vessels were sometimes redeployed as privateers, with some, such as the *Dover's Prize* of London and *Kitty's Amelia* of Liverpool, having their names altered to bear testimony to their origin. Private men-of-war embarked on cruises rather than voyages, carrying little, if any, cargo. Generally, they were heavily armed and naval terminology was applied to the officers and crew; thus, privateers carried lieutenants rather than mates, midshipmen instead of apprentices, and the crew often included a surgeon and a gunner.[13] Indeed, the size and composition of its crew were probably the most distinctive features of the eighteenth-century private man-of-war. Invariably this predator would be heavily manned in relation to her size. Large crews were necessary to man the extra guns normally carried by the private man-of-war and, most significantly, to provide prize crews to navigate captured vessels to a friendly port. A successful cruise might involve the seizure of a number of prizes and large crews were necessary to secure prizes and allow the private man-of-war to remain at sea.

A further distinctive feature of a private man-of-war's crew was that, unlike its counterpart in the merchant service or the Royal Navy, it received no regular wages. An advance, or bounty, was usually paid to the men as they enlisted,[14] but any further remuneration normally depended upon the seizure and condemnation of a prize. The articles of agreement drawn up before the commencement of each cruise laid down the division of any spoils. In Britain the proceeds of a cruise were generally divided into two parts, with the owners of the vessel receiving one half, the other going to the crew.[15] The latter portion would then be divided amongst the crew according to the number of shares allocated to each man. In the case of the *Southwell* of Bristol, the crew's half was divided into $262\frac{1}{2}$ shares, with the commander owning 12 shares, the first lieutenant, master, and doctor holding 6 shares each, the "able sailers" holding a single share apiece, and the "ordinary sailers" allotted three-quarters of a share each. Thus, when the *Southwell's* fifth cruise produced net receipts of £251 7s 3d, each of the twelve owners received £11 16s 3d and Commander John Engledue pocketed £5 15s 0d, each share being worth 9s 7d.[16]

Regulatory Devices

While the armed merchantman and the private man-of-war embarked with different intentions, both types of privateer were subject to an identical system of regulation. This system had evolved over time, its greatest development occurring in the seventeenth century as the rapid growth of overseas trade and state navies obliged the maritime powers to formalize their relations. Within the code of international maritime law which developed to meet this need, the control of privateering—and its definition as a legitimate activity, distinct from piracy—assumed a principal position. In Britain, privateering activity was regulated by the High Court of Admiralty, a body responsible for the issue of letters of marque and privateer commissions and the condemnation of prizes. To obtain a license, the intending privateer commander, or someone acting on his behalf, was required to attend the Admiralty Court, in Doctors' Commons, London,[17] and produce a "warrant from the Lord High Admiral of England and Ireland for the granting of a letter of marque or commission." Then he was obliged to make a declaration before the Admiralty judge consisting of a "particular true and exact account of the ship or vessel" to be commissioned.[18] Furthermore, a bail or surety had to be provided by reputable guarantors of the good behavior of the commander and his crew.

These two devices—the commander's declaration and the guarantor's bond—were the principal means by which the Admiralty Court controlled the issue of letters of marque. The declaration, first introduced in 1689, detailed the characteristics of the vessel and named the officers and principal owners, clearly identifying the ship and those responsible for her actions. The taking of sureties was the method traditionally employed by the authorities to ensure that privateers acted in accordance with the Admiralty's "instructions to privateers," drafted at the commencement of hostilities. If the instructions were contravened the bond was liable to prosecution in the Admiralty Court. Its amount, fixed by the Anglo-Dutch Marine Treaty of 1674, varied with crew size; if more than one hundred fifty men were on board the bail was £3,000, and if less, it was £1500.[19] Under the terms of the 1708 Cruisers and Convoys Act the Court was obliged to grant a letter of marque to any commander making a declaration and providing bail. However, complaints from neutrals about the excesses of British privateers forced the government to pass the Privateers' Act of 1759,[20] which imposed some restrictions on the issue of commissions. This legislation gave the Admiralty the discretion to refuse licenses to privateers under 100 tons burden carrying fewer than 12 guns of 4 lbs weight of shot and 40 men, although their issue remained obligatory for larger ships.[21] Furthermore, it tightened up the regulations on sureties, forbidding the commanders and owners to stand bail for themselves, obliging the guarantors to swear that they were worth the sum in which they were bound, and instructing the marshal of the Court to inquire into their circumstances.

The declaration having been made and the bail provided, the commander was granted a letter of marque authorizing him to attack enemy property. Before leaving port, however, the commissioned vessel had to be examined by the local Customs Collector who issued a certificate as to the size, manning, and armaments of the ship. If the privateer embarked without this clearance pass or if the force of the ship was less than that stated in the letter of marque, the latter was null and void and the commander liable to imprisonment. Once at sea the conduct of the cruise was bounded by the "instructions to privateers" issued to each recipient of a letter of marque. In addition, privateer owners often provided their commanders with copies of relevant treaties and books to guide their behavior. Thus, John Engledue of the *Southwell* privateer was presented with a "Book of maritime affairs and Copy of the Marine Treaty between us and the Dutch,"[22] while Richard Fitzherbert of the *Dreadnought* was given a copy of "Naval Trade and Commerce" and instructed to comply with its provisions, particularly with regard to the 1674 Anglo-Dutch treaty.[23]

These various instructions embodied a code of conduct within which the commander and crew were supposed to operate. The code was modified over time, but five main areas of control were evident.[24] First, the rights of neutrals were to be respected, hence the concern of owners that the 1674 Marine Treaty should be observed. The spoliation of neutrals, particularly the Dutch, sometimes embarrassed the British government which made sporadic attempts to limit the privateering attack to contraband goods.[25] The second aim of the instructions was to prevent cruelty to the crews of captured vessels; thus, Francis Ingram, managing owner of the *Enterprize* of Liverpool, implored her commander, James Haslam, to refrain from plundering any prisoners of their clothes and bedding and to treat them "with all tenderness and humanity, consistent with your own safety."[26]

Third, the instructions were designed to eradicate any suppression or distortion of evidence. Captors were required, therefore, to bring three or four members of the prize vessel's crew into port for examination as to the nature of the voyage and the capture. Papers, sea briefs, bills of lading, and any other documents found on board the prize were to be brought into port intact and without interference to help determine the legality of the capture. The fourth area of regulation forbade the embezzlement of cargoes and the sale of goods before condemnation. The fifth concern of the instructions was to ensure that prizes should be brought to trial. Thus, captors were obliged to convey their prizes to a British, colonial, or friendly port where examination of the prize, witnesses, and evidence could take place. The practice of ransoming vessels at sea was gradually restricted, and finally outlawed in the American Revolutionary War,[27] thereby ensuring that prizes could be properly adjudicated.

Penalties were fixed for those who transgressed the instructions, although how rigorously they were enforced is open to some doubt, particularly in the colonies.[28] However, the instructions constituted a set of rules for the proper conduct of the privateer at sea. If a vessel was arrested by the commissioned vessel and there were sufficient grounds for its prosecution it was to be dispatched to a home or friendly port with at least three of its crew as witnesses, its bulk unbroken, and any documentary evidence intact.[29] When a prize was landed, its arrival was to be reported to the customs officials of the port and subsequently a libel was exhibited against it in the Admiralty Court.

Members of the prize vessel's crew, preferably the captain and two officers, were then subjected to a preparatory examination as to the legality of the capture. This examination was normally conducted in the port of landing, often at an inn, before the local magistrate and public notary. Witnesses were obliged to answer a set of standing interrogatories, some twenty or so questions intended to discover the nationality of the prize, its crew and owners, the origin and destination of its cargo, and the nature and location of its seizure. On the completion of the preparatory examinations a monition was set up in a public place, usually outside the Royal Exchange in London, ordering all persons interested in the prize vessel or cargo to stake their claim within twenty days. If nobody claimed within the stipulated time the judge of the Admiralty Court was to take into consideration the preparatory examinations, together with any evidence taken from the prize, and pronounce sentence.

This procedure was straightforward and swift in cases where the prize was uncontested, but in other cases, when interested parties made a claim to the property in question, the system was more complex. If the evidence of distant witnesses was required, the judge ordered an appraisement of the disputed vessel or goods to be made before awarding them to the claimant, by interlocutory decree. On receipt of the property the claimant was required to give security to restore the appraised value should the sentence go against him. Either party could appeal against the decision to a superior court, the Court of Prize Appeals, which could delay the final pronouncement for months or even years.

Thus, from the issue of his letter of marque to the condemnation of his prizes a variety of devices, amounting to a system of control, restrained the activities of the British privateersman. The competence of this system is difficult to judge. However, it is clear that its application not only involved a number of agencies, but also required a substantial contribution from the privateersman himself.

Policing the Privateersman

The regulatory framework within which British privateers operated was well established by the eighteenth century. Its chief function, as far as the state was concerned, was to maximize the military utility of private ships-of-war by restricting their predatory designs to the trade and shipping of enemy nations. The extent to which the authorities could control privateers depended upon two main factors: the efficiency of the legal and administrative system erected to deal with general reprisals, and the effectiveness of the means deployed to police private warships on the high seas. In essence, this entailed the smooth operation of the prize division of the High Court of Admiralty, and, at sea, the vigilance and impartiality of the Navy, together with a degree of self-discipline on the part of the privateersman.

The evidence relating to these matters is somewhat fragmentary, largely because those who successfully transgressed the rules of the predatory game were naturally reluctant to chronicle their misdemeanors. However, there is sufficient information to suggest that the system of control and the methods of policing private men-of-war were sufficient to curb the worst excesses of privateersmen and to ensure that commerce raiding only rarely jeopardized Britain's relations with neutrals and allies. The High Court of Admiralty, for instance, seems to have discharged its prize duties with some competence. This was a somewhat quixotic tribunal, a bastion of the civil law in which the interests of litigants were represented by proctors who presented the depositions of witnesses, exhibits, and other forms of evidence to a judge presiding and adjudicating without a jury.[30] It was an institution which experienced its share of administrative problems; for instance, in 1778, it was reported that the

> warrants granted to privateers for making reprisals on the French were, either through negligence, inattention or design, sealed with a wrong seal; the consequence thereof is that they must be resealed, which will protract their sailing for seven or eight days at least.[31]

Moreover, as the Admiralty Court was the only place in which prize law could be dispensed, the proctors were in a monopoly position, a factor reflected in the heavy fees charged for their services.[32] Political pressure could also influence the Court's decisions. For instance, in 1758–59, with the neutral United Provinces threatening to declare war, a number of privateersmen were sentenced to death for plundering Dutch ships, while a series of contentious cases were settled in favor of Dutch claimants in the Prize Appeals Court, verdicts which owed more to diplomatic considerations than to natural justice.[33]

Yet for all its idiosyncrasies and occasional lapses, the High Court of Admiralty dealt effectively with a large volume of prize business during wartime. This is clearly apparent in the vast extent and remarkable internal consistency of the archive which survives. Hundreds of thousands of documents relating to countless predators and captures are preserved and logically arranged in the HCA collection. In these holdings, the expertise of the Court's servants in negotiating the complexities of prize law, the technicalities of life at sea, and the conflicting interpretations of international treaties are readily apparent.[34] Furthermore, this specialist tribunal regularly invoked its power to punish British privateersmen who exceeded their authority. The papers of the Prize Appeals Court abound with the successful claims of wronged neutral or allied citizens, with costs and damages generally awarded against the errant captor.[35]

That such impartiality had a wider impact is suggested by the orders given to Captain Patrick Galloway by his employers. Thus, he was to desist from bringing in neutral ships,

> as it will never answer our ends, & on the contrary would make us odious to all traders here [London], & at the Court of Admiralty, & put us to great charges and damages.[36]

Of course, the High Court of Admiralty could only act upon the cases brought before it and the evidence submitted by litigants. The extent to which privateersmen plundered vessels, mistreated prisoners, distorted evidence, or otherwise ignored their instructions is uncertain. However, it is clear that there were means of detecting, and of deterring, such misdemeanors. The Navy was the principal detective agency. There were occasions when the discipline of errant privateersmen formed a specific part of a naval captain's duty. For instance, in 1760, "the commanders of all the King's ships" were ordered to locate the infamous privateersman John Patrick and "to take him out of his ship wherever they meet with him."[37] Generally, however, it was on an incidental basis that men-of-warsmen were called upon to administer discipline to privateersmen. A chance encounter at sea, for instance, revealed to Lord Hervey, captain of H.M.S. *Daphne,* that James Vercoe, commander of the *Fox* privateer of Plymouth, had plundered a neutral merchantman, while the officers of H.M.S. *Berwick* discovered stolen and smuggled goods aboard the *Dreadnought* privateer of Newcastle during a similar meeting.[38]

This policing role was just one facet of the complex relationship which existed between public and private naval forces in the eighteenth century. In theory, private men-of-war supplemented the state navy in the attack upon enemy trade and the defense of home shipping. There were innumerable occasions when privateers performed such a supportive role, though their contributions were usually small in scale and of an incidental nature.[39] But it was competition rather than cooperation that generally characterized the relations between naval and privateering personnel. Thus, as service in both forms of warship was rewarded by a share in any properties taken, there was invariably a degree of rivalry in the pursuit of prizes. Disputes over the division of spoils between privateersmen and men-of-warsmen frequently occupied the time of the Prize and Prize Appeals Courts, particularly during those phases when the commerce-raiding war was at its height.[40]

The search for seamen was a further source of friction. Private men-of-war were labor-intensive vessels and attracted large numbers of men at times when naval requirements meant that demand far exceeded supply in the seafaring labor market.[41] Though privateersmen were normally protected from impressment, complaints from privateer owners indicate that such immunities were often ignored.[42] Here, the Navy's recruitment drive might harmonize conveniently with its policing function, for as well as delivering miscreants to the proper authorities, naval officers sometimes took a more direct form of disciplinary action by pressing guilty men into naval service. Such immediate retribution was visited upon twenty-nine privateersmen who mutinied aboard the *Princess Augusta of* Bristol, on the thieves and smugglers discovered in the *Dreadnought* of Newcastle, on the angry members of the *Winchelsea*'s crew in their violent efforts to obtain compensation from the vessel's owners, and no doubt on countless other troublesome seafarers.[43] To the privateersman, therefore, the naval officer might appear as both press-master and policeman, an authoritarian duality which perhaps explains the bitterness evident in the "New Song on the *Blandford* Privateer":

> Why should we here our time delay, in London void of pleasure,
> Let's haste away to Biscay Bay and ransack there for treasure,

> Here we must weep and play bo-peep to shun the damn'd press-masters,
> We live in strife, even die in life, confin'd by catch-pole bastards.[44]

While irregularities in the privateersman's behavior at sea might be detected and summarily punished, deterrence was probably a much more effective means of control. This is not to suggest that offenders faced extraordinarily harsh physical punishments if apprehended. Rather, the chief deterrent—and probably the single most important facet of the regulatory system—at work aboard a British private man-of-war was the self-discipline that the economic rationale of the commerce-raiding business instilled into her crew. In general, privateersmen earned no wages, their sole remuneration arising out of the proceeds of any prizes taken and subsequently condemned. Each seafarer was therefore a shareholder in the profits of the venture. Accordingly, it was in the interests of all concerned, men as well as owners, to maximize the prize fund to be divided at the conclusion of the enterprise. While this vested interest served to discourage plunder and embezzlement, it positively encouraged the commanders and crew of commissioned vessels to follow their instructions, for behaviorial and procedural irregularities might precipitate a rash of claims in the Admiralty Court, thereby protracting the legal proceedings and adding to the costs of the venture. Such threats to the earnings of privateersmen, many of whom viewed their transitory occupation as a once-in-a-lifetime opportunity to secure a fortune, were instrumental in ensuring that the great majority of ventures did not stray beyond the regulatory limits laid down by the state. Quite simply, observing the guidelines enhanced the chances of securing the extraordinary profits which commerce raiding promised. While this may not always have been the case in earlier times, by the eighteenth century British privateering enterprise, that ancient, tense amalgam of private interest and public service, had developed a regulatory logic of its own.

NOTES

1. The issues discussed in this paper are treated at length in David J. Starkey, *British Privateering Enterprise in the Eighteenth Century* (Exeter: University of Exeter Press, 1990).

2. John W. Damer Powell, *Bristol Privateers and Ships of War* (Bristol: Arrowsmith, 1930), xvi.

3. For a detailed analysis of the theory and practice of reprisals in medieval Europe, see Maurice H. Keen, *The Laws of War in the Late Middle Ages* (London: Routledge and Kegan Paul, 1965), 218–38.

4. This was sometimes "mark," "mart," or "march." Although its etymological source is unclear it seems likely that the word "marque" derived from "march," from the marcher's right to avenge his wrongs by armed force. Keen, *Laws of War,* 231.

5. Francis R. Stark, *The Abolition of Privateering and the Declaration of Paris* (New York: Columbia University Press, 1897), 51–55.

6. Stark, *Abolition,* 50–51.

7. Reginald G. Marsden, ed., *Documents relating to Law and Custom of the Sea*, 2 vols. (London: Navy Records Society, 1915–1916), 1: 115–18.

8. Privateer commissions against the colonists were authorized by 17 George III, c.7. "An Act for Enabling the Commissioners . . . to Grant Commissions . . ."

9. Public Record Office (PRO), High Court of Admiralty (HCA), 26/4. "Instructions to Privateers," 29 March 1744.

10. Such ships were known as "runners."

11. John Knox Laughton, *Studies in Naval History: Biographies* (London: Longmans, Green, and Co., 1887), 201.

12. Powell, *Bristol Privateers,* 137.

13. Walter E. Minchinton, "Piracy and Privateering in the Atlantic, 1702–76," in *Course et piraterie: Études presentées à la Commission Internationale d'Histoire Maritime à l'occasion de son XVè colloque international pendant le XIVè Congrès International des Sciences Historiques (San Francisco, août 1975)*, ed. Michel Mollat (Paris: Institut de Recherche et d'Histoire des Textes, Centre National de la Recherche Scientifique, 1975), 1: 299–330, reference here to 300.

14. For instance, a total of £518 3s 6d was advanced to the crew of the *Southwell* before her fifth cruise in May 1746. The officers received 5 guineas each, 3 guineas went to the "able sailers," with 2 guineas advanced to every "ordinary sailer." Avon County Library (ACL) papers of *Southwell* privateer, 24651.

15. There were regional variations, however. See Starkey, *British Privateering,* 73–78.

16. ACL, Papers of the *Southwell* privateer, 24651.

17. In the colonies, the vice-admiralty courts granted commissions and condemned prizes, though abuse of the system appears to have been common. See Richard Pares, *Colonial Blockade and Neutral Rights, 1739–1763* (Philadelphia: Porcupine Press, 1975), 53–64.

18. Quoted from "Instructions to Privateers," PRO, HCA 26/60.

19. The declarations made in the Admiralty Court between 1689 and 1815 are to be found in PRO, HCA 26/1–104; the respective bail documents are included in the HCA 25 classification.

20. 32 George II, c.25. The preamble states that "whereas repeated complaints have of late been made of divers outrageous Acts of piracy and robbery, committed on board great numbers of ships, more particularly by the crews of small ships, vessels or boats being, or pretending to be, English privateers . . ."

21. The alleged depredations were blamed on the smaller privateers, especially those operating in the Channel.

22. ACL, Papers of the *Southwell* privateer, 24651.

23. ACL, Papers of the *Southwell* privateer, 24651.

24. For a detailed discussion of the privateers' instructions, see Pares, *Colonial Blockade,* 53–64.

25. The definition of contraband varied over time and from country to country and was always a source of diplomatic tension between Britain and neutral powers. See Stark, *Abolition,* 68–98; Pares, *Colonial Blockade,* 92–94.

26. Liverpool Record Office (LRO), Account books of the *Enterprize,* 387 MD 45.

27. See Pares, *Colonial Blockade,* 19–26. Ransoms were finally prohibited by the 1778 Prize Act, 19 George II, c.67.

28. The many irregularities of colonial privateers and prize courts are discussed by Pares, *Colonial Blockade,* 109–32.

29. Commanders were generally directed by their employers to escort valuable prizes to port to reduce the risk of recapture by an enemy man-of-war or privateer, or repossession by the prize vessel's crew. Prize crews usually navigated less valuable prizes to the nearest home port, leaving the privateer to pursue its cruise.

30. F. L. Wiswall, *The Development of Admiralty Jurisdiction and Practice since 1800: An English Study with American Comparisons* (Cambridge: Cambridge University Press, 1970).

31. *Morning Chronicle and London Advertiser,* 19 August 1778.

32. See Starkey, *British Privateering,* 308–15.

33. *Gentleman's Magazine,* 29 (1759): 496, 604.

34. See John C. Appleby and David J. Starkey, "The Records of the High Court of Admiralty as a Source for Maritime Historians," in *Sources for a New Maritime History of Devon,* ed. David J. Starkey (Exeter: Devon County Council, 1986), 70–86.

35. See PRO, HCA 42 and 45.

36. PRO, C 108/318, Creagh and Fallet to Patrick Galloway, 2–3 March 1703.

37. Powell, *Bristol Privateers,* 207–13.

38. PRO, HCA 45/12; *Newcastle Chronicle,* 9 June 1781.

39. David J. Starkey, "The Economic and Military Significance of British Privateering, 1702–83," *Journal of Transport History* 9 (1988): 50–59.

40. See David J. Starkey, "British Privateering against the Dutch in the American Revolutionary War, 1780–1783," in *Studies in British Privateering, Trading Enterprise and Seamen's Welfare, 1775–1900,* ed. Stephen Fisher (Exeter: University of Exeter Press, 1987), 1–17.

41. David J. Starkey, "War and the Market for Seafarers in Britain, 1736–1742," in *Shipping and Trade 1750–1950: Essays in International Maritime Economic History,* ed. L. R. Fischer and H. W. Nordvik (Pontefract: Lofthouse, 1990), 25–42.

42. For instance, see Francis Ingram's complaints in LRO, Account books of the *Enterprize,* 387 MD 45.

43. Powell, *Bristol Privateers,* 157; *Newcastle Chronicle,* 9 June 1781; PRO, C 103/130, Richard Taunton to Thomas Hall, 26 August 1746.

44. Powell, *Bristol Privateers,* 140–41.

Chapter 5

Piracy and World History
An Economic Perspective on Maritime Predation

John L. Anderson

Oceans and seas have always provided opportunities for the relatively cheap transport of products and persons, and the resulting movement of vulnerable assets has attracted from earliest times predators called pirates. These generally behaved as a species of William H. McNeill's metaphorical macroparasites, human groups that draw sustenance from the toil and enterprise of others, offering nothing in return.[1] The form of maritime macroparasitism termed piracy adversely affected trade and so productivity in ways not always recognized. It also had political implications when it was an expression of conflict between the practice of indigenous peoples and the economic expansion of a power from beyond the region.[2]

The purpose of this chapter is to present an overview, with analysis based on legal and economic concepts, of the nature and significance of piracy. This form of predation has been global in its incidence and, at times, at least partly global in its structure. The patterns that emerge from a study of several historical examples are the reflections of wider contexts of commerce and politics, and often of remote events and policies formulated far from the scene of a particular action. In the Caribbean, piracy originated in and was fueled by Old World rivalries. The predation on merchant shipping in the Mediterranean Sea in early modern times was sustained not simply by ideological animosity and individual greed but also by economic rivalry between European nation-states. In the eastern seas in the nineteenth century, piracy was indirectly stimulated and eventually suppressed by the economic and technical changes associated with the British industrial revolution, half a world away.[3] The story of maritime predation involves much more than localized incidents or enterprising and colorful individuals.

Piracy is a subset of violent maritime predation in that it is not part of a declared or widely recognized war. Within the general category of maritime predation, a precise definition of piracy universally acceptable over time and be-

tween places has eluded jurists. A broad definition that emerges from historical writing is that of the essentially *indiscriminate* taking of property (or persons) with violence, on or by descent from the sea.[4] This concept of piracy certainly includes one of the widely accepted elements of stealing—that is, the
taking and carrying away of the property of another—but doubt may arise
about a further element, the lack of "color of right." This further element relates to whether there was reasonable belief that the relevant conduct was justifiable. While some may see a partial justification for piracy in Marxist terms
as an expropriation of the expropriators, comment on the question of culpability generally focuses on the question of the traditional rights of members of
communities to appropriate to themselves the property of others and the associated question of whether interference with those rights was anything more
than the manifest imperialism of an expansionist power.

The problem of framing and securing international recognition for laws
that would rid the seas of pirates, without infringing on the rights of sovereign
states, appears not to have been resolved for many reasons, some relating to
the nature of the offense.[5] Private purpose *(animus furandi)* has generally been
held to be a necessary element of piracy, to distinguish the crime from political
activity. If a pirate claims to be acting on behalf of a state rather than from
private motives, then the issue turns first on whether the state is one entitled to
authorize such actions and then on whether it accepts responsibility for them
or not and whether it can or will act responsibly in either case. Throughout
history, many officials at all levels of authority have found it expedient and
usually profitable to ignore or even covertly to sponsor acts of piracy.[6] It was
precisely the inaction or ineffectiveness of ancient and medieval European
states in relation to theft by sea that led to the practice of reprisal, whereby an
aggrieved party was given license to recover from any member of the offender's community the value of property stolen. The path from that action to
random piracy is short and clear.

It has been argued that some societies, stigmatized as having been piratical,
were merely claiming or exercising a historical right to levy "taxes" on
passers-by. For example, Alfred H. Rubin writes of the Mediterranean Sea in
the sixteenth century, when predation was unarguably intense, that "the picture is actually, legally, one of lively and dangerous commerce and conflicting
claims to authority that might be called an authority to tax nearby shipping
lanes with capture of the vessel, confiscation of its cargo, and the enslavement
of the crew the penalty for tax evasion."[7] He writes also of "waters historically claimed as within the taxing jurisdiction of Tunis" and refers to a British
legal decision in the nineteenth century as implicitly denying Borneo Dyaks "a
jurisdiction of their own to control commerce, tax it, or forbid it in waters
they might claim as part of their own territory."[8]

This approach raises interesting questions about the origin of and justification for such levies. If the rights claimed were established and maintained by force, can there be complaint if a superior force extinguishes those rights? Further, reference to "tax" in this context is inappropriate. The term tax, with its aura of legitimacy, implies revenues collected from a community in return for the provision of public goods, such as defense and law at a minimum, and perhaps public works and services designed to improve the life and livelihood of those taxed. If the arrangement lacks this reciprocity, then the exactions are more properly termed tribute. Tribute may be defined as unrequited, systematic exactions effected by force or threat of force, such as were made, for example, by medieval European robber barons and modern protection-racketeering gangsters.

The legal problem of suppression of piracy is further compounded by the question of jurisdiction. The emergence of nation-states in Europe led to the establishment of clear (though often disputed) frontiers between territorial units, and within each unit jurisdiction was by definition not in question. By contrast, the sea offered no such defined frontiers other than coastlines, variously defined at law. Therefore, strictly speaking, there could be no lawful general policing of the oceans by a party willing to intervene in an incident between nationals of two other states or their ships.[9] By the same reasoning, however, it seems difficult to allow any group a right of jurisdiction over the high seas for the purpose of collecting tribute, or for that purpose even over vessels making "innocent passage" through what the group might arbitrarily choose to consider its territorial waters.[10]

The legal aspects of piracy affect expected returns and costs in what was essentially a business. The problems of legal definition and jurisdiction in cases of alleged piracy, when a given state's laws do not clearly apply, would tend to lessen the probability of a pirate's being brought to trial and successfully prosecuted, which would in turn reduce the "costs" pirates might expect as a consequence of their activities. Similarly, the elusiveness and anonymity of a ship in the expanse of oceans and the ease of disposal of incriminating evidence (and witnesses) make detection and apprehension difficult, which further reduces the probability of punishment in the pirates' calculus of profit and loss. The expectation of punishment would be lowered still further if the pirate had the open or tacit protection and support of powerful individuals or enjoyed the benign indifference of a state administration. On the other side of the ledger, high returns could be expected from piracy; wealth is concentrated in ships themselves and in their holds, and ships are easy to intercept as they predictably double capes or negotiate narrow straits and other "choke points" on trade routes.

The consequences of piracy and, more broadly, maritime predation can be further examined in economic terms. The economic significance of predation in history extends beyond the transfer of commodities or destruction of vessels that it occasioned. It also includes the implications of the reduction in tradable assets that results from predatory activity. For analytical purposes, the losses may be considered as immediate, both direct and indirect, and as dynamic, resulting from the adverse effects on future production.

Direct losses to the violence of predation were the destruction of capital in the form of ships and cargo, and of labor with the death of crew members. Indirect losses, which are less obvious and less noticed in the literature on piracy, were the resources used for protection against the predators and so lost to direct productive activity. These losses occur because piracy does not represent a simple transaction that is economically neutral; rather, the resources of both predator and victim are consumed in contesting the transfer of the assets.[11] The pirate's labor and capital could probably, although not necessarily, have been used in ways that would have added to the total of desirable goods and services, and it is certain that a mercantile victim would have found more productive use for the assets devoted to protection. These assets could include taxes paid for defense or sums paid for guns, for crew to defend the vessel in addition to those necessary to work it, and for various forms of insurance.

The immediate effect of theft associated with piracy would be to reduce the supply of commodities available in the normal channels of trade. Both the producers and consumers of such commodities are likely to suffer loss. Fewer goods would be available to the consumer, and those probably at a higher price. Even if the pirate placed the stolen goods on the market, the producer would have suffered a loss, leading to a contraction in production and in the trade dependent on it.

In dynamic terms, losses that result over time from pirates' acquisition of part of the benefits of trade lie in the reduction of incentives for existing producers and merchants to continue with or to expand their activities, or for others to enter those industries. Indeed, reduction of productive effort, which reduces assets at risk, is one way of self-insuring against predation.[12] Another way to reduce risk is to reduce the proportion of capital in the production process, despite the consequent fall in productivity. The random nature of piratical predation, with concomitant business uncertainty, would compound disincentives.[13] A reduction of trade tends to limit the opportunity for exchange and so reduces the scope for increased satisfaction through diversity in consumption. It also limits the specialization in production upon which advances of productivity overwhelmingly depended, directly or indirectly, in the preindustrial world.

Losses in general could be reduced in two ways: through a reduction of predation, effected perhaps by more efficient naval patrols, and through a reduction in the costs of providing a given level of protection, as could result from the deployment of fewer but individually more effective warships. In the first case, the shipowners and merchants—and the crews—would obviously benefit. In the second case, the benefits might be retained by the providers of protection, but even so, the savings in resources could permit an increase in investment and trade, and that result would almost certainly follow if political arrangements were such that the reduction in protection costs was passed on to the merchants. Despite the conspicuous consumption of individual merchants, their function as a group was to invest and expand their activities in search of profits.[14]

At particular times in world history, and over the long term, costs of protection fell. The benefits of reduced costs, however, accrued differentially to merchant groups, the differences depending on a variety of technical and political circumstances.[15] Those merchants who enjoyed relatively low costs of protection had a competitive advantage over their mercantile rivals who did not. The net surplus acquired through this advantage in premodern times is plausibly argued by Frederic C. Lane to have been "a more important source of profits . . . than superiority in industrial techniques or industrial organization."[16] In this analysis, protection costs are central to the process of capital accumulation and differential economic growth, and the costs of protection to the mercantile sector, when so much trade was seaborne and vulnerable, were in turn significantly affected by the intensity of maritime predation.[17] It has been shown, for example, that a substantial part of the fall in freight rates on the North Atlantic between the sixteenth and eighteenth centuries reflected the savings made in costs of protection as a result of the suppression of piracy.[18]

For analytical purposes, piracy, or predation of a more ambiguous nature, may be broadly classified in terms of its form or expression. It may be parasitic, dependent on the extent of seaborne trade or the wealth of vulnerable littorals; episodic, occasioned by a disruption or distortion of normal trading patterns; or intrinsic, a situation in which piracy (or at least predation) is part of the fiscal and even commercial fabric of the society concerned. These classifications relate to the causes of predatory activity and so necessarily to its suppression.

The analogy of pirate with parasite is useful in understanding the argument that rejects the assertions that, if trade was flourishing, then reported piracy could not have been a significant problem.[19] With parasitic piracy, it is precisely when trade is flourishing that piracy is likely to be a problem: parasites flourish when hosts are readily available, and an efficient parasite at worst debilitates rather than destroys the host that sustains it. The trade data say nothing about the counterfactual probability of "what might have been" if there had been no piracy.

The simple parasite analogy, however, cannot carry too great a weight of analysis. The functional relationship between this form of piracy and trade expansion is not one of constant proportions, as might be expected between parasite and host. Instead, after a certain point, parasitic piracy is likely to be reduced as trade increases. This follows from economies of scale in defense—the probability of there being a reduction in cost of defense per ship or unit of cargo with an expansion of trade. As the volume of trade increases, the form of protection can change with increased cost-effectiveness. Initially, each ship may carry soldiers and their provisions, which would be expensive directly and also indirectly through reduction of cargo-carrying capacity. At a greater scale of activity, merchants might jointly hire an armed ship to convoy their vessels. At a still greater scale of operation, they may form a group (or pay a government) to deploy cruisers and perhaps to dominate, annex, or destroy predatory societies.

This increasing efficiency of defense with increased scale of mercantile activity would reduce unit costs of protection and loss from predation. Assuming the political structure to be such that these benefits flowed onward to the merchants, their greater share in the gains of trade would provide an incentive to increase trade still further. This process depends ultimately on the society having sufficient resources to prevail in the conflict with the predators. The Roman empire and the great trading companies and nation-states of France, Britain, and the Netherlands had such resources, but city-states with significant dependence on revenues from trade were more vulnerable. Singapore merchants in the early nineteenth century were highly sensitive to the problem, but were able to gain the support of metropolitan power. Venice, standing alone at the end of the sixteenth century against powerful adversaries, was not so fortunate.

Venice is a documented case in which piracy contributed to the decline of an established commercial center.[20] The city-state was subjected to a predatory onslaught on its seaborne commerce in the late sixteenth century. At that time, Venetian ships were at hazard from Uskok boats in the northern Adriatic Sea, from Algerian and Tunisian corsairs at the entrance to the Adriatic, and from Turks, Dutch, English, and others in the Mediterranean.[21] The effect of this situation on Venetian trade can be gauged by one of the few available estimates of losses of ships and profits as a consequence of piratical activity. Between 250 and 300 Venetian ships (with a total of about ten times that number of ships in general) are estimated to have been taken between 1592 and 1609—not many fewer than the 350 that suffered shipwreck.[22] Around the turn of the century, insurance rates rose; even normal rates more than doubled, and some rose to more than 50 percent of the value of the goods insured—when insurance could be had.[23] It is estimated that from an expected return of 10,000 ducats on a voyage in 1607, 8,500 would have been consumed in expenses for port dues, soldiers, sailors, and insurance.[24] In the late sixteenth century, Venetian capital and enterprise began to turn from the sea. Although the fundamental causes of the long-term decline of the Venetian economy were the rise both of the Atlantic nations and of Islamic power in the Levant and the Mediterranean, "the pirates, and especially their activities in the years 1595–1605, brought the organization of Venetian trade and shipping to a crisis which could only accentuate the results of a secular trend."[25]

Returning to the analysis of the nature of piracy, it can be accepted that defense is not the only activity enjoying economies of scale; piracy does also. Philip Gosse identifies and outlines the nature and dynamics of a "piracy cycle."[26] In this, piracy is initially conducted by small and independent groups of individuals using their boats for piracy as desperation of poverty dictates or as the opportunity presents. Success in this venture equips the groups with more and larger vessels, and an organization can emerge to coordinate their activities, these changes making predation increasingly effective. With further success the pirates' strength becomes such as to make them a virtually independent power, when they may choose to enter into an alliance with some recognized state. At that point the pirates have become in effect a mercenary navy, paid by plunder. Success will legitimize their power; failure and defeat will lead to disintegration of the organization into the small, furtive outlaw groups from which the force originated.

This "piracy cycle" is evident in the Mediterranean in Roman times. The organization of the Cilician pirates on the coast of Anatolia moved from bands to squadrons to a navy, which early in the first century B.C.E. was allied with Mithridates of Asia Minor in a war against Rome. The Cilicians survived their ally's defeat to become an independent and troublesome force. The Cilicians had been increasingly active in the Mediterranean and along its coasts from about the middle of the second century, but had been tolerated by Rome for the slaves that they provided. However, the developing dominance of the seas by Cilicians, along with the threat they posed to the grain supply of Rome, stirred the Senate in 67 B.C.E. to give the general Pompey, titled "the Great," what was effectively plenary power over the Mediterranean and Black Seas and their littorals. With a comprehensive and systematic strategy, and an astutely humane policy to the vanquished, Pompey destroyed the pirate power in a few months.[27]

Elements of the "piracy cycle" can also be seen in the semipiratical careers of the English Sea-Dogs who emerged from the tradition of West Country piracy, and who came to form the core of the English navy. Their Dutch contemporaries, the *Watergeuzen* (Sea Beggars), driven to predation at sea by troubles in their mercantile and maritime homeland, became organized on a scale adequate to seize the politically significant Dutch port of Den Briel, and they continued as the maritime arm of the Netherlands in the rebellion against

Spain.[28] Further examples of the "piracy cycle" can be found in the rise of the city-states of the North African littoral, the so-called Barbary States,[29] which menaced the Mediterranean sea-lanes in alliance with or independent of the Ottoman empire, and in the patterns of Chinese piracy in the sixteenth and nineteenth centuries.

The involvement of elements of a navy, mentioned above in reference to a process of suppression of piracy, bespeaks the entry of a political force into the contest between pirates and merchants, usually as the result of an increase in the scale of trade. In the Caribbean and colonial waters, increased volume of trade in the eighteenth century meant that governors, as well as planters and merchants, could benefit more from legitimate activities than from corruptly supporting or clandestinely supplying the pirates.[30] Increased American trade in the Mediterranean following independence led to the punitive expeditions conducted in the Mediterranean by units of the fledgling U.S. Navy. In the first century B.C.E. the Roman state, with increasing commerce and power, took action, at first relatively ineffectually, against piratical activity in the eastern Mediterranean. The British pursued a similar course of action in the eastern seas. At the stage when state power is enlisted to suppress predation upon shipping, however, the predators themselves are likely to be at the apogee of the "piracy cycle" and to form part of an organized society if not of a state, whether recognized or not. The situation then becomes legally and politically unclear.

At the point when predation is de facto or de jure a part of the commercial or fiscal functioning of an organized community, it may be classified as "intrinsic." Any attempt by another state to interfere with that activity by definition impinges on the customs, revenues, prestige, and perhaps territorial integrity of the indigenous peoples concerned—whether of the cities of the North African and Indian littorals in early modern times or of Malayan sultanates in the nineteenth century. In this situation, the circumstances surrounding the predation and its suppression cloud the issue of right. A merely reactive resistance by potential prey to attack by maritime predators is a hazardous if not wholly ineffective policy, as it gives the predator a probably decisive tactical advantage. Consequently, warships have commonly cruised to actively protect seaborne trade and to destroy predators' vessels, and armed forces have at times engaged in punitive expeditions ashore. The question then arises whether these initiatives were police actions justifiable by an extension of the natural rights of property and self-defense or whether they represented the naval edge of imperialism.[31]

A possible test of the nature and intent of antipiracy patrols and expeditions is whether as in police doctrine the action involved no more force than was necessary for the purpose or whether as in military practice the maximum force was applied and the territorial intrusions became permanent occupations. By these criteria, European activity in the Mediterranean and British activity in the eastern seas to suppress interference with shipping were perhaps less imperialistic than a strict interpretation of law might suggest. In each case, for quite some time only limited force was applied, and that generally intermittently; the territorial control or occupation that effectively eliminated predation came late in the process.

In the Mediterranean Sea, from the sixteenth to the eighteenth centuries, the line between piracy, privateering, and trading was seldom easily discernible.[32] Rhetoric in the Atlantic powers, charged with mercantile self-interest and colored by hostility toward Islam, condemned as piracy the activities of corsairs sailing from the North African ports of Algiers, Tunis, Tripoli, and Salé, cities for which predation was an intrinsic part of public finance and of commerce.[33] However, there was little to distinguish the behavior of corsairs from those cities from that of the Christian Knights of St. John based at Malta and of those of St. Stephen at Pisa and Livorno, for example, or from the behavior of many individual European mariners sailing under their national flags or as renegades under the flags of their North African bases.[34] Predation was generally but not necessarily directed across ideological lines, Christian versus Muslim, but both sides enthusiastically attacked the richly laden Venetian ships.[35] Indeed, Fernand Braudel observes of the Mediterranean at this time that "privateering often had little to do with either country or faith, but was merely a means of making a living." When failure in the enterprise meant famine at home, "privateers in these circumstances took no heed of persons, nationalities or creeds, but became mere sea-robbers."[36]

Ironically, it was the consolidation of the nation-states of Atlantic Europe, with the establishment of law and order within their boundaries, that brought lawlessness to a new level of intensity on the Mediterranean Sea. The policy of ideological homogeneity adopted by the nascent nation-state of Spain led to expulsions of Muslims and suspected Muslims, which provided at the beginning of the seventeenth century and perhaps earlier a flow of aggrieved Moriscos to man the raiders of the North African cities of Algiers and Salé.[37] The rivalry between France and Spain set upon the sea corsairs of dubious commission and doubtful integrity. A French alliance even allowed a Turkish fleet under the command of Khayr al-Din, known as Barbarossa, the opportunity to harass Spanish shipping and raid coasts from the French base at Toulon. The English and Dutch entered the Mediterranean with heavily armed merchantmen and with little respect for the property of French or Spanish nationals—or, often enough, for that of any nationals, whatever the diplomatic relations between states happened to be.[38]

This behavior foreshadowed and led into the more systematically competitive mercantilist era of the seventeenth century, when it was assumed that in the competition for trade, one party's gain was another's loss. The term *mercantilist* reflects the symbiotic alliance between the state and the commercial interests in pursuit of power and wealth at the expense of other states.[39] The aggressive spirit of mercantilism was perhaps as well expressed by the behavior of the Europeans in the armed merchantmen as it was later by the warfare between nation-states, partly for explicitly economic ends, that punctuated the second half of the seventeenth and all of the eighteenth century. The geography of the Mediterranean Sea, together with the technology and logistics of naval warfare, meant that the ideological and commercial conflict there was of necessity carried on not by fleet actions but by raid and counterraid.[40] This was undertaken in large part by private enterprise, often in the fullest sense of the term, for the acquisition of profit and the power on which profit in those times largely depended.

The same mercantilist pursuit of profit and power led nation-states of Europe to come to an accommodation with the states of the Maghrib, whose corsairs the Europeans often termed "pirates." By this accommodation, the European states competitively served their own interests by paying tribute for the safe passage of their ships, which they hoped would be denied to their commercial competitors. In practice, safe-conduct passes could be unreliable protection in the absence of adequate naval power to ensure that they were accepted.[41] Diplomatic relations were established between the states of Europe and the Maghrib, but these were generally fragile and often ruptured. Nevertheless, such recognition of the sovereignty of the Maghribi states gave increased weight to the claim that predators acting under their patronage were privateers rather than pirates.[42]

In the eighteenth century relations between Christian and Islamic powers in the Mediterranean Sea were regularized and became less overtly hostile. This is not surprising, since with the development of the East Asian trade, European commercial interest in the Levant had declined relatively. Also, northern navies were more powerful and therefore more threatening, while their expansion provided employment for restless seamen who in earlier centuries might have "gone on the account" and even "turned Turk" to do so. Further, in the global wars between European nations in the eighteenth century, in which navies were important instruments, the alliance or at least respectful neutrality of the North African states was a useful strategic asset, confirmed by the regular payment of tribute.[43]

These comfortable arrangements were disrupted in the early nineteenth century by the nascent power of the newly independent United States. That country had come into conflict with Tripoli over a dispute concerning tribute payments. Action by U.S. naval forces and marines obliged the pasha of Tripoli to undertake to refrain from interfering with American ships and from demanding tribute. Corsair attacks continued, however, and a further naval expedition to Algiers, Tunis, and again Tripoli in 1815 temporarily restrained (but failed to subdue) the rulers of those cities.[44]

Almost immediately after the American action, the power of the Maghribi states was further challenged by Britain, but again with limited effect. The Royal Navy, acting on earlier precedents and with Dutch support, in 1816 bombarded Algiers into accepting peace and the abolition of the slave trade. As on many previous occasions, however, punitive actions and naval demonstrations by one or two nations brought only a temporary respite from interference with seaborne commerce—naturally so, as predation had long been intrinsic to the structure and functioning of the maritime states of North Africa. The threat that their corsairs posed for the safe passage of ships on the Mediterranean Sea was all but eliminated a few years later, not through occasional naval action but through a novel cooperation between the major European maritime powers, at that time Britain and France.[45] About a decade later, France occupied Algeria as part of the nineteenth-century movement of European colonial expansion.

A similar situation developed in the seas of Southeast Asia in the early nineteenth century, though on a smaller scale and involving weaker predatory groups.[46] For the purpose of predation, the environment was ideal. The flow of maritime trade between the Indian Ocean and the South China Sea was concentrated in the Straits of Malacca, on the littorals of which and on nearby islands dwelled groups that possessed few natural resources other than their location. Predation increased in the nineteenth century with the expansion of trade in and through the region, but predation had been endemic from the earliest times. The hazard of pirates was referred to with apprehension as early as the fifth century by Chinese who sailed in those waters.[47]

The interest of political and legal historians in piracy in the Malaysian seas has been focused not on the opportunistic activities of individuals or small independent groups, which constituted piracy by any definition, but on the systematic and large-scale predation that was an intrinsic part of organized indigenous communities, tolerated or supported by their chiefs or sultans. The nature of that predation could be less easily defined; it has been argued that tradition had given the practice "color of right" and that the right of the British in law and morality to suppress it by armed intervention may be questioned.[48]

The victims of predation were generally Chinese or Indochinese merchants and seamen and relatively defenseless Malay peoples: villagers, fishermen, and merchants trading locally or who had been drawn from the Indonesian seas to the British entrepots of Penang, Malacca, or Singapore. In 1824, a year of troublesome pirate activity, it was noted that only one (European) brig had been taken, but that pirates "harassed the trading prahus [native craft] incessantly, cutting them off and murdering or making slaves of the crews.[49] Whatever the precise legal status of the predatory activity, it imposed costs upon the economy in terms of reduced trade and hence reduced specialization, exchange, and productivity, while fear and uncertainty would have restricted capital accumulation. In some cases fear even led to the abandonment of land and the depopulation of coastal and island areas.[50] These effects must have been a handicap to economic development in the region.

Much of the raiding, particularly by predators coming from the Sulu Sea and southern Philippines, was for slaves. Although the compulsion implicit in slavery may have increased the net productivity of the units of labor taken, it is doubtful whether that would have significantly offset the wastage involved in capture and coercion. Slaving is a business inherently wasteful of human life. In addition to those killed in the raids, some new captives "died from hunger, some from being handcuffed, some from grief. . . . If prisoners were sick so they could not pull on an oar they were thrown overboard."[51] Similarly, when captives were traded for use in ritual sacrifice, their labor was lost to a region in which labor was already the scarce factor of production.[52]

In the early nineteenth century, British efforts to suppress predation in Malayan waters were feeble. Because their trade was little affected, they were reluctant to become embroiled in local affairs. It was in the material interest of neither the British government nor the East India Company to expend their resources in the protection of the persons or property of Malay traders or Chinese merchants. As a result of the increasing trade of the newly established Singapore, however, the problem of parasitic predation became so acute that the naval presence was increasingly strengthened. Eventually punitive expeditions were mounted up the rivers of Borneo to destroy the principal predators' bases.

In a close analysis of the legality of British efforts afloat and ashore to suppress predation in the eastern seas, Alfred H. Rubin remarks incidentally that "the political effect of the raid in Borneo was to help James Brooke, an English adventurer, in his attempts to get control personally of the government of Sarawak."[53] Quite so, but the achievement of that objective and the destruction of the predators' power made the region safer for maritime commerce and for littoral dwellers. It was followed by a freeing of trade through the Straits of Malacca and a sustained increase in trade with Borneo, to the apparent contentment of the indigenous people—though perhaps not of their leaders. Even the formerly "piratical" Sea Dyaks remained loyal to Brooke in later risings fostered by Chinese secret societies and discontented chiefs.[54]

A further type of piracy, differing from parasitic and intrinsic piracy in its cause and cure, may be termed episodic. The episodes in question may be political or economic. A surge of piracy may accompany the weakening of a political power that had restrained, on either a regional or local scale, the predatory proclivities of some mariners or some maritime communities. In the seventeenth century, with the decline of the Iberian, Ottoman, Mughal, and Ming empires, a "great pirate belt" developed from the Caribbean to the South China Sea.[55] Weak or disputed political authority in an area would also permit an analytically distinct form of episodic piracy to flourish: piracy caused by a disruption or distortion in the normal patterns of trade.

Disruption of trade resulted in the unemployment of both seamen and ships, leading those whose livelihood was derived from maritime activity to seek alternatives, which included smuggling and piracy. When normal levels or patterns of trade were restored, the fundamental cause of this form of piracy was removed.[56] Employment was then available for seamen and ships, and merchants who had supplied vessels or received cargo without questions being asked when trade had been disrupted could then find adequate outlets for their capital in legitimate trade. At that point, piracy presented a threat, rather than an opportunity, to the business community and to government officials. Episodic piracy essentially of this nature occurred in the Indian Ocean, the Caribbean Sea, and the South China Sea.

In the Indian Ocean, a conjuncture of alien intrusions and local political weakness formed the conditions for a spectacular episode of piracy in the late seventeenth and early eighteenth centuries. Piracy in some form, often intrinsic, had been endemic in the Indian Ocean from the earliest times, and merchant vessels carried warriors for protection.[57] Nevertheless, regular trade had been conducted peaceably by merchants, and the large, cosmopolitan ports were neutral places. All that changed with the arrival of the Europeans.[58] The Portuguese, driven by a crusading zeal and a thirst for wealth, sought to control the trade of the eastern seas through their superior naval power and the seizure of bases.[59] This turned Muslim shipping operating from the coast of India into "an armed trade diaspora that made little distinction between the legitimacy of trade and plunder after a century of maritime guerilla warfare."[60] In the late seventeenth century, with the weakening of Mughal rule, this predation was systematized under the leadership of the Angria family, initially on behalf of the rising Hindu Maratha power and later for itself when Angria squadrons menaced all shipping off the west coast of India.[61] In addition, pirates from the Caribbean also had established themselves in the Indian Ocean in the late seventeenth century, adding to the European pirates who had been preying on shipping in the region for much of the century.

The Caribbean pirates had been drawn to the Indian Ocean in search of cruising grounds that offered richer prizes and more secure refuges than did the West Indies at that time. From bases on Madagascar they marauded indiscriminately, but their chief prey were the merchant and pilgrim vessels plying the Arabian Sea. Some of the pirates were British—Avery and Kidd being the most notorious—while others often wore English colors. The East India Company accordingly suffered embarrassment as well as losses; it was initially held to account by the Great Mughal for the depredations of those who were or appeared to be its countrymen.

As the East India Company became more capable in the defense of its vessels, the focus of piracy perpetrated by Europeans shifted back to the Caribbean. There, with the early eighteenth-century dislocations of war and of the following peace, piracy reached the apogee of its "classic age." By that time, piracy had become a business global in its reach, with plundered assets being no less mobile than the mariners who acquired them. While the pirates were operating in the Indian Ocean, New York and other colonial ports made profits from supplying them and purchasing their loot.[62] However, as the century progressed, the growth in America of domestic production and trade afforded alternative employment for labor and capital and led to a demand for the suppression of piracy. Meanwhile, that objective was being pursued with increasing assiduity by agents of the state, civil and naval, of improved efficiency and increased integrity.[63]

Piracy in the Caribbean was not confined to the major episode in the early eighteenth century or to the time of buccaneering—a mixture of piracy and privateering—that occupied much of the preceding century.[64] There were further notable episodes, which, like that of the early eighteenth century, were in large part a response to events occurring beyond the region—in these cases the conclusion of European wars. The peace made between England and Spain in 1603 and between Spain and the Netherlands in 1609 was followed by increased piracy.[65] Although the Treaty of Utrecht in 1713 brought peace to the warring states of Europe, by 1718 piracy is said to have brought the trade of the West Indies and the North American coast "to a virtual standstill."[66] There was a further surge of piracy in the Caribbean and in the eastern Mediterranean after the end of the Napoleonic wars in the early nineteenth century.

There were clear economic reasons for the episodes of increased piracy at the close of major European wars. Peace was usually followed by readjustment or recession, which threw merchant seamen out of employment, while at the same time sailors from privateers and men-of-war were discharged to glut the maritime labor market.[67] Ships lay idle, and merchants could find fewer profitable outlets for their capital; piracy offered an alternative to starvation or bankruptcy. The nature of the surge of piracy in the Caribbean after the Napoleonic wars was more complex, because the Latin American colonies of Spain were in a state of rebellion. Then, as in the eastern Mediterranean where the Greeks had risen against their Ottoman overlords, predation ranged from insurgent action, recognized in international law, to simple piracy.[68] The United States, which had a major trading interest in the West Indies, began effective naval action in 1821 to eliminate piracy in the Caribbean. The West India Squadron, deployed for this purpose, reflected President Monroe's policy that the U.S. Navy be structured for police purposes, rather than for command of the sea.[69]

In Chinese waters, a major episode of piracy occurred in the sixteenth century.[70] The fundamental cause was again economic hardship suffered by maritime communities, but in this case it was caused by a prohibition on overseas trade imposed by imperial authorities in an attempt to eliminate petty parasitic piracy. For decades early in the century, a flourishing clandestine trade fused with the mounting maritime power of the so-called *wakō*. Although the term means "Japanese pirate," it is clear that Chinese personnel predominated and provided leadership.[71] Official control was ineffective: the Ming dynasty was in decline, and in Japan the Ashikaga shogunate was in the process of disintegration.

The Ming administration's prohibition of overseas trade in response to petty piracy was a quintessentially bureaucratic solution to an irritant associated with an economic activity in which the administration had no official interest, philosophically or materially. Not surprisingly, the prohibition was not accepted by coastal communities. The wealthy continued to provide finance, officials charged with the suppression of trade still functioned as intermediaries, and the ordinary people continued in their employment in maritime and ancillary occupations, one of which, when opportunity presented, could be piracy.[72] With the passage of time, the merchant-pirates became better organized and more powerful, as groups coalesced and operated from bases on offshore islands beyond official reach. Even then, trade rather than pillage appears to have been the primary desideratum: the most influential of the pirates, Wang Ji, had cooperated with officials to suppress pirates who obstructed trade.[73]

At the same time, private trade with the Japanese had been opened by Chinese merchants. Trade between China and Japan had been limited and formalized within the traditional tribute system, but frustration with this led the Japanese, quasi-feudal and unconstrained by any central authority, to establish commercial and piratical links with Chinese merchants. Pirate bands that emerged from these associations, reinforced by desperate peasants suffering from the droughts and famines of the years 1543–46, cruised in large, well-armed fleets and ravaged the central coast of China, where they established fortified bases on land, frequently defeated imperial troops, and even threatened the imperial grain barges in the Yangzi delta.

This episode of piracy was brought to an end in the 1560s as a result of divisions in the pirate leadership, official astuteness (and duplicity), and campaigns mounted with locally raised, well-trained, and well-led troops.[74] The cause of large-scale piracy was eliminated in the 1560s when the ban on overseas trade was rescinded and a tax system was formulated that was less burdensome on the agricultural peasantry.[75] The threat of Japanese participation in piracy waned as Japan came increasingly under centralized political control, and without Japanese allies, Chinese pirates could be defeated in detail.[76]

Extensive piracy reemerged on the South China coast in the early seventeenth century, as the Ming dynasty declined in famine and rebellion toward its demise at the hands of Manchu invaders. Zheng Chenggong (Koxinga), the son of a high Ming official who had made his wealth in trade and illicit activity, led the resistance to the Manchu in the southern coastal areas and later expelled the Dutch from Taiwan.[77] In these activities he was patriot rather than pirate, at least in purpose, if not always in practice: problems of supply obliged Zheng to raid coastal areas.[78] The episode is interesting because despite the specific circumstances and the particular motivations involved, the actions of Zheng and his Manchu adversaries conformed to the patterns characteristic of large-scale piracy and its suppression in China both before and since. These patterns are the deployment against the dynasty of large, well-organized, and well-disciplined fleets, with pitched battles against imperial forces on land and sea; the banning of maritime trade by imperial authorities to deny prey to the predators (with, on this occasion, the clearing of population from the southern coastal strip for some years in the 1660s); and the termination of the episode of piracy by some combination of internal dissension, imperial diplomacy, and the military force that was available to the empire.

The next large-scale episode of piracy in Chinese waters followed the cessation of a war between factions in northern and southern Vietnam in the late eighteenth century, again a time of famine and civil disturbance in China. Chinese naval mercenaries moved north to their home waters and put their naval, organizational, and strategic skills to use in large-scale and systematic predation for about two decades. Such was the scale of their operations that they were able regularly to engage and defeat fleets of imperial war—junks. The pirates levied tribute in the land areas over which they had some control.[79] In effect, they set up a pirate state, mimicking some aspects of the structure and functioning of the increasingly ineffectual imperial Qing state and adding to the burdens of an already impoverished peasantry.

Although the power of the pirate "state" was broken by internal divisions and the official diplomacy that exploited those divisions, there were further regular outbreaks of Chinese piracy during the nineteenth century. These episodes were generally associated with the crises characteristic of a dynasty in decline and the consequent poverty, lawlessness, and weakening of government control both on land and at sea. In addition, the illicit opium trade in the first half of the century was associated with an increase in parasitic piracy.

Although European vessels carrying opium or the proceeds of its sale were desirable prizes, the burden of piracy in Chinese as in Southeast Asian waters appears to have fallen most heavily on relatively defenseless seafarers and inhabitants of the littorals, rather than on the better armed Europeans. Profit, in piracy as in any business, depends on the difference between returns and costs, with the difference being multiplied by the number of transactions. While opium clippers and other European ships offered the prospect of high returns to predators, European ships were generally well armed and therefore costly to engage, except perhaps if there was an opportunity to employ stealth or deception.[80] Local craft, such as market boats, generally offered in themselves and in their cargo a lower return as prizes, but were numerous and relatively defenseless. Grace Estelle Fox notes of this period that "pirates . . . attacked and plundered some European ships, and they captured an incalculable number of native cargoes."[81]

The episode of piracy most costly of life in modern times took place in nearby seas and again followed the cessation of a conflict in Vietnam. With the establishment of a new regime in South Vietnam in 1975, hundreds of thousands of Vietnamese sought to leave their homeland, many doing so in a variety of small, often overcrowded and unseaworthy boats. These refugees, with their wealth—such as it was—necessarily in portable and easily negotiable form, attracted opportunistic maritime predators with hideously tragic results. Problems of jurisdiction and detection impeded effective action to suppress the pirates. States in the region had jurisdiction but not necessarily control over the acts of their nationals at sea. Vietnam had unequivocal legal standing in international law to act or to seek action to protect its citizens, but it did neither. Other states, whatever their revulsion at the occurrences, had no legal standing to act directly.[82] Despite efforts that were made within the region to suppress the evil and those made, necessarily indirectly, by states outside the region, predation waned only as the prey diminished.

In that episode of piracy, and commonly in other cases in modern times, difficulties of detection have impeded its suppression.[83] Modern piracy committed on commercial shipping, although perhaps organized by criminal groups and essentially parasitic, can have elements of intrinsic predation. Pirates and their vessels are often able to blend undetectably into communities that may knowingly give them shelter and support, but which in any case have legitimate dealings with boats and the sea. In those situations, patrols cannot easily distinguish predators from mariners going about their lawful business, and later investigations cannot easily identify offenders or prosecute with a level of proof beyond reasonable doubt.

The problem of piracy—parasitic, intrinsic, episodic—will continue to exist as long as there are criminally inclined persons and maritime zones of ineffective law enforcement. In addition, as this review suggests, piracy is likely to exist while there are littoral communities that are sunk in poverty or vulnerable to economic fluctuations and in which local traditional practice is more respected than the law of a remote central authority. The availability of appropriate technology for maritime surveillance and the apprehension of offenders is—and has been from the remote past—a necessary but not sufficient condition for the effective suppression of piracy. Further requirements are national resolve, international cooperation, and economic development that improves the material conditions of maritime communities.

NOTES

I gratefully acknowledge the helpful comments and suggestions given by participants at the World History Association Conference, Honolulu, Hawaii, June 1993, particularly K. N. Chaudhuri and K. R. Robinson. I attribute the sharpening of some definitions and some of the analysis in this paper to the comments of anonymous referees. Remaining inadequacies are my own responsibility.

1. William H. McNeill, *The Human Condition: An Ecological and Historical View* (Princeton: Princeton University Press, 1980), 6–8. Macroparasites contrast with microparasites, or disease organisms, in size, number, scale of effect, and historical impact, but not in function.

2. See both Anne Pérotin-Dumon, "The Pirate and the Emperor: Power and the Law on the Seas, 1450–1850," and David J. Starkey, "Pirates and Markets," in this collection.

3. The industrial revolution was associated with an increase in oceanic trade and produced the technology that helped to defend that trade—in particular the steam gunboat and the electric telegraph. See Daniel R. Headrick, *The Tools of Empire: Technology and European Imperialism in the Nineteenth Century* (New York: Oxford University Press, 1981), 43–57.

4. A distinction between piracy and privateering can be drawn in theory but not always easily in practice. A privateer was an armed vessel, privately owned, carrying formal authority to attack the shipping and to take in a regulated way the property of a specified enemy in time of war. This form of predation on commerce was abandoned in 1856 by most nations by the Declaration of Paris. A recent study of privateering, with useful bibliography, is that of David Starkey, *British Privateering Enterprise in the Eighteenth Century* (Exeter: University of Exeter Press, 1990).

5. Alfred P. Rubin, *The Law of Piracy* (Newport, R.I.: Naval War College Press, 1988), 305–37.

6. On "officially sanctioned piracy," see Robert C. Ritchie, *Captain Kidd and the War against the Pirates* (Cambridge, Mass.: Harvard University Press, 1986), 11–16.

7. Rubin, *Law of Piracy*, 14. However, the most vigorous and effective predators seldom confined their activities to their home waters. In the first half of the seventeenth century, Algerian raiders operated regularly off the southwest coast of England from April to October. Todd Gray, "Turkish Piracy and Early Stuart Devon," *Reports of the Transactions of the Devonshire Association for the Advancement of Science* 121 (1989): 159–71, reference here to 161. Similarly, predators from the Sulu archipelago, with bases in Borneo, habitually used the monsoon—the "pirate wind"—to cruise extensively in the eastern seas: James F. Warren, *The Sulu Zone, 1768–1898: The Dynamics of External Trade, Slavery and Ethnicity in the Transformation of a Southeast Asian Maritime State* (Singapore: Singapore University Press, 1981), 154.

8. Rubin, *Law of Piracy*, 211, 231. See also the exculpatory arguments in Sir Godfrey Fisher, *Barbary Legend: War, Trade, and Piracy in North Africa, 1415–1830* (Westport, Conn.: Greenwood Press, 1974).

9. This legal opinion is pressed in Rubin, *Law of Piracy*, 337–46. Rubin argues the point at length in relation to the global Pax Britannica and the earlier Mediterranean Pax Romana.

10. The developed convention of a "three-mile limit" of territorial water, insofar as it was based on the extreme range of a cannon, reflected the extent of a territorial authority's effective reach. See D. P. O'Connell, *The International Law of the Sea*, 2 vols. (Oxford: Clarendon Press, 1982), 1: chapter 7.

11. R. W. Anderson, *The Economics of Crime* (London: Macmillan, 1976), 38.

12. Ibid., 41. The threat of predation can severely restrict all maritime activity, with consequent economic dislocation to industries and regions. In England in 1625, for example, it was reported of so-called "Turkish pirates" that "in the west parts they made the coast so dangerous through their spoils as few dared put forth of their harbors." See Gray, "Turkish Piracy," 161. In the same century, according to a former chaplain at Surat, European pirates in Arabian seas "so impoverish'd . . . some of the Mogul's people that they must either cease to carry on a trade or resolve to be made a prey." G. V. Scammell, "European Exiles, Renegades and Outlaws and the Maritime Economy of Asia, c. 1500–1750," *Modern Asian Studies* 26, no. 4 (1992): 641–61. For the Philippines, see Warren, *Sulu Zone*, 168, 181. For parts of the Caribbean, see Kenneth R. Andrews, *The Spanish Caribbean: Trade and Plunder, 1530–1630* (New Haven: Yale University Press, 1978), 165.

13. A large part of the explanation of economic development in Europe may be argued to have been the reduction, through impersonal law, of predation on the business community by those not under authority—and by those in authority. See E. L. Jones, *The European Miracle: Environments, Economies, and Geopolitics in the History of Europe and Asia*, 2d ed. (Cambridge: Cambridge University Press, 1987), 85–149.

14. The analysis in this and the following paragraph is drawn from F. C. Lane, "Economic Consequences of Organised Violence," *Journal of Economic History* 18, no. 4 (1958). On page 8 Lane refers to merchants' propensity to invest. A model of the dynamics of early mercantile expansion can be found in Sir John Hicks, *A Theory of Economic History* (Oxford: Clarendon Press, 1969), 43–46.

15. At a different level, Jones, *European Miracle*, argues that competition between

nation-states in politically fragmented Europe restrained governments in their revenue raising and also reduced transaction costs. This was to the economic advantage of early modern Europeans, relative to their contemporaries in comparatively monolithic Asian empires.

16. Lane, "Economic Consequences," 410.

17. Piracy, in Marxist analysis, could have contributed to primitive accumulation of capital by Europeans, but its quasi-universal and random nature and its costs to all parties could hardly have yielded Europe a significant surplus, if any. Quantitatively, piracy would be inconsequential relative to the other forms of plunder and expropriation discussed in part 8 of Karl Marx, *Capital: A Critique of Political Economy* (Harmondsworth: Penguin, 1976–81). This point might be considered with P. K. O'Brien's calculations of the limited contribution that even lawful overseas trade made to European economic growth. P. K. O'Brien, "European Economic Development: The Contribution of the Periphery," *Economic History Review* 2d ser., 35 (1982): 1–18. This is not to deny that the transfer of assets effected by successful predation could provide a net profit for particular individuals or groups.

18. Douglass C. North, "Sources of Productivity Change in Ocean Shipping 1600–1850," *Journal of Political Economy,* 76 (1968): 953–67.

19. Fisher, *Barbary Legend,* 157, 176. The point is raised also in Carl Trocki, *Prince of Pirates: The Temenggongs and the Development of Johor and Singapore 1784–1885* (Singapore: Singapore University Press, 1979), 86–87.

20. Alberto Tenenti, *Piracy and the Decline of Venice 1580–1615*, trans. Janet and Brian Pullan (Berkeley: University of California Press, 1967).

21. Christopher Lloyd, *English Corsairs on the Barbary Coast* (London: Collins, 1981), 60. The term corsair is generally (but not necessarily) used to describe sea raiders, most notably in the Mediterranean region, who unlike pirates acted in at least some respects with the approval, or on behalf of an established political authority, but who were not universally acknowledged to be privateers. See Peter Kemp, ed., *The Oxford Companion to Ships and the Sea* (London: Oxford University Press, 1976), 207.

22. Fernand Braudel, *The Mediterranean and the Mediterranean World in the Age of Philip II*, trans. Siân Reynolds, 2 vols. (London: Collins, 1972–73), 2: 887.

23. Tenenti, *Piracy and the Decline of Venice,* 101–3.

24. Ibid., 107.

25. Ibid., 109.

26. Philip Gosse, *The History of Piracy* (London: Longmans, Green, 1932), 1–2.

27. Henry A. Ormerod, *Piracy in the Ancient World: An Essay in Mediterranean History* (Liverpool: Liverpool University Press, 1924), chapter 6.

28. Given their circumstances and motivation, even the early Sea-Beggars could more reasonably be seen as privateers than as pirates, but "unfortunately, they but too often made their demands upon both friend and foe." John Lothrop Motley, *The Rise of the Dutch Republic: A History,* 3 vols. (London: Dent, 1906), 2: 285.

29. The term *Barbary* has been commonly if vaguely used to refer to the whole or part of the region of North Africa that lies to the west of Egypt, including part of the Atlantic coast. The region is more properly called the Maghrib.

30. Ritchie, *Captain Kidd,* 17–19, 233.

31. Rubin argues, inter alia, that the Pax Britannica in the eastern seas, similar to and in some ways patterned on the Pax Romana in the Mediterranean of two thousand years before, was wrong at law. Rubin, *Law of Piracy,* chapters 1 and 4. See also A. P. Rubin, *Piracy, Paramountcy and Protectorates* (Kuala Lumpur: Penerbit Universiti Malaya, 1974).

32. John Francis Guilmartin, *Gunpowder and Galleys: Changing Technology and Mediterranean Warfare at Sea in the Sixteenth Century* (London: Cambridge University Press, 1974), 22–23.

33. See Jamil M. Abun-Nasr, *A History of the Maghrib in the Islamic Period* (Cambridge: Cambridge University Press, 1987), esp. 159, 165 (Algiers); 177 (Tunis); 194 (Tripoli); 221 (Salé). It is observed (p. 165) that the intrinsic nature of predation in the first three of these cities persisted because of the exclusion of their shipping from European ports and the predatory activities of the Knights of St. John.

34. Lloyd, *English Corsairs,* 38; C. M. Senior, *A Nation of Pirates: English Piracy in Its Heyday* (Newton Abbot: David and Charles, 1976), 9.

35. Tenenti, *Piracy and the Decline of Venice,* 18.

36. Braudel, *The Mediterranean,* 2: 867. Weakening domestic political control could also result in corsairs crossing the line between regulated predation and criminality. See Abun-Nasr, *History of the Maghrib,* 194.

37. Lloyd, *English Corsairs,* 94.

38. The English and Dutch carried into the Mediterranean their developed practice of predation by private enterprise, sharpened by the bitterness of the conflicts of the Reformation.

39. The nature and significance for the economic development of Europe of the mutually supportive relationship between state power and commercial enterprise that was mercantilism is succinctly put in William H. McNeill, *The Pursuit of Power: Technology, Armed force, and Society since A.D. 1000* (Oxford: Blackwell, 1983), 150–51.

40. Guilmartin, *Gunpowder and Galleys,* 264.

41. The power of the Royal Navy, from the late seventeenth century on, meant that British ships were less at risk in the Mediterranean than those of their commercial rivals and so could carry smaller crews. This gave them a cost advantage and with it a large share of the carrying trade. Ralph Davis, "England and the Mediterranean, 1570–1670," in *Essays in the Economic and Political History of Tudor and Stuart England,* ed. F. J. Fisher (Cambridge: University Press, 1961), 117–37, reference here to 131–32.

42. One purpose of the establishment of relations was the facilitation of the ransom or exchange of captives. Predators in the Mediterranean took captives as a matter of course for ransom or for use as slaves ashore or aboard galleys.

43. Lloyd, *English Corsairs,* 14 7, 156–58.

44. Edward L. Beach, *The United States Navy: Two Hundred Years* (New York: H. Holt, 1986), 46–48, 136.

45. Seaton Dearden, *A Nest of Corsairs: The Fighting Karamanlis of the Barbary Coast* (London: John Murray, 1976), 244. The corsair activities of the Knights of St.

John at Malta also became negligible during the eighteenth century. See Lloyd, *English Corsairs,* 146–47.

46. Aspects of nineteenth-century piracy in Malaysian and Chinese waters are considered in more detail in John Anderson, "Piracy in the Eastern Seas 1750–1850: Some Economic Implications," in *Pirates and Privateers: New Perspectives on the War on Trade in the Eighteenth and Nineteenth Centuries,* ed. David J. Starkey, van Eyck van Heslinga, and J. A. de Moor (Exeter: University of Exeter Press, 1997), 87–105.

47. Paul Wheatley, *The Golden Khersonese: Studies in the Historical Geography of the Malay Peninsula before* A.D. *1500* (Kuala Lumpur: University of Malaya Press, 1961), 38, 57, 82, 91.

48. See Rubin, *Law of Piracy,* 240–58; also Nicholas Tarling, *Piracy and Politics in the Malay World: A Study in British Imperialism in Nineteenth-Century South-East Asia* (Melbourne: Cheshire, 1963), 58. For the Persian Gulf, the existence of any such right is rejected by Sultan ibn Muhammad al-Qasimi, *The Myth of Arab Piracy in the Gulf* (London: Croom Helm, 1986).

49. Anonymous, "The Piracy and Slave Trade of the Indian Archipelago," *Journal of the Indian Archipelago* ser. 1, 3 (1849): 632. Other reports support this assessment; see Tarling, *Piracy and Politics,* 28–29, 166. Of the dozen or so British ships reported as having been lost to pirates in the 1840s, some seem to have been looted after grounding and others were simply lost without trace. See *British Parliamentary Papers:* Accounts and Papers, 1850, 55: 9, "Return of British Vessels Attacked or Plundered by Malay or Dyak Pirates off the Coast of Borneo, August 1839–1849."

50. D. G. E. Hall, *A History of South-East Asia,* 2d ed. (London: Macmillan, 1966), 499; Warren, *Sulu Zone,* 29. Similar effects occurred elsewhere. Of ancient times in the Mediterranean, Henry A. Ormerod notes that "as a result of this general insecurity and continued harrying of the coasts, wide tracts of country passed out of cultivation." Ormerod, *Piracy in the Ancient World,* 49. For examples from later times, see Braudel, *The Mediterranean,* 1: 32, 154.

51. Deposition of a former captive dealing with events in 1847, quoted in Warren, *Sulu Zone,* 242.

52. Ibid., 199, 249. On labor as the scarce resource, see Anthony Reid, *Southeast Asia in the Age of Commerce, 1450–1680,* 2 vols. (New Haven: Yale University Press, 1988–1993), 1: 129.

53. Rubin, *Law of Piracy,* 230.

54. Hall, *A History,* 505. Data on Borneo trade are given in Wong Lin Ken, "The Trade of Singapore 1819–1869," *Journal of the Malayan Branch of the Royal Asiatic Society* 23, no. 4 (1960): 283.

55. Braudel, *The Mediterranean,* 2: 865, citing Louis Dermigny, *La Chine et l'Occident: Le commerce à Canton au XVII1è siècle, 1719–1833.*

56. Restoration of trade in Europe followed the disruptions of war and the depressions of peace. However, when trade disruption resulted from the intrusion of a power that established a monopoly of trade in the area, as happened in the eastern seas, the protracted "episode" could originate or stimulate intrinsic piracy. For a view of the effects of Dutch intrusion into the Indonesian archipelago, see Hall, *A History,* 497–98.

For some of the antecedents of raiding in the area, see Philip D. Curtin, *Cross-Cultural Trade in World History* (Cambridge: Cambridge University Press, 1984), 159–60.

57. Simon Digby, "The Maritime Trade of India," in *The Cambridge Economic History of India,* ed. Tapan Raychaudhuri and Irfan Habib (Cambridge: Cambridge University Press, 1982), 152–54. See also Radhakumud Mookerji, *Indian Shipping: A History of the Sea-Borne Trade and Maritime Activity of the Indians from the Earliest Times,* 2d ed. (Allahabad: K. Mahal, 1962), 133. Digby notes that it was the practice of the pirates of which he writes neither to enslave nor to kill their victims. This is an example of an efficient parasite, which may debilitate but does not kill its host. Further, a known policy of clemency toward those who had not resisted would reduce the probability of resistance. For the European experience, see Senior, *Nation of Pirates,* 22–23. For China, and the brutality inflicted on those who did resist, see Robert J. Antony, "Aspects of the Socio-Political Culture of South China's Water World, 1740–1840," *Great Circle* 15, no. 2 (1993): 75–90, reference here to 84; see also Ormerod, *Piracy in the Ancient World,* 228.

58. K. N. Chaudhuri, *Trade and Civilisation in the Indian Ocean: An Economic History from the Rise of Islam to 1750* (Cambridge: Cambridge University Press, 1985), 63–64.

59. The later Dutch and English intrusions into the eastern seas were also inextricably associated with predation and outright piracy. See Scammell, "European Exiles," 649–56.

60. Curtin, *Cross-Cultural Trade,* 147.

61. Colonel John Biddulph, *The Pirates of Malabar; and an Englishwoman in India Two Hundred Years Ago* (London: Smith, Elder, 1907), 83. On Angrian independence, see also Sir Richard Burn, ed., *The Cambridge History of India,* 6 vols. (Delhi: S. Chand, 1963), 4: 394, 404.

62. Neville Williams, *Captains Outrageous* (London: Barrie and Rockliff, 1961), 132–34; Ritchie, *Captain Kidd,* 37–38.

63. Clinton V. Black, *Pirates of the West Indies* (Cambridge: Cambridge University Press, 1989), 25.

64. The nature of buccaneering, which originated in the Caribbean Sea as a colonial extension of European national conflicts exacerbated by trading exclusivity, is outlined in Gosse, *History of Piracy,* book 3, chapter 1. See also the bibliographical review in Larry Schweikart and B. R. Burg, "Stand by to Repel Historians: Modern Scholarship and Caribbean Pirates, 1650–1725," *Historian* 46, no. 2 (1984): 219–34. In the West Indies of the seventeenth century, "it was left to entrepreneurs to carry out state policy by private means." Ritchie, *Captain Kidd,* 15.

65. For England, see Senior, *A Nation of Pirates,* 7–11.

66. Black, *Pirates of the West Indies,* 11.

67. Surplus labor resulted in poor wages and conditions as well as unemployment: see Ritchie, *Captain Kidd,* 234; and Marcus Rediker, *Between the Devil and the Deep Blue Sea: Merchant Seamen, Pirates and the Anglo American Maritime Worlds 1700–1726* (Cambridge: Cambridge University Press, 1987), 281–82.

68. Sir Edward Codrington, *Piracy in the Levant, 1827–8; Selected from the Pa-*

pers of Admiral Sir Edward Codrington, ed. C. G. Pitcairn Jones, *Publications of the Navy Records Society*, vol. 72 (London: Navy Records Society, 1934); Francis B. C. Bradlee, *Piracy in the West Indies and Its Suppression*, 2d ed., *American Maritime History* (Salem, Mass.: Essex Institute, 1923), gives numerous examples from contemporary sources.

69. Kenneth J. Hagan, *This People's Navy: The Making of American Sea Power* (New York: Free Press, 1991), 94–96.

70. Kwan-wai So, *Japanese Piracy in Ming China during the Sixteenth Century* (East Lansing: Michigan State University Press, 1975).

71. Ibid., chapter 1.

72. Denis Crispin Twitchett and John K. Fairbank, eds., *The Cambridge History of China*, 15 vols. (Cambridge: Cambridge University Press, 1978–1998), 7: 490.

73. So, *Japanese Piracy*, 34.

74. *Cambridge History of China*, 7: 503.

75. So, *Japanese Piracy*, 154–55.

76. *Cambridge History of China*, 7: 504. Korea dealt with earlier Japanese piracy more adroitly; see Kenneth R. Robinson, "From Raiders to Traders: Border Security and Border Control in Early Choson, 1392–1450," *Korean Studies* 16 (1992): 94–115.

77. The career of Zheng Chenggong and the course of his campaigns are outlined in *The Cambridge History of China*, 7: 666–67, 710–25. An appraisal of the episode is found in Ralph Crozier, *Koxinga and Chinese Nationalism: History, Myth, and Hero* (Canbridge, Mass.: Harvard University Press: 1977).

78. John E. Wills, "Maritime China from Wang Chih to Shih Lang: Themes in Maritime History," in *From Ming to Ching: Conquest, Region, and Continuity in Seventeenth-Century China*, ed. Jonathan D. Spence and John E. Wills (New Haven: Yale University Press, 1979), 201–38, reference here to 226.

79. Dian H. Murray, *Pirates of the South China Coast, 1790–1810* (Stanford: Stanford University Press, 1987), 89–90. Control by pirate confederations was established "through formal systems of terrorism, extortion and bribery. . . . Through the systematic use of violence and brutality pirates would intimidate . . . their victims into submission." Antony, "Aspects of South China's Water World," 84.

80. In the 1850s there were many relatively small European vessels—schooners of about 200 registered tons—operating in the opium trade on the coast of China. One such, for example, was "armed with four eighteen-pounders of a side; a long eighteen on the forecastle and a sixty-eight pounder amidships—these two last being pivot guns." Captain Lindsay Anderson, *A Cruise in an Opium Clipper*, reprint ed. (Melbourne: Ibex, 1989), 35. The armament was comparable to that of a small British warship. Pirate junks appear to have mounted up to a dozen guns, but a pirate ship mentioned as being "a large one" had only four six-pounders, though it had a crew of one hundred twenty men. Basil Lubbock, *The Opium Clippers* (Glasgow: Brown, Son, and Ferguson, 1933), 292–93, 339.

81. Grace Fox, *British Admirals and Chinese Pirates, 1832–1869* (London: Paul, Trench, Trubner, 1940), 187.

82. Rubin, *Law of Piracy,* 340–42. This episode is briefly surveyed in *Vietnamese Boat People* (New York: UN Commission for Refugees, 1984).

83. A further problem can be a reluctance on the part of victims to report incidents for fear of offending trading partners or of suffering an increase in insurance premiums. Captain Roger Villar, *Piracy Today: Robbery and Violence at Sea since 1980* (London: Conway Maritime Press, 1985), 14. A survey of modern criminality at sea is provided by G. O. W Mueller and Freda Adler, *Outlaws of the Ocean: The Complete Book of Contemporary Crime on the High Seas* (New York: Hearst Marine Books, 1985). Piracy in the South China Sea, in the waters of Southeast Asia, Africa, and South America still can give cause for concern; for examples, see reports in the *Economist* (26 March 1994); *Time* (5 October 1992); *Asiaweek* (3 July 1992); and *Fortune* (15 July 1991).

Chapter 6

Pirates and Markets

David J. Starkey

Attacks upon seaborne trade were a persistent and important feature of the Atlantic empires established by European maritime powers in the early modern era. Such assaults were often perpetrated by the crews of naval and privateering vessels sanctioned by their respective states to commit acts of violence upon specified targets—usually enemy traders in wartime. At the same time, this colonial and commercial world attracted and spawned a range of predators whose operations were deemed illegal by contemporaries. Such commerce raiders were viewed as pirates. Of course, this was a highly subjective viewpoint, for the law of the sea was more a reflection of the prevailing balance of state power than an impartial interpretation of natural justice.[1] In reality, the pirates included not only stereotypical, stateless sea robbers, but also such predators as the Barbary corsairs and Caribbean buccaneers, whose actions were licensed by authorities largely beyond the control of the metropolitan seats of imperial power. This paper is concerned with the various forms of piracy which fell within this imprecise parameter.

At the heart of the discussion is the contention that piracy, for all its political and social ramifications, was essentially an economic activity; that men, and occasionally women, attacked and plundered shipping to generate income for themselves.[2] Though its extent and impact fluctuated greatly, piracy at certain times and in particular regions assumed the proportions of a large-scale business, significant enough to attract the repressive attentions of maritime states. Often located physically and socially on the margins of the Atlantic economy, this business was inextricably linked to its market mechanisms. In providing goods and services to a range of consumers by deploying a variety of resources, piracy was a facet of the markets which governed trading and shipping activity. At the same time, it was largely a function of these markets, for it tended to emerge and thrive at the junctures when disequilibria were evident between demand and supply. The extent to which such market inefficiencies precipitated piratical activity is the main concern of this paper. To this end, attention is focused on three aspects of the subject. First, the principal forms of Atlantic piracy in the early modern era are identified; then, the market forces which conditioned the pirate's business are analyzed; and finally, the causes and incidence of piratical activity are related to the wider question of the efficiency of the market for seafarers in the age of sail.[3]

Waves of Piracy

Piracy is a service industry, a business concerned with the transport and distribution, rather than the production, of commodities. Seaborne trade is a prerequisite of this activity, although as in any form of predatory enterprise the very success of the hunter necessarily affects the extent of the prey. Market forces condition the scale, incidence, and character of this business. On the demand side, pirates consume the goods they steal, or else deliver them to buyers who are rarely the intended recipients but consumers in alternative markets.[4] Moreover, while the interests of states might be served by piratical activity, for this consumer the service provided is usually military rather than commercial. On the supply side, piracy is sustained by three principal production factors— land (ports and bases), labor (seafarers), and capital (vessels, provisions, arms, etc.). Yet instead of competing in factor markets, the pirate obtains resources by stealing or else by deploying idle vessels, equipment, and labor. Intervening substantially in this market, of course, is the state. While piracy by definition is illegal, variable factors like political will, commercial interest, and naval capability greatly influence the color and effectiveness of a government's interventionist policies.

This market structure strongly resembles the shipping industry. Shippers, like pirates, depend on the existence of seaborne trade, as well as serving the needs of consumers and states and drawing upon supplies of land, capital, and labor. But there are critical differences between the two. The role of government differs, for states generally seek to encourage their shipping industries; protection against pirates was one measure customarily adopted to meet this end. A further contrast lies in the relationships between shipping and piracy on the one hand, and trade on the other. Shipping relates to trade symbiotically, an increase or decrease in one normally leading to gains or losses in the other. Piracy, by contrast, is parasitic, feeding not only on the goods transported but also on the resources deployed by the carrier. The markets which shippers serve, and in which they engage, are therefore highly significant to the level of piratical as well as shipping activity. But piracy is not a simple parasite, expanding or contracting in line with its host.[5] Rather, as a rival with— and predator upon—the interests of traders and shippers, piracy tends to exploit market deficiencies, flourishing at times when substantial disequilibria emerge between the demand and supply of commodities, military services, and the production factors of shippers.

Activity rates reflect the contrasts between shipping and piracy. Whereas the former is a more or less constant, albeit fluctuating, form of enterprise, piracy is largely a product of particular, often short-term, conditions. It is therefore volatile, a contention borne out by the pattern of piratical activity evident in the Atlantic between the early seventeenth century and the 1830s. Of course, measuring the scale of piracy with any precision is difficult due to the fragmentary nature of the surviving evidence. Nevertheless, sufficient data exist to offer an outline of the course of the business of piracy in the Atlantic economy of the early modern era. Though countless, incidental, petty acts of maritime lawlessness doubtless occurred, piracy as a large-scale business activity proceeded in five waves of varying duration and amplitude. Originating in, and impacting upon, different regions and facets of this trading system, each of the waves constituted a problem, and sometimes an opportunity, for the European maritime states.

Two of these piratical phenomena—Barbary piracy and Caribbean buccaneering—might be described as "long" waves, in that both were relatively durable maritime activities. While the so-called Barbary pirates were active more or less continuously in the Mediterranean, and occasionally in the eastern Atlantic, from the Middle Ages to the nineteenth century, buccaneering emerged in the early seventeenth century and remained a factor in the Caribbean until at least the 1690s.[6] There were other similarities between these two commerce-raiding genres. In the strictest sense, neither was piratical. The corsairs of North Africa cruised against Christian shipping with the spiritual blessing of Muhammad and the temporal authority of the Sultan, although they were generally regarded as pirates by European statesmen who likened their activities to a thorn in the foot, a painful irritant requiring a remedy.[7] Likewise, many of the great buccaneering forays against the Spanish Main were afforded a veneer of legitimacy by letters of marque issued by colonial authorities, even though the aims and means of these operations were clearly piratical.[8] Significantly, despite their dubious legality, both the Barbary corsairs and the Caribbean buccaneers served the interests of states, though not always overtly and sometimes inadvertently, by preying upon the commerce of political and commercial rivals.

In other respects, these long waves of piracy differed greatly. Essentially, the Barbary corsairs were the naval arm of Islam engaged in Eternal War with Christendom. Their operations therefore threatened the commerce and shipping of the principal European maritime states, though the nature and extent of the menace varied. In the early seventeenth century, the trading interests of

England, Holland, and Spain were damaged extensively by commerce raiders based in Algiers, Salé, Tunis, and other North African ports. Abandoning oared galleys for sailing vessels, the Barbary corsairs ventured from their customary Mediterranean grounds to prey on the shipping lanes of the eastern Atlantic. While Spanish coastal and short-sea trade suffered great losses, it was the English who were most vexed by their depredations, not least because they raided the coasts of southwestern England. With a "staggering" total of approximately 400 vessels and above 8,000 captives carried to Barbary between 1616 and 1642, the English government was stirred to mount two naval campaigns and a series of diplomatic offensives to free hostages and reduce the "pirate scourge."[9] While these efforts had mixed results, the "Turkish menace" gradually receded from the 1640s by dint of treaties, tribute, and threats of naval reprisal. Thereafter, the Barbary corsairs rarely passed the Straits—though as late as 1710 English East Indiamen were instructed to sail to the Orient "not in the way of the Algerine cruisers"—and focused their aggression instead on the Christian privateers of Malta.[10] Though the scale of this activity diminished greatly in the eighteenth century, the coffers of the Barbary regencies nevertheless continued to be replenished by "safe passages" procured by Britain, France, and other maritime powers.[11]

Buccaneering rendered military rather than financial services to the state. The origins of this somewhat nebulous breed of piracy can be traced to the outcasts, outlaws, and interlopers who gained footholds in the Caribbean islands on the fringes of Spain's American empire during the late sixteenth and early seventeenth centuries.[12] Surviving by hunting wild cattle, their number swelled in the 1630s and 1640s by those forced off the land by the advance of the plantation system, and by political refugees from Europe, these *boucaniers* gradually widened their predatory horizons to include Spanish vessels and goods passing close to their bases.[13] From such roots sprang the buccaneers of yore, who formed a potent, if irregular, military force in the Caribbean during the second half of the seventeenth century. Disowned in London, Paris, and Amsterdam, yet commissioned concurrently in the West Indies, the buccaneers in effect were one of the main weapons with which Britain, France, and the United Provinces sought to breach Spain's New World monopoly. Amid this war of attrition, the sack of Panama in 1670 by a division of buccaneers under Henry Morgan, the incursion of Bartholomew Sharp and over 1,000 men into the Pacific in 1680–81, and the attack on Veracruz by thirteen ships and 1,400 buccaneers point to the scale and wider significance of this activity during an era in which there really was "no peace beyond the line."[14] But toward the end of the seventeenth century, the conditions in which buccaneering developed and functioned passed, a change signaled by the French assault on Cartagena in 1697, in which "two societies, two conceptions of justice, collaborated and collided" in the combined force of regular troops from France and a company of unruly and increasingly anachronistic buccaneers.[15]

Such long waves of piratical activity were inextricably linked to the political and economic aspirations of the states, colonies, or communities from which they emanated. Somewhat different in origin and effect were the comparatively brief surges of maritime lawlessness which occurred in the Atlantic between 1603 and 1616, 1714 and 1726, and 1815 and 1835. Similar patterns and characteristics can be perceived in these "short" waves of piracy. For instance, each followed a prolonged, wide-ranging war. Thus, the cessation of the Anglo-Spanish conflict of 1585–1603 heralded a burst of piratical aggression which originated in England but quickly spread to bases in southern Ireland and North Africa. Active in British coastal waters, the Western Approaches, off the Iberian peninsula and as far west as Newfoundland, these Jacobean pirates represented a serious threat to European traders and shippers, as well as a considerable diplomatic embarrassment to James I, the self-righteous, pirate-hating king of a "nation of pirates." At its height in 1608–14, as many as 300 ships and 1,000 men were engaged in piratical activity under the command of "admirals" such as Bishop Jennings, Peter Easton, and Henry Mainwaring. By 1615, however, this wave of piracy had lost momentum and within a year, much to James I's relief, the pirate menace had almost completely vanished.[16]

A century later, a similar cycle of lawlessness followed the peace of Utrecht. Though the epicentre of this eruption was the Caribbean, its tremors were felt in the Bahamas, the Carolinas, and as far away as West Africa and the Indian Ocean. It has been estimated that up to 5,000 freebooters were active at some stage during this wave of North American piracy in which such legendary characters as Edward Teach ("Blackbeard"), William Sawkins, Stede Bonnet, and Bartholomew Roberts played prominent roles.[17] Related in a number of respects to the buccaneering of the previous generation, this wave of piracy was marked by an anarchic, antiauthoritarian strain which has become the stuff of legend. It was a passing phase, however, lasting for a decade or so, before abating amid much violence in the mid-1720s.[18]

In the early nineteenth century, a further piratical wave developed in the Caribbean. This *course indépendante,* like buccaneering and Barbary commerce raiding, had pretensions of legitimacy in that it was integral to the wars of liberation which convulsed Spain's American empire during and after the Napoleonic wars. As such, much piratical activity was undertaken by predators armed with commissions granted by revolutionary regimes, most notably the Carthaginian Republic and the Confederation of South American States.[19] Yet it was more akin to the lawless surges of 1603–16 and 1714–26. While it was closely linked to the onset of peace, it was also relatively short-lived and spatially dynamic, the focus of operations shifting from the West Indies to Colombia, Mexico, Buenos Aires, and thence to Cuba, around whose shores fishermen-pirates continued to operate to great effect into the 1830s. As in the earlier short waves, pirate operations were on a large scale and, significantly, did not serve but threatened the commercial interests of European maritime states. The business of piracy, in each case, was therefore deemed beyond the law and confronted by naval forces dispatched to eradicate, reduce, or at least police it. In the early seventeenth century, Dutch warships cruised against pirates based in southern Ireland while a Spanish fleet destroyed the pirate stronghold of Mamora in North Africa in July 1614.[20] Likewise, the British navy, supported by the bureaucracy and courts of the Admiralty, was charged with eliminating North American piracy in the 1710s and 1720s.[21] A century later it performed more of a restraining role, diverting the energies of the *course indépendante* away from British interests in the Western hemisphere.[22]

A further common trait lay in the composition and structure of pirate crews and communities. The short waves of piracy—and buccaneering—were marked by the cosmopolitan character of the personnel involved and the egalitarian, democratic values which permeated their activities. All contained clear anti-Spanish tendencies, but in a mercantilist world in which ships, cargoes, and seafarers were rigorously categorized by nationality, pirates discriminated as little in their recruitment policies as in their choice of targets. Often mixed in nationality and race, though rarely in gender, companies of pirates from the early seventeenth century to the 1830s were generally organized along extraordinary lines. Unlike seafarers in the shipping industry, these maritime laborers were part-owners of their vessels, owned shares in the profits of their ventures, and were entitled to select (or remove) their commanders and officers. Extending such "alternative," collective principles beyond the workplace, pirate settlements were established almost in defiance of "normal" society. Thus, in locations as distant in time and space as Lundy Island and Barataria, men such as Thomas Sockwell and Jean Laffitte led pirate communities, while the fraternal tendencies of groups that styled themselves the "Confederation of Deep-Sea Pirates," the "Brethren of the Coast," or the "Brethren of the Gulf" further attest to the self-conscious "otherness" of pirate life.[23]

Such brotherhoods were essentially transitory. They belonged to, and symbolized, an extraordinary business which fed off the trade and shipping of European maritime states for relatively short periods in the early modern era. With the commerce raiders of the Islamic world from time to time preying on the same targets, the level of piratical activity in the Atlantic fluctuated dramatically. Though many factors were at play, economic forces chiefly explain this pattern.

Causalities

In the vast literature on piracy, there are numerous attempts to identify its causes. Implicit in many accounts is the notion that piracy is a product of weak and immature political, economic, and social structures, that it will inevitably die out as civilization progresses. The Atlantic experience offers some support for this Whiggish interpretation, for piracy was much more prevalent before the 1730s than after and generally less of a threat as the institutions and military capabilities of states developed. But the outbreak of large-scale maritime lawlessness in the early nineteenth century, albeit in the context of the terminal disintegration of the Spanish empire, tends to weaken such a thesis. Others have followed contemporaries in linking piratical activity to the cycles of war and peace, and certainly the demobilizations of 1603, 1714, and 1815 provided thousands of idle hands to do the devil's work. Yet piracy did not erupt once the peace treaties of 1748, 1763, and 1783 were signed.[24]

A further line of reasoning has looked to the unit of production—the pirate crew and community—to explain the ebb and flow of piracy. While the attractions of a libertarian lifestyle or, more important, an alternative form of social organization may well have enticed many oppressed seafarers or political outcasts to serve under the black flag, this elucidates how a wave of piracy might be sustained rather than the reasons for its genesis.[25] Equally inadequate is the contention that piracy was precipitated by change in the political realm. This was clearly an important factor, the interimperial rivalries of the early modern era providing the unstable political climate in which piracy often flourished, while state policies, whether designed to nurture commercial hegemony over an area or to exclude competitors from established trades, frequently cast interlopers or rivals as pirates.[26] Yet context and definition are not the same as causality. Accordingly, to assert that the "dynamic" underlying piracy was political is to ignore the essential truth that the motive which "spurs men on to the undertaking of the most difficult Adventures is the sacred hunger of gold"—that pirates appropriated the vessels and properties of others to earn profits.[27] This might have important political ramifications, but the chief causal dynamic, as the waves of maritime lawlessness in the Atlantic demonstrate, was economic and was found in the forces of demand and supply which conditioned trading and shipping activity.

Analysis of these market forces suggests that some were more passive than others in instigating and sustaining piratical activity. On the demand side, pirates provided goods and services for three forms of consumer. In the first place, there is a self-satisfying element to any piratical activity and there are many instances of seafarers or others plundering vessels and goods to meet their own needs. In this sense, piracy might be viewed as demand-led, the resort of people or societies lacking basic necessities. The *boucaniers* of the early seventeenth-century Caribbean conform to this type, hunting cattle and preying upon passing ships principally for reasons of self-sufficiency.[28] While this impetus might account for some piratical attacks, it hardly explains the scale of the various waves of piracy which rippled through the Atlantic for at least a decade. During these phases, pirates undoubtedly used or destroyed some of the properties they seized. But even the most wanton, ostentatious, or dissolute commerce raider was unlikely to consume all that was taken. Prize goods surplus to requirements therefore gave rise to a market, a black market in which cheap stolen properties were purchased by merchants and dealers who generally supplied the established, respectable communities of the Atlantic world.

This second form of demand tended to sustain waves of piratical activity. Once pirates had generated supplies of commodities for sale at discount prices, buyers were attracted to the entrepôts which invariably developed to handle this business. In the early seventeenth century, for instance, English and Dutch merchants regularly visited Leamcon in southern Ireland to treat with the pirate community, while traders from Leghorn, Venice, Genoa, and elsewhere in the Mediterranean formed strong commercial ties with the raiders who furnished the thriving mart of Mamora in North Africa with sugar, spices, wine, cloth, and a host of more mundane commodities.[29] Likewise, in the Caribbean, buccaneers and pirates were central to a transport system which saw the goods of the European maritime powers, especially Spain and her empire, redistributed within the West Indies and diverted in significant quantities to the ports of colonial North America.[30]

The services of pirates were also deployed by a third type of consumer, the state. Such demand generally arose from infant or weak authorities who lacked the resources to equip and maintain regular armed forces and therefore turned to opportunistic commerce raiders for the military muscle they required. Again, this was not demand-led, for such employers did not establish new forces but called upon existing predatory units as a short-term solution to their deficiencies. Such a cheap option was regularly pursued in the seventeenth-century Caribbean, where buccaneers supplied much of the physical force needed by the local representatives of the British, French, and Dutch states in their long war of attrition with the Spaniards.[31] A similar pragmatic arrangement pertained in the same theater in the early nineteenth century as insurgents relied on the violence of pirates in the maritime facet of their wars of liberation. In such instances, the service provided and price agreed amounted to the same thing—the unlimited plunder of Spanish property, a goal thought to weaken the enemy as well as reward the predator. The long wave of piracy based in the Barbary regencies worked on the same premise, though here the exchange between state and commerce raider was financial as well as military, for the corsairs generated income in the form of taxes and tributes for the littoral communities of North Africa.

While demand for the services of pirates did not initiate waves of maritime lawlessness, it played an important part in maintaining the momentum of predatory surges. Once the commercial, military, or fiscal utility of piracy was demonstrated, the business might swiftly become an important, sometimes intrinsic, feature of the economic and political life of a society. This points to clear weaknesses in the structure of "normal," legal markets. Thus, pirates furnished goods and military services to communities unable to obtain sufficient, affordable supplies through prescribed mechanisms. Mediterranean markets short of Northern European commodities, Spanish colonies forlornly awaiting supply vessels from Seville, North American communities obliged to purchase only British manufactures, European settlements in the Caribbean left unguarded due to the inadequacies of metropolitan resources, North African states impoverished by the limitations of their economic base—such were the consumers of piratical services. Of course, once legitimate traders and regular armed forces began to meet these needs, the demand for piracy fell and its practitioners were obliged to modify their operations or retire from the business.

On the supply side, piracy was only marginally conditioned by the availability of land. Bases were an important factor in that all pirates, even the most self-sufficient of marauders, needed a safe haven where vessels and crews could be replenished. While there was no shortage of such facilities in the comparatively undeveloped and sparsely populated Atlantic of the seventeenth and eighteenth centuries, the need for more substantial port amenities for the discharge of cargoes and exchange of goods might influence piratical activity. Such entrepôts emerged, of course; Leamcon, Mamora, Algiers, Salé, Tortuga, Port Royal, the Bahamas, Madagascar, Havana, Galveston, and many other places served at one time or another as pirate marts and strongholds. Though these "nests" were vulnerable to the violence of naval forces, as the reduction of Mamora in 1614, the assault on Salé in 1637, the "cleansing" of the Bahamas in 1718, and the attack on Jean Laffitte's community at Galveston in 1821 clearly demonstrate, the pest was generally inconvenienced rather than eliminated by the measures taken.[32]

Capital requirements were more of an influence upon the level of piratical activity. Of course, such needs might be minimal, for many piracies were committed with equipment as rudimentary as the canoes and muskets used by the early *boucaniers*. Moreover, a high proportion of piratical forays were self-sustaining. In the very nature of the business, vessels, arms, stores, provisions, and other necessities were taken and put to commerce raiding, an ad hoc means of investment and accumulation by which more successful pirates improved and extended their capital stock at little expense. But more substantial investments were needed to mount large-scale, deep-water ventures. The funds to purchase and equip vessels, procure armaments and provisions, and recruit labor came in some cases from legitimate mercantile and government sources. For instance, the depredations of the Turkish corsairs were funded by the merchants of Algiers, Salé, and other Moorish ports, while Governor Modyforde and other colonial officials invested in the buccaneering campaigns of Morgan, Sharp, Coxon, and others.[33] Likewise, William Kidd's infamous cruise in the *Adventure Gally,* a privateering venture which degenerated into piracy, was funded by a consortium led by Lord Bellomont, Governor of New York.[34]

On occasion, "foreign" capital was invested in piracy. In the seventeenth century, merchants in French Mediterranean ports provided funds for Barbary corsairs even as their government was negotiating ways of reducing the menace.[35] Similarly, though to a much greater degree, capital resources in the United States were deployed in the *course indépendante.* Vessels built for, and funds generated by, the carrying trade and privateering which American shippers successively and lucratively exploited during the Revolutionary and Napoleonic wars, lay idle once the peace of 1814 was signed. Now prohibited from carrying for, or cruising against, the European powers, with funds and vessels surplus to the needs of home trade, American merchants and shipowners invested in potentially profitable, if dubiously legal, trading, smuggling, and piratical activity in the Caribbean and South America.[36]

This was unusual, however, for capital, and land even less so, rarely precipitated surges of piracy. The supply of labor, by contrast, was invariably critical. Piracy was essentially labor-intensive, with comparatively large crews required to overhaul and overwhelm prizes. Though quantitative evidence is sparse, estimates suggest that in the Jacobean era the average pirate company was over fifty strong, twice the size of the crew of an English merchantman trading in the Mediterranean and three times that of the typical crew working in Northern European waters.[37] Barbary corsairs had even more substantial complements, the larger galleys and sailing vessels carrying between one hundred forty and two hundred soldiers to board their victims.[38] In the early eighteenth century, about eighty men worked the typical pirate ships of the Caribbean and North America at a time when complements on trans-Atlantic merchantmen were falling to between fifteen and twenty men.[39] Typically, pirate crews comprised men who worked not for shipowners or the state but for themselves. They were "on the account," self-employed maritime laborers whose remuneration came from a share in the spoils. While such terms of service meant that pirates might earn windfall profits from the capture of a valuable prize, they also entailed high risks, for negative earnings would accrue from a barren sortie. This prospect of "no purchase, no pay," together with the physical danger and, most significant, the illegality of piratical work, implies that employment opportunities, or conditions of service, in more regular, secure occupations must have been lacking for laborers to turn to this hazardous work.[40]

Such flaws in the labor market were at the root of the business of piracy in the Atlantic during the early modern era. Underlying each wave of lawlessness were discrepancies between the demand for, and supply of, labor. In some instances, the weakness was chronic and broadly based, and a steady flow of pirate recruits was forthcoming for long periods. The persistence and extent of Barbary piracy, for example, was in many ways symptomatic of the unemployment, underemployment, and widespread poverty which characterized the economics of the North African regencies. Though the immediate hinterlands of Algiers, Tunis, and Tripoli were relatively fertile and productive, it was the sea and commerce raiding which provided manufactures, raw materials, and slaves for distribution through a trading network which extended throughout the Islamic world.[41] In the very different setting of the early seventeenth-century Caribbean, a similar pattern was evident. The infant economics of the region, hindered by Spain's monopolistic policies, could not employ the miscellany of Europeans who gravitated toward the fabled wealth of the Americas. As cattle-hunting *boucaniers* evolved into commerce-raiding buccaneers, so the development of large-scale sugar plantations intensified the chronic oversupply of labor by squeezing a veritable class of smallholders off the land. Piratical forays were one solution to this crisis and over time a necessary search for sustenance became not only a viable business but also a way of life.[42]

Exacerbating these market inefficiencies in the Caribbean were similar problems in Europe. In England, Spain, France, and elsewhere, the late sixteenth and early seventeenth centuries were marked by rapid population growth and economic stagnation, a combination which led to high and sustained levels of unemployment. Together with the political and religious crises of the period, this helped fuel the flow of emigrants to the New World, thereby adding to the oversupply of labor and the wave of buccaneering it generated. It was also a factor contributing to the short wave of piracy which originated in Jacobean England in the early seventeenth century. Though evidence relating to the occupational background of those engaged in this wave of piracy is sparse, it would seem that a sizable proportion, perhaps as large as 30 percent, of the pirate population was drawn from land-based occupations. While a number, like J. M. Barrie's aptly-named "Gentleman" Starkey,[43] came from the professions and the ranks of the well-to-do, there were artisans, husbandmen, and even a poet among those who sailed with the "Confederation of

Deep-Sea Pirates."[44] The inference to be drawn from such data is that high and chronic levels of unemployment in the domestic economy encouraged some to seek a livelihood in lawless activity at sea.

More central to the outbreak of short waves of piracy was oversupply in the seafaring labor market. This was a large, diverse market in which labor was procured by shipowners in exchange for wages. It was notable for its fluctuations, a trait directly linked to the cycle of war and peace. But in meeting the demands of the navy and privateers in wartime, generally aided by state intervention, the seafaring labor market tended to generate a capacity difficult to maintain in peacetime, leading on occasion to outbreaks of lawlessness. This pattern is clear in the English market for seafarers in the early seventeenth century.[45] Largely as a result of the war against Spain, which formally commenced in 1585, the number of seafarers engaged in English naval, privateering, and merchant vessels increased from an estimated 16,000 in the early 1580s to nearly 50,000 in the last years of Elizabeth's reign.[46] When naval demobilization and the suspension of letters of marque occurred suddenly in the summer of 1603, a large proportion of the maritime workforce was rendered idle. This acute crisis, together with the chronic shortage of work in the economy as a whole, meant that relatively few sailors could obtain employment ashore or afloat. Contemporaries readily recognized the piratical implications of such a situation, officials in numerous English port towns warning the central authorities of the threat to law, order, and property posed by the "great number of sailors, mariners and other masterless men that heretofore have been at sea in men-of-war."[47] And, of course, once the efficacy and rewards of predatory activity were demonstrated, the urge to prey upon trade gathered a momentum of its own and the wave of piracy was sustained by new recruits and by prizes taken in a widening operational theater.

A similar pattern can be detected a century or so later. The demand for seafarers in the long wars of 1689–1714, the first Anglo-French struggle to assume truly global proportions, was unprecedented. In France, the manning requirements of the great fleets of Louis XIV were immense, while in this era of Jean Bart, de Forbin, and *l'apogée de la course* a considerable number of seafarers were recruited by privateering armateurs.[48] Likewise, in England and the United Provinces the navy exerted substantial pressure on the market for seafarers, with almost 50,000 men serving in Queen Anne's fleets in the closing years of the war. At the same time, the irregular buccaneering forces which had harassed and plundered Spanish trade before the war were now given the authority to continue their business as privateers and, moreover, to add a significant anti-French or anti-English string to their bows. But on the cessation of hostilities, a by now familiar pattern can be observed. Navies demobilized—within a year, the British navy had cut its workforce to under 14,000—privateering came to an end, and a large body of seamen were left without work.[49] And large-scale seafaring unemployment, as contemporaries noted, especially in the Caribbean and North America, where buccaneers-turned-privateersmen were left idle, bred the piratical wave which ensued in the years following the Peace of Utrecht. With wage reductions and harsher terms of service—those companions of unemployment—also featuring strongly during this period, a flow of recruits to the black flag was forthcoming for the next decade or so.[50]

Labor surpluses also underpinned the *course indépendante* of the early nineteenth century. Again, the end of a long war with an important privateering dimension led to unemployment and, as a century earlier, the bulk of overcapacity was located in the Caribbean.[51] At the same time, the rapid expansion in the carrying, privateering, and shipping interests of the United States, which had generated so much maritime capital in the French Revolutionary and Napoleonic conflicts, was mirrored in the growth of the seafaring labor force. With the dismantling in 1815 of the hothouse in which this American enterprise had flourished, seafarers, as well as ships and funds, were relatively abundant in Baltimore, New York, Boston, and other northern ports. In such a context, the profitable potential of the uncertain political and commercial situation in the Caribbean attracted a flow of surplus maritime resources from New England and the Middle States to the West Indies and South America.[52] This flow of Baltimore schooners and American seafarers, together with the picaroons of former Spanish and French privateersmen, contributed significantly to the *course indépendante* and the wars of liberation.

While the short waves of piracy were largely a consequence of market deficiencies, such conditions did not persist. Pirates might have supplied communities with goods and provisions, and colonies with military services, for a number of years, but theirs was essentially a short-term business.[53] In all instances, it was only a matter of time before "regular" merchants and the state began to encroach on the pirates by providing competitive, legitimate services and by using the law to criminalize those who dealt with pirates.[54] While such measures reduced the demand for piratical services, attempts were made to cut the supply of recruits to this labor-intensive activity. Thus, the violence of the courts and the navy were deployed to eliminate pirates and to deter would-be volunteers, and pardons were offered to make gamekeepers out of poachers. But the main precipitant of maritime lawlessness—the supply of labor—was also its main constraint. In this, the business of piracy provides an unusual vantage point from which to consider the efficiency of the market for seafarers.

Piracy and the Efficiency of the Market for Seafarers

The various waves of piracy which swept the Atlantic in the early modern era were essentially a function of economic factors, chief among these being disequilibria between supply and demand in the labor market. While the long waves reflected chronic deficiencies in the underdeveloped economies of the Caribbean and North Africa, the short waves were causally related to the over-supply in the market for seafarers at the end of war in 1603, 1714, and 1815. This latter conclusion, in particular, tends to support the notion that the seafaring labor market in the age of sail exhibited many aspects of inefficiency.[55]

Yet this is not to suggest that the market was inherently defective. Significantly, piratical waves were comparatively brief, lasting from ten to twenty years. In each case, piracy reached its peak some years after the onset of peace.[56] While state violence generally hastened the end, the operation of the labor market was largely responsible for the demise of these waves of piracy. In postwar years, unemployment, wage reductions, and harsher conditions of service may have encouraged large numbers of seafarers to go "on the account," but it persuaded many more to leave the sea altogether and deterred others from seeking employment afloat. Over time, the labor surplus cleared. As the supply of seafarers largely conditioned the supply of pirates, this return to equilibrium curtailed the flow of potential freebooters. Accordingly, once pirate crews were depleted by death, retirement, and the courts, a shortage of replacement labor made the productive unit less effective and the business entered a downward spiral. That it took at least a decade to complete this piratical cycle suggests that the market was slow to readjust to "normal" conditions rather than perpetually inefficient.

Moreover, lawless surges were not always evident in the aftermath of maritime conflicts, as the relative calm following the great imperial struggles of 1739–48, 1756–63, and 1776–83 testify. Two interrelated factors explain this differential pattern. First, the symbiotic relationship between trade and shipping was seriously disrupted by wars, which spawned short waves of piracy. In each instance, the expansion of shipping was disproportionate to the level of trade in particular regions of the Atlantic. Accordingly, in England the three-fold expansion in the seafaring labor force of the late sixteenth and early seventeenth centuries was linked to the major and unprecedented growth of privateering, which emerged as "the characteristic form of maritime warfare" in the period.[57] Likewise, in the Caribbean the long wars of 1689–1714 boosted predatory activity and maritime resources but depressed aggregate levels of trade. And in the northern ports of the United States, the windfall profits of neutrality and privateering rather than any expansion in domestic imports and exports stimulated the extraordinary growth in shipping which marked the years 1793–1814.[58] With the end of each war, the "artificial" conditions which had stimulated the expansion of shipping—privateering or neutrality—swiftly evaporated and a surplus of shipping resources, especially labor, remained.

At such junctures, a second factor, the depressed level of foreign trade, ensured that an adequate transfer of resources from belligerent to commercial employment did not occur. Again, this was evident in each case. While sluggish growth characterized English overseas commerce in the early seventeenth century, and the British imperial system from the 1690s to the 1740s, it was also a feature of the U.S. economy in the decades after Waterloo.[59] The situation in the mid-eighteenth century was rather different. While privateering was a prominent feature of the midcentury wars, it was significant only during short phases of these conflicts and was conducted while trade proceeded, and in a number of cases flourished.[60] Moreover, in each of the postwar eras—1749–55, 1764–75, and 1784–93—trans-Atlantic commerce boomed, so that the demands placed on European shipping were sufficient to absorb enough resources, including labor, to obviate any major disequilibrium in the seafaring labor market. In other words, the divergence between shipping and trade in the wars of the mid-eighteenth century was never wide enough to foster large-scale unemployment and its child, piracy.

Insofar as piracy was a barometer of labor market efficiency, this implies that the market functioned relatively well in postwar years from the 1740s to the 1790s, but at other times was much slower to adjust to the dislocations of war.[61] It also offers a new perspective on the argument that the eradication of piracy in the eighteenth century contributed significantly to productivity gains in shipping.[62] On the contrary, it would seem that it was the relative efficiency of the commercial and shipping markets that largely explains why piracy was much less prevalent in the Atlantic after the 1720s.

NOTES

1. Anne Pérotin-Dumon, "The Pirate and the Emperor: Power and the Law on the Seas, 1450–1850," in this volume.

2. See John Anderson, "Piracy in the Eastern Seas 1750–1850: Some Economic Implications," in *Pirates and Privateers: New Perspectives on the War on Trade in the Eighteenth and Nineteenth Centuries*, ed. David J. Starkey, E. S. van Eyck van Heslinga, and J. A. de Moor (Exeter: University of Exeter Press, 1997), 87–105.

3. Charles P. Kindleberger, *Mariners and Markets* (New York: New York University Press, 1992), 83.

4. In this respect, piracy may be viewed as a form of social banditry. See E. J. Hobsbawm, *Bandits* (London: Weidenfeld and Nicolson, 1969), 71–79.

5. Anderson, "Eastern Seas."

6. See Peter Earle, *Corsairs of Malta and Barbary* (London: Sidgwick and Jackson, 1970).

7. David Delison Hebb, *Piracy and the English Government, 1616–1642* (Aldershot: Scolar Press, 1994), 3.

8. See Robert C. Ritchie, *Captain Kidd and the War against the Pirates* (Cambridge, Mass.: Harvard University Press, 1986).

9. Hebb, *Piracy,* 139–140.

10. Great Britain, Public Record Office (PRO), High Court of Admiralty Papers (HCA) 26/14 Letter of marque declaration of Edmund Godfrey, captain of the *Katherine,* 6 April 1710.

11. Earle, *Corsairs,* 36–46.

12. Some interesting case studies are provided by David Marley, *Pirates and Engineers: Dutch and Flemish Adventurers in New Spain (1607–1697)* (Windsor, Ontario: Netherlandic Press, 1992). For more general accounts, see A. H. Cooper-Pritchard, *The Buccaneers: A Brief History* (Paris: 1927).

13. Carl Bridenbaugh and Roberta Bridenbaugh, *No Peace beyond the Line: The English in the Caribbean, 1624–1690* (New York: Oxford University Press, 1972), Christopher Hill, "Radical Pirates?" in *The Collected Essays of Christopher Hill* (Brighton, Sussex: Harvester Press, 1985).

14. Alexander O. Exquemelin, *The Buccaneers of America* (Amsterdam, 1678; reprint, Annapolis: Naval Institute Press, 1993); Derek Howse and Norman J. W. Thrower, eds., *A Buccaneer's Atlas: Basil Ringrose's South Sea Waggoner* (Berkeley: University of California Press, 1992); David F. Marley, *Sack of Veracruz: The Great Pirate Raid of 1683* (Windsor, Ontario: Netherlandic Press, 1993).

15. J. S. Bromley, "Outlaws at Sea, 1660–1720: Liberty, Equality, and Fraternity among the Caribbean Freebooters," in this volume.

16. C. M. Senior, *A Nation of Pirates: English Piracy in Its Heyday* (Newton Abbot: David and Charles, 1976); Hebb, *Piracy,* 7–11.

17. See Philip Gosse, *The History of Piracy* (London: Longmans, Green, 1932), 176–212.

18. Ritchie, *Captain Kidd,* 1–26; Marcus Rediker, *Between the Devil and the Deep Blue Sea: Merchant Seamen, Pirates and the Anglo American Maritime World 1700–1750* (Cambridge: Cambridge University Press, 1987), 254–287.

19. Anne Pérotin-Dumon, "La contribution de *corsarios insurgentes* à l'indépendence américaine 1810–1830," in *Course et piraterie,* ed. Michel Mollat (Paris: Institut de Recherche et Histoire des Textes, Centre National de la Recherche Scientifique, 1975), 2:666–675; Basil Lubbock, *Cruisers, Corsairs and Slavers: An Account of the Suppression of the Picaroon, Pirate and Slaver by the Royal Navy during the 19th Century,* 1st ed. (Glasgow: Brown, Son and Ferguson, 1993), 59–72.

20. Clive M. Senior, "The Confederation of Deep-Sea Pirates: English Pirates in the Atlantic 1603–25," in *Course et piraterie,* ed. Mollat, 1:347–348.

21. Rediker, *Between the Devil,* 254–287; Carl E. Swanson, *Predators and Prizes: American Privateering and Imperial Warfare, 1739–1748* (Columbia, S.C.: University of South Carolina Press, 1991), 29–48.

22. Gerald S. Graham and R. A. Humphreys, eds., *The Navy and South America, 1807–1823: Correspondence of the Commanders-in-Chief on the South American Station* (London: Navy Records Society 1962), xxiii–xxxiv.

23. See Senior, *Nation,* 30–33: Senior, "Confederation," 332; Marcus Rediker,

"Hydrarchy and Libertalia: The Utopian Dimensions of Atlantic Piracy in the Early Eighteenth Century," in *Pirates and Privateers: New Perspectives on the War on Trade in the Eighteenth and Nineteenth Centuries*, ed. David J. Starkey, E. S. van Eyck van Heslinga, and J. A. de Moor (Exeter: University of Exeter Press, 1997), 29–46; Lubbock, *Cruisers*, 59–72.

24. For instance, see Senior, "Confederation," 331–333; Rediker, *Between the Devil*, 281–283; Lubbock, *Cruisers*, 59.

25. Hill, "Radical Pirates?"; Rediker, *Between the Devil*, 254–287.

26. These arguments are developed in Pérotin-Dumon, "The Pirate and the Emperor," in this volume.

27. The opening to the first published account of Sharp's buccaneering voyage of 1680, cited in Howse and Thrower, *Buccaneer's Atlas*.

28. Cooper-Pritchard, *Buccaneers*, 13–36.

29. See John C. Appleby, "A Nursery of Pirates: The English Pirate Community in Ireland in the Early 17th Century," *International Journal of Maritime History* 2, no. 1 (1990): 1–27; Senior, "Confederation."

30. Ritchie, *Captain Kidd*, 1–26.

31. This partly explains why Bartholomew Sharp and others were acquitted of piracy on their return to London. See Howse and Thrower, *Buccaneer's Atlas*, 27–28.

32. See Senior, "Confederation"; Hebb, *Piracy*; Rediker, *Between the Devil*, 254–287; Lubbock, *Cruisers*, 59–72.

33. Earle, *Corsairs*; Gosse, *History*, 157–158.

34. Ritchie, *Captain Kidd*, 52–54.

35. Earle, *Corsairs*, 15–16.

36. Jerome R. Garitee, *The Republic's Private Navy: The American Privateering Business as Practiced by Baltimore during the War of 1812* (Middletown, Conn.: Wesleyan University Press, 1977), 224–230; Howard I. Chapelle, *The History of American Sailing Ships* (New York: W. W. Norton, 1985), 238–239.

37. Senior, *Nation of Pirates*, 30; Ralph Davis, *The Rise of the English Shipping Industry in the Seventeenth and Eighteenth Centuries* (London: Macmillan, 1962), 110.

38. Earle, *Corsairs*, 53.

39. Rediker, *Between the Devil*, 265; Davis, *English Shipping Industry*, 111.

40. Similar prospects faced privateersmen. See David J. Starkey, *British Privateering Enterprise in the Eighteenth Century* (Exeter: University of Exeter Press, 1990).

41. Earle, *Corsairs*, 32–36.

42. Bridenbaugh and Bridenbaugh, *No Peace*, 175–176.

43. "Gentleman Starkey, once an usher in a public school, and still dainty in his ways of killing." J. M. Barrie, *Peter Pan* (London: Everyman's Library, 1992, originally published in 1911), 173.

44. Senior, "Confederation," passim.

45. David J. Starkey, "War and the Market for Seafarers in Britain, 1736–1742," in *Shipping and Trade 1750–1950: Essays in International Maritime Economic History*, ed. L. R. Fischer and H. W. Nordvik (Pontefract: Lofthouse, 1990), 25–42.

46. Senior, "Confederation," 331.

47. Senior, *Nation of Pirates*, 10.

48. Ernest H. Jenkins, *A History of the French Navy, from Its Beginnings to the Present Day* (London: Macdonald and Jane's, 1973); J. S. Bromley, "The French Privateering War," in *Corsairs and Navies, 1660–1760* (London: Hambledon Press, 1987), 231–242.

49. Christopher Lloyd, *The British Seaman 1200–1860: A Social Survey* (London: Collins, 1968), 286–287.

50. Rediker, *Between the Devil*, 254–287.

51. Lubbock, *Cruisers*, 59–61.

52. Garitee, *Private Navy*, 224–230.

53. This is symbolized in the inclusion of a timepiece in pirate flags of the early eighteenth century. See Rediker, *Between the Devil*, 278–281.

54. See Senior, "Confederation," passim.

55. Kindleberger, *Mariners and Markets*, 90.

56. The cyclical pattern of piracy is apparent in Senior, *Nation of Pirates*; and Rediker, *Between the Devil*.

57. Kenneth R. Andrews, *Elizabethan Privateering: English Privateering during the Spanish War, 1585–1603* (Cambridge: Cambridge University Press, 1964), 6.

58. Ralph Davis, "English Foreign Trade, 1700–1774," *Economic History Review* 15 (1962): 285–303; Garitee, *Private Navy*, 219–237.

59. Davis, "English Foreign Trade"; Garitee, *Private Navy*.

60. Starkey, *British Privateering*, in particular chapter 9, pp. 245–252.

61. Starkey, "War and the Market."

62. James F. Shepherd and Gary M. Walton, *Shipping, Maritime Trade and the Economic Development of Colonial North America* (Cambridge: Cambridge University Press, 1972).

Chapter 7

Corsairing as a Commercial System
The Edges of Legitimate Trade

Gonçal López Nadal

In essence, corsairing had two functions for the societies—be they cities or states—that practiced it: it was an instrument both of commerce and of naval activity.[1] As a result, this sort of maritime behavior became an internationally recognized instrument both of warfare and commerce and, over time, was increasingly stamped by a legitimizing process. Thus a phenomenon that began with the preparation and fitting out of the corsairing vessel and ended with the distribution of the prize or booty can best be described in institutional terms. There were four essential stages in this process.

First of all a captain had to apply for, and be granted a letter of marque (*patente*) that set out the conditions under which he was allowed to raid the shipping of other states; then he had to provide a bond or security, a (not always symbolic) sum of money, as a guarantee that the expedition would be carried out according to the regulations outlined in the letter of marque; third, just before the ship sailed, the captain, a public notary, and two qualified witnesses had to sign a document in which he agreed to obey the regulations governing corsairing; finally, when he returned, the port authorities had to adjudicate all the prizes, to determine whether or not they were "good" (that is, legal), before the proceeds could be distributed to the different participants in the enterprise.

Taken alongside the right of the government to tax the proceeds, these requirements clearly show the legalistic nature of corsairing, and it is that which really distinguishes it from its illegal counterpart, piracy. The basic difference between corsairing and piracy lay precisely in this juridical quality: that is, a distinction "*de droit.*" Michel Mollat de Jourdin has made the useful distinction between "une course réglementée" and "une piraterie sauvage,"[2] describing corsairing as a violent, but *institutionalized,* maritime activity—it was the institutional element that distinguished it from piracy. Otherwise the two phenomena were practically identical.[3]

Although all corsairing clearly had a military aspect, this chapter concentrates on corsairing as a commercial, or more strictly an economic, activity. It will begin by trying to pin down exactly what it is we are dealing with, a task that seems never-ending. It is certainly something I seem to have to do every time I write on this topic. In the past I used a number of adjectives, all rather similar in meaning, in an effort to bring out the distinctive nature of this commercial aspect of corsairing. I experimented with terms like "atypical" or "irregular" commerce but these provoked the comment (by Josep Fontana) that they were too similar to the dissembling and obfuscatory euphemisms ("obscure transactions," for example) used by bankers in cahoots with the ruling groups in the present-day Catalan government![4]

Later, I used the term "forced" to describe corsairing as a commercial system,[5] but this may have been misleading because it contains a double meaning. In fact, that double meaning was quite apposite since it referred to both the commercial system that the islanders developed in response to an economic crisis, and to the consequences of corsairing on the shipping of other Mediterranean countries, particularly that of France. Those countries that suffered from the attentions of Mallorcan corsairs found themselves obliged to develop a very specialized form of commercial shipping, relying on convoys, escorts, carriage in neutral ships, and so on. This duality in the end produced a convergence, since the "forced" commerce of the Mallorcans caused a general distortion of commerce in the western Mediterranean.

My use of the phrase "unconventional commercial system"[6] was perhaps a less happy choice. Intended as a halfway house between "atypical" and "alternative" commerce, the term "unconventional" carried with it an ambiguity and a nuance that made it resemble "irregular" commerce—and it too looked like a euphemism. Even so, such a usage also carried with it a second idea: that corsairing was an occasional method of commerce, one that could only be employed at certain times, which were of course those when the circumstances were favorable and, by implication, not propitious for peaceful commerce. This second point does rescue the idea of "unconventional" commerce, since the more one looks at the commercial aspects of corsairing, the harder it gets to make a clear distinction between the two.

Later still, I decided to describe corsairing as an "alternative strategy," that is, one that defines it as a commercial practice that substituted in part for what was usually considered the "regular" structure of commercial practices. In this sense corsairing was but one of several alternative systems, perhaps the most common, that were adopted when certain very specific circumstances made it profitable. Corsairing could then be explained as a simple commercial system that was adopted by societies like those in Mallorca, Sicily, Sardinia, and the North African states. So before we go further and deal with the nub of the question—the limits to legitimate commerce—it would be useful to identify the ways in which corsairing functioned as a form of alternative commerce, especially as it developed in the Mediterranean in the early modern period.

Between the sixteenth and eighteenth centuries, indeed until well into the nineteenth, there were clear differences in the systems through which maritime societies organized their commercial relations. Almost always, the determining factor was economic, but corsairing was influenced by the prevailing political instability and, to a lesser extent, by long-standing and deeply held ideological (or "religious") prejudices. It is these factors that explain the growth and development of alternative commercial methods that maritime merchants used to make money. The Mediterranean, sunk in an economic slump, was the quintessential setting for these "other forms of commerce."

On the one hand there was what is usually considered regular commerce: coastal trade, point-to-point trade, and company trade. On the other, there were the alternative systems: trade in neutral vessels, smuggling, and corsairing. Between the sixteenth and eighteenth centuries, these latter systems became common practice. Consequently, it is hard to decide what importance should be attached to the purely commercial activities such as the operations of fleets or commercial interchanges involving distribution and exchange. It is difficult to describe these methods of economic activity in terms that are conceptually distinct from commerce in general. In any event, they were certainly not the product of chance: these alternative methods of commerce were not adopted at the whim of office-bound financiers; quite the contrary, they were the most convenient, the simplest, and the cheapest way of doing what their practitioners had always done: trade.

There is no space to deal with the first two alternatives, trade in neutral vessels and smuggling. Our purpose here is to deal with the third, corsairing. Josep Fontana put his finger on the nub of the problem (although his concern at the time was the rather different one of the interpretive value of different historical sources) when he wrote:

> Our history books say, for example, that France took over Algiers to defend itself against the piracy of petty Muslim kings. But they do not tell us that these North African kingdoms were, in their turn, victims of European piracy that prevented them from developing normal trade and forced them into corsairing.[7]

To be sure, it is encouraging to see this deliberate twisting of the popular concepts of piracy and corsairing (contrasting the first as seen from a Christian viewpoint with the second in terms of its consequences for the Islamic world), and refreshing to see the attempt to go beyond the usual tired clichés like "nest of pirates" and "corsair republics" when talking about the North African states. Yet underlying this paragraph are two other crucial considerations: the idea of "normal" commerce and of being "forced" into corsairing. Both these terms should be understood in the terms we used before when we described corsairing as a forced trade. However, given Fontana's reservations about the use of the term "atypical" commerce to describe corsairing, we still have to face a number of awkward questions: Is there such a thing as "normal" commerce? What should we understand that to be? What sorts of transactions does it consist of? How can we study it? What sort of documentary sources should we use? Or, to turn these questions on their head: What does "abnormal" commerce mean? Who does it? How, when, and why? Before trying to answer those questions, we might also ask ourselves not about "abnormal commerce" but about the resort to "corsairing." These questions would give rise to similar if not identical replies. In practice, once we get to grips with actual events, things are confused. This is particularly true when what is "normal" is what people are forced to "have recourse to"; in short, when corsairing has become commerce pure and simple.

Let us continue to examine corsairing in its commercial manifestation: we can talk of it as a commerce of war, or perhaps a commerce of crisis. I do not think it would stretch the point too far if we were to suggest a relationship between the development of corsairing and the various stages of an economic recession, something that may apply to earlier periods than the one we are considering here. Specialists in the late medieval period are apparently undecided on the relationship between corsairing and economics, and there is clearly much work still to be done on the subject.[8] But if we restrict ourselves to the period between the Battle of Lepanto (1571) and the Treaty of Utrecht (1713), we clearly can talk about a link—almost a cause and effect relationship—between corsairing and economic recession. Indeed, we can go further and describe corsairing as a phenomenon that is peculiar to a crisis economy. In contrast to the classic view, formulated by Braudel, that it was a "parasitic commerce,"[9] Michel Fontenay has repeatedly put forward the idea that corsairing was a means of last resort, placing the relationship in the context of the decline of the Mediterranean relative to the rise of the Atlantic.[10] My own analysis of the corsairs of Mallorca in the second half of the seventeenth century has led me to agree with Fontenay's thesis. Their activities can be seen from two points of view: how they fit into corsairing in the Mediterranean, but also how they can be compared with some of the events in the northern seas.

Between the end of the sixteenth and the first quarter of the eighteenth centuries, the functional nature of Mediterranean corsairing is clear enough. Big merchants armed corsair ships because the business could reap them large profits.[11] But they only did so when the political and economic circumstances combined to make it necessary. For the majority of our period, those circumstances were indeed favorable: war and commerce lay at the very heart of corsairing: otherwise there would have been no commercial point in corsairing at all. There was, of course, a third motivation, the ideological impulse, reflected in the survival of the holy war (crusade or jihad).[12] But this was not enough by itself to explain the long-term infrastructure that corsairing required, the arming of powerful vessels, and the organization of year-long expeditions. Indeed, in the case of European corsairing, it never has been enough. By the eighteenth century "Spanish" corsairing, not to speak of its Mallorcan manifestation, was quite different from the sort of corsairing that reached its peak in the second half of the century before.[13] In the seventeenth century, the inhabitants of the islands, like those of several mainland ports in the western Mediterranean, took up the practice of corsairing as a simple (but vital) means of development and even of economic growth. Because they carried on doing it, virtually without interruption, corsairing was transformed into a normal part of economic life.

That this was so is clearly shown by the role of corsairing in supplying grain when it was in short supply.[14] Mallorcans, Sardinians, Sicilians, Maltese, Tuscans, Neapolitans, and others hunted the ships carrying grain from southern France, from the coast of North Africa, or from the Ottoman Levant. Once they started obtaining wheat in this manner, it increased the temptation for other institutions, the public authorities, to act in the same way. Thus port officials, claiming ancient medieval precedent, would impound merchant ships carrying grain that were anchored in their waters.[15] So would the officers of the galleys of the French and Spanish kings when they intercepted shipping carrying these products in time of war. The commanders of naval squadrons of the Spanish king would seize French vessels that, despite having a safe conduct signed by his viceroys, were actually carrying supplies to Spanish ports.

Although the lack of grain may have been less of a compulsion in the North African provinces, it was there that this type of commerce was most clearly to be seen, to the extent that it had become quite a normal operation.[16] Corsairing was quite clearly a response to the progressive economic marginalization of the North African states from the international community, and it was this that made the conjunction of the military and commercial functions so clear.[17] Of course there are differences in the way that corsairing was done on the two sides of the Mediterranean but, particularly if it is examined as a method of trade, these are not as great as might at first be supposed.

There is a second, closely connected, aspect of corsairing: in Europe it appeared mainly in societies that found themselves thwarted by an unchallengeable commercial competitor. Not surprisingly, the ports that were most prone to turn to force were the strictly second-rate trading centers, while the major trading centers suffered the most from raiding. Valencia, Barcelona, Genoa, and Venice did very little corsairing. Venice is an excellent example of this: its decline from the end of the sixteenth century onward owes a great deal to the ravages of corsairs.[18] The maritime communities on the eastern side of the Iberian peninsula suffered frequent threats from North African corsairs: Valencia after the expulsion of the Moriscos and particularly the Catalans throughout the eighteenth century.[19] Marseilles and Genoa suffered the same harmful effects from corsairs who circulated throughout the Mediterranean, even in waters very close to their coasts.[20] Their captors were men from cities and ports that were economically less advanced who had put to sea to find not only a means of subsistence but also of economic development.

Something similar seems to have happened in the Atlantic world. The seamen of Flushing (Vlissingen) were corsairs, while those of Amsterdam hardly bothered with it; presumably they were more occupied with the opportunities provided by the Dutch East and West India Companies. With some slight variations, that is what happened in the English Channel too, where the ports of St. Malo and Dunkirk were much more feared for their corsairs than Nantes or Rennes. One could see the same pattern, presumably, in the Mediterranean. A comparative study is needed, contrasting Northern Europe with the Mediterranean.[21]

Although there is no such study yet, it is still possible and useful to make a broad general comparison between the main corsairing bases of the Atlantic and the Mediterranean. This would draw out the convergence between raiding and economic crisis. The ports we are talking of derived considerable profit from the corsairing activities of their seamen and captains, and such men were honored and defended by their fellow citizens. Saint-Malo was widely known as "the corsairing city," and the city of Ibiza put up a prominent monument to its corsairs. It was the "people" of the City of Mallorca who refused to back down before the threat of the French fleet to invade their island and rescue the ships that local corsairs had taken after the peace of Nijmwegen.[22] These are striking social responses that reflect the extreme importance of corsairing in the economic life of these towns.

Even if we confine ourselves to this one example, the similarities between Christian and Muslim corsairing crop up in all sorts of places. In the North African states, the social image of the "great corsairs" stands out clearly when they were recognized as "founders" of those states. It is hardly surprising that the Barbarossa brothers have been made into heroes, and ones far more popular than their equivalents in St. Malo, Jean Bart, and Duguay-Trouin, or Mallorcan corsairs like Jaume Canals, or Pere Flexes, or the Ibizan Riquer family (perhaps dynasty would be a better word for the Riquers). The comparison, of course, is not simply one of folkloric representations of the past, but one that must be understood in economic terms. On both sides of the Mediterranean, in North Africa and in Mallorca, the commercial aspect of corsairing is clear even when corsairing was not taking place because the circumstances of the time were unpropitious.

It is precisely at these moments that the place of corsairing in the general mercantile structures stands out: corsairing and commerce were associated, even indistinguishable, because those responsible were one and the same. The men who equipped a ship for corsairing also did so in order to sell their wares, raiding and trading at the same time: Mallorcan merchants sent out corsairing expeditions that would carry oil to Genoa and return with the prizes they had captured in the Ligurian Sea.

The confusion between privateers and merchants reached its climax when the same financiers started to invest both in corsairing and in marine insurance. In these two branches of maritime commerce the men who created the risk interacted with those who profited from it.[23] Much the same thing seems to have happened in Mallorca, where the same people were involved in both corsairing and insurance: some of them from the nobility, others from the class of big merchants, along with a few artisans and, above all, a large number of Chuetas, descendants of converts from Judaism whose own loyalty to Catholicism was often suspect. They needed to set up guarantees, a surety, against the activities that they themselves were promoting.[24] It is a neat prefiguring of *The Kid*: Charlie Chaplin as glazier while his companion throws stones.

Between the seventeenth and the beginning of the twentieth centuries there was, in the port of Palma de Mallorca, a synergetic alternation—one might even say it was structural—between ordinary commerce and corsairing commerce.[25] An analysis of the commercial registers shows the frequent arrival and departure of corsairing vessels. Of course, circumstance ruled: such activity coincided with the long years of war between the Spanish and French monarchies (1652–59, 1674–97). Sometimes the registers indicate (although at others they do not) whether a particular voyage was made for purposes of corsairing. The very fact that such a mention is made is an eloquent testimony to whether corsairing really was (or was not) a distinctive type of commerce. Moreover, although it would be a mistake to push the point too far, one can clearly discern the role of corsairing in bringing goods of very high value into port: almost certainly these were from French merchant ships coming from the Levant. This explains the duties imposed on such merchants when their ships were registered as leaving the port; they were high, but equitable.[26]

These and many other examples draw one to the conclusion that "regularity" or "normality" in commercial systems knew no other limits than merely institutional, or purely theoretical, ones. Even so, when it suited them, as documentary evidence makes only too plain, the corsairs were quick to fling the rules aside. A case in point was when corsair captains took in their prizes, and sold them, in other ports of call, Livorno in particular. They "justified" their behavior by the risk of losing the prize altogether if they had to take it all the way home, although like any trader what they really were up to was tax avoidance. Any strategy, however and wherever it was performed, was valid, provided it worked and was profitable. What we are talking about is not a choice between merchant and corsairs, but men who were sometimes one, sometimes the other, sometimes both simultaneously.

NOTES

1. I have made this point at greater length in Gonçal López Nadal, *El corsarisme mallorqui a la Mediterránea occidental 1652–1698: Un comerç forçat* (Barcelona: Conselleria d'Educació i Cultura de les Illes Balears, 1986), and "El corsarisme mallorqui a l'edat moderna," *Cuaderns Cultura Fi de Segle*, number entitled "Quinze anys de premis d'invetigació *Ciutat de Palma* (1970–1984)" (1986): 21–39. On the question of the nature of piracy, see also Paul Adam, "Esquisse d'une typologie de la course," in *Course et piraterie: Études presentées à la Commission Internationale d'Histoire Maritime à l'occasion de son XVè colloque international pendant le XIVè Congrès International des Sciences Historiques (San Francisco, août 1975)*, ed. Michel Mollat (Paris: Institut de Recherche et d'Histoire des Textes, Centre National de la Recherche Scientifique, 1975), 915–955; this article was revised and republished as "Histoire raisonné de la piraterie," in *Stratégies maritimes et économie*, ed. Paul Adam (Perthes-en-Gâtinais: Ed. du Grand Moulin, 1980), 69–119.

2. Michel Mollat was a pioneer in attempts to define piracy and corsairing. His "Essai d'orientation pour l'étude de la guerre de course et la piraterie (XII–XV siècles)," *Anuario de Estudios Medievales* 10 (1980): 743–749, was originally given as a paper presented at the I Congreso Internacional de Historia Mediterránea, at Palma de Mallorca in 1953; see also his "De la piraterie sauvage à la course réglementée (XIVè–XVè siècles)," in *Course et piraterie: Études presentées à la Commission Internationale d'Histoire Maritime à l'occasion de son XVè colloque international pendant le XIVè Congrès International des Sciences Historiques* (San Francisco, August 1975), ed. Michel Mollat (Paris: Institut de Recherche et d'Histoire des Textes, Centre National de la Recherche Scientifique, 1975), 162–184.

3. Equally suggestive is the English expression "commerce raiding" used to define privateering. See Patrick Crowhurst, "'Guerre de course' et 'Privateering': Vers une étude comparative," in *Guerre et paix, 1600–1815* (Vincennes: N.p., 1987), 311–322.

4. The comment was made by Josep Fontana at the oral examination of my doctoral thesis, given at the Universitat Autònoma de Barcelona in September 1984. His remarks and those of Jaume Torras and Alberto Tenenti provided me with useful guidance when the thesis was prepared for publication.

5. This was a concept that drew on the ideas of Miguel Barceló, who used "forced commerce" to describe corsairing in Mallorca.

6. Gonçal López Nadal, "Contribution à l'étude du revenue dans un système com-

mercial maritime non conventionnel: La course européene en Méditerranée pendant le XVII et le XVIII siècles," *Studia Historia Oeconomica* (1993): 119–129.

7. Josep Fontana, *La historía* (Barcelona: Salvat, 1972).

8. See, for example, the articles in the first section of Gonçal López Nadal, ed., *El comerç alternatiu: Corsarisme i contraban (ss. xv–xviii)* (Palma de Mallorca: Conselleria de Cultura, Educació i Esports, Govern Balear, 1990), 29–116.

9. Fernand Braudel, *The Mediterranean and the Mediterranean World in the Age of Philip II*, trans. Siân Reynolds, 2 vols. (London: Collins, 1972–73), 2: 866–867 and especially 887.

10. Michel Fontenay, "Los fenómenos corsarios el la "periferazión" del Mediterráneo en el siglo XVII," *Areas (Murcia)* (1984): 116–121.

11. G. López Nadal, "La course et les societés méditerranéennes: Une voie alternative," paper presented at the conference "Perception de la Méditerranée d'après les cartes et les récits des voyageurs," Tunis, 1989; López Nadal, "Contribution à l'étude."

12. Gonçal López Nadal, "Entre la Cruz y la Media Luna," in *Felipe II y el Mediterráneo*, ed. Ernest Belenguer (Madrid: Sociedad Estatal para la Conmemoración de los Centenarios de Felipe II y Carlos V, 1999), 409–425.

13. Gonçal López Nadal, "Mediterranean Privateering between the Treaties of Utrecht and Paris, 1715–1856: First Reflections," in *Pirates and Privateers: New Perspectives on the War on Trade in the Eighteenth and Nineteenth Centuries*, ed. David J. Starkey, E. S. van Eyck van Heslinga, and J. A. de Moor (Exeter: University of Exeter Press, 1997), 106–125.

14. Gonçal López Nadal, "Privateering and Wheat Supply in the West Mediterranean in Modern Times." Paper presented at the 17 Congreso International de Ciencias Históricas Sección Cronológica: Edad Moderna I, "Los cereales en la historia moderna," Madrid, 1990. On the specific case of Mallorca, see Gonçal López Nadal, "Corsarismo y abastecimiento de grano en Mallorca durante la segunda mitad del siglo xvii," *Estudis d'Història Econòmica* 2 (1990): 27–49.

15. In these cases they would be activating what were called "rights of lordship" (*derechos de señoría*). See J. Pons, "El risc a la mar: Les asseguances marítimes a Mallorca durant la segona mitad del segle XVII" (Tesis de licenciatura, Universitat de les Iles Balears, 1990). There are also references to this practice in U. Casanova, "El déficit alimentico del Reino de Mallorca a lo largo del siglo XVII y sus problemas de abastecimiento," *Mayurqa* (1985–87): 217–232; J. Juan, "Crisis de subsistencies i aprovisionament blader de Mallorca durant el segle XVIII," *Randa* 26 (1990); López Nadal, "El corsarisme mallorqui"; and López Nadal, "Corsarismo y abastecimiento."

16. Taoufik Bachrouch, *Formation sociale barbaresque et pouvoir à Tunis au xviiè siècle* (Tunis: Publications de l'Université de Tunis, 1977); Ciro Manca, *Il modello di sviluppo economico delle città marittime barbaresche dopo Lepanto* (Napoli: Giannini Editore, 1982); Boubaker Sadok, *La régence de Tunis au XVIIe siècle: Ses relations commerciales avec les ports de l'Europe méditerranéenne, Marseille et Livourne* (Zaghouan: Ceroma, 1987).

17. A. Djeghloul, "La formation sociale algérienne à la veille de la colonization," *La Pensée* 185 (1976): 61–81; J. Weiner, "New Approaches to the Study of the

Barbary Corsairs," *Revue d'Histoire Maghrébine* 13–14 (1979): 204–208. Earlier British historians put forward similar explanations: G. N. Clark, "The Barbary Corsairs in the Seventeenth Century," *Cambridge Historical Journal* 8 (1944): 22–25; Sir Godfrey Fisher, *Barbary Legend: War, Trade, and Piracy in North Africa, 1415–1830* (Westport, Conn.: Greenwood Press, 1974); Peter Earle, *Corsairs of Malta and Barbary* (London: Sidgwick and Jackson, 1970). See also J. De Courcy Ireland, "The Corsairs of North Africa," *Mariner's Mirror* 66 (1980): 271–283.

18. Alberto Tenenti, *Piracy and the Decline of Venice 1580–1615*, trans. Janet and Brian Pullan (Berkeley: University of California Press, 1967).

19. Plenty of books have been written about the North African depredations on the Valencian coast, although few of them have much to offer in terms of new information. The most useful are: Juan Reglá, *Bandolers pirates i Hugonots a la Catalunya del segle XVI* (Barcelona: Editorial Selecta, 1969); Vicente Graullera Sanz, *La esclavitud en Valencia en los siglos XVI y XVII* (Valencia: Instituto Valenciano de Estudios Históricos, 1978); and Sebastià Garcia Martínez, *Bandolers, corsaris i moriscos* (Valencia: Eliseu Climent, 1980). Fortunately the coverage of Cataluña is far better, thanks to the works of Eloy Martín Corrales. See Eloy Martín Corrales, "Dos obstáculos en las relaciones comerciales entre Cataluña y los países musulmanes en el siglo xviii: El corso y la peste," in *Primer Congrés d'Història Moderna de Catalunya*, 2 vols. (Barcelona: Universitat de Barcelona, 1984), 1: 611–617; Eloy Martín Corrales, "Impulso de la actividad maritima catalana y corsarismo norteafricano (1680–1714)," in *XIII Congrés d'Història de la Corona d'Aragó* (Palma de Mallorca: Institut d'Estudis Baleàrics, 1990), 185–194; Eloy Martín Corrales, "El corsarismo norteafricano y las embarcaciones catalanas de la Carrera de Indias," *Manuscrits* 10 (1992): 375–393; Eloy Martín Corrales, "La huella del corso norteafricano en la mentalidad colectiva catalana del siglo xviii," in *El Comerç Alternatiu: Corsarisme i contraban (ss.xv–xviii)*, ed. Gonçal López Nadal (Palma de Mallorca: Conselleria de Cultura, Educació i Esports, Govern Balear, 1990), 217–230; Eloy Martín Corrales, "El comercio de Cataluña con el Mediterráneo musulmán, 1680–1830" (Tesis doctoral, Universidad de Barcelona, 1993). See also M. Barrio Gozalo, "El corso norteafricano y su incidencia en el principado de Cataluña durante el siglo xviii," *Annals de l'Institut d'Estudis Gironis* 18 (1984): 313–327.

20. For Genoa, see C. Constantini, "Aspetti della politica navale genovesca nel seicento," in *Guerra e commercio nell'evoluzione della marina genovesa tra XV e XVIII secolo* (Genoa-Milan: Idos, 1973), 207–235, and G. C. Calcagno, "La navigazione convogliata a Genova nella seconda metà del seicento," in ibid., 265–293, and other articles in the same collection. For Marseille, see L. Bergasse and G. Rambert, *Histoire du commerce de Marseille*, vol. 4, *de 1599 à 1789* (Paris: Plon, 1954); and Robert Paris, *Histoire du commerce de Marseille*, vol. 6, *Le Levant de 1660 à 1789* (Paris: Plon, 1957); Gonçal López Nadal, "Corsarisme mallorqui a les costes meridionales franceses," in *Mallorca i el sud francés: IV jornades de estudis històrics locals* (Palma: Institut d'Estudis Baleàrics, 1986), 21–39. López Nadal, "El corsarisme mallorqui" covers both places.

21. Such a study would use the work of the late John Bromley, of Jean Meyer, and

André Lespagnole, for northern Europe. See, for example, the chapter by John Bromley in this collection, and others among his collected articles: J. S. Bromley, *Corsairs and Navies, 1660–1760* (London: Hambledon Press, 1987); also Jean Meyer, "La course: Romantisme: Exutoire social, réalité économique?" *Annales de Bretagne* 78 (1971): 308–344; André Lespagnole, *Messiers de Saint-Malo: Une élite négotiante au temps de Louis XIV* (Saint-Malo: Editions de l'Ancre de Marine, 1991); and André Lespagnole, "La course comme mode d'entreé dans les trafics internationaux," in *El comerç alternatiu: Corsarisme i contraban (ss.xv–xviii)*, ed. Gonçal López Nadal (Palma de Mallorca: Conselleria de Cultura, Educació i Esports, Govern Balear, 1990), 175–185. For the Mediterranean it would draw on Michel Fontenay's studies on Malta in particular: Michel Fontenay, "Corsaire de la foi ou rentiers du sol? Les Chevaliers de Malte dans le corso méditerrenéen au xvii siècle," *Revue d'Histoire Moderne et Contemporaine* 25 (1988): 361–384; "La place de la course dans l'économie portuaire: L'exemple de Malte et des ports barbaresques," in *I porti come impresa economica: Atti della "Diciannovesima Settimana di studi,"* 2–6 May 1987 (Florence: Le Monnier, 1988), 843–879 (reprinted in *Annales ESC* [1988]: 1321–1347); "Les missions des galères de Malte, 1530–1798," in *Guerre et commerce en Méditerranée: IX–XXe siècles*, ed. Michel Vergé-Franceschi (Paris: Editions Veyrier, 1991), 103–122; "Le développement urbain du port de Malte du XVI au XVIII siècles," *Revue du monde Musulman et de la Méditerranée* 71 (1994): 101–108. For an overview of the Mediterranean as a whole, see Michel Fontenay and Alberto Tenenti, "Course et piraterie meditéranéennes de la fin du moyen âge au début du XIXè siècle," in *Course et piraterie: Études presentées à la Commission Internationale d'Histoire Maritime à l'occasion de son XVè colloque international pendant le XIVè Congrès International des Sciences Historiques* (San Francisco, August 1975), ed. Michel Mollat (Paris: Institut de Recherche et d'Histoire des Textes, Centre National de la Recherche Scientifique, 1975), 78–136.

22. Gonçal López Nadal, "The Peace Treaty of Nijmegen and the Decline of Majorcan Privateering, 1676–1684" (Ph.D. dissertation, Leeds University, 1995).

23. Alberto Tenenti, *Naufrages, corsaires et assurances maritimes à Venise, 1592–1609* (Paris: S.E.V.P.E.N., 1959); Alberto Tenenti, "Risque et sécurité: Course et assurances entre le Levant et Ponent du bas moyen âge à l'époque moderne," in *Économies méditerranéennes: Équilibres et intercommunications, XIIIè–XIXè siècles: Actes du IIè Colloque International d'Histoire, Athènes*, 18–25 September 1983 (Athens: Centre de Recherches Néohelléniques de la Fondation Nationale de la Recherche Scientifique, 1985–86), 285–400; Alberto Tenenti and Branislava Tenenti, *Il prezzo del rischio: L'assicurazione mediterranea vista da Ragusa, 1563–1591* (Rome: Jouvence, 1985).

24. See the various works of Jerònia Pons, "Asseguorances i canvis maritims a Mallorca: Les companyies (1660–1680)," *Estudis d'Historia Econòmica*, no. 2 (1988): 43–67; "Les companyies en el sistema asseguratiu mallorquí (1660–1680)," *Mayurqa* 22, no. 2 (1988): 885–893; "El pago del seguro marítimo y los conflictos ante el Tribunal Consular," *Pedralbes* 12 (1992): 71–94; and *Companyies i mercat assegurador a Mallorca (1650–1715)* (Palma de Mallorca: El Tall, 1996); Gonçal López Nadal,

"Actividades financieras de los Chuetas en al segunda mitad del siglo XVII: Armamentos en corso y seguros marítimos," in *A Face Not Turned to the Wall: Essays on Hispanic Themes for Gareth Alban Davies*, ed. C. A. Longhurst (Leeds: Department of Spanish and Portuguese, University of Leeds, 1987), 110–136.

25. Andreu Bibiloni, Miquel Deià, Carles Manera, and Jerònia Pons, "Comerç i dependència: Els intercanvis del port de Palma 1600–1900," unpublished paper; see also Andreu Bibiloni Amengual, *El comerç exterior de Mallorca: Homes, mercats i productes d'intercanvi (1650–1720)* (Mallorca: El Tall, 1995).

26. Gonçal López Nadal, "Comentaris a uns aranzels comercials de mitjan segle XVII," *Estudis d'Història Econòmica*, no. 1 (1987): 21–31.

Part II

Pirates in Action

Chapter 8

The Seaman as Pirate
Plunder and Social Banditry at Sea

Marcus Rediker

Writing to the Board of Trade in 1724, Governor Alexander Spotswood of Virginia lamented his lack of "some safe opportunity to get home" to London. He insisted that he would travel only in a well-armed man-of-war.

> Your Lordships will easily conceive my Meaning when you reflect on the Vigorous part I've acted to suppress Pirates: and if those barbarous Wretches can be moved to cut off the Nose & Ears of a Master for but correcting his own Sailors, what inhuman treatment must I expect, should I fall within their power, who have been markt as the principle object of their vengeance, for cutting off their arch Pirate Thatch [Teach, also known as Blackbeard], with all his grand Designs, & making so many of their Fraternity to swing in the open air of Virginia.[1]

Spotswood knew these pirates well. He had authorized the expedition that returned to Virginia boasting Blackbeard's head as a trophy. He had done his share to see that many pirates swung on Virginia gallows. He knew that pirates had a fondness for revenge, that they often punished ship captains for "correcting" their crews, and that a kind of "fraternity" prevailed among them. He had good reason to fear them.

Anglo-American pirates created an imperial crisis with their relentless and successful attacks upon merchants' property and international commerce between 1716 and 1726. Accordingly, these freebooters occupy a grand position in the long history of robbery at sea. Their numbers, near five thousand, were extraordinary, and their plunderings were exceptional in both volume and value.[2] This chapter explores the social and cultural dimensions of piracy, focusing on pirates' experience, the organization of their ships, and their social relations and consciousness. It concludes with observations on the social and economic context of the crime and its culture. Piracy represented "crime" on a massive scale. It was a way of life voluntarily chosen, for the most part, by large numbers of men who directly challenged the ways of the society from which they excepted themselves. The main intent of this chapter is to see how piracy looked from the inside and to examine the kinds of social order that pirates forged beyond the reach of traditional authority. Beneath the Jolly Roger, "the banner of King Death," a new social world took shape once pirates had, as one of them put it, "the choice in themselves."[3] It was a world profoundly shaped and textured by the experiences of work, wages, culture, and authority accumulated in the normal, rugged course of maritime life and labor in the early eighteenth century.

Contemporary estimates of the pirate population during the period under consideration placed the number between 1,000 and 2,000 at any one time. This range seems generally accurate. From records that describe the activities of pirate ships and from reports or projections of crew sizes, it appears that 1,800 to 2,400 Anglo-American pirates prowled the seas between 1716 and 1718, 1,500 to 2,000 between 1719 and 1722, and 1,000 to 1,500, declining to fewer than 200, between 1723 and 1726. In the only estimate we have from the other side of the law, a band of pirates in 1716 claimed that "30 Company of them," or roughly 2,400 men, plied the oceans of the globe. In all, some 4,500 to 5,500 men went, as they called it, "upon the account." The pirates' chief military enemy, the Royal Navy, employed an average of only 13,000 men in any given year between 1716 and 1726.[4]

These sea robbers followed lucrative trade and, like their predecessors, sought bases for their depredations in the Caribbean Sea and the Indian Ocean. The Bahama Islands, undefended and ungoverned by the Crown, began in 1716 to attract pirates by the hundreds. By 1718 a torrent of complaints had moved George I to commission Woodes Rogers to lead an expedition to bring the islands under control. Rogers's efforts largely succeeded, and pirates scattered to the unpeopled inlets of the Carolinas and to Africa. They had frequented African shores as early as 1691; by 1718, Madagascar served as both an entrepôt for booty and a spot for temporary settlement. At the mouth of the Sierra Leone River on Africa's western coast, pirates stopped off for "whoring and drinking" and to unload goods. Theaters of operation among pirates shifted, however, according to the policing designs of the Royal Navy. Pirates favored the Caribbean's small, unsettled cays and shallow waters, which proved hard to negotiate for men-of-war that offered chase. But generally, as one pirate noted, these rovers were "dispers't into several parts of the World." Sea robbers sought and usually found bases near major trade routes, as distant as possible from the powers of the state.[5]

Almost all pirates had labored as merchant seamen, Royal Navy sailors, or privateersmen.[6] The vast majority came from captured merchantmen as volunteers, for reasons suggested by Dr. Samuel Johnson's observation that "no man will be a sailor who has contrivance enough to get himself into a jail; for being in a ship is being in jail with the chance of being drowned. . . . A man in jail has more room, better food, and commonly better company."[7] Dr. Johnson's class condescension aside, he had a point. Incarceration on a ship did not differ essentially from incarceration in a jail. As previous chapters have suggested, merchant seamen had an extremely difficult lot in the early eighteenth century. They got a hard, close look at death. Disease and accidents were commonplace in their occupation, natural disasters threatened incessantly, rations were often meager, and discipline was brutal, even murderous on occasion. Peacetime wages were low, fraud and irregularities in the distribution of pay general. A prime purpose of eighteenth-century maritime laws was "to assure a ready supply of cheap, docile labor."[8] Merchant seamen also had to contend with impressment by the Royal Navy.

Some pirates had served in the navy, where conditions aboard ship were no less harsh. Food supplies often ran short, wages were low, mortality was high, discipline severe, and desertion consequently chronic. As one officer reported, the navy had trouble fighting pirates because the king's ships were "so much disabled by sickness, death, and desertion of their seamen."[9] In 1722 the Crown sent the *Weymouth* and the *Swallow* in search of a pirate convoy. Royal surgeon John Atkins, noting that merchant seamen were frequently pressed, underlined precisely what these sailors had to fear when he recorded that the *"Weymouth, who* brought out of *England* a Compliment [*sic*] Of 240 Men," had "at the end of the Voyage 280 dead upon her Books." The same point was made by the captain of a man-of-war sent to Jamaica to guard against pirates in 1720–21. He faithfully recorded the names of the thirty-five seamen who died during the year of duty.[10] Epidemics, consumption, and scurvy raged on royal ships, and the men were "caught in a machine from which there was no escape, bar desertion, incapacitation, or death."[11] Or piracy.

Pirates who had served on privateering vessels knew well that such employment was far less onerous than on merchant or naval ships. Food was usually more plentiful, the pay considerably higher, and the work shifts generally shorter.[12] Even so, owing to rigid discipline and other grievances, mutinies were not uncommon. On Woodes Rogers's spectacularly successful privateering expedition of 1708–11, Peter Clark was thrown into irons for wishing himself "aboard a Pirate" and saying that "he should be glad that an Enemy, who could over-power us, was a-long-side of us."[13]

Most men became pirates when their merchant vessels were taken. Colonel Benjamin Bennet wrote to the Council of Trade and Plantations in 1718, setting forth his worries about freebooters in the West Indies: "I fear they will soon multiply for so many are willing to joyn with them when taken." The seizure of a merchant ship was followed by a moment of great confrontational drama. The pirate captain or quartermaster asked the seamen of the captured vessel who among them would serve under the death's head and black colors, and frequently several stepped forward. Many fewer pirates originated as mutineers who had boldly and collectively seized control of a merchant vessel. But regardless of their methods, pirates necessarily came from seafaring employments, whether the merchant service, the navy, or privateering. Piracy emphatically was not an option open to landlubbers, since sea robbers "entertain'd so contemptible a Notion of Landmen."[14] Men who became pirates were grimly familiar with the rigors of life at sea and with a single-sex community of work.

Ages are known for 117 pirates active between 1716 and 1726. The range was 17 to 50 years, the mean 27.4, and the median 27; the 20–24 and 25–29 age categories had the highest concentrations, with thirty-nine and thirty-seven men, respectively. Three in five were 25 or older. The age distribution was almost identical to that of the merchant service as a whole, suggesting that piracy held roughly equal attraction for sailors of all ages.[15] Though evidence is sketchy, most pirates seem not to have been bound to land and home by familial ties or obligations. Wives and children were rarely mentioned in the records of trials of pirates, and pirate vessels, to forestall desertion, often would "take no Married Man."[16] Almost without exception, pirates, like the larger body of seafaring men, came from the lowest social classes. They were, as a royal official condescendingly observed, "desperate Rogues" who could have little hope in life ashore.[17] These traits served as bases of unity when men of the sea decided, in search of something better, to become pirates.

These characteristics had a vital bearing on the ways pirates organized their daily activities. Contemporaries who claimed that pirates had "no regular command among them" mistook a different social order—different from the ordering of merchant naval, and privateering vessels—for disorder.[18] This social order, articulated in the organization of the pirate ship, was conceived and deliberately constructed by the pirates themselves. Its hallmark was a rough, improvised, but effective egalitarianism that placed authority in the collective hands of the crew. A core value in the broader culture of the common tar, egalitarianism was institutionalized aboard the pirate slip.

A striking uniformity of rules and customs prevailed aboard pirate ships, each of which functioned under the terms of written articles, a compact drawn up at the beginning of a voyage or upon election of a new captain, and agreed to by the crew. By these articles crews allocated authority, distributed plunder, and enforced discipline.[19] These arrangements made the captain the creature of his crew. Demanding someone both bold of temper and skilled in navigation, the men elected their captain. They gave him few privileges. He "or any other Officer is allowed no more [food] than another man, nay, the Captain cannot keep his Cabbin to himself."[20] Some pirates "messed with the Captain, but withal no Body look'd on it, as a Mark of Favour, or Distinction, for every one came and eat and drank with him at their Humour." A merchant captain held captive by pirates noted with displeasure that crew members slept on the ship wherever they pleased, "the Captain himself not being allowed a Bed."[21] The determined reorganization of space and privilege aboard the ship was crucial to the remaking of maritime social relations.

The crew granted the captain unquestioned authority "in fighting, chasing, or being chased," but "in all other Matters whatsoever" he was "governed by a Majority."[22] As the majority elected, so did it depose. Captains were snatched from their positions for cowardice, cruelty, or refusing "to take and plunder English Vessels."[23] One captain incurred the class-conscious wrath of his crew for being too "Gentleman-like."[24] Occasionally, a despotic captain was summarily executed. As pirate Francis Kennedy explained, most sea robbers "having suffered formerly from the ill-treatment of their officers, provided carefully against any such evil" once they arranged their own command. The democratic selection of officers echoed similar demands within the New Model Army in the English Revolution and stood in stark, telling contrast to the near-dictatorial arrangement of command in the merchant service and the Royal Navy.[25]

To prevent the misuse of authority, pirates delegated countervailing powers to the quartermaster, who was elected to represent and protect "the Interest of the Crew."[26] The quartermaster, who was not considered an officer in the merchant service, was elevated to a valued position of trust and authority. His tasks were to adjudicate minor disputes, to distribute food and money, and in some instances to lead the attacks on prize vessels. He served as a "civil Magistrate" and dispensed necessaries "with an Equality to them all," carefully guarding against the galling and divisive use of privilege and preferment that characterized the distribution of the necessaries of life in other maritime occupations.[27] The quartermaster often became the captain of a captured ship when the captor was overcrowded or divided by discord. This containment of authority within a dual and representative executive was a distinctive feature of social organization among pirates.[28]

The decisions that had the greatest bearing on the welfare of the crew were generally reserved to the council, the highest authority on the pirate ship. Pirates drew upon an ancient custom, largely lapsed by the early modern era, in which the master consulted his entire crew in making crucial decisions. Freebooters also knew of the naval tradition, the council of war, in which the top officers in a fleet or ship met to plan strategy. But pirates democratized the naval custom. Their councils usually included every man on the ship. The council determined such matters as where the best prizes could be taken and how disruptive dissension was to be resolved. Some crews continually used the council, "carrying every thing by a majority of votes"; others set up the council as a court. The decisions made by this body were sacrosanct, and even the boldest captain dared not challenge a council's mandate.[29]

The distribution of plunder was regulated explicitly by the ship's articles, which allocated booty according to skills and duties. Pirates used the precapitalist share system to allocate their take. Captain and quartermaster received between one and one-half and two shares; gunners, boatswains, mates, carpenters, and doctors, one and one-quarter or one and one-half; all others got one share each.[30] This pay system represented a radical departure from practices in the merchant service, Royal Navy, or privateering. It leveled an elaborate hierarchy of pay ranks and decisively reduced the disparity between the top and bottom of the scale. Indeed, this must have been one of the most egalitarian plans for the disposition of resources to be found anywhere in the early eighteenth century. The scheme revealingly indicates that pirates did not consider themselves wage laborers but rather risk-sharing partners. If, as a noted historian of piracy, Philip Gosse, has suggested, "the pick of all seamen were pirates,"[31] the equitable distribution of plunder and the conception of the partnership were the work of men who valued and respected the skills of their comrades. But not all booty was dispensed this way. A portion went into a "common fund" to provide for the men who sustained injury of lasting effect.[32] The loss of eyesight or any appendage merited compensation. By this welfare system pirates attempted to guard against debilities caused by accidents, to protect skills, to enhance recruitment, and to promote loyalty within the group.

The articles also regulated discipline aboard ship, though "discipline" is perhaps a misnomer for a system of rules that left large ranges of behavior uncontrolled. Less arbitrary than that of the merchant service and less codified than that of the navy, discipline among pirates always depended on a collective sense of transgression. Many misdeeds were accorded "what Punishment the Captain and Majority of the Company shall think fit," and it is noteworthy that pirates did not often resort to the whip. Their discipline, if no less severe in certain cases, was generally tolerant of behavior that provoked punishment in other maritime occupations. Three major methods of discipline were employed, all conditioned by the fact that pirate ships were crowded; an average crew numbered near eighty on a 250-ton vessel. The articles of Bartholomew Roberts's ship revealed one tactic for maintaining order: "No striking one another on board, but every Man's Quarrels to be ended on Shore at Sword and Pistol." The antagonists were to fight a duel with pistols, but if both missed their first shots, they then seized swords, and the first to draw blood was declared the victor. By taking such conflicts off the ship (and symbolically off the sea), this practice promoted harmony in the crowded quarters below decks.[33] The ideal of harmony was also reflected when pirates made a crew member the "Governor of an Island." Men who were incorrigibly disruptive or who transgressed important rules were marooned. For defrauding his mates by taking more than a proper share of plunder, for deserting or malingering during battle, for keeping secrets from the crew, or for stealing, a pirate risked being deposited "where he was sure to encounter Hardships."[34] The ultimate method of maintaining order was execution. This penalty was exacted for bringing on board "a Boy or a Woman" or for meddling with a "prudent Woman" on a prize ship, but was most commonly invoked to punish a captain who abused his authority.[35]

Some crews attempted to circumvent disciplinary problems by taking "no Body against their Wills."[36] By the same logic, they would keep no unwilling person. The confession of pirate Edward Davis in 1718 indicates that oaths of honor were used to cement the loyalty of new members:

> at first the old Pirates were a little shy of the new ones. . . . yet in a short time the *New Men* being sworn to be faithful, and not to cheat the Company to the Value of a *Piece of Eight,* they all consulted and acted together with great unanimity, and no distinction was made between Old and *New.*[37]

Yet for all their efforts to blunt the cutting edge of authority and to maintain harmony and cohesion, conflict could not always be contained. Occasionally upon election of a new captain, men who favored other leadership drew up new articles and sailed away from their former mates.[38] The social organization constructed by pirates, although flexible, was unable to accommodate severe, sustained conflict. Those who had experienced the claustrophobic and authoritarian world of the merchant ship cherished the freedom to separate. The egalitarian and collective exercise of authority by pirates had both negative and positive effects. Although it produced a chronic instability, it also guaranteed continuity. The very process by which new crews were established helped to ensure a social uniformity and, as we shall see, a consciousness of kind among pirates.[39]

One important mechanism in this continuity can be seen by charting the connections among pirate crews. The accompanying diagram, arranged according to vessel captaincy, demonstrates that by splintering, by sailing in consorts, or by other associations, roughly 3,600 pirates—more than 70 percent of all those active between 1716 and 1726—fit into two main lines of genealogical descent. Captain Benjamin Hornigold and the pirate rendezvous in the Bahamas stood at the origin of an intricate lineage that ended with the hanging of John Phillips's crew in June 1724. The second line, spawned in the chance meeting of the lately mutinous crews of George Lowther and Edward

Low in 1722, culminated in the executions of William Fly and his men in July 1726. It was primarily within and through this network that the social organization of the pirate ship took on its significance, transmitting and preserving customs and meanings and helping to structure and perpetuate the pirates' social world.[40]

Pirates constructed that world in defiant contradistinction to the ways of the world they had left behind, in particular to its salient figures of power, the merchant captain and the royal official, and to the system of authority those figures represented and enforced. When eight pirates were tried in Boston in 1718, merchant captain Thomas Checkley told of the capture of his ship by pirates who "pretended," he said, "to be Robbin Hoods Men."[41] Eric Hobsbawm has defined social banditry as a "universal and virtually unchanging phenomenon," an "endemic peasant protest against oppression and poverty: a cry for vengeance on the rich and the oppressors." Its goal is "a traditional world in which men are justly dealt with, not a new and perfect world"; Hobsbawm calls its advocates "revolutionary traditionalists."[42] Pirates, of course, were not peasants, but they fit Hobsbawm's formulation in every other respect. Of special importance was their "cry for vengeance."

Spotswood told no more than the simple truth when he expressed his fear of pirate vengeance, for the very names of pirate ships made the same threat. Edward Teach, whom Spotswood's men cut off, called his vessel *Queen Anne's Revenge;* other notorious craft were Stede Bonnet's *Revenge* and John Cole's *New York Revenge's Revenge.*[43] The foremost target of vengeance was the merchant captain. Frequently, "in a far distant latitude," as one seaman put it, "unlimited power, bad views, ill nature and ill principles all concur[red]" in a ship's commander. Here was a man "past all restraint" who often made life miserable for his crew.[44] Spotswood also noted how pirates avenged the captain's "correcting" of his sailors. In 1722, merchant captains Isham Randolph, Constantine Cane, and William Halladay petitioned Spotswood "in behalf of themselves and other Masters of Ships" for "some certain method . . . for punishing mutinous & disobedient Seamen." They explained that captains faced great danger "in case of meeting with Pyrates, where we are sure to suffer all the tortures w[hi]ch such an abandoned crew can invent, upon the least intimation of our Striking any of our men."[45] Pirates acted the part of a floating mob with its own distinctive sense of popular justice.

Upon seizing a merchantman, pirates often administered the "Distribution of Justice," "enquiring into the Manner of the Commander's Behaviour to their Men, and those, against whom Complaint was made" were "whipp'd and pickled."[46] Bartholomew Roberts's crew considered such inquiry so important that they formally designated one of their men, George Willson, as the "Dispencer of Justice." In 1724 merchant captain Richard Hawkins described another form of retribution, a torture known as the "Sweat":

Between decks they stick Candles round the Mizen-Mast, and about twenty-five men surround it with Points of Swords, Penknives, Compasses, Forks &c in each of their hands: Culprit enters the Circle; the Violin plays a merry jig; and he must run for about ten Minutes, while each man runs his Instrument into his Posteriors.[47]

Many captured captains were "barbarously used," and some were summarily executed. Pirate Philip Lyne carried this vengeance to its bloodiest extremity, confessing when apprehended in 1726 that "during the time of his Piracy" he "had killed 37 Masters of Vessels."[48] The search for vengeance was in many ways a fierce, embittered response to the violent, personal, and arbitrary authority wielded by the merchant captain.

Still, the punishment of captains was not indiscriminate, for a captain who had been "an honest Fellow that never abused any Sailors" was often rewarded by pirates.[49] The best description of pirates' notions of justice comes from merchant captain William Snelgrave's account of his capture in 1719. On April 1, Snelgrave's ship was seized by Thomas Cooklyn's crew of rovers at the mouth of the Sierra Leone River. Cooklyn was soon joined by men captained by Oliver LaBouche and Howell Davis, and Snelgrave spent the next thirty days among two hundred forty pirates.[50]

The capture was effected when twelve pirates in a small boat came alongside Snelgrave's ship, which was manned by forty-five sailors. Snelgrave ordered his crew to arms. They refused, but the pirate quartermaster, infuriated by the command, drew a pistol and then, Snelgrave testified, "with the but-end [he] endeavoured to beat out my Brains" until "some of my People . . . cried out aloud 'For God sake don't kill our Captain, for we never were with a better Man.'" The quartermaster, Snelgrave noted, "told me, 'my Life was safe provided none of My People complained against me.' I replied, 'I was sure none of them could.'"[51]

Snelgrave was taken to Cocklyn, who told him, "I am sorry you have met with bad usage after Quarter given, but 'tis the Fortune of War sometimes. . . . [I]f you tell the truth, and your Men make no Complaints against you, you shall be kindly used." Howell Davis, commander of the largest of the pirate ships, reprimanded Cocklyn's men for their roughness and, by Snelgrave's account, expressed himself

ashamed to hear how I had been used by them. That they should remember their reasons for going a pirating were to revenge themselves on base Merchants and cruel commanders of Ships. . . . [N]o one of my People, even those that had entered with them gave me the least ill-character. . . . [I]t was plain they loved me.[52]

Snelgrave's men may not have loved him, but they surely did respect him. Indeed, Snelgrave's character proved so respectable that the pirates proposed to give him a captured ship with full cargo and to sell the goods for him. Then they would capture a Portuguese slaver, sell the slaves, and give the proceeds to Snelgrave so that he could "return with a large sum of Money to London, and bid the Merchants defiance."[53] Pirates hoped to show these merchants that good fortunes befell good captains. The proposal was "unanimously approved" by the pirates, but fearing a charge of complicity, Snelgrave hesitated to accept it. Davis then interceded, saying that he favored "allowing every Body to go to the Devil in their own way" and that he knew that Snelgrave feared for "his Reputation." The refusal was graciously accepted, Snelgrave claiming that "the Tide being turned, they were as kind to me, as they had been at first severe."[54]

Snelgrave related another revealing episode. While he remained in pirate hands, a decrepit schooner belonging to the Royal African Company sailed into the Sierra Leone and was taken by his captors. Simon Jones, a member of Cocklyn's crew, urged his mates to burn the ship, since he had been poorly treated while in the company's employ. The pirates were about to do so when another of them, James Stubbs, protested that such action would only "serve the Company's interests," since the ship was worth but little. He also pointed out that "the poor People that now belong to her, and have been on so long a voyage, will lose their Wages, which I am sure is Three times the Value of the Vessel." The pirates concurred and returned the ship to its crew, who "came safe home to England in it." Captain Snelgrave also returned to England soon after this incident, but eleven of his seamen remained behind as pirates.[55] Snelgrave's experience revealed how pirates attempted to intervene against—and modify—the standard brutalities that marked the social relations of production in merchant shipping. That they sometimes chose to do so with brutalities of their own shows that they could not escape the system of which they were a part.

Snelgrave seems to have been an exceptionally decent captain. Pirates like Howell Davis claimed that abusive treatment by masters of merchantmen contributed mightily to their willingness to become sea robbers. John Archer, whose career as a pirate dated from 1718 when he sailed with Edward Teach, uttered a final protest before his execution in 1724:

> I could wish that Masters of Vessels would not use their Men with so much Severity, as many of them do, which exposes us to great Temptations.[56]

William Fly, facing the gallows for murder and piracy in 1726, angrily announced,

> I can't charge myself,—I shan't own myself Guilty of any Murder,—Our Captain and his Mate used us Barbarously. We poor Men can't have justice done us. There is nothing said to our Commanders, let them never so much abuse us, and use us like Dogs.[57]

To pirates revenge was justice; punishment was meted out to barbarous captains, as befitted the captains' crimes.

Sea robbers who fell into the hands of the state received the full force of penalties for crimes against property. The official view of piracy as crime was outlined in 1718 by Vice-Admiralty Judge Nicholas Trott in his charge to the jury in the trial of Stede Bonnet and thirty-three members of his crew at Charleston, South Carolina. Declaring that "the Sea was given by God for the use of Men, and is subject to Dominion and Property, as well as the Land," Trott observed of the accused that "the Law of Nations never granted to them a Power to change the Right of Property." Pirates on trial were denied benefit of clergy, were "called *Hostis Humani Generis*, with whom neither Faith nor Oath" were to be kept, and were regarded as *"Brutes*, and *Beasts of Prey."* Turning from the jury to the accused, Trott circumspectly surmised that "no further Good or Benefit can be expected from you but by the Example of your Deaths."[58]

The insistence on obtaining this final benefit locked royal officials and pirates into a system of reciprocal terror. As royal authorities offered bounties for captured pirates, so too did pirates "offer any price" for certain officials.[59] In Virginia in 1720, one of six pirates facing the gallows "called for a Bottle of Wine, and taking a Glass of it, he Drank Damnation to the Governour and Confusion to the Colony, which the rest pledged." Not to be outdone, Governor Spotswood thought it "necessary for the greater Terrour to hang up four of them in Chains."[60] Pirates demonstrated an antinomian disdain for state authority when George I extended general pardons for piracy in 1717 and 1718. Some accepted the grace but refused to reform; others "seem'd to slight it," and the most defiant "used the King's Proclamation with great contempt, and tore it into pieces."[61] One pirate crew downed its punch, proclaiming, "Curse the King and all the Higher Powers."[62] The social relations of piracy were marked by vigorous, often violent, antipathy toward traditional authority. The pervasive antiauthoritarianism of the culture of the common seafarer found many expressions beneath the Jolly Roger.

At the Charleston trial over which Trott presided, Richard Allen, attorney general of South Carolina, told the jury that "pirates prey upon all Mankind, their own Species and Fellow-Creatures without Distinction of Nations or Religions."[63] Allen was right in claiming that pirates did not respect nationality in their plunders, but he was wrong in claiming that they did not respect their "Fellow-Creatures." Pirates did not prey on one another. Rather, they consistently expressed in numerous and subtle ways a highly developed consciousness of kind. Here we turn from the external social relations of piracy to the internal in order to examine this consciousness of kind—in a sense, a strategy for survival—and the collectivistic ethos it expressed.

Pirates showed a recurrent willingness to join forces at sea and in port. In April 1719, when Howell Davis and crew sailed into the Sierra Leone River, the pirates captained by Thomas Cocklyn were wary until they saw on the approaching ship "her Black Flag"; then "immediately they were easy in their minds," and a little time after, "the crews saluted one another with their Cannon." Other crews exchanged similar greetings and, like Davis and Cocklyn who combined their powers, frequently invoked an unwritten code of hospitality to forge spontaneous alliances.[64]

This communitarian urge was perhaps most evident in the pirate strongholds of Madagascar and Sierra Leone. Sea robbers occasionally chose more sedentary lifeways on various thinly populated islands, and they contributed a notorious number of men to the community of logwood cutters at the Bay of Campeche in the Gulf of Mexico. In 1718 a royal official complained of a "nest of pirates" in the Bahamas "who already esteem themselves a community, and to have one common interest."[65]

To perpetuate such community, it was necessary to minimize conflict not only on each ship but also among separate bands of pirates. Indeed, one of the strongest indicators of consciousness of kind is the manifest absence of discord between different pirate crews. To some extent, this was even a transnational matter: French, Dutch, Spanish, and Anglo-American pirates usually cooperated peaceably, only occasionally exchanging cannon fire. Anglo-American crews consistently refused to attack one another.[66]

In no way was the pirate sense of fraternity, which Spotswood and others noted, more forcefully expressed than in the threats and acts of revenge taken by pirates. Theirs was truly a case of hanging together or being hanged separately. In April 1717, the pirate ship *Whydah* was wrecked near Boston. Most of its crew perished; the survivors were jailed. In July, Thomas Fox, a Boston ship captain, was taken by pirates who "Questioned him whether anything was done to the Pyrates in Boston Goall," promising "that if the Prisoners Suffered they would Kill every Body they took belonging to New England."[67] Shortly after this incident, Teach's sea rovers captured a merchant vessel and, "because she belonged to Boston, [Teach] alledging the People of Boston had hanged some of the Pirates, so burnt her." Teach declared that all Boston ships deserved a similar fate."[68] Charles Vane, reputedly a most fearsome pirate, "would give no quarter to the Bermudians" and punished them and "cut away their masts upon account of one Thomas Brown who was (some time) detain'd in these Islands upon suspicion of piracy." Brown apparently planned to sail as Vane's consort until foiled by his capture.[69]

In September 1720, pirates captained by Bartholomew Roberts "openly and in the daytime burnt and destroyed vessels in the Road of Basseterre [St. Kitts] and had the audaciousness to insult H. M. Fort," avenging the execution of "their comrades at Nevis." Roberts then sent word to the governor that "they would Come and Burn the Town [Sandy Point] about his Ears for hanging the Pyrates there."[70] In 1721 Spotswood relayed information to the Council of Trade and Plantations that Roberts "said he expected to be joined by another ship and would then visit Virginia, and avenge the pirates who have been executed here."[71] The credibility of the threat was confirmed by the unanimous resolution of the Virginia Executive Council that "the Country be put into an immediate posture of Defense." Lookouts and beacons were quickly provided and communications with neighboring colonies effected. "Near 60 Cannon," Spotswood later reported, were "mounted on sundry Substantial Batteries."[72]

In 1723 pirate captain Francis Spriggs vowed to find a Captain Moore "and put him to death for being the cause of the death of [pirate] Lowther," and, shortly after, similarly pledged to go "in quest of Captain Solgard," who had overpowered a pirate ship commanded by Charles Harris.[73] In January 1724, Lieutenant Governor Charles Hope of Bermuda wrote to the Board of Trade that he found it difficult to procure trial evidence against pirates because residents "feared that this very execution wou'd make our vessels fare the worse for it, when they happen'd to fall into pirate hands."[74] The threats of revenge were sometimes effective.

Pirates also affirmed their unity symbolically. Some evidence indicates that sea robbers may have had a sense of belonging to a separate, in some manner exclusive, speech community. Philip Ashton, who spent sixteen months among pirates in 1722–23, noted that "according to the Pirates usual Custom, and *in their proper Dialect,* asked me, If I would sign their Articles."[75] Many sources suggest that cursing, swearing, and blaspheming may have been defining traits of this style of speech, perhaps to an even greater extent than among the larger population of seafaring men. For example, near the Sierra Leone River, a British official named Plunkett pretended to cooperate with, but then attacked, the pirates with Bartholomew Roberts. Plunkett was captured, and Roberts

> upon the first sight of Plunkett swore at him like any Devil, for his Irish Impudence in daring to resist him. Old Plunkett, finding he had got into bad Company, fell a swearing and cursing as fast or faster than Roberts; which made the rest of the Pirates laugh heartily, desiring Roberts to sit down and hold his Peace, for he had no Share in the Pallaver with Plunkett at all. So that by meer Dint of Cursing and Damning, Old Plunkett . . . sav'd his life.[76]

We can see only outlines here, but it appears that the symbolic connectedness, the consciousness of kind, extended to the domain of language.

Certainly the best-known symbol of piracy is the flag, the Jolly Roger. Less known and appreciated is the fact that the flag was very widely used.

No fewer, and probably a great many more, than 2,500 men sailed under it.[77] So general an adoption indicates an advanced state of group identification. The Jolly Roger was described as a "black Ensign, in the Middle of which is a large white Skeleton with a Dart in one hand striking a bleeding Heart, and in the other an Hour Glass."[78] Although there was considerable variation in particulars among these flags, there was also a general uniformity of chosen images. The flag's background was black, adorned with white representational figures. The most common symbol was the human skull, or "death's head," sometimes isolated but more frequently the most prominent feature of an entire skeleton. Other recurring items were a weapon—cutlass, sword, or dart—and an hourglass.[79]

The flag was intended to terrify the pirates' prey, but its triad of interlocking symbols—death, violence, limited time—simultaneously pointed to meaningful parts of the seaman's experience and eloquently bespoke the pirates' own consciousness of themselves as preyed upon in turn. Pirates seized the symbol of mortality from ship captains who used the skull "as a marginal sign in their logs to indicate the record of a death."[80] Seamen who became pirates escaped from one closed system only to find themselves encased in another. But as pirates—and, some believed, only as pirates—these men were able to fight back beneath the somber colors of "King Death" against those captains, merchants, and officials who waved banners of authority.[81] Moreover, pirates self-righteously perceived their situation and the excesses of these powerful figures through a collectivistic ethos that had been forged in the struggle for survival.

The self-righteousness of pirates was strongly linked to a world—traditional, mythical, or utopian—"in which men are justly dealt with," as described by Hobsbawm.[82] It found expression in their social rules, their egalitarian social organization, and their notions of revenge and justice. By walking "to the Gallows without a Tear," by calling themselves "Honest Men" and "Gentlemen," and by speaking self-servingly but proudly of their "Conscience" and "Honor," pirates flaunted their certitude.[83] When, in 1720, ruling groups concluded that "nothing but force will subdue them," many pirates responded by intensifying their commitment.[84] Edward Low's crew in 1724 swore "with the most direful Imprecations, that if ever they should find themselves overpower'd they would immediately blow their ship up rather than suffer themselves to be hang'd like Dogs." These sea robbers would not "do Jolly Roger the Disgrace to be struck."[85]

The consciousness of kind among pirates manifested itself in an elaborate social code. Through rule, custom, and symbol, the code prescribed specific behavioral standards intended to preserve the social world that pirates had creatively built for themselves. As the examples of revenge reveal, royal officials recognized the threat of the pirates' alternative order. Some authorities feared that pirates might "set up a sort of Commonwealth"[86]—and they were precisely correct in their designation—in uninhabited regions, since "no Power in those Parts of the World could have been able to dispute it with them."[87] But the consciousness of kind never took national shape, and piracy was soon suppressed.

Contemporary observers usually attributed the rise of piracy to the demobilization of the Royal Navy at the end of the War of the Spanish Succession. A group of Virginia merchants, for instance, wrote to the Admiralty in 1713, setting forth "the apprehensions they have of Pyrates molesting their trade in the time of Peace."[88] The navy plunged from 49,860 men at the end of the war to 13,475 just two years later, and only by 1740 did it increase to as many as 30,000 again.[89] At the same time, the expiration of privateering licenses—bills of marque—added to the number of seamen loose and looking for work in the port cities of the empire. Such underemployment contributed significantly to the rise of piracy,[90] but it is not a sufficient explanation, since, as already noted, the vast majority of those who became pirates were working in the merchant service at the moment of their joining.

The surplus of labor at the end of the war had extensive, sometimes jarring social and economic effects. It produced an immediate contraction of wages; merchant seamen who made 45–55s. per month in 1707 made only half that amount in 1713. It provoked greater competition for seafaring jobs, which favored the hiring of older, more experienced seamen. And over time, it affected the social conditions and relations of life at sea, cutting back material benefits and hardening discipline.[91] War years, despite their deadly dangers, provided seafarers with tangible benefits. The Anglo-American seamen of 1713 had performed wartime labor for twenty of the previous twenty-five years and for eleven years consecutively.

Conditions did not worsen immediately after the war. As Ralph Davis explained,

> the years 1713–1715 saw—as did immediate post-war years throughout the eighteenth century—the shifting of heaped-up surpluses of colonial goods, the movement of great quantities of English goods to colonial and other markets, and a general filling in of stocks of imported goods which had been allowed to run down.[92]

This small-scale boom gave employment to some of the seamen who had been dropped from naval rolls. But by late 1715 a slump in trade began, to last into the 1730s. All these difficulties were exacerbated by the intensification of maritime discipline over the course of the eighteenth century.[93] Many seamen knew that things had once been different and, for many, decisively better.

By 1726, the menace of piracy had been effectively suppressed by governmental action. Circumstantial factors such as the remobilization of the Royal Navy cannot account fully for its demise. The number of men in the Navy increased from 6,298 in 1725 to 16,872 in 1726 and again to 20,697 in 1727, which had some bearing on the declining number of sea robbers. Yet some 20,000 sailors had been in the navy in 1719 and 1720, years when pirates were numerous.[94] In addition, seafaring wages only occasionally rose above 30s. per month between 1713 and the mid-1730s.[95] The conditions of life at sea did not change appreciably until war broke out in 1739.

The pardons offered to pirates in 1717 and 1718 failed to rid the sea of robbers. Since the graces specified that only crimes committed at certain times and in particular regions would be forgiven, many pirates saw enormous latitude for official trickery and refused to surrender. Moreover, accepting and abiding by the rules of the pardon would have meant for most men a return to the dismal conditions they had escaped. Their tactic failing, royal officials intensified the naval campaign against piracy—with great and gruesome effect. Corpses dangled in chains in British ports around the world "as a Spectacle for the Warning of others."[96] No fewer than four hundred, and probably five hundred to six hundred Anglo-American pirates were executed between 1716 and 1726. The state also passed harsh legislation that criminalized all contact with pirates. Anyone who "truck[ed], barter[ed], exchange[d]" with pirates, furnished them with stores, or even consulted with them might be punished with death.[97]

The campaign to cleanse the seas was supported by clergymen, royal officials, and publicists who sought through sermons, proclamations, pamphlets, and the newspaper press to create an image of the pirate that would legitimate his extermination. Piracy had always depended in some measure on the rumors and tales of its successes, especially among seamen and dealers in stolen cargo. In 1722 and 1723, after a spate of hangings and a burst of propaganda, the pirate population began to decline. By 1726, only a handful of the fraternity remained.

Pirates themselves unwittingly took a hand in their own destruction. From the outset, theirs had been a fragile social world. They produced nothing and had no secure place in the economic order. They had no nation, no home; they were widely dispersed; their community had virtually no geographic boundaries. Try as they might, they were unable to create reliable mechanisms through which they could either replenish their ranks or mobilize their collective strength. These deficiencies of social organization made them, in the long run, relatively easy prey.

The pirate was, perhaps above all else, an unremarkable man caught in harsh, often deadly circumstances. Wealth he surely desired, but a strong social logic informed both his motivation and his behavior. Emerging from working-class backgrounds and maritime employments, and loosed from familial bonds, pirates developed common symbols and standards of conduct. They forged spontaneous alliances, refused to fight each other, swore to avenge injury to their own kind, and even retired to pirate communities. They erected their own ideal of justice, insisted upon an egalitarian, if unstable, form of social organization, and defined themselves against other social groups and types. So, too, did they perceive many of their activities as ethical and justified, not unlike the eighteenth-century crowds described by E. P. Thompson.[98] But pirates, experienced as cooperative seafaring laborers and no longer disciplined by law, were both familiar with the workings of an international market economy and little affected by the uncertainties of economic change. Their experience as free wage laborers and as members of an uncontrolled, freewheeling subculture gave them the perspective and occasion to fight back against brutal and unjust authority and to construct a new social order where King Death would not reign supreme. Theirs was probably a contradictory pursuit. For many, piracy, as a strategy of survival, was ill-fated.

Piracy, in the end, offers us an extraordinary opportunity. Here we can see how a sizable group of Anglo-Americans—poor men in canvas jackets and tarred breeches—constructed a social world where they had "the choice in themselves."[99] The choice did not exist on the merchant ship or the man-of-war. The social order and practices established by pirates recalled several key features of ancient and medieval maritime life. They divided their money and goods into shares; they consulted collectively and democratically on matters of moment; they elected a quartermaster, who, like the medieval "consul," adjudicated the differences between captain and crew.[100]

Pirates constructed a culture of masterless men. They were as far removed from traditional authority as any men could be in the early eighteenth century. Beyond the church, beyond the family, beyond disciplinary labor, and using the sea to distance themselves from the powers of the state, they carried out a strange experiment. The social constellation of piracy, in particular the complex consciousness and egalitarian impulses that developed once the shackles were off, provides valuable clarification of more general social and cultural patterns among seamen in particular and the laboring poor in general. Here we can see aspirations and achievements that under normal circumstances were heavily muted, if not in many cases rendered imperceptible altogether, by the power relationships of everyday life.

The final word on piracy must belong to Barnaby Slush, the man who understood and gave poetic expression to so many aspects of the common seaman's life in the early eighteenth century:

Pyrates and *Buccaneers,* are Princes to [Seamen], for there, as none are exempt from the General Toil and Danger; so if the Chief have a Supream Share beyond his Comrades, 'tis because he's always the Leading Man in e'ry daring Enterprize; and yet as bold as he is in all other Attempts, he dares not offer to infringe the common laws of Equity; but every Associate has his due Quota . . . thus these *Hostes Humani Generis* as great robbers as they are to all besides, are precisely just among themselves; without which they could no more Subsist than a Structure without a Foundation.[101]

Thus did pirates express the collectivistic ethos of life at sea by the egalitarian and comradely distribution of life chances, the refusal to grant privilege or exemption from danger, and the just allocation of shares. Their notion of justice—among themselves and in their dealings with their class enemies—was indeed the foundation of their enterprise. Equally, piracy itself was a "structure" formed upon a "foundation" of the culture and society of Anglo-American deep-sea sailors in the first half of the eighteenth century.

NOTES

1. PRO CO 5/1319, Alexander Spotswood to the Board of Trade, 16 June 1724.

2. Studies of piracy include general surveys, descriptive chronicles of exploits, and specific, often monographic examinations of certain features of pirate life. The first historian of these pirates was "Captain Charles Johnson," sometimes identified as Daniel Defoe. In 1724 (reprinted in 1728) he published an invaluable collection of mostly accurate information, *A General History of the Pyrates.* The edition cited in this article is Captain Charles Johnson, *A General History of the Robberies and Murders of the Most Notorious Pyrates and also their Policies, Discipline and Government from their first Rise and Settlement in the Island of Providence, in 1717, to the Present Year, 1724, with the Remarkable Actions and Adventures of the two Female Pyrates, Mary Read and Anne Bonny, to which is Prefix'd an Account of the famous Captain Avery and his Companions; with the Manner of his Death in England,* ed. Manuel Schonhorn (London: Dent, 1972) who does ascribe the book to Defoe. George Roberts, *The four years voyages of Capt. George Roberts; being a series of uncommon events, which befell him in a voyage to the islands of the Canaries, Cape de Verde, and Barbadoes, from whence he was bound to the coast of Guiney . . . Together with observations on the minerals, mineral waters, metals, and salts, and of the nitre with which some of these islands abound* (London: A. Bettesworth [etc.], 1726), contains believable accounts of pirates. Roberts is also believed by some to have been Defoe. The best recent study is Hugh F. Rankin, *The Golden Age of Piracy* (Williamsburg: Colonial Williamsburg, 1969). More ambitious are Philip Gosse, *The History of Piracy* (London: Longmans, Green, 1932); Neville Williams, *Captains Outrageous* (London: Barrie and Rockliff, 1961); and Peter Kemp and Christopher Lloyd, *The Brethren of the Coast: The British and French Buccaneers in the South Seas* (London:

Heinemann, 1960); Patrick Pringle, *Jolly Roger: The Story of the Great Age of Piracy* (New York: W. W. Norton, 1953), a piece of popular history, has some fine insights. Charles Grey, *Pirates of the Eastern Seas (1618–1723): A Lurid Page of History*, ed. Sir George MacMunn, reprint of London, S. Low, Marston 1933 ed. (Port Washington, N.Y.: Kennikat Press, 1971); George Francis Dow and John Henry Edmonds, *The Pirates of the New England Coast*, reprint of Salem, Mass., 1923 ed. (New York: Argosy-Antiquarian, 1968; and John Biddulph, *The Pirates of Malabar; and an Englishwoman in India Two Hundred Years Ago* (London: Smith, Elder, 1907), are somewhat descriptive but contain important data. Stanley Richards, *Black Bart* (Llandybie, Carmarthenshire: C. Davies, 1966), is a biography of Bartholomew Roberts. See also Shirley Carter Hughson, *The Carolina Pirates and Colonial Commerce, 1670–1740*, Johns Hopkins University Studies in Historical and Political Science, ser. no. 5–7 (Baltimore: Johns Hopkins University, 1894); B. R. Burg, "Legitimacy and Authority, Case-Study of Pirate Commanders in the 17th and 18th Centuries," *American Neptune* 37, 1 (1977): 40–49; James Gavin Lydon, *Pirates, Privateers, and Profits* (Upper Saddle River, N.J.: Gregg Press, 1970); and Richard B. Morris, "The Ghost of Captain Kidd," *New York History* 19 (1938): 280–97. The literature on piracy is vast. For the newcomer, these works provide a solid beginning.

3. S. Charles Hill, "Episodes of Piracy in Eastern Waters," *Indian Antiquary* 49 (1920), 37; Arthur L. Hayward, ed., *Lives of the Most Remarkable Criminals: Who have been Condemed and Executed for Murder, the Highway, Housebreaking, Street Robberies, Coining or Other Offences*, reprint of 1735 London ed. (London and New York: Routledge and Dodd, Mead, 1927), 37. Following E. P. Thompson, *Whigs and Hunters: The Origin of the Black Act* (New York: Pantheon Books, 1975), and Douglas Hay et al., eds., *Albion's Fatal Tree: Crime and Society in Eighteenth-Century England* (New York: Pantheon Books, 1975), this chapter uses the social history of crime as access to working-class life in the eighteenth century. I define a pirate as one who willingly participates in robbery on the sea, not discriminating among nationalities in the choice of victims. Part of the empirical base of this chapter was accumulated in piecemeal fashion from documents of all varieties. Individual pirates were recorded by name and dates of activity, and information on age, labor, class, family background, and miscellaneous detail was noted. This file *(519 men, 2 women)* can be replicated only by consulting all the sources that follow in the notes. Since I have found mention of only two female pirates, and since the maritime world was predominantly male, the latter gender is used in the references.

4. James Logan (1717) estimated 1,500 in Hughson, *Carolina Pirates, 59*; Governor of Bermuda (1717) "at least 1,000" in Pringle, *Jolly Roger*, 181, and in PRO HCA 1/54 (1717), f. 113; Woodes Rogers (1718) "near a thousand" quoted in Johnson, *General History*, 615; Daniel Defoe *(1720)*, 1,500, ibid., 132; Governor of South Carolina (1718) "near 2,000" in *CPSCS America and the West Indies*, 31: 10; Anonymous (1721), 1,500 in Abel Boyer, ed., *The Political State of Great Britain . . .* (London: 1711–40), 21: 659. Quotation from Representation from Several Merchants Trading to Virginia to Board of Trade, PRO CO 5/1318, 15 April 1717. Estimates of the sizes of crews are available for thirty-seven pirate ships: The mean is 79.5. I have

found reference to seventy-nine crews through mention of the ship or captain. Totals were obtained by arranging ships according to periods of activity and multiplying by the mean crew size. If this mean holds, the total population would have been 6,281. Yet this figure counts some pirates more than once. For example, many who sailed with both Howell Davis and Bartholomew Roberts are counted twice. The range 4,000–5,500 expresses the uncertainty of the calculations. It seems that, in all, some five thousand men were involved. For estimates of the number of men in the Royal Navy, see Christopher Lloyd, *The British Seaman 1200–1860: A Social Survey*, 1st American ed. (Rutherford, N.J.: Fairleigh Dickinson University Press, 1970), 287, and Marcus Rediker, "Society and Culture among Anglo-American Deep-Sea Sailors, 1700–1750" (Ph.D. dissertation, University of Pennsylvania, 1982), 49, 317.

5. Deposition of John Vickers, PRO CO 5/1317 (1716); Spotswood to Council of Trade and Plantations (hereafter CTP), PRO CO 5/1364 (31 May 1717); Johnson, *General History*, 31–34; Great Britain, Parliament, *Proceedings and Debates of the British Parliaments respecting North America*, ed. Leo Francis Stock, 5 vols. (Washington, D.C.: Carnegie Institution of Washington, 1924–41), 3: 399; Deposition of Adam Baldridge in J. F. Jameson, *Privateering and Piracy in the Colonial Period: Illustrative Documents* (New York: Macmillan, 1923), 180–87; R. A. Brock, ed., *The Official Letters of Alexander Spotswood Lieutenant-Governor of the Colony of Virginia, 1710–1722*, Virginia Historical Society, Collections, N.S. , 1–2 (Richmond, Va.: 1882), 168; William Snelgrave, *A New Account of Some Parts of Guinea and the Slave-Trade*, reprint of 1734 ed. (London: Frank Cass, 1971), 197; Abbé Rochon, "A Voyage to Madagascar and the East Indies," in *A General Collection of the Best and Most Interesting Voyages and Travels in all Parts of the World: Many of which are now First Translated into English*, ed. John Pinkerton (London: Longman, Hurst, Rees, and Orme, 1808–14), 767–71; William Smith, *A New Voyage to Guinea: Describing the Customs, Manners, Soil, Climate, Habits, Buildings, Education . . . Habitations, Diversions, Marriages, and Whatever Else is Memorable among the Inhabitants* (London: J. Nourse, 1744): On Johnson/Defoe's credibility, see Schonhorn's introduction to Johnson, *General History*, xxvii–xl; Gosse, *History of Piracy*, 182; and Rankin, *Golden Age*, 161.

6. Biographical data indicate that 155 of the 157 whose labor background is known came from one of these employments; 144 had been in the merchant service. Probably fewer than 5 percent of pirates originated as mutineers. See Johnson, *General History*, 116, 196, 215–16; Snelgrave, *Account of the Slave-Trade*, 203; Deposition of Richard Simes, CSPCS 32: 319; and 33: 365 on volunteers.

7. James Boswell, *The Life of Samuel Johnson, LL. D. Comprehending an Account of his Studies and Numerous Works* (London: Printed by Henry Baldwin for Charles Dilly, 1791), 86.

8. Jesse Lemisch, "Jack Tar in the Streets: Merchant Seamen in the Politics of Revolutionary America," *William and Mary Quarterly* 25 (1968): 371–407, reference here to 379, 375–76, 406; Richard Brandon Morris, *Government and Labor in Early America* (New York: Columbia University Press, 1946), 246–47, 257, 262–68; Johnson, *General History*, 244, 359; A. G. Course, *The Merchant Navy: A Social*

History (London: F. Muller, 1963), 61; Samuel Cox to CTP, *CSPCS* 31: 393; Ralph Davis, *The Rise of the English Shipping Industry in the Seventeenth and Eighteenth Centuries* (London: Macmillan, 1962), 144, 154–55; Nathaniel Uring, *The Voyages and Travels of Captain Nathaniel Uring*, ed. Alfred Dewar (London: Cassell, 1928; originally published in 1726), xxviii, 176–78; Arthur Pierce Middleton, *Tobacco Coast: A Maritime History of Chesapeake Bay in the Colonial Era* (Newport News: Mariners' Museum, 1953), 8, 13, 15, 18, 271, 281; Lloyd, *British Seaman*, 249, 264; John Atkins, *A Voyage to Guinea, Brasil, and the West-Indies; in His Majesty's Ships, the Swallow and Weymouth* (London and Scarborough: Caesar Ward and Richard Chandler, 1735), 261; G. T. Crook and J. L. Rayner, eds., *The Complete Newgate Calendar; being Captain Charles Johnson's General History of the Lives and Adventures of the Most Famous Highwaymen, Murderers, Street-Robbers and Account of the Voyages and Plunders of the Most Notorious Pyrates, 1734; Captain Alexander Smith's Compleat History of the Lives and Robberies of the Most Notorious Highwaymen, Footpads, Shop-lifts and Cheats, 1719; The Tyburn Chronicle, 1768; The Malefactors' Register, 1796; George Borrow's Celebrated Trials, 1825; The Newgate Calendar, by Andrew Knapp and William Baldwin, 1826; Camden Pelham's Chronicles of Crime, 1841*, 5 vols. (London: Navarre Society, 1926), 3:57–58; S. Charles Hill, "Notes on Piracy in Eastern Waters," *Indian Antiquary* 46 (1927), 130; Hayward, *Remarkable Criminals*, 126.

9. Gov. Lowther to CTP, *CSPCS* 29:350; Morris, *Government and Labor*, 247; Lemisch, "Jack Tar," 379; Davis, *English Shipping*, 133–37; R. D. Merriman, ed., *Queen Anne's Navy: Documents concerning the Administration of the Navy of Queen Anne, 1702–1714* (London, Navy Records Society: 1961), 170–72, 174, 221–22, 250; Lloyd, *British Seaman*, 44–46, 124–49; Peter Kemp, *The British Sailor: A Social History of the Lower Deck* (London: Dent, 1970), chapters 4, 5; Arthur Gilbert, "Buggery and the British Navy 1700–1861," *Journal of Social History* 10, 1 (1976): 72–98.

10. Atkins, *Voyage to Guinea*, 139, 187; Captain's logbook, "At Jamaica, 1720–1721," Rawlinson Manuscripts A-299, Bodleian Library, Oxford; *The Historical Register, Containing an Impartial Relation of all Transactions, . . . With a Chronological Diary . . . Volume VII. For the Year 1722* (London: 1722), 344.

11. Merriman, *Queen Anne's Navy*, 171. Lloyd, *British Seaman*, 44, estimates that one-half of all men pressed between 1600 and 1800 died at sea.

12. Course, *Merchant Navy*, 84; Lloyd, *British Seaman*, 57; Edward Cooke, *A Voyage to the South Sea, and Round the World, Perform'd in the years 1708, 1709, 1710, and 1711. Containing a Journal of all Memorable Transactions . . . With a New Map and Description of the mighty River of the Amazons. Wherein an Account is given of Mr. Alexander Selkirk*, 2 vols. (London: 1712), v–vi, 14–16; Woodes Rogers, *A Cruising Voyage Round the World*, ed. G. E. Manwaring (New York: Longmans, Green and Co, 1928), 34–36, 38, 46, 157, 214, 217 (Rogers's book was originally published in 1713); William Betagh, *A Voyage Round the World: Being an Account of a Remarkable Enterprize, Begun in the Year 1719, Chiefly to Cruise on the Spaniards in the Great South Ocean . . . by William Betagh, Captain of Marines in that Expedition* (London: Printed for T. Combes, J. Lacy, and J. Clarke, 1728), 4.

13. Rogers, *Cruising Voyage*, 205. See also George Shelvocke, *A Privateer's Voyage Round the World* (1726; London: Jonathan Cape, 1930), 43, 221–25.

14. Col. Benjamin Bennet to Council of Trade and Plantations, PRO CO 37/10 (31 May 1718 and 30 July 1717), f. 18; Johnson, *General History*, 228. On volunteers, see note 6 of this chapter.

15. See note 3 of this chapter. Ages were taken at the time of the first known piracy. See also Appendix A of Marcus Rediker, *Between the Devil and the Deep Blue Sea: Merchant Seamen, Pirates and the Anglo American Maritime Worlds 1700–1726* (Cambridge: Cambridge University Press, 1987). In Marcus Rediker, "'Under the Banner of King Death': The Social World of Anglo-American Pirates 1716–1726," *William and Mary Quarterly* 38 (1981): 203–27, on page 208, I mistakenly argued that pirates were older than the seafaring population as a whole.

16. Only 23 in the sample of 521 are known to have been married. In pirate confessions, regrets were often expressed to parents, seldom to wives or children. See Cotton Mather, *Useful remarks. An Essay upon Remarkables in the Way of Wicked Men. A Sermon on the Tragical End, unto which the Way of Twenty-six Pirates brought them; at New Port on Rhode-Island, July 19, 1723. With an Account of their Speeches, Letters, & Actions, before their execution* (New-London, Conn.: T. Green, 1723), 38–42; and *The Trials of Eight Persons Indited for Piracy &c. Of Whom Two were Acquitted, and the Rest Found Guilty. At a Justiciary Court of Admiralty Assembled and Held in Boston Within His Majesty's Province of the Massachusetts-Bay in New-England, on the 18th of October 1717. And by Several Adjournments Continued to the 30th. Pursuant to His Majesty's Commission and Instruction, Founded on the Act of Parliament Made in the 11th. & 12th of King William IIID. Intituled, An Act for the More Effectual Suppression of Piracy: with an Appendix, Containing the Substance of Their Confessions Given Before His Excellency the Governour, when They Were First Brought to Boston, and Committed to Gaol* (Boston: B. Green for John Edwards, 1718), 24, 25. Quotation from John Barnard, *Ashton's Memorial. An History of the Strange Adventures, and Signal Deliverances, of Mr. Philip Ashton, who, after he had Made his Escape from the Pirates, Liv'd Alone on a Desolate Island for about Sixteen Months, &c. With a Short Account of Mr. Nicholas Merritt, who was Taken at the Same Time. To Which is Added a Sermon on Dan. 3. 17.* (Boston: Samuel Gerrish, 1725), 3.

17. Peter Haywood to CTP, PRO CO 137112, 3 December 1716; Lemisch, "Jack Tar," 377; Davis, *English Shipping*, 114. Biographical data show that seventy-one of seventy-five pirates came from working-class backgrounds.

18. Betagh, *Voyage*, 148.

19. Johnson, *General History*, 167, 211–13, 298, 307–8, 321; Hayward, *Remarkable Criminals*, 37; Information of Alexander Thompson, PRO HCA 1/55 (1723), f. 23; Snelgrave, *Account of the Slave-Trade*, 220; Jameson, *Privateering and Piracy*, 337; Rankin, *Golden Age*, 31. The vast differences between pirate and privateer articles can be seen by comparing the preceding to Rogers, *Cruising Voyage*, xiv, xxv, 22–23; Shelvocke, *Voyage*, 34–36, 159, 218, 223; Cooke, *Voyage*, iv–vi; and Betagh, *Voyage*, 205–6.

20. Clement Downing, *A History of the Indian Wars* (London: Oxford University Press, 1924), 99 (this is a reprint of *A Compendious History of the Indian Wars; with an account of . . . Angria the Pyrate. Also the Transactions of a Squadron of Men of War under Commodore Matthews, sent to the East-Indies to Suppress the Pyrates. To which is Annex'd, an Additional History of the Wars between the Great Mogul, Angria, and his Allies. With an Account of the Life and Actions of John Plantain, a Notorious Pyrate at Madagascar* (London: 1737); Johnson, *General History,* 121, 139, 167–68, 195, 208, 214, 340, 352; Snelgrave, *Account of the Slave-Trade,* 199; *Trials of Eight Persons,* 24; Boyer, *Political State,* 37: 152; Roberts, *Four Years Voyages,* 39.

21. "Proceedings of the Court held on the Coast of Africa upon Trying of 100 Pirates taken by his Maj[es]ties Ship *Swallow,*" PRO HCA 1/99 (1722), f. 59; Snelgrave, *Account of the Slave-Trade,* 217; Johnson, *General History,* 213–14.

22. Johnson, *General History,* 139; Hayward, *Remarkable Criminals,* 37; Boyer, *Political State,* 38: 153; Burg, "Legitimacy and Authority," 40–49.

23. Jameson, *Privateering and Piracy,* 294; Johnson, *General History,* 139, 167; Dow and Edmonds, *Pirates of New England,* 217; *Trials of Eight Persons,* 23; Morris, "Ghost of Kidd," 282.

24. Snelgrave, *Account of the Slave-Trade,* 199; Burg, "Legitimacy and Authority," 44–48.

25. Hayward, *Remarkable Criminals,* 37; Johnson, *General History,* 42, 296, 337. Christopher Hill, *The World Turned Upside Down: Radical Ideas during the English Revolution* (New York: Viking Press, 1972).

26. Johnson, *General History,* 423; Lloyd Haynes Williams, *Pirates of Colonial Virginia* (Richmond, Va.: Dietz Press, 1937), 19.

27. Roberts, *Four Years Voyages,* 37, 80; *The Tryals of Major Stede Bonnet, and Other Pirates, Viz. Robert Tucker, Edward Robinson, Neal Paterson [And Others] . . . Who Were All Condemn'd for Piracy. As Also the Tryals of Thomas Nichols, Rowland Sharp, Jonathan Clarke, and Thomas Gerrat, for Piracy, Who Were Acquitted. At the Admiralty Sessions Held at Charlestown, in the Province of South Carolina, on Tuesday the 28th of October, 1718, and by Several Adjournments Continued to Wednesday the 12th of November, Following, to Which is Prefix'd, An Account of the Taking of the Said Major Bonnet, and the Rest of the Pirates* (London: Printed for B. Cowse, 1719), 37; Snelgrave, *Account of the Slave-Trade,* 199–200, 238–39; Boyer, *Political State,* 37: 153; Johnson, *General History,* 213–25; *Trials of Eight Persons,* 24, 25; Great Britain, High Court of Admiralty (Rhode Island), *Tryals of Thirty-six Persons for Piracy, Twenty-eight of Them upon Full Evidence were Found Guilty, and the Rest Acquitted. At a Court of Admiralty for Tryal of Pirates, held at Newport within His Majesties Colony of Rhode-Island and Providence-Plantations in America, on the tenth, eleventh and twelfth days of July, anno Dom. 1723. Pursuant to His Majesties Commission, Founded on an Act of Parliament, Made in the eleventh & twelfth Years of King William the Third, entituled, An act for the More Effectual Suppression of Piracy. And Made Perpetual by an Act of the Sixth of King George* (Boston: Samuel Kneeland, 1723), 9; *Boston News-Letter,* 15–22 July 1717; quotations from Johnson, *General History,* 213; Downing, *Indian Wars,* 99.

28. Boyer, *Political State*, 38: 151; Snelgrave, *Account of the Slave-Trade*, 272; Johnson, *General History*, 138–39, 312. Davis, *English Shipping*, 113, discusses the quite different role of the quartermaster in the merchant service; see also Rediker, *Between the Devil*, 85.

29. Johnson, *General History*, 88–89, 117, 145, 167, 222–25, 292, 595; *Trials of Eight Persons*, 24; Downing, *Indian Wars*, 44, 103; Hill, "Episodes of Piracy," 41–42, 59; Roberts, *Four Years Voyages*, 55, 86; Boyer, *Political State*, 37: 153. Quotation from Betagh, *Voyage*, 148.

30. Johnson, *General History*, 211–12, 307–8, 342–43; Dow and Edmonds, *Pirates of New England*, 146–47; Hayward, *Remarkable Criminals*, 37; *Tryals of Bonnet*, 22; Morris, "Ghost of Kidd," 283.

31. See note 20, this chapter; Gosse, *History of Piracy*, 103; Biddulph, *Pirates of Malabar*, x, 155; "A Narrative of the Singular Sufferings of John Fillmore and Others on Board the Noted Pirate Vessel Commanded by Captain Phillips," Buffalo Historical Society, *Publications*, 10 (1907): 32.

32. Johnson, *General History*, 212, 308, 343; Dow and Edmonds, *Pirates of New England*, 147; pirate Jeremiah Huggins, quoted in Morris, "Ghost of Kidd," 292; Hill, "Episodes of Piracy," 57.

33. Johnson, *General History*, 307, 212, 157–58, 339; see note 4 to this chapter. James F. Shepherd and Gary M. Walton, *Shipping, Maritime Trade and the Economic Development of Colonial North America* (Cambridge: Cambridge University Press, 1972), 201–3, show that for the ports of Jamaica (1729–31), Barbados (1696–98), and Charleston (1735–39), respectively, merchant seamen in vessels over 150 tons handled 8, 6, 10.7, and 12.0 tons of storage per man. Pirates, by more general calculations, handled only 3.1 tons per man; the difference reveals how much more crowded their vessels were.

34. *Tryals of Bonnet*, 30; Johnson, *General History*, 211, 212, 343; Biddulph, *Pirates of Malabar*, 163–64; Rankin, *Golden Age*, 37.

35. Johnson, *General History*, 212, 343; Snelgrave, *Account of the Slave-Trade*, 256; *American Weekly Mercury* (Philadelphia), 30 May–6 June 1723. The discussion of discipline takes into account not only the articles themselves but also observations on actual punishments from other sources.

36. Jameson, *Privateering and Piracy*, 304; *Trials of Eight Persons*, 19, 21; Brock, *Letters of Spotswood*, 249; Johnson, *General History*, 260. Some men, usually those with important skills, were occasionally pressed; see *CPSCS* 33: 365.

37. *Trials of Eight Persons*, 221; Deposition of Samuel Cooper, PRO CO 37/10 (1718), f. 35; Johnson, *General History*, 116, 196, 216, 228; Boyer, *Political State*, 38: 148; Governor of Bermuda quoted in Pringle, *Jolly Roger*, 181; Deposition of Richard Symes, PRO CO 152/14 (1721), f. 33; *American Weekly Mercury*, 17 March 1720; *New-England Courant* (Boston), 25 June–2 July 1722.

38. Dow and Edmonds, *Pirates of New England*, 278; Johnson, *General History*, 225, 313; Lt. Gov. Bennett to Mr. Popple, 31 March 1720, *CPSCS* 37: 19.

39. Hayward, *Remarkable Criminals*, 37; Johnson, *General History*, 226, 342.

40. The total of 3,600 is reached by multiplying the number of ship captains shown

in the figure by the average crew size of 79.5. See Johnson, *General History*, 41–42, 72, 121, 137, 138, 174, 210, 225, 277, 281, 296, 312, 352, 355, 671; *New-England Courant*, 11–18 June 1722; *American Weekly Mercury*, 6–13 July 1721, 5–12 January and 16–23 September 1725; Pringle, *Jolly Roger*, 181, 190, 244; Biddulph, *Pirates of Malabar*, 135, 187; Snelgrave, *Account of the Slave-Trade*, 196–97, 199, 272, 280; Hughson, *Carolina Pirates*, 70; *Boston News-Letter*, 12–19 August 1717, 13–20 October and 10–17 November 1718, 4–11 February 1725, 30 June–7 July 1726; Downing, *Indian Wars*, 51, 101; Morris, "Ghost of Kidd," 282, 283, 296; *Tryals of Bonnet*, iii, 44–45; Dow and Edmonds, *Pirates of New England*, 117, 135, 201, 283, 287; *Trials of Eight Persons*, 23; Jameson, *Privateering and Piracy*, 304, 341; Boyer, *Political State*, 25: 198–99; Hill, "Notes on Piracy," 148, 150; Capt. Matthew Musson to CTP, *CSPCS* 29: 338; ibid., 31: 21, 118; ibid., 33: 274; John F. Watson, *Annals of Philadelphia, and Pennsylvania, in the Olden Time; Being a Collection of Memoirs, Anecdotes, and Incidents of the City and its Inhabitants, and of the Earliest Settlements of the Inland Part of Pennsylvania*, 3 vols. (Philadelphia: E. S. Stuart, 1884–1909), 2: 227; *Boston Gazette*, 27 April–4 May 1724; BL, Add. Mss. 0806, 40812, 40813.

41. Testimony of Thomas Checkley (1717) in Jameson, *Privateering and Piracy*, 304; *Trials of Eight Persons*, 11.

42. Eric J. Hobsbawm, *Primitive Rebels: Studies in Archaic Forms of Social Movement in the 19th and 20th Centuries* (New York: W. W. Norton, 1959), 5, 17, 18, 27, 28; see also his *Bandits* (London: Weidenfeld and Nicolson, and New York: Delacorte Press, 1969), 24–29.

43. *The Tryals of Sixteen Persons for Piracy, &c. Four of which were Found Guilty, and the Rest Acquitted. At a Special Court of Admiralty for the Tryal of Pirates, Held at Boston Within the Province of the Masachusetts-bay in New-England, on Monday the Fourth Day of July, Anno Dom. 1726. Pursuant to His Majesty's Commission, Founded on an Act of Parliament, Made in the Eleventh and Twelfth Years of the Reign of King William the Third, Intitled, An Act for the More Effectual Suppression of Piracy. And Made Perpetual by an Act of the Sixth of King George* (Boston: Joseph Edwards, 1726), 5; *Tryals of Bonnet*, iii, iv; Crook and Rayner, *Newgate Calendar*, 61; Hughson, *Carolina Pirates*, 121; Rankin, *Golden Age*, 28; Johnson, *General History*, 116, 342; Downing, *Indian Wars*, 98. An analysis of the names of forty-four pirate ships reveals the following patterns: eight (18.2 percent) made reference to revenge; seven (15.9 percent) were named *Ranger* or *Rover*, suggesting mobility and perhaps, as discussed subsequently, a watchfulness over the way captains treated their sailors; five (11.4 percent) referred to royalty. It is noteworthy that only two names referred to wealth. Other names indicated that places *(Lancaster)*, unidentifiable people *(Mary Anne)*, and animals *(Black Robin)* constituted less significant themes. Two names, *Batchelor's Delight* and *Batchelor's Adventure*, tend to support the probability (note 16, this chapter) that most pirates were unmarried; see Johnson, *General History*, 220, 313; Virginia, *Calendar of Virginia State Papers and other Manuscripts, 1652–1869 Preserved in the Capitol at Richmond*, ed. William Pitt Palmer, 11 vols. (Richmond: 1875–93), 1: 194, and *CSPCS* 30: 263.

44. Betagh, *Voyage*, 41.

45. Petition of Randolph, Cane, and Halladay (1722) in *Calendar of Virginia State Papers*, 202.

46. "Proceedings of the Court held on the Coast of Africa," PRO HCA 1/99 (1722), f. 101; Johnson, *General History*, 338, 582; Snelgrave, *Account of the Slave-Trade*, 212, 225; Dow and Edmonds, *Pirates of New England*, 301; *Voyages and Travels of Captain Nathaniel Uring*, xxviii. See Rediker, *Between the Devil*, 217 n. 27.

47. Hawkins in Boyer, *Political State*, 38: 149–50; Johnson, *General History*, 352–53; Dow and Edmonds, *Pirates of New England*, 278; Betagh, *Voyage*, 26. This torture may have exploited that meaning of the verb "to sweat," which was to drive hard, to overwork. The construction of a literally vicious circle here seems hardly coincidental. See *Oxford English Dictionary*, s.v. "sweat"; *Tryals of Sixteen Persons*, 14. Knowledge of this ritualized violence was evidently widespread. In 1722, Bristol merchants informed Parliament that pirates "study how to torture"; see Stock, *Proceedings and Debates of Parliaments*, 453. Torture was also applied to captains who refused to reveal the whereabouts of their loot. It seems that Spanish captains received especially harsh treatment.

48. Crook and Rayner, *Newgate Calendar*, 59; Boyer, *Political State*, 32: 272; *Boston Gazette*, 24–31 October 1720; Rankin, *Golden Age*, 35, 135, 148; Cotton Mather, *The Vial Poured Out upon the Sea. A Remarkable Relation of Certain Pirates Brought unto a Tragical and Untimely End. Some Conferences with Them, after their Condemnation. Their Behaviour at their Execution. And a Sermon Preached on that Occasion* (Boston: N. Belknap, 1726), 227, quotation from *Boston Gazette*, 21–28 March 1726. It should be stressed that Lyne's bloodletting was exceptional.

49. *Boston News-Letter*, 14–21 November 1720.

50. Snelgrave, *Account of the Slave-Trade*, 196, 199. This is a marvelous work written by an intelligent and perceptive man of long experience at sea. The book mainly concerns the slave trade, was addressed to the merchants of London, and apparently was not intended as popular reading.

51. Ibid., 202–8.

52. Ibid., 212, 225. Piracy was perceived by many as an activity akin to war. See also Johnson, *General History*, 168, 319. Francis R. Stark, *The Abolition of Privateering and the Declaration of Paris* (New York: Columbia University Press, 1897), 14, 13, 22, claims that war in the seventeenth and early eighteenth centuries was understood more in terms of "individual enmity" than national struggle. Victors had "absolute right over (1) hostile persons and (2) hostile property." This might partially explain pirates' violence and destructiveness. Rankin, *Golden Age*, 146, correctly observes that "as more pirates were captured and hanged, the greater cruelty was practiced by those who were still alive."

53. Snelgrave, *Account of the Slave-Trade*, 241. For other examples of giving cargo to ship captains and treating them "civilly," see Deposition of Robert Dunn, PRO CO 152/13 (1720), f. 26; Deposition of Richard Symes, PRO CO 152/14 (1721), f. 33; Biddulph, *Pirates of Malabar*, 139; Brock, *Letters of Spotswood*, 339–43; *Boston Gazette*, 21 August 1721; Hill, "Episodes of Piracy," 57; Morris, "Ghost of Kidd," 283; Elizabeth Donnan, ed., *Documents Illustrative of the History of the Slave Trade*

to America, 4 vols. (Washington, D.C.: Carnegie Institution of Washington, 1930–35), 4: 96; *Tryals of Bonnet,* 13; Boyer, *Political State,* 27: 616; Deposition of Henry Bostock, *CSPCS* 30: 150–51; *Boston News-Letter,* 14–21 November 1720; and Spotswood to Craggs: "it is a common practice with those Rovers upon the pillageing of a Ship to make presents of other Commodity's to such Masters as they take a fancy to in Lieu of that they have plundered them of": PRO CO 5/1319, 20 May 1720.

54. Snelgrave, *Account of the Slave-Trade,* 241, 242, 243.

55. Ibid., 275, 276, 284.

56. Johnson, *General History,* 351; Jameson, *Privateering and Piracy,* 341.

57. Mather, *Vial Poured Out,* 21, 48; Boyer, *Political State,* 32: 272; Benjamin Colman, *It is a Fearful Thing to Fall Into the Hands of the Living God. A Sermon Preached to Some Miserable Pirates July 10. 1726. On the Lord's Day, Before Their Execution. By Benjamin Colman, Pastor of a Church in Boston. To Which is Added Some Account of Said Pirates* (Boston: John Phillips and Thomas Hancock, 1726), 39.

58. *Tryals of Bonnet,* 2, 4, 3, 34. See also Hughson, *Carolina Pirates,* 5; Johnson, *General History,* 264, 377–79; Dow and Edmonds, *Pirates of New England,* 297; Brock, *Letters of Spotswood,* 339.

59. Boyer, *Political State,* 24: 194; 34: 295; 35: 662; Johnson, *General History,* 79; *CPSCS* 32: 168; Hill, "Episodes of Piracy," 39; *American Weekly Mercury,* 13–20 July 1721.

60. *American Weekly Mercury,* 17 March 1720; Brock, *Letters of Spotswood,* 338. For other cases of hanging in chains, see *Letters of Spotswood,* 342; Jameson, *Privateering and Piracy,* 344; *Tryals of Sixteen Persons,* 19; Johnson, *General History,* 151; *Boston Gazette,* 27 August–3 September 1722; Boyer, *Political State,* 24: 201; and Gov. Hart to CTP, *CSPCS,* 33: 275. For an analysis of this type of terror, see Michel Foucault, *Discipline and Punish: The Birth of the Prison,* trans. Alan Sheridan (New York: Pantheon Books, 1977), chapter 2.

61. Deposition of Henry Bostock, PRO CO 152/12 (1717); Snelgrave, *Account of the Slave-Trade,* 253; Johnson, *General History,* 217; Spotswood to Board of Trade, PRO CO 5/1318, 31 May 1717; Jameson, *Privateering and Piracy,* 315.

62. Deposition of Edward North, PRO CO 37/10 (1718).

63. *Tryals of Bonnet,* 8.

64. Snelgrave, *Account of the Slave-Trade,* 199; Johnson, *General History,* 138, 174; Morris, "Ghost of Kidd," 282.

65. James Craggs to CTP, *CSPCS* 31: 10; Board of Trade to J. Methuen, PRO CO 23/12, 3 September 1716; Johnson, *General History,* 315, 582; Downing, *Indian Wars,* 98, 104–5; *Voyages and Travels of Captain Nathaniel Uring,* 241; Shelvocke, *Voyage,* 242; Virginia, Council, *Executive Journals of the Council of Colonial Virginia,* ed. H. R. McIlwaine (Richmond: Davis Bottom, 1925–), 3: 612; Dow and Edmonds, *Pirates of New England,* 341; Deposition of R. Lazenby in Hill, "Episodes of Piracy," 60; "Voyage to Guinea, Antego, Bay of Campeachy, Cuba, Barbadoes, &c, 1714–1723," BL, Add. Ms. 39946.

66. *Boston News-Letter,* 15–22 August 1720; *American Weekly Mercury,* 6–13 September 1722.

67. Trial of Thomas Davis (1717) in Jameson, *Privateering and Piracy,* 308; *Boston News-Letter,* 4–11 November 1717.

68. *Tryals of Bonnet,* 45.

69. Lt. Gov. Benjamin Bennet to CTP, *CSPCS* 30: 263; *Tryals of Bonnet,* 29, 50; Johnson, *General History,* 195.

70. Gov. Walter Hamilton to CTP, *CSPCS* 32: 165; *American Weekly Mercury,* 27 October 1720; *Boston Gazette,* 24–31 October 1720.

71. Spotswood to CTP, *CSPCS* 32: 328.

72. Council Meeting of 3 May 1721, *Council of Colonial Virginia,* 542; abstract of Spotswood to Board of Trade, PRO CO 5/1370, 11 June 1722; Spotswood to Board of Trade, PRO CO 5/1319, 31 May 1721.

73. Dow and Edmonds, *Pirates of New England,* 281–82; Johnson, *General History,* 355; *American Weekly Mercury,* 21–28 May 1724.

74. Hope to CTP, PRO CO 37/11, 14 January 1724, f. 37. See also Treasury Warrant to Capt. Knott, PRO T52/32 10 August 1722), Captain Luke Knott, after turning over eight pirates to authorities, prayed relief for "his being obliged to quit the Merchant Service, the Pirates threatning to Torture him to death if ever he should fall into their hands." Robert Walpole personally awarded Knott £230 for the loss of his career.

75. Barnard, *Ashton's Memorial,* 2, 4; emphasis added. Perhaps this was what M. A. K. Halliday has called an antilanguage. This is "the acting out of a distinct social structure [in speech]; and this social structure is, in turn, the bearer of an alternative social reality." An antilanguage exists in "the context of resocialization." See his "Anti-Languages," *American Anthropologist* 78 (1976): 570–84, reference here to 572, 575.

76. Smith, *New Voyage,* 42–43. See also Morris, "Ghost of Kidd," 286.

77. Anthropologist Raymond Firth argues that flags function as instruments of both power and sentiment, creating solidarity and symbolizing unity. See Raymond William Firth, *Symbols: Public and Private* (Ithaca, N.Y.: Cornell University Press, 1973), 328, 339; Hill, "Notes on Piracy," 147. For particular pirate crews known to have sailed under the Jolly Roger, see *Boston Gazette,* 29 November–6 December 1725 (Lyne); *Boston News-Letter,* 10–17 September 1716 (Jennings? Leslie?); ibid., 12–19 August 1717 (Napin, Nichols); ibid., 2–9 March 1719 (Thompson); ibid., 28 May–4 June 1724 (Phillips); ibid., 5–8 June 1721 (Rackam?); Jameson, *Privateering and Piracy,* 317 (Roberts); *Tryals of Sixteen Persons,* 5 (Fly); Snelgrave, *Account of the Slave-Trade,* 199 (Cocklyn, LaBouche, Davis); *Trials of Eight Persons,* 24 (Bellamy); Hughson, *Carolina Pirates,* 113 (Moody); *Tryals of Bonnet,* 44–45 (Bonnet, Teach, Richards); Dow and Edmonds, *Pirates of New England,* 208 (Harris), 213 (Low); Boyer, *Political State,* 28:152 (Spriggs); Biddulph, *Pirates of Malabar,* 135 (Taylor); Donnan, *Documents of the Slave Trade,* 96 (England); and Johnson, *General History,* 240–41 (Skyrm), 67–68 (Martel), 144 (Vane), 371 (captain unknown), 628 (Macarty, Bunce), 299 (Worley). Royal officials affirmed and attempted to reroute the power of this symbolism by raising the Jolly Roger on the gallows when hanging pirates. See Johnson, *General History,* 658; *New-England Courant,* 22 July 1723; and *Boston News-Letter,* 28 May–4 June 1724. The symbols were commonly used in the grave-

stone art of this period and did not originate with piracy. The argument here is that new meanings, derived from maritime experience, were attached to them.

78. Boyer, *Political State,* 28: 152. Pirates also occasionally used red or "bloody" flags.

79. Ibid.

80. Hill, "Episodes of Piracy," 37.

81. Ibid.; Snelgrave, *Account of the Slave-Trade,* 236.

82. See note 42 of this chapter.

83. Johnson, *General History,* 28, 43, 159, 244, 285, 628, 656, 660; Hayward, *Remarkable Criminals,* 39; Rankin, *Golden Age,* 155; Mather, *Vial Poured Out,* 47; Jameson, *Privateering and Piracy,* 341; Lt. Gen. Mathew to Gov. Hamilton, *CSPCS* 32: 167; Bartholomew Roberts, the pirate, to Lt. Gen. Mathew, ibid., 169.

84. Gov. Hamilton to CTP, *CSPCS* 32: 165.

85. Boyer, *Political State,* 28: 153. For similar vows and actual attempts, see *Tryals of Bonnet,* 18; Johnson, *General History,* 143, 241, 245, 298, 317; *CSPCS* 32: 168; Dow and Edmonds, *Pirates of New England,* 239, 292; Watson, *Annals of Philadelphia,* 227; Hayward, *Remarkable Criminals,* 296–97; Atkins, *Voyage,* 12; Jameson, *Privateering and Piracy,* 315; Arthur L. Cooke, "British Newspaper Accounts of Blackbeard's Death," *Virginia Magazine of History and Biography* 56 (1953): 305–6; *American Weekly Mercury,* 16–23 June 1720; *Tryals of Thirty-Six Persons,* 9; Spotswood to Board of Trade, PRO CO 5/1318, 22 December 1718.

86. Cotton Mather, *Instructions to the Living, From the Condition of the Dead. A Brief Relation of Remarkables in the Shipwreck of Above One Hundred Pirates, Who Were Cast Away in the Ship Whido, on the Coast of New-England, April 26. 1717. And in the Death of Six, Who After A Fair Trial At Boston, Were Convicted & Condemned, Octob. 22. And Executed, Novemb. 15. 1717. With Some Account of the Discourse Had with Them on the Way to Their Execution. And A Sermon Preached on Their Occasion* (Boston: 1717), 4; meeting of 1 April 1717, in Great Britain, Board of Trade, *Journal of the Commissioners for Trade and Plantations . . . Preserved in the Public Record Office,* 4 vols. (London: H.M. Stationery Office, 1920–24), 3: 359.

87. Johnson, *General History,* 7.

88. Virginia Merchants to Admiralty, PRO CO 389/42 (1713).

89. Lloyd, *British Seaman,* 287, Table 3.

90. Jameson, *Privateering and Piracy,* 291; Pringle, *Jolly Roger,* 95; Lydon, *Pirates, Privateers, and Profits,* 17–20; Rankin, *Golden Age,* 23; Nellis Maynard Crouse, *The French Struggle for the West Indies, 1665–1713* (New York: Columbia University Press, 1943), 310.

91. Davis, *English Shipping,* 136–37; see also Rediker, *Between the Devil,* Appendix C.

92. Davis, *English Shipping,* 27.

93. Ibid., 154.

94. Lloyd, *British Seaman,* 287, Table 3; Davis, *English Shipping,* 27, 31.

95. Davis, *English Shipping,* 136–37; Rediker, "Society and Culture," 318–28. See also Rediker, *Between the Devil,* Appendix C.

96. Pringle, *Jolly Roger,* 266–67; Violet Barbour, "Privateers and Pirates of the West Indies," *American Historical Review* 16 (1910–11): 529–66, reference here to 566; Boyer, *Political State,* 28: 152; Hayward, *Remarkable Criminals,* 37; "A Scheme for Stationing Men of War in the West Indies for better Securing the Trade there from Pirates," PRO CO 323/8 (1723); *Boston News-Letter,* 7–14 July 1726. Gary M. Walton, "Sources of Productivity Change in American Colonial Shipping, 1675–1775," *Economic History Review* 2d Series 20 (1967): 67–78, reference here to 77, notes that the economic uncertainty occasioned by piracy declined after 1725. See chapter 1 of Rediker, *Between the Devil.*

97. See "An Act for the More Effectual Suppressing of Piracy" (8 George I, c. 24, 1721), in Sir Thomas Parker, *The Laws of Shipping and Insurance, with a Digest of Adjudged Cases* (London: 1775), republished in *British Maritime Cases, 1648–1871,* 36 vols. (Abingdon: Professional Books, 1978), 24. 94–95. If the population range discussed previously is accurate, about one pirate in thirteen died on the gallows, which would have represented a vastly higher ratio than in any other period of piracy.

98. E. P. Thompson, "The Moral Economy of the English Crowd in the Eighteenth Century," *Past and Present* 50 (1971): 76–136.

99. Hayward, *Remarkable Criminals,* 37. See also Hill, *The World Turned Upside Down.*

100. William McFee, *The Law of the Sea* (Philadelphia: Lippincott, 1950), 50, 54, 59, 72.

101. Barnaby Slush, *The Navy Royal: Or a Sea-cook Turn'd Projector. Containing a Few Thoughts, About Manning Our Ships of War with the Best of Sailors, Without Violences, and in the Most Pleasing Manner* (London: printed for B. Bragge, 1709), viii.

Chapter 9

Outlaws at Sea, 1660–1720
Liberty, Equality, and Fraternity among the Caribbean Freebooters

J. S. Bromley

Two societies, two conceptions of justice, collaborated and collided when French forces stormed Cartagena of the Indies in May 1697. For their commander, the Baron de Pointis, a naval captain in the mold of Drake, this bloody if strategically pointless success fulfilled a long-postponed design "that might be both honourable and advantageous," with ships lent and soldiers (but not seamen) paid by the King. He in return would take the Crown's usual one-fifth interest in such "prêts de vaisseaux," the remaining costs falling on private subscribers, in this case no less than 666 of them, headed by courtiers, financiers, naval contractors and officers of both pen and sword.[1] According to Pointis, peace rumors restricted the flow of advances and the expedition, nearly 4,000 strong when it sailed out of Brest, was weaker than he had planned, especially if it should prove difficult to use the ships' crews ashore. At St. Domingue, however, the experienced governor Jean Ducasse, who had risen by his own business abilities from relatively humble origins in Béarn, had orders to place another thousand men at the baron's disposal, in locally armed frigates and sloops. Some of these seasoned warriors were garrison soldiers, others militiamen and small settlers; there were also 180 negroes, some free and others lent by their owners with a promise of manumission if the enterprise went well. But the majority, at least 650 and probably more, were *flibustiers*, freebooters whom Ducasse had called from the sea and detained for months pending the late arrival of the squadron. With their long, light muskets known as *boucaniers*—from their original use by those earlier huntsmen who smoke-dried their meat *(boucane)* Indian fashion—these were crack marksmen, well able to board ships or Spanish trenches, if not ramparts, with little use for artillery.

According to the careful historian, Fr Charlevoix, who had access to government records as well as to the manuscripts of a fellow Jesuit, Le Pers, who was serving on the coast of St. Domingue at the time, Ducasse's contingent, amounting in the end to more than a fifth of the whole force, acquitted themselves with their usual audacity and resourcefulness.[2] Even Pointis, in his *Relation,* praised the negroes. The *flibustiers,* however, were "a troop of *Banditti* . . . idle Spectators of a great Action . . . this Rabble . . . that base Kind of Life," gifted only with "a particular Talent at discovering hidden Treasures." He had resented having "to court them in the most flattering Terms." They, in their turn, were quick to object to "le bâton haut" of naval officers, as happened again when Le Moyne d'Iberville brought his last privateering armament to Martinique in 1706.[3] It was because they would serve immediately only under a man they knew, preferably one whom they had elected, that Governor Ducasse himself joined the expedition. Even so, they would have sulked in the woods had he not obtained from Pointis some prior agreement about sharing the plunder. A notice was accordingly posted at Petit Goave—by this date as much the principal privateering base of the Coast as the island of Tortuga had been in the earlier decades of "la flibuste"— announcing simply that the St. Domingue contingent would participate "homme par homme" with the crews of His Majesty's ships.

Ducasse took this vague undertaking to mean that his men would share in the booty in the same proportion as their numbers bore to those from France. Pointis, mindful of the claims of his shareholders but entirely overlooking the modest investors of the Coast, allowed this assumption to rest until he was ready to embark the booty, provisionally estimated at not more than nine million in *livres tournois.* Ducasse and his followers, who had not been allowed into the countinghouse where the gold and silver and precious stones had been collected, suspected that it would add up to twice as much; in any case, they expected over two million for themselves. Word came back, for the two leaders were no longer on speaking terms, that they were entitled to 160,000 *livres tournois* in silver crowns or pieces of eight as their proper proportion of what was due to the French crews—a tenth of the first million and a mere thirtieth of the rest. This worked out at twenty-five crowns a man instead of an anticipated 1,500 or 1,600, including three months' wages. The freebooters' answer was to return to the city, against the appeals of Ducasse, and sack it all over again. They came away with enough precious metal to distribute a thousand crowns to each man by weight, as their custom was, before sailing, but also with fabrics and other merchandise which they would later have parted with for much less than they were worth. Four of their larger ships were soon intercepted by the British navy, the cargo of the *Cerf Volant* allegedly being sold in Jamaica for £100,000.[4]

The quarrel between Pointis and Ducasse reverberated for years. A royal *arrêt* awarded the *flibustiers* something near 17 percent of the ultimate net sum available for distribution, but it was remitted to St. Domingue in goods, piecemeal, and much of this "masse de Cartagennes" never reached its intended destination, partly because it passed through dishonest hands but also because many of the tropical claimants had dispersed or died.[5] It was precisely the flight of its warriors that every good governor of St. Domingue, thinly populated and exposed to attack from many quarters, most feared; and Ducasse too had a substantial personal stake in the *masse* or stock out of which the tropical investors should recover their outlay. Nevertheless, the "perfidy" of Pointis rankled most in that he had caused the governor to break faith with his prickly following.[6] He had already experienced their stubborn refusal to go to sea whenever they had money to spend, and their strong preference for the occasional Spanish prize over regular cruising against the English or Dutch, as distinct from tip-and-run descents on Jamaica for slaves. Moreover, they were still grumbling that they had not received justice after Ducasse's own attack on Jamaica in 1694. Beeston, governor of Jamaica, referred to this when reporting the state of mutiny which preceded the departure for Cartagena—"they to fight and the great only to take away the money from them."[7]

This feeling about "the great" marks the whole history of seventeenth-century privateering in the West Indies, and indeed finds echoes among the pirates, properly so called, documented by Defoe. "They were poor rogues," said some, of those hung up at Cape Coast in 1722, "and so hanged, while others, no less guilty in other way, escaped."[8] The resentments of pirates, generally recruited from merchantmen, were most specifically directed at the despotism of shipmasters: after seizing a ship, Captain Johnson tells us, "the Pirates began to take upon themselves the distribution of justice, examining the men concerning their master's usage of them, according to the custom of other Pirates."[9] On privateers, impeccably commissioned by a sovereign prince, a kind of class consciousness revolted against the larger shares of prize and plunder allotted to the officers, often numerous because crews were not under naval discipline; and there was sometimes distrust of the owners as well. Although usually entitled in France and Britain to two-thirds of the net takings, there was no rule about this and it looks as if such gentlemen adventurers came to be contented with half at a later date. The well-known cruises of Woodes Rogers and George Shelvocke into the Pacific, respectively in 1708–11 and 1719–22, provide rich evidence of both attitudes, and are especially relevant here because they carried old campaigners from "the Jamaica [buccaneering] discipline." They evidently drew on what William Dampier, himself a buccaneer from 1679 to 1688 and chief pilot to Rogers, calls "the Law of Privateers," meaning in effect what in St. Domingue was known as "the Custom of the Coast"—a corpus of practices which also left a strong mark on those of the common pirates, many of whom originated in the Caribbean after the proclamations of peace in 1697 and 1713, and sometimes while formal hostilities continued between their princes.

Shelvocke's account largely consists of his encounters with mutineers. Their first petition, moderately worded by comparison with what was to come, he described as "needless tautologies, insignificant expressions, and dull confusion." It referred to the treatment of Rogers's two crews, who carried their "Case" against the Bristol owners to the House of Lords, though in vain.[10] The agreements Shelvocke had to make at sea defining and dividing plunder— those articles in a prize to which the captors had sole claim, such as the personal possessions of prisoners— follow almost word for word those made by Woodes Rogers and his fellow captain, Stephen Courtney, whose grand stroke was to surrender "the whole Cabin-Plunder," that is, the contents of "the Great Cabbins" of captured shipmasters and often therefore the best of the pillage. Their object was to prevent both indiscriminate plunder and its concealment by securing every man's interest. To do so they had to extend their definition well outside the limits (all above deck, roughly) recognized in European courts and eventually to shut their eyes to the embezzlement of "Arms, Chests, Knives, Roman Relicks, Scizzars, Tobacco, loose Books, Pictures, and worthless Tools and Toys, and Bedding in use." Shelvocke's chief enemy, William Betagh, his captain of marines, wanted to go much further—"to oppose the owners having a part of any thing but what was upon freight, or mentioned in bills of lading."[11]

Cheating the owners by excessive pillage was inherent in privateering. Thanks to "riflinge," Elizabethan "owners and victuallers" may have received less than half the value of their prizes, instead of the nominal two-thirds; and the *armateurs* of Louis XIV's numerous corsairs never ceased to complain of pillage, and of the laxity of the courts in repressing it. Temptation mounted when wages were substituted for shares, for then a ship's company was entitled in France only to a tenth of the prize money in place of a third, the same as in the navy. The naval bureaucracy preferred wages ("à la solde") to shares ("à la part") in privateers, because of the tricks and delays for which the directors of armaments were notorious; but "à la part" remained the prevailing system at Dunkirk and St. Malo, if not in Provence.

Rogers's "undertakers" neatly combined wages and shares, wages halving a man's share whatever his rank. There was no universal method and no uniform tariff of shares, though Trinity House had long ago tried to establish one.[12] At St. Malo the company's portion was distributed by a panel of ship's officers in the light of performance, but at Calais and probably Dunkirk shares were allotted before sailing as was the English practice, where all depended on the negotiating strength of owners, officers, and seamen in each case. Thus Woodes Rogers was to enjoy twenty-four shares in his company's third, the master and surgeon ten each, and so on down the scale to the sailor at two and a half and the landman at one and a half. Exactly the same subdivision was observed in their agreements about plunder. Rogers exchanged his "Cabin Plunder" for an extra 5 percent on his shares. These were high in proportion to the sailor's; at Calais, for example, a captain got only four or six times the "lot" of a *matelot*.[13] But Rogers, who was about to cruise for as many years as a small Calais corsair, would be away for months; the investment, risks, and objectives were in no way comparable. Nevertheless, his company alleged that the officers "could not possibly in a Privateer deserve what they were allow'd in proportion to the rest." Shelvocke's boatswain called them all "*Blood-suckers.*" The *syndic* of St. Malo implied as much of some of his own captains.[14] That Shelvocke was on the British navy's half-pay list would not have worked in his favor either. Naval officers were notoriously avaricious about prize money, which engendered constant friction between them. One who knew them well told King William in 1699 that some commanders kept their men out of their money for years, "until not a man concerned was to be found," while James Vernon, a secretary of state and prize commissioner, considered that this particular fraud contributed to desertion and piracy.[15]

Although their codes of punishment were wide apart, harsh treatment in navy and merchant navy alike fed these animosities. In the latter, however, arbitrary and even savage conduct by a master was less likely to be corrected by other officers or the employer. There was a great gulf between shipmasters, in terms of their powers and responsibilities and prospects, and even their first mates. The powers and responsibilities were as old as the Laws of Wisby and Oléron, themselves only compilations of earlier decisions or customs; masters were responsible to their owners for the offenses of their crews, a member of whom had little right to defend himself against the boss's physical blows, while any refusal of duty might forfeit all title to wages. Once he had signed articles, a seaman's life was no longer his own. Meanwhile, the privileges and social position of masters had gone forward by leaps and bounds, at least in England. In the late seventeenth century a body of attorneys is said to have lived on encouraging seamen's claims against them.[16]

It is essential to keep this background in mind if we are to understand the originality of the Caribbean freebooters in dealing with plunder, and indeed freebooting itself. However, it would be wholly erroneous to suppose that "*flibustier*," alias "buccaneer," necessarily implies a seaman. This "fanciful kind of inversion" itself implies that the English were confused by the interchangeability of *flibustier* and *boucanier,* who in the opinion of James Burney, still the best of their English historians, "are to be considered as the same character, exercising sometimes one, sometimes the other employ-ment."[17] Charlevoix, steeped in the "société des ordres," distinguished func-tions rather than men in describing them as separate "corps," as he did also the settlers *(habitants)* and their indentured white servants *(engagés)* in that "République des Aventuriers" which preceded royal government in St. Domingue and long lived side by side with it. It was all a matter of less or more, the *gens du métier* (without fixed property unless or until they settled down, as some did) and the part-timers, who might also be settlers or traders rather than huntsmen—a dying profession long before 1700.[18]

What *flibustier* and *boucanier* most obviously had in common was their ac-curacy with small arms, the principal weapon of the privateering *barques* or sloops, which called for the minimum of seamanship. Fr Labat, who some-times sailed with them and counted some of their captains among his friends, attributes their preference for a simple sail-rig to a dislike of work in the first place; Pointis's sailors were "nègres blancs" to them.[19] In any case, "roving on the account" included land operations, all the way from Trinidad to Campeche and ultimately the Spanish Pacific coasts as well. Sir Henry Mor-gan's ransom of Panama in 1671, to recall only the most famous of these episodes, was the reward of sound military tactics as well as tough marching by a miscellaneous Anglo-French force which knew how to draw itself up "in the form of a tertia"; in Cuba earlier, says Esquemelin, "the Pirates marched in very good rank and file, at the sound of their drums and with flying colours."[20] Their standard method of levying contributions from coastal vil-lages, under threat of burning, is reminiscent of the Thirty Years War. In Dampier's and other contemporary narratives there is mention of "the for-lorn," the European soldiers' term for the advance guard, also known among the freebooters as the "enfants perdus."[21] Their habit of assuming *noms de guerre* was also common with those impoverished noblemen and others who made a profession of war in mercenary armies; and we know that privateering captains from Europe could often be described, like Nathaniel Butler of the Old Providence Company, as "an ancient soldier at sea and land."[22]

Even more evocative of the European military background, ignored by our buccaneering historians, was the role assigned to the quartermaster, the sec-ond man to the freebooter captain and elected like him, but more especially entrusted with the interests of "les garçons," above all in the distribution of booty, "une espèce de procureur pernicieux qui règle leurs comptes," as an un-kind planter official put it. This "trustee for the whole," as Defoe described him, enjoyed the chief authority also on pirate vessels, except in chase or ac-tion: among the Caribbean privateersmen, "his opinion is like the Mufti's among the Turks."[23] Such a magistracy can have had little to do with the hum-ble role of quartermasters at sea, who were petty officers ranking only a shade above the ordinary seaman. This fact may well have rendered his title agreeable, and it is true that seagoing quartermasters took charge of boats during disembarkations; but, as an infallible sign of "the Jamaica discipline," he resembled those officers who saw to the billetting, feeding, clothing, and accounts of a body of troops, once known as harbingers, highly respectable and well enough remunerated for their duties to be worth the attention of commissioned officers.[24]

Freebooters—a "softer" word than "pirates" and not yet common robbers—got their name from an old tradition of soldiers serving for booty only, like those privateersmen who signed "on the old pleasing account of no purchase no pay [*à la part*]."[25] Even after 1700, while pay mutinies remained "so endemic that they were almost condoned" in Europe, "plentiful campaigns" meant good plunder.[26] The prospect of loot was a friend to the recruiting sergeant, conjuring up that dream of sudden wealth which was also a powerful if illusory inducement to many a West Indian immigrant, thanks to travelers' tales and the eloquence of those who traded in indentured servants. To illustrate the lure of pillage to officers as well as men, we need look no further than the restlessness of the land forces engaged in Cromwell's Western Design when it was at first proposed to "dispose of all Preys and Booties . . . towards the carrying on of the present Service," many officers, on the contrary, "coming in hopes of Pillage into a country where they conceiv'd Gold as plentiful as Stones." Venables and Perm wished to meet this pressure, in effect, in much the same way as the *flibustiers* managed their booty, by throwing all into a common stock, with fierce penalties on concealment and a view to distribution "according to every Mans quality and Merit." There was no reference to special recompense for the loss of limbs or eyes, characteristic of privateering and piratical charter parties, but the generals referred to David's military law (1st Sam. xxx. 24) "to give equal share to every person of the Army though not present in the Action."[27] Whether or not Levelling teachings came to the West Indies in 1655, we can be certain that the civil war experience abundantly did—and Irish experience long before that, especially through its victims. So, too, through Dutch and French, the pitiless, *sauve-qui-peut* mentality of the long Continental strife, as we see it through the eyes of *Simplicissimus*. Whether any significant number of our Caribbean freebooters had endured the tyranny and rapacity of military commanders there is no means of telling, but in nothing were these "pay-grabbers" and "military enterprisers" more distrusted than in the sharing of loot. What is of even more interest for present purposes, military workforces showed talent in organizing their mutinies, under elected leaders—the *Ambosat* or *electo* of the sixteenth century.[28]

We shall never know the individual buccaneer, not even most of the captains, with anything like the intimacy which the devotion of George Rudé has

recovered for participants in urban riots, or even as well as we know the leading figures in Warwick's and Pym's Old Providence Company. This is because
buccaneering proper, unlike the long history of earlier privateering and armed
trade in the Caribbean, was by definition locally based and early West Indian
records are scarce. It is conventionally dated from about 1640, from the use of
Tortuga, with its comfortable anchorage and strong natural defenses, by
bands of rovers from the recently settled British and French islands in the
outer chain of the Antilles, as distinct from earlier occupation by the *boucaniers* who hunted hogs and cattle for barter with vessels from Normandy,
which frequented those parts well before 1600.[29] Under the suggestive name
of Association Island, Tortuga had also been briefly taken over by the Old
Providence Company in the 1630s. There is no need to recapitulate the early
vicissitudes of this privateering nursery, except to stress the brutality of Spanish attempts to expel the intruders. Like the harsh treatment of prisoners
later—though these were more usually treated as convicts than pirates—it was
enough to feed the flames of hispanophobia, so harsh a characteristic of some
of the earlier *flibustiers* as to afford their marauding an ideology of sorts.

Tortuga, alternately dominated by French and English leaders, always
elected but sometimes tyrannical, until formally adopted by the French Crown
in 1657, received several increments of Huguenots, beginning with the fall of
La Rochelle: St. Domingue itself, with its English and especially Dutch elements, offered them a more attractive asylum than the more strictly governed
Martinique.[30] Whether Montbars of Languedoc, soaked in Las Casas, or the
merciless l'Olonnais (of Sables) were of Protestant origin is unproven, but two
other leaders particularly feared by the Spaniards, Roche Brasiliano and Laurens de Graaf, were Dutchmen. Calvinism, it is true, did not flourish in the
West Indies, as the example of Providence Island (Santa Catalina) showed, and
such traces of religion as we find among the *flibustiers* were Roman: Ravenau
de Lussan, referring to one of the many discords which marred their collaboration with the British in the South Sea (after 1680), expresses shock at the
iconoclasm of the buccaneers, who were yet capable of sabbath observance
"by command and common consent" under Captains Sawkins and Watling.
Ravenau, a Parisian and an example of the gentleman adventurer in debt, was
shrewd enough to see that Creole hatred of impiety rubbed off on French
Catholics.[31] Walking off with the altar candlesticks, on the contrary, was necessary—"la bonne guerre"—and we are not obliged to believe Labat's assertion that the Martinique privateers always donated captured church orna-
ments to sacred uses.[32] Spanish churches were also regularly used as the *corps
de garde* for prisoners and pillage, apart from the intrinsic value of their contents. The aggressors had their own share of superstition, however, and there
were good and able men among them, like the incomparable Dampier and his
"ingenious Friend Mr Ringrose."[33]

If the ideological bitterness of the sixteenth century was receding, it is hardly credible that the freebooters could have acted so fiercely toward Spanish Creole civilians without the moral self-righteousness conferred, in their turn, by Spanish atrocities and intolerance, real or mythical. It was still what the Elizabethans called a war of reprisals: "our Men," wrote Dampier, "were very squeamish of plundering without Licence," even if it meant getting one from an Asian prince in the faraway Philippines. This was in 1686, several years after the supply of French or Portuguese commissions had dried up.[34]

In the violent, mobile West Indian scene the freebooters necessarily suffered heavy casualties. Losses were particularly heavy following the grand exodus to the Pacific in the 1680s, so much so as to create anxiety for the security of Jamaica and St. Domingue when the islands were divided by the Nine Years War. Yet, so long as Spain was the enemy, their forces soon built up again. Ducasse once remarked that the *flibuste* renewed itself every ten years.[35] A reliable analysis of 1706, admittedly from Martinique, which succeeded where St. Domingue failed in organizing a prosperous cruising war against English and Dutch, breaks it down into three human elements: a sprinkling of young men from the best families; impoverished settlers "et des engagés qui ne veulent point s'assujetir au travail de la terre"; and ("la plus forte de la flibuste") deserters from merchantmen, hiding behind their *noms de guerre*.[36] Sailors from Europe, however, needed time to become acclimatized and there is evidence that they did not take to the staple diet of the freebooters, manioc. Morgan in 1680, when he had turned King's evidence, told London that buccaneering tempted "white servants and all men of unfortunate and desperate condition."[37] Pointis saw them as seamen deserters or else vagabonds sent out to work in the plantations: "at the End of the Term of Servitude, some Body lends them a Gun, and to Sea they go a Buccaniering."[38] As an excellent intendant of Martinique pointed out, the *engagé*, though he served shorter articles than his British counterpart, usually wanted to go home after eighteen months: the habit of hard work had to be acquired, and there were also bad masters who underfed them and worked them beyond their strength.[39] The blacks were said to be better treated, unless the bond-servant exercised some skill as artisan, in which case he was more like a European apprentice, though earning higher wages. But artisans too joined the freebooters. "We had Sawyers, Carpenters, Joyners, Brickmakers, Bricklayers, Shoemakers, Taylors, &c.," says Dampier.[40] Because they frequently adapted prizes for their own use, and were as often wrecked, the buccaneers set a high value on carpenters, as on surgeons or apprentice surgeons.

Paid off with a few hundred pounds of tobacco at the end of his articles, the *engagé* had not the means to set up as a planter, as the English often had before Barbados and the Leewards filled up; but even there, as is well known, the "sugar revolution" (1640–60) spelled doom to the small planter.

Captain William Jackson, who "kept the Indies in an uproar," could have manned his ships threefold at Barbados in 1642, on the basis of no purchase no pay, "every one that was denied entertainement reputing himselfe most unfortunate."[41]

Jackson and his "vice-admiral," both old Providence hands, armed ships in England, but increased their fleet to seven in Barbados and St. Christopher with an additional 750 men. Can we doubt that the obscure beginnings of a Caribbean-based privateering industry are connected with the midcentury decades of growing displacement and indebtedness, when the struggle for existence, among those who survived the appalling mortality rate of immigrants, quickened movement from island to island? In these conditions a bond-servant might change masters many times, as bankrupt planters swelled the ranks of runaways and derelicts, naturally disposed to soak the wealthy Spaniard.

The plight of the British has been movingly described by Carl and Roberta Bridenbaugh, who consider that from 1640 the "parent islands" contained "the greatest concentration of poverty-stricken freemen in any of England's dominions before 1776," boom or slump.[42] The parent islands of the French reached demographic saturation somewhat later, but their social experience was not dissimilar. In both cases, of course, the run of first-generation immigrants were men and women without resources, buying their passage by selling themselves to a known or more often unknown settler. Some would have borne the scars of pressures and oppressions, if not persecutions, at home. More than half the population of the British West Indies in 1650 were Irishmen, the latest arrivals soldiers from Drogheda; Barbados alone received thousands of war prisoners before the transportation of felons began in 1655. Numerous Anabaptists came out with Penn and Venables in that year.[43]

Gabriel Debien's patient combing of the "actes d'engagement" in the notarial minutes of La Rochelle, Nantes, and Dieppe points to a preponderance of day laborers, textile workers, and other *ruraux* making for the islands, and not least St. Domingue, where one might become a "valet de boucanier"? many sailed in the winter months, when jobs were relatively scarce.[44] Although we are now more vividly aware of seasonal and other kinds of vagabondage along French roads and rivers, it seems significant that so many came from areas affected by peasant risings against the royal fisc and the proliferation of crown agents, not to mention plunder by unpaid soldiers, in the 1630s; the *Croquants* of Saintonge, Angoumois, and Poitou, the *Nu-Pieds* of Normandy. These violent events would not have been soon forgotten. Emotive, visceral, spontaneous gestures they may have been, devoid of revolutionary content: nevertheless, large assemblies of aggrieved taxpayers had shown a capacity for self-organization, the constitution of "communes," election of deputies, and promulgation of *Ordonnances:* "L'assemblée du Commun peuple, le Conseil tenant, a esté ordonné ce qui s'ensuit." Revealing, indeed startling, is the image they had of themselves as forgotten men, "comme si on ne songeait à nous que comme des pièces perdues."[45]

Well might Mazarin fear the contagion of English example in 1647.[46] Two years later republican placards appeared in Paris, also a major source of West Indian grants, often from the building trades. The presence of a substantial, literate working-class élite among the emigrants is fully established. A rector of Kingston was to say that in the Jamaica of 1720 there were not six families of "gentle descent": tavern keepers, tailors, carpenters, and joiners called themselves Colonel, Major, Captain, Honorable, or Esquire.[47] So respectable a picture may be corrected, however, by the critical comments of the priest who sailed with an ill-fated party for Cayenne in 1652: "toutes sortes de personnes . . . enfants incorrigibles . . . gens qui avoient fait faillite . . . Plusieurs jeunes débauchez . . . des Moines Apostats . . . Et le pire de tout, quantité de femmes." They had not got far before their "General" accused them of aiming at "un corps de Republique, voulant y establir des Présidents, Conseillers . . . un Parlement."[48]

A president, councillors, and other officers were certainly elected for the baptismal ceremonies, followed by protracted drinking, when newcomers to the tropics crossed the Line. Charlevoix has it that these mysteries were held in St. Domingue to release a man from all antecedent contracts.[49] Even there life was never so simple, but for some decades it preserved in exaggerated forms that libertarianism which in some degree splintered all the English colonies, as was demonstrated from the start in the radical politics of Bermuda and Barbados. A governor of Jamaica, within ten years of conquest, could describe his people as "generally easy to be governed, yet rather by persuasion than severity"; as late as 1692, Ducasse wrote of "cette colonie n'ayant esté formée que selon le caprice de chaque particulier, elle a subsisté dans le désordre"; not a man, said another, "qui ne se croie plus que nous officiers du Roy."[50]

The early history of "the Coast" was stamped by a series of revolts, especially against French monopoly companies, from the time when Governor d'Ogeron (1665–75), "whom nature had formed to be great in himself," began "to establish the regularity of society upon the ruins of a ferocious anarchy."[51] The supreme embodiment of this impatience of authority, this drive to absolute freedom, was la *flibuste,* in Jamaica "roving on the account." Dampier, who called it "the other loose roving way of Life," notes that "Privateers are not obliged to any Ship, but free to go ashore where they please, or to go into any other Ship that will entertain them."[52] The authorities agree on their self-will, caprice, dislike of work; on their disordered and unwashed clothing, their habit of singing while companions tried to sleep and shooting to make a noise; on their blasphemies and debaucheries. So long as they had cash to spend, it was difficult to persuade them to the sea. In this they resemble typical *pícaro*, willing to lose everything on the throw of a dice, then begin all over again; and the picaresque novel, though seldom set in the New World, contains some profound truths about it. Living from day to day, at the mercy of events, the picaresque rogue is seldom his own master for long, yet living on his wits he can assert his independence and turn the table on masters no more virtuous than himself.[53] There was more than this, however, to the libertinism of the buccaneers. They were not merely escaping from bondage. In their enterprises at least, they practiced notions of liberty and equality, even of fraternity, which for most inhabitants of the old world and the new remained frustrated dreams, so far as they were dreamed at all—more than we usually suppose, perhaps.

The first such notion was familiar enough to Croquants and Levellers: the right to be consulted. Elizabethan seamen, according to Monson, had claimed a say in the conduct of their voyages and freedom to adopt at sea a casual privateering consort—unpremeditated agreements which owners might disown.[54] Both were standard features of buccaneering practice. Before ever a ship's company left on the account, however, articles had to be agreed regarding future dividends, and captains and quartermasters elected. Later might follow "consults" about consortship with other companies encountered, or about tactics, especially in tight situations. Thus l'Olonnais "called a council of the whole fleet, wherein he told them he intended to go to Guatemala. Upon this point they divided into several sentiments. . . . But the major part of the company, judging the propounded voyage little fit for their purpose, separated from l'Olonnais and the rest."[55]

Far from base, especially on the far side of the Isthmus of Darien, such secessions were commonplace. After the death of Richard Sawkins, "the best beloved of all our company or the most part thereof," records the scholarly Basil Ringrose, Captain Sharp "asked our men in full council who of them were willing to go or stay, and prosecute the design Captain Sawkins had undertaken, which was to remain in the South Sea."[56] Those who stayed later deposed Sharp and subsequently reinstated him. So even when captains only consulted each other, they must have kept a finger on the pulses of their followings. Morgan seems only to have taken counsel with "the chiefest of his companions—, but he had a record of success which removed all obstacles."[57] No doubt this and a reputation for personal valor go far to explain the election of other leaders. Yet powers of verbal persuasion must always have been requisite, another quality Morgan had in abundance. Governor Nathaniel Butler of Old Providence noted in his diary that Captain Parker "and his two Counsellors being obstinate to their owne Endes, went about to satisfie," with words, a starving crew which "in temperate waye desired to know what he meant to doe with them"—and buccaneers could be far more intractable than that.[58] It is unlikely that they could have been ruled by the methods of terror and delation attributed to Tuscan captains in the Levant by one who sailed with them in the 1690s.[59] As late as 1708, the Board of Trade in London thought that the "ill practices too frequently committed" by Bermudian privateers (clearly influenced by the Jamaica discipline) could be prevented if captains enjoyed "the sole command . . . whereas, as we have been informed, every seaman on board a privateer having a vote, it is not in the captain's power."[60]

The balance between privateering democracy and dominant personalities is hard to strike, and commanders certainly enjoyed absolute power in action; but in this as in other respects there is a strong indication of the consolidation of a body of regulatory customs among the freebooters in the survival of references to them into the Spanish Succession War. In 1706 the "gouverneur par intérim" on the Coast, Charitte, in writing home, used such phrases as "les charteparties qui se font aux Isles Françoises" or simply "charteparties de l'Amérique." He was referring to the distribution of booty and provision for the maimed. The principles are the same as those briefly described by Exquemelin and Charlevoix for an earlier period.[61] No text of a "chasse-partie," as it was known (neatly translated by Burney as a "chasing agreement"), has come to light before 1688. It does not restate the basic egalitarian principle, "à compagnon bon lot," presumably because this could be taken for granted; it is an agreement between Captain Charpin and Mathurin Desmaretz "quartier maistre de l'équipage" and deals expressly with a very few departures from that rule in defining the captain's dividend—ten *lots* and first choice of any captured vessels—and those of two surgeons, who in addition to the usual allowance for their chests were to keep captured instruments "qui ne seront point garnys d'argent."[62] Pillage included "or, argent, perle, diamant, musq, ambre, sivette, et toutes sortes de pierreries" as well as "tous balots entammez entre deux ponts ou au fond." That this was clarified is a sure sign that their ship, *St. Roze*, was not owned by captain and crew.

The typical privateer seems usually to have been the crew's common property or that of their leader, in which case the leader was awarded extra shares. Morgan's captains in 1670 drew the shares of eight men for the expenses of their ships, besides their usual allotment, which Esquemelin elsewhere states as "five or six portions to what the ordinary seamen have."[63] It is to be noted that the largest part of the outlay in a European privateer consisted in victuals, arms, and cash advances to the crew. None these items counted for much or at all with the freebooters, each of whom contributed the essential weaponry and often also his provisions, so far as they did not rely on what they shot or fished, gathered or seized. With a week's supply of food to start with, the only big capital item was the ship and this itself might well be a cheap prize. Only a frigate would call for such resources as those of the royal officers on the Coast (usually also planters) could supply, and they might invest with the object of stimulating the "course aux ennemis," especially governors who shared the admiralty tenth in prizes.[64]

At the same time there was nothing to stop settlers from taking out an interest, and we have to allow for the debts piled up by freebooters with innkeepers and others; the *cabaretiers* gave credit to the *flibustiers* in 1690, for example, to buy victuals, allegedly at inflated prices.[65] In St. Domingue privateering retained the approval of the community long after it had begun to be opposed by a powerful interest in Jamaica, the Spanish traders. In 1709 Choiseul Beaupré, a governor who set himself to revive the waning *course*, claimed credit for restoring the classical "*A compagnon bon lot*," which meant that the chief fitter-out agreed with the ship's company for a certain number of lots amounting to never more than an eighth of the produce of a cruise, in place of his usual third—in metropolitan France, two-thirds.[66] As an interesting Guernsey charter party of 1703 suggests, this difference of a third may be accounted for by the fact that the crew provided their own food and drink; in earlier times, when *armateurs* were divided into owners and victuallers, armaments, including trading voyages to the Caribbean, had been split into thirds, so that "*tiercement*" in France came to be a synonym for whatever was owing to a crew. On the other hand, the buccaneering sloop was so cheap that it could have been mainly the cost of victualling that fell on the fitters-out, whether ship's company or not, allowing "victualling" to include such items as powder, lanterns, and "menus ustensiles."[67]

The freebooters allowed "extraordinary shares" to other ship's officers besides the captain, but on a narrow scale: "the Master's Mate only two," says Esquemelin, "and other Officers proportionable to their employment." On a small sloop or brigantine they were not numerous. Defoe's pirates, who drew directly on the model of the freebooters, offered a bonus only to half a dozen officers, even captain and quartermaster receiving only twice (or less) the common dividend.[68] This was what they called "a free ship, that is, they agreed every man should have an equal share in all prizes."[69] Labat's friends among the freebooting captains received only a present in addition to the equal dividend when their ship was common property, though it might be substantial enough to multiply his dividend three or four times; otherwise the only special beneficiaries, rateably, were the quartermaster, surgeon, and pilot.[70] But the freebooters liked to make merit awards. Morgan offered fifty pieces of eight for "entering the first any castle, or taking down the Spanish colours"; Rogers, twenty "to him that first sees a Prize of Good Value, or exceeding 50

Tuns in Burden," and "a good Suit of Clothes to be made for each Man that went up the River above Guiaquil [*sic*]." His owners had already agreed to a scale of compensation for widows and those "so disabled as not to get a Livelihood," as well as further rewards for "Whoever shall in Fight, or otherwise, signalize himself," notably in boarding.[71] Time had passed since it was possible to assert that English privateers could not afford to take care of their wounded or the relatives of their dead, and since the mercenary soldier's wage was expected to cover the cost of his injuries.[72]

The shipowners' duty to provide for a sick seaman is at least as old as the Laws of Oléron, but awards to the disabled originated much later. The mutual benevolent fund created by Drake and Hawkins in 1590, the Chatham Chest, marked a giant step forward for seamen, although its resources fell far below the claims made on it in wartime: by 1675 it was granting disability pensions for war wounds, "in its historic condition of insolvency."[73] At about that date the French government blazed a similar trail for its *troupes de terre,* and it was the first, though not until 1703, to set up a state fund for granting half pay to men disabled in private armaments at sea, with small lump sums for widows. The idea was born of a small tax on prizes levied in Brittany for the redemption of Barbary slaves, and its extension opposed by the Dunkirk owners, who pointed to the traditional responsibility of its *magistrat* for finding public employments, short of the "maison des pauvres"; even at St. Malo there were many claims for unpaid nursing expenses in the admiralty court.[74]

Against this background it is not surprising that Exquemelin, who qualified as a surgeon at Amsterdam a year after his book was first published there, makes much of the smart money awarded in the *chasse-parties* for the loss of limbs and eyes. As with all such articles, there was room for variety, and doubtless evolution: an eye worth only a hundred piastres even in Morgan's grand scale—1,800 crowns for the two hands as against 600 for one and 1,500 for both legs—equated with a thumb or index finger at 300 in Labat's account, in which the wearing of a cannula had gone up to as much as an arm (600 écus without distinction between right and left). Defoe's pirates offered 600 dollars (about £15 0) to a cripple, according to the three sets of articles he came by—about the same as the governor of St. Domingue offered for its defense in 1709, with the alternative of a life annuity.[75]

There is clear evidence of custom at work in these tariffs, except that the freebooters had no thought for pensions. That would have contradicted their mentality, which was to distribute dividends on the first possible occasion. Nor was there anything like a hospital on the Coast until 1710, when Choiseul created one for soldiers and *flibustiers,* partly to be funded by the *lots* of those killed without heirs.[76] But there were captured slaves. Negroes, though sometimes freed when they could be placed, served as slaves until they

could be sold. After money, plate, and precious stones, they were the most easily convertible booty. Indeed, the crippled freebooter might elect to take a
slave in lieu of 100 pieces of eight. That might prove a sounder pension than
any annuity—with up to six slaves in return for a wooden leg, a retired freebooter might set up as a planter, though he would need to be a good husband
of his shares, as some were.[77]

Charlevoix tells us that the practice was for cruises to go on until enough
had been earned to pay for the lamed and wounded—first charge on the common stock. There were other prior charges, including the claims of owners or
victuallers ashore (if any) and the admiralty tenth, payable in Jamaica from
the start and on the Coast by the 1690s, to judge by the disputes of Ducasse
with the governor-general in Martinique.[78] Given a flexible attitude to plunder, which by definition belonged to the captors exclusively, and the sale of
prize goods in neutral islands, especially Danish St. Thomas, it is unlikely that
these tithes were ever surrendered in full. But no doubt whatsoever hangs over
the basic rule of the common stock. All our authorities refer to this, or to the
punishment of theft, at the least by forfeiture of shares, at worst by maroon-
ing. The articles drawn up in 1697 for d'Iberville's projected Mississippi expedition—describing his Canadians as *flibustiers,* interestingly enough—impose
both penalties, unless "selon le vol" the offender deserved shooting: the same
with the pirates' articles. Woodes Rogers preferred to get agreement to a fine
of twenty times the value for concealing plunder worth more than half a
crown, besides loss of shares, the original penalty: that the terms were stiff-
ened suggests trouble in the intervening year, but also that it was reprobated
by the majority. It means something that Dampier never accused his fellows of
the "many hundreds of little deceitful Acts" which he noticed among Dutch
seamen in the Far East; in his "new voyage" of 1683–91, moreover, he reported only one case of theft, the offender being condemned "to have three
Blows from each Man in the Ship."[79]

Cheating would self-evidently be least tolerable under the system of "à
compagnon bon lot," virtually a Rousseauistic contract rooted in self-interest.
By this device the freebooters' democracy may be thought to have achieved an
objective which eluded most commanders on land or sea, "everybody thinking
they have a right to get what they can."[80] "Captain Johnson," who enjoyed
exposing the hypocrisy of his readers, noted the paradox: "For these men
whom we term, and not without reason, the scandal of human nature . . .
when they judged it for their interest . . . were strictly just."[81] It is reasonable
to assume that besides a cut in expectations, an outraged sense of justice
played its part in the Cartagena affair, and for that matter in the "obloquies
and detractions" which drove Morgan to leave most of his followers behind
when he sailed home from the Isthmus in 1671.[82]

Defoe relates with gusto a mock trial conducted by a crew of Caribbean pirates under the greenwood tree about 1720—a parody of English institutions typical, apparently, of these outlaws.[83] But freebooter justice was deeply flawed in its own turn. We need not make too much of the fact, so much deplored by the earliest historian of the Coast, the Dominican Père du Tertre, that they were apt to be self-appointed judges in their own cause;[84] nor perhaps of acknowledged cruelties to Spanish civilians, which seem to have been largely confined to the extraction of information and of ransoms—manners in which they had little to teach European privateersmen, and nothing to European warlords. As Ducasse wrote after his descent on Jamaica in 1694, "nous avons fait la guerre en gens désintéressés, ayant tout brulé"; at Cartagena, thought Charlevoix, "the flibustiers showed more ruse than violence, much of it feigned."[85] A calculated terrorism, as distinct from gratuitous cruelty, was inherent in this type of banditry, approximating most nearly to the "haiduk" variety in Eric Hobsbawm's classification.[86] Among the pirates proper, examples of sheer brutality are not hard to find; they made a point of recruiting prisoners, the freebooters in the end released them; but even the pirates, it was said, were most to be feared in the first flush of success.

The test of fraternity is how they treated each other. The freebooters' care for their sick and their solemn funeral rites are indications of that.[87] Further, Esquemelin remarks that, among themselves, the buccaneers "are very civil and charitable . . . if any wants what another has, with great liberality they give it to one another." Liberality, indeed a generosity "mieux qu'en aucun lieu du monde" (as Labat says of their hospitable customs), was as characteristic of the *flibustiers* as intemperate drinking, and neither trait was perhaps without a touch of that ostentation which to them would stamp a gentleman, "ce sont des dîners éternels."[88] But if high spending was a rule of "la bonne flibuste," as it was a habit of the European *pícaro*, so was gambling. What Bartholomew Sharp called "Confusion and strong Contests among the Men" were a necessary consequence of their "Consults," but drink and gaming engendered faction. A buccaneer would wager the clothes off his back. "The main Division," says Dampier of Swan's men at Mindanao in 1687, "was between those that had Money and those that had none." A little earlier, Sharp himself, wishing to go home with "almost a thousand pound," had been supported by the thrifty and turned out by those "scarce worth a groat," who were for staying in the South Sea.[89] Ravenau de Lussan had an even sorrier tale to tell of his return across the Isthmus in 1688: "Eighteen of those whom the luck of the play had most despoiled had determined to massacre those who were rich." To save their heads, but also to solve a problem of portage, "the rich" shared again with "the poor," on condition of receiving back a half or two-thirds after reaching St. Domingue.[90] No wonder d'Iberville, Rogers, and the pirate John Phillips, to mention but a few, treated gambling as an abuse only less heinous than theft, or that Sawkins cast the dice overboard.[91]

Fraternity "on the account," therefore, under stress of monotony and rum, might be less apparent than in times of danger or dividend distribution. Was it anything more than the camaraderie of the camp or the sociability of the village? "Pebble-Smasher" and "Never-Fail" were only variants of "Chasse-Marée" or "Passe-Partout," and of a thousand other such familiar vulgarities as helped cement the fellowship of military "chambers" and the inescapable collectivity of country communities.[92] Guildsmen were supposed to be brothers too—and George Rudé has taught us not to underrate the solidarity of the shop floor, of the mentality common to masters and men among the *sans-culottes*. One could also invoke Roland Mousnier's "société des fidélités" for the seventeenth century, although his examples of total devotion are all of high-born men.[93] Further down the scale, however, out on the Coast, there was the well-established institution of *matelotage,* first among the *boucaniers,* who shared any property they had with their "mess-mate" and might bequeath it to him: when the early *habitants* combined to cultivate a plot, "ils s'a-matelotaient."[94] What is less well known, something like *matelotage* prevailed among the log cutters of Campeche and Honduras, the "Baymen" whose "Trade had its Rise from the decay of Privateering."[95] An anonymous but intelligent visitor to those parts in 1714–15 noted that they were hard drinkers and very quarrelsome, but that neighbors lived in common, under two elected governors and a short compendium of laws "very severe against theft and Encroachments."[96] Forty years earlier Dampier noticed there that "every Man is left to his choice to carry what he pleaseth and commonly they agree very well about it." And on Saturdays at least they hunted.[97] It looks as though "the Custom of the Coast," originally that of the *boucaniers,* being rooted in the wilderness and doubtless subject to Carib, Cuna, and other Indian influences, possessed an extraordinary power of survival in suitable circumstances. But between Coast and Bay we need look for no stranger agency than the freebooters themselves. The code survived even while its adherents might fail it, as is true of any social group.

Among "fellow adventurers" as impulsive as the Brethren of the Coast it would be surprising to find consistency of conduct, especially with English and Dutch admixtures of differing backgrounds. And yet the outlines of a fairly homogeneous portrait can be put together. That Captain Andreas who called one morning on the Scots in Darien, and who claimed Swan and Davis as "his particular Friends," stands forth as a recognizable type: "He (as generally those People are) is of a small Stature. In his Garb affects the Spaniard as alsoe in the Gravity of his Carriage. He had a red loose Stuff coat on with an old hatt and a pair of Drawers, but noe Shoes or Stockins."[98] The skills of a

Rudé could uncover a crowd of such forgotten men.[99] There are sources still to be mined, especially Spanish, and short of them ample room for new perspectives. The freebooters astonished the world in their day and have attracted some sensational literature since. Sadly, very little has come from professional historians. As Una said to Puck in one of Kipling's stories, "pirates aren't lessons." But did she wish they were? And why not?

NOTES

1. Jean-Bernard-Louis Desjean Pointis, *An Authentick and Particular Account of the Taking of Carthagena by the French, in the Year 1697* (London: Printed for O. Payne, 1740). This is a late edition of the 1698 translation of the *Relation de l'expédition de Carthagene* (Amsterdam: 1698), 1; France, Archives Nationales (henceforth AN), 1 Marine B4/17, fos. 404–5; France, Bibliothèque Nationale (henceforth BN), Thoisy 91, 515. There is a modern narrative of this expedition in Nellis Maynard Crouse, *The French Struggle for the West Indies, 1665–1713* (New York: Columbia University Press, 1943), chapter 7.

2. Pierre-François-Xavier de Charlevoix, *Histoire de l'île espagnole ou de S.-Domingue, écrite particulièrement sur des mémoires manuscrits du P. Jean-Baptiste Le Pers, . . . et sur les pièces originales qui se conservent au dépôt de la marine*, 4 vols. (Amsterdam: F. L'Honoré, 1733), 4:123 ff.

3. Pointis, *Account*, 42–43, 62, 69; AN, Col[onies] C8A/16, Vaucresson, 10 May 1706.

4. AN, Col. C9A/3, fos. 303 ff., 370 ff.; George Everett, *An answer to Mr. Paschal's Letter to his friend in the countrey, stating the case of Mr. Parkhurst and himself, &c. Being a vindication of the House of Commons, against those gentleman commissioners for prizes* (London,: A. Baldwin, 1702), 5; Charlevoix, *Histoire*, 4:106, 150 ff.

5. Charlevoix, *Histoire*, 4:167–68; AN, Col. C8A/12 folios, 190 ff.; C9A/8, f.337^v; BN, Thoisy 91, 515–32.

6. AN, Col. C9A/4, fos. 272–74.

7. Charlevoix, *Histoire*, 4:44–45, 105, 110; *CSPCS*, 1696–97, 403.

8. Captain Charles Johnson, *A General History of the Robberies and Murders of the Most Notorious Pyrates and also their Policies, Discipline and Government from their first Rise and Settlement in the Island of Providence, in 1717, to the Present Year, 1724, with the Remarkable Actions and Adventures of the two Female Pyrates, Mary Read and Anne Bonny, to which is Prefix'd an Account of the famous Captain Avery and his Companions; with the Manner of his Death in England*, ed. Manuel Schonhorn (London: Dent, 1972), 286. For Defoe's authorship, see John Robert Moore, *Defoe in the Pillory and Other Studies* (Bloomington: Indiana University Press, 1939), 126–88.

9. Johnson, *General History*, 338.

10. George Shelvocke, *A Privateer's Voyage Round the World*, reprint of 1726 ed.

(London: Jonathan Cape, 1930), 43–46; Great Britain, Royal Commission on Historical Manuscripts, *The Manuscripts of the House of Lords, New Series* (London: H.M. Stationery Office) 12 (1970): 235–36.

11. Woodes Rogers, *A Cruising Voyage Round the World* (New York: Longmans, Green and Co., 1928), 22–23, 114–16, 170–71, 206–7; Shelvocke, *Privateer's Voyage*, 114.

12. Kenneth R. Andrews, *Elizabethan Privateering: English Privateering during the Spanish War, 1585–1603* (Cambridge: Cambridge University Press, 1964), 39–44, 167; Oxford, Bodleian Library, Rawl. A 171, fos. 634; AN, Marine G 144 and B 3/115, fo. 532.

13. Rennes, Archive du Département de Ille-et-Vilaine, *fonds de notaires*, Pitot and Vercoutère-Le Roy *(actes d'engagement);* Arras, Archives du Département du Pas de Calais, 13 B 156, 13 February and 2 March 1694; Edward Cooke, *A Voyage to the South Sea, and Round the World, Perform'd in the years 1708, 1709, 1710, and 1711. Containing a Journal of all Memorable Transactions . . . With a New Map and Description of the mighty River of the Amazons. Wherein an Account is given of Mr. Alexander Selkirk,* 2 vols. (London: 1712) sig. b4[r-v].

14. Rogers, *Cruising Voyage*, 173; Shelvocke, *Privateer's Voyage*, 40; AN, Marine B3/115, fos. 544–48.

15. Charles Sergison, *The Sergison Papers*, ed. R. D. Merriman, *Publications of the Navy Records Society*, v. 89 (London: Navy Records Society, 1950), 8–9; G. P. R. James, ed., *Letters Illustrative of the Reign of William III, from 1696 to 1708, Addressed to the Duke of Shrewsbury, by James Vernon*, 3 vols. (London: H. Colburn, 1841), 2:187.

16. Charles Molloy, *De Jure Maritimo et Navali: or, a Treatise of Affairs Maritime and of Commerce*, 5th ed. (London: Printed for R. Vincent and John Walthoe, 1701), 220–24; Ralph Davis, *The Rise of the English Shipping Industry in the Seventeenth and Eighteenth Centuries* (London: Macmillan, 1962), 149–54.

17. James Burney, *History of the Buccaneers of America* (London: Unit Library, 1902), 40. In 1657 the first of Jamaica's governors referred to "buckaneers" as "French and English that kill cattle" in Hispaniola: "Edward D'Oyley's Journal, Part 2," *Jamaica Historical Review*, 9 (1978): 69.

18. Charlevoix, *Histoire*, 3:11, 54–67; P. Constantin, "Jacques Yvon sieur des Landes (1645–1698), Lieutenant du roi à Saint-Domingue," *La Province du Maine*, 26–27 (Laval, 1957), 7–48.

19. Jean-Baptiste Labat, *Nouveau voyage aux isles de l'Amérique, contenant l'histoire naturelle de ces pays, l'origine, les moeurs, la religion et le gouvernement des habitans anciens et modernes, les guerres et les événemens singuliers qui y sont arrivez . . . le commerce et les manufactures qui y sont établies,* 2 vols. (The Hague: P. Husson, 1724), 1:ii, 77; Charlevoix, *Histoire*, 4:137.

20. CSPCS, 1669–1674, 202; A. O. Exquemelin, *The Buccaneers of America: A True Account of the Most Remarkable Assaults Committed of Late Years upon the Coast of the West Indies by the Buccaneers of Jamaica and Tortuga, both English and French Written originally in Dutch by John Esquemeling, one of the Buccaneers . . .* (New York: Dorset Press, 1987), 131.

21. Cf. Defoe's description of seamen as "Les Enfants Perdus, the Forlorn hope of the World." Daniel Defoe, *An Essay upon Projects* (London: Printed by R. R. for T. Cockerill at the Three Legs in the Poultrey, 1697), 124. A modern edition of this book was brought out by Scolar Press in 1969.

22. Fritz Redlich, *The German Military Enterpriser and his Work Force; a Study in European Economic and Social History*, 2 vols. (Wiesbaden: F. Steiner, 1964), 1:117; Arthur Percival Newton, *The Colonising Activities of the English Puritans* (New Haven: Yale University Press, 1914), 252.

23. AN, Col. C9A/9, fo. 217; Johnson, *General History,* 213, 423.

24. Charles Greig Cruickshank, *Elizabeth's Army* (Oxford: Clarendon Press, 1966), 49; R. E. Scouller, *The Armies of Queen Anne* (Oxford: Clarendon Press, 1966), 66.

25. Shelvocke, *Privateer's Voyage,* 30; Redlich, *German Military Enterpriser,* 1: 134; Michael Pawson and David Buisseret, *Port Royal, Jamaica* (Oxford: Clarendon Press, 1975), 29.

26. Scouller, *Armies,* 130, 267.

27. Robert Venables, *The Narrative of General Venables, with an Appendix of Papers Relating to the Expedition to the West Indies and the Conquest of Jamaica, 1654–1655,* ed. C. H. Firth *Camden New series,* v. 60 (London: Longmans Green, 1900), 14–16.

28. Redlich, *German Military Enterpriser,* 1:135; Geoffrey Parker, *The Army of Flanders and the Spanish Road, 1567–1659: The Logistics of Spanish Victory and Defeat in the Low Countries' Wars* (Cambridge: Cambridge University Press, 1972), 188–90.

29. See Kenneth R. Andrews, *The Spanish Caribbean: Trade and Plunder, 1530–1630* (New Haven: Yale University Press, 1978), esp. 181–87.

30. Gabriel Debien, *Les engagés pour les Antilles (1634–1715)* (Paris: Société de l'histoire des colonies françaises, 1952), 188–89; Newton, *Colonising Activities,* 103–10, 192–93, 211–16, 279–82; cf. Charlevoix, *Histoire,* 3:46.

31. I have used the translation of his "Journey to the Southern Sea from 1685 to 1686" in Maurice Besson, *The Scourge of the Indies, Buccaneers, Corsairs and Filibusters* (London: G. Routledge, 1929), see 115–16. Cf. Basil Ringrose's journal in Exquemelin, *Buccaneers of America,* part 4, 398.

32. *Labat, Nouveau voyage,* 1:I, 75–76. Louis XIV did his best to return the church treasures taken by Pointis: France Archives Nationales, Marine B 4/18, fos. 348–65. It should be recalled that Spanish American churches were "the place of all publick Meetings, and all Plays and Pastimes are acted there also." William Dampier, *A New Voyage Round the World* (London: Argonaut Press, 1927), 93.

33. Dampier, *New Voyage,* 189. Dampier's veracity can be checked by reference to Ringrose's journal (and vice versa) till the latter's death in 1686.

34. Dampier, *New Voyage,* 211. Jamaican commissions were no longer obtainable after 1670, when many buccaneers resorted to St. Domingue. Conversely, some of the *flibustiers* served in Jamaican privateers during the Spanish Succession War. See generally Arthur Percival Newton, *The European Nations in the West Indies, 1493–1688*

(London: A. and C. Black, 1933), 286ff; and C. H. Haring, *The Buccaneers in the West Indies in the XVIIth Century*, reprint of 1910 ed. (Hamden, Conn.: Archon Books, 1966). Cf. the design of Capt. Nathaniel North's men, "not intending to Pirate among the Europeans, but honestly and quietly to rob what Moors fell in their way, and return home with clear consciences."

35. AN, Col. C9A/4, fo. 446, 15 October 1698.

36. AN, Col. C8A/16, "Mémoire sur l'état présent des Isles. Remis par Mr Mithon et Mr de Vaucresson . . . à son arrivée," 10 May 1706; AN, Col. C9A/4, fo. 75, Blénac to Pontchartrain, Martinique, 23 March 1694.

37. *CSPCS*, 1677–1680, 565.

38. Pointis, *Account*, 10.

39. AN, Col. C8A/10, fos. 350–53, Robert to Pontchartrain, 11 July 1698.

40. Dampier, *New Voyage*, 240. Carl Bridenbaugh and Roberta Bridenbaugh, *No Peace beyond the Line: The English in the Caribbean, 1624–1690* (New York: Oxford University Press, 1972), 106, 118–20. Half a dozen types of *engagement* are described in G. Debien, "L'émigration poitevine vers l'Amérique au XVIIe siècle," *Bulletin de la Société des Antiquaires de l'Ouest*, sér. 4, 2 (1952), 273–80.

41. *The Voyages of Captain William Jackson, 1642–1645*, ed. V. T. Harlow (Camden 3rd ser. no. 34), 2; cf. Newton, *Colonising Activities*, 267–68, 315–17.

42. Bridenbaugh and Bridenbaugh, *No Peace*, 113.

43. Ibid., 17, 102–3, 196; Arthur Pryor Watts, *Une histoire des colonies anglaises aux Antilles (de 1649 à 1660)* (Paris: Les Presses Universitaires de France, 1924), 134.

44. Debien, *Engagés*, chapter 5.

45. Roland Mousnier, *Fureurs paysannes, les paysans dans les révoltes du XVIIè siècle (France, Russie, Chine)* (Paris: Calmann-Lévy, 1967), 72, 90; there is an English translation of this book entitled *Peasant Uprisings in Seventeenth-Century France, Russia, and China* (New York: Harper and Row, 1970), and a review by R. Mandrou in *Revue Historique*, 242 (1969): 29–40.

46. Christopher Hill, *Puritanism and Revolution: Studies in Interpretation of the English Revolution of the Seventeenth Century* (London: Secker and Warburg, 1958), 136.

47. Debien, *Engagés*, 109, 131; L. Lewis, "English Commemorative Sculpture in Jamaica," *Jamaica Historical Review* 9 (1972): 12.

48. Antoine Biet, *Voyage de la France equinoxiale en l'isle de Cayenne, entrepris par les François en l'année M.DC.LII.* (Paris: F. Clovzier, 1664), 8, 56f.

49. Charlevoix, *Histoire*, 3:55.

50. Sir Charles Lyttleton, quoted by Frank Cundall, *The Governors of Jamaica in the Seventeenth Century* (London: The West India Committee, 1936), 19; Pierre de Vaissière, *Saint-Domingue: La société et la vie créoles sous l'ancien régime (1629–1789)* (Paris: Perrin, 1909), 55.

51. Abbé Raynal, *A Philosophical and Political History of the Settlements and Trade of the Europeans in the East and West Indies*, trans. J. O. Justamond (London: Printed for W. Strahan; and T. Cadell, 1783), 6:125–26.

52. Dampier, *New Voyage*, 30, 238.

53. Frank Wadleigh Chandler, *Romances of Roguery; an Episode in the History of the Novel. The Picaresque Novel in Spain* (New York: B. Franklin, 1961), especially 47 ff., and Angel Valbuena Prat, ed., *La Novela picaresca española*, 3 ed. (Madrid: Aguilar, 1956), 14ff.

54. M. Oppenheim, ed., *The Naval Tracts of Sir William Monson*, 4 vols. (London: Navy Records Society, 1912); Kenneth R. Andrews, ed., *English Privateering Voyages to the West Indies, 1588–1595* (Cambridge: Hakluyt Society, 1959), 162.

55. Exquemelin, *Buccaneers of America*, 112.

56. Ibid., 333–34.

57. Ibid., 130.

58. [London,] British Library, Sloane MS. 758, entry for 25 August 1639.

59. See the account of Roberts's voyage in William Hacke et al., *A Collection of Original Voyages: Containing I. Capt. Cowley's Voyage round the Globe. II. Captain Sharp's Journey over the Isthmus of Darien, and Expedition into the South seas, Written by Himself. III. Capt. Wood's Voyage thro' the Streights of Magellan. IV. Mr. Roberts's Adventures among the Corsairs of the Levant; his account of their way of living; description of the Archipelago islands, taking of Scio, &c* (London: Printed for J. Knapton, 1699); cf. AN, Col. C8A/6, fos. 446v–47.

60. Quoted by Henry Campbell Wilkinson, *Bermuda in the Old Empire; a History of the Island from the Dissolution of then Somers Island Company until the End of the American Revolutionary War: 1684–1784* (London: Oxford University Press, 1950), 24.

61. AN, Col. C9A/7, fos. 322–23.

62. AN, Col. C9A/2, fo. 357, Isle à Vache, 18 February 1688.

63. Exquemelin, *Buccaneers of America* 60, 177. Charlevoix, *Histoire*, 3:68 grants the captains only a double lot.

64. Ducasse's running quarrel with Blénac, the governor-general at Martinique, who claimed the *dixième*, suggests not only that it was a useful source of income, but that the disposal of prizes was now coming under official control, although Danish St. Thomas remained a favorite mart for them: see (e.g.) AN, Col. C9A/2, fos. 322, 328–29, 362, 418–20, 471. Ducasse lost this battle in 1696 (ibid., 3, fo. 231), but in 1702 the Amiral de France awarded half his tenths to the governors of both islands (ibid., 6, fo. 130v). Governor d'Ogeron's more direct involvement in the *flibuste* should be clarified by the edition of his correspondence now being prepared by M. Michel Camus.

65. AN, Col. C9A/2, 2, fo. 130.

66. AN, Col. C9A/2, 8, fo. 394.

67. I am most grateful to Dr. Alan Jamieson of University College, London, for communicating a copy of the charter party of the *Defiance* of Guernsey, possessed by the Priaulx Library; it is impossible to be sure that it was typical of the numerous Channel Island privateers of the time. For illuminating examples of *tiercements*, see Charles Bréard and Paul Bréard, *Documents relatifs à la marine normande et à ses armements aux XVIe et XVIIe siècles pour le Canada, l'Afrique, les Antilles, le Brésil et les Indes*, ed. Société de l'histoire de Normandie, *Publications* (Rouen: A. Lestringant, 1889), 11–25.

68. Exquemelin, *Buccaneers of America*, 60; Johnson, *General History*, 212, 308, 343.

69. Johnson, *General History*, 517.

70. Labat, *Nouveau voyage*, 1:i, 74–75.

71. Exquemelin, *Buccaneers of America*, 178; Rogers, *Cruising Voyage*, 23, 171; Cooke, *Voyage to the South Sea*, i, sig, b4.

72. G. St Lo, *England's Safety (1693)*, in *Somers Tracts: A Collection of Scarce and Valuable Tracts: On the Most Interesting and Entertaining Subjects, but Chiefly such as Relate to the History and Constitution of these Kingdoms. Selected from an Infinite Number in Print and Manuscript, in the Royal, Cotton, Sion, and other Public, as well as Private, Libraries Particularly that of the Late Lord Somers*, 2d ed., 13 vols. (London: Printed for T. Cadell, 1809–15), 72; Redlich, *German Military Enterpriser*, i, 122.

73. John J. Keevil, Jack Leonard Sagar Coulter, and Christopher Lloyd, *Medicine and the Navy, 1200–1900* (Edinburgh: E. and S. Livingstone, 1957–63), 2:135–36.

74. Arrêt du Conseil, 31 March 1693, text in (Citoyen) Sylvain Lebeau, ed., *Nouveau code des prises, ou Recueil des édits, déclarations, lettres patentes . . . sur la course et l'administration des prises, depuis 1400 . . . jusqu'à présent . . .* , 4 vols. (Paris: an 7–9 (=1799–1801)), 1:137, 273–75; AN, Marine B4/25, fos. 410–11; Henri-François Buffet, ed., *Archives d'Ille-et-Vilaine. Répertoire numérique de la sous-série 9B Amirauté de Saint-Malo* (Rennes: Impr. Réunies, 1962), 188–206.

75. Exquemelin, *Buccaneers of America*, 60, 177–78; Labat, *Nouveau voyage*, 1:i, 75; Johnson, 184, 274, 307; AN, Col. C9A/8, fos. 402–3. I have found only one French agreement, probably of 1702, offering compensation for disablement, but the sums are well below West Indian rates—e.g., 150 *livres tournois,* or roughly thirty-eight piastres, for an eye. AN, Marine B4/23, fo. 134.

76. AN, Col. C9A/9, fo. 51; cf. ibid., 2, fo. 204.

77. The phrase is Dampier's, *New Voyage*, p. 246. Cf. Pawson and Buisseret, *Port Royal*, 31; Gabriel Debien, *Une plantation de Saint-Domingue: La sucrerie Galbaud du Fort (1690–1802)* (Le Caire: Les Presses de l'Institut français d'archéologie orientale du Caire, 1941), 34; Labat, *Nouveau voyage*, 2:237.

78. Charlevoix, *Histoire*, 3:68; AN, Col. C8A/6, fo. 407 (on provisions, 1691). On admiralty tenths, see Helen Josephine Crump, *Colonial Admiralty Jurisdiction in the Seventeenth Century* (London: Longmans Green and Co., 1931), 5, and supra, n. 64.

79. Pierre Margry, ed., *Découvertes et établissements des Français dans l'ouest et dans le sud de l'Amérique septentrionale. 4, Découverte par mer des bouches du Mississipi et établissements de Lemoyne d'Iberville sur le Golfe du Mexique 1614–1754: Mémoires et documents originaux: 1694–1703* (Paris: Maisonneuve, 1880–81), 17; Johnson, *General History*, 211, 308, 343; Rogers, *Cruising Voyage*, 22, 206; Dampier, *New Voyage*, 195, 219.

80. Sir C. Wager to Admiralty, 1727, cited in Reginald G. Marsden, ed., *Documents Relating to Law and Custom of the Sea*, 2 vols. (London: Navy Records Society, 1915–16), 2:266. Cf. T. Hesketh, *A Discourse concerning Plunder* (London: 1703), arguing, with reference to the plunder of St. Mary's and of the Vigo galleons in 1702,

that booty belongs to him who takes it; and more generally, Fritz Redlich, *De Praeda Militari: Looting and Booty, 1500–1815* (Wiesbaden: F. Steiner, 1956).

81. Johnson, *General History*, 527.

82. Exquemelin, *Buccaneers of America*, 222–23: pace Dudley Pope, *Harry Morgan's Way: The Biography of Sir Henry Morgan, 1635–1684* (London: Secker and Warburg, 1977), 246. The charge was supported by Morgan's surgeon-general, Richard Browne, in *CSPCS*, 1669–1674, 252.

83. Johnson, *General History*, 292–94. Cf. the parody of Lords and Commons in ibid., 194–95.

84. Jean-Baptiste du Tertre, *Histoire générale des Antilles habitées par les Français*, 4 vols. (Paris: T. Jolly, 1667–71), 3:151.

85. AN, Col. C9A/3, fo. 47; Charlevoix, *Histoire*, 4:163–84.

86. E. J. Hobsbawm, *Bandits* (London and New York: Weidenfeld and Nicolson, and Delacorte Press, 1969), especially 50, 62–64.

87. Charlevoix, *Histoire*, 3:246–47. Ravenau de Lussan suggests a care for sick comrades reminiscent of the Yugoslav partisans: Besson, *Scourge*, 98, 137, 147. Dampier, *New Voyage*, 155, notes the willingness of his companions to stay behind on one of their marches to protect "a stout old Grey-headed Man, aged about 84, who had served under *Oliver*." Cf. Lionel Wafer, *A New Voyage & Description of the Isthmus of America*, ed. L. E. Elliott Joyce, *Hakluyt Society 2d ser., no. 73* (Oxford: Printed for the Hakluyt Society, 1934), 5: "There had been an Order made among us at our first Landing, to kill any who should flag in the Journey. But this was made only to terrify any from loitering, and being taken by the Spaniards; who by Tortures might extort from them a Discovery of our March." The wounded Wafer owed his life to the kindliness of the "wild," unconquered Cuna Indians of the Isthmus, indispensable allies of the buccaneers.

88. Exquemelin, *Buccaneers of America*, 61; Labat, *Nouveau voyage*, 2:244, 249.

89. See the account of Sharp's voyage in Hacke, *Original Voyages*, 14; Dampier, *New Voyage*, 252; Exquemelin, *Buccaneers of America*, 273, 341, 398.

90. Besson, *Scourge*, 153; cf. Charlevoix, *Histoire*, 3:243.

91. Margry, *Découvertes*, 4:17; Rogers, *Cruising Voyage*, 207; Johnson, *General History*, 342; Ringrose, *apud* Exquemelin, *Buccaneers of America*, 398.

92. On the sharing of possessions and profits by the half-dozen men who composed a *camera* in the Army of Flanders, see Parker, *Army of Flanders*, 177; and Cruickshank, *Elizabeth's Army*, 114, for Elizabethan *cameradas*. Debien, *Engagés*, 136–37, offers a rich selection of nicknames in France.

93. Roland Mousnier, *Les institutions de la France sous la monarchie absolue: 1598–1789*, 2 vols. (Paris: Presses Universitaires de France, 1974), 1:85–89. There is an English translation of this book: *The Institutions of France under the Absolute Monarchy, 1598–1789* (Chicago: University of Chicago Press, 1979).

94. Charlevoix, *Histoire*, 3:55; Labat, *Nouveau voyage*, 1:i, 75; Debien, *Galbaud du Fort*, 33; Burney, *History*, 41. Cf. London, Public Record Office, Admiralty 1/3930, Paris, 28 October 1701, reporting a new Line of Battle: "the *Prompt is* in the midst of them as being Matelot, or assistant to the Vice-Admirall."

95. Dampier, *New Voyage*, 163.

96. BL. Add. MSS 39, 946, fo. 10^v.

97. William Dampier, *Voyages and Discoveries* (London: Argonaut Press, 1931), 181.

98. George Insh, ed., *Papers Relating to the Ships and Voyages of the Company of Scotland Trading to Africa and the Indies, 1696–1707, Publications of the Scottish History Society; 3d. ser.*, vol. VI (Edinburgh: Edinburgh University Press, 1924), 81.

99. Some freebooter captains, mostly English, are to be found in Philip Gosse, *The Pirates' Who's Who, Giving Particulars of the Lives & Deaths of the Pirates & Buccaneers* (London: Dulau and Company, 1924) which draws on a narrow range of well-known sources. Gosse at least considered that more of them deserved a place in the *Dictionary* of *National Biography*.

Chapter 10

Black Men under the Black Flag

Kenneth J. Kinkor

Nobody can give you freedom. Nobody can give
you equality or justice or anything. If you're a man,
you take it.   —Malcolm X

Victims of good movies and bad scholarship, pirates have long stood shrouded
in mists of myth and myopia. Utterly divorced from historical reality, the romantic appeal of fiction such as *Treasure Island* and *Captain Blood* is both
undeniable and pervasive. Even nonfiction is often conscripted as entertainment for the casual reader. The portrayal of pirates as aberrant and predatory
individuals prompted by greed, adventurism, and/or simple perversity also
safely insulates audiences from the broader socioeconomic implications of
piracy. That pirates and other social bandits might have been a logical by-
product of seventeenth- and eighteenth-century European "progress" is not
only less than edifying to juvenile readers, but also counters such historio-
graphic icons as Macauley and Trevelyan.

Until recently, the emphasis has therefore been on pirate crimes, and not on
the motivation for those crimes. The focus was on the voyages, and not on the
context of those voyages. Much more attention has been paid to pirate personalities than to their principles. This is understandable, for only recently has
a scholar dared to rank pirates above slave traders in a moral hierarchy.[1]

When not simply ignored, as once were the "Buffalo Soldiers" and black
cowboys, racial stereotypes and the expectations of a predominantly white
middle-class audience heavily conditioned the fictional depictions of pirates of
African descent. Frequently used as stock characters who could be conveniently killed off to serve as spectral sentinels for the treasure caches of tradition, black pirates were, in other instances, used to exploit fear and prejudice
by being characterized as particularly demonic creatures within an especially
heinous category of crime.[2] While inciting such *frisson* may once have passed

for literary fun in some circles, its intellectual bankruptcy is apparent. Treating European piracy as either dime novel or morality play does not explain the impact, longevity and extent of piratical operations through far-flung shipping lanes between 1680 and 1725. Nor does it explain how such "motley crews" transcended the boundaries of race, nation, class and creed.

Understanding black participation in piracy and related issues is not an easy task. Deviant subcultures are secretive by nature, and eighteenth-century European piracy was an especially inarticulate movement. It produced no recorded theoreticians, ideologues, or apologists.[3] Only fleeting glimpses of pirate attitudes can be glimpsed through the perspectives of victims or persecutors. There is enough evidence, however, to prompt some to view eighteenth-century pirates not as simple seaborne thieves, but as "marginal men" driven by desperation and rage to vengeful acts of theft and violence against an oppressive and unjust society.[4]

In 1984, divers led by Barry Clifford discovered *The Whydah Galley* off Cape Cod, the only pirate shipwreck so far authenticated. Research accompanying the ongoing archaeological recovery of over one hundred thousand artifacts from this site has also dispelled some of the mystery swirling around these legendary men, leading to new insights about the role of blacks in eighteenth-century piracy. Rather than chance associations of individual criminals, eighteenth-century European pirates can now be seen as a socially deviant subculture engaged in an inchoate maritime revolt: "a blind popular uprising, a *jacquerie* directed against sea captains and merchants, almost a slave revolt."[5] This spasmodic uprising was characterized more by the centrifugal binding ethos of a primitive, yet definable, protoideology than by centripetal motives of individual greed. It is this *gestalt* which nourished the revolt as it waged war on the entire world with astounding vigor.

Insofar as it was hostile to socioeconomic trends within European society as a whole, as well as to certain political events within the British Isles in particular, eighteenth-century piracy was fundamentally a reactionary movement. Like other outbreaks of "social banditry," its goal was not a new world, but rather "a traditional world in which men are justly dealt with." The expression of this goal was "a protest against oppression and poverty: a cry for vengeance on the rich and oppressors."[6] In so doing, pirates and other social bandits adopted social mechanisms which can be summarized as libertarian, democratic, federal, egalitarian, fraternal, and communal. It may well be argued that these "floating commonwealths" are examples of a form of pre-Englightenment radicalism.

If the revolutionary formula "Liberty, Equality, Fraternity" is expanded to include the concept of transnationalism, pirates still fit this paradigm insofar as they were far less divided by national, religious, and racial differences than

The classic image of the evil pirate: François l'Olonnais cuts out the heart of one of his victims and forces another to eat it. From the 1684 English edition of Exquemelin's *The Buccaneers of America: A True Account of the Most Remarkable Assaults Committed of Late Years upon the Coasts of the West Indies by the Buccaneers of Jamaica and Tortuga, both English and French: Wherein Are Contained More Especially the Unparalleled Exploits of Sir Henry Morgan, Our English Jamaican Hero, who Sacked Porto Bello, Burnt Panama, Etc. Written Originally in Dutch by John Esquemeling; Now Faithfully Rendered Into English with Facsimiles of All the Original Engravings, Etc.*

Pirates and death. *(Top)* Two North African ships pull a victim apart. *(Bottom)* Clinton and Purser hanged between the high and low water marks. From *The Lives and Deaths of Two English Pyrats Purser and Clinton* (London, 1639).

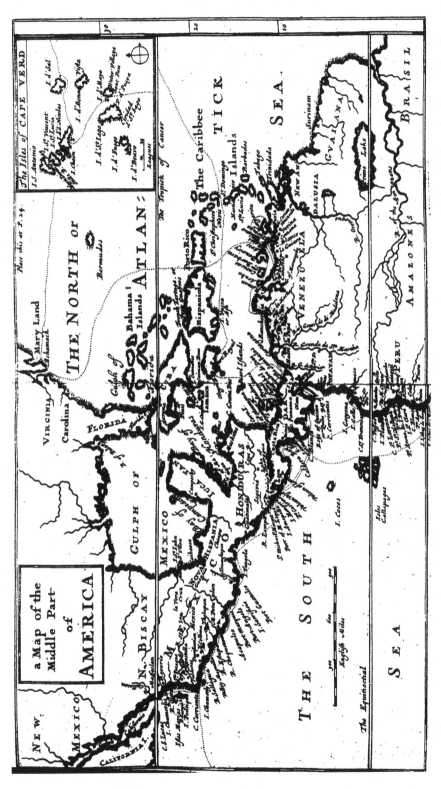

The pirate's own map: the Caribbean and the East Coast of America in the seventeenth century as mapped in the fourth edition of William Dampier, *A New Voyage Round the World* (London, 1699).

Benito Soto, leader of the pirates of the Defensor de Pedro. A line drawing made in Gibraltar shortly before his execution and reproduced in Joaquín María Lagaza, *Los Piratas del Defensor de Pedro: Extracto de las causas y proceso formados contra los piratas del bergantín brasileño Defenso de Pedro que fueron ahorcados en Cádiz en los días 11 y 12 de enero de 1830* (Madrid, 1892). (See chapter 1, "Introduction: Brought to Book.")

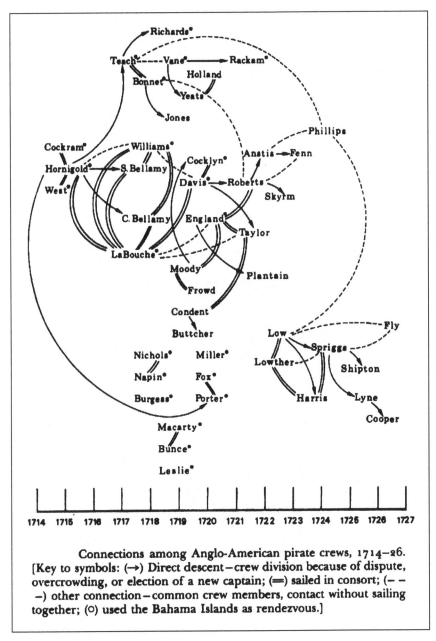

Connections among Anglo-American pirate crews, 1714–26.
[Key to symbols: (→) Direct descent—crew division because of dispute,
overcrowding, or election of a new captain; (═) sailed in consort; (– –
–) other connection—common crew members, contact without sailing
together; (○) used the Bahama Islands as rendezvous.]

Connections among the Anglo-American Pirates. From Marcus Rediker, *Between the Devil and the Deep Blue Sea: Merchant Seamen, Pirates, and the Anglo American Maritime Worlds, 1700–1726* (Cambridge: Cambridge University Press, 1987).

(Top) Captain Jacob Bevan drew these skulls and cross-bones in his ship's log to indicate the death of two of his seamen. On February 22, 1686, Bevan noted that a storm "kild 2 of our men Right and broke our 3d Mat[e]s arme, our mans thigh and 5 more men brused." The symbol of the death's head was appropriated by pirates and used to emblazon the Jolly Roger, the notorious pirate flag. *(Bottom)* A late sixteenth-century English ship of war. The crews from these ships provided some of the early pirate crews. Picture from *The Lives and Deaths of the Two English Pyrats Purser and Clinton* (London, 1639).

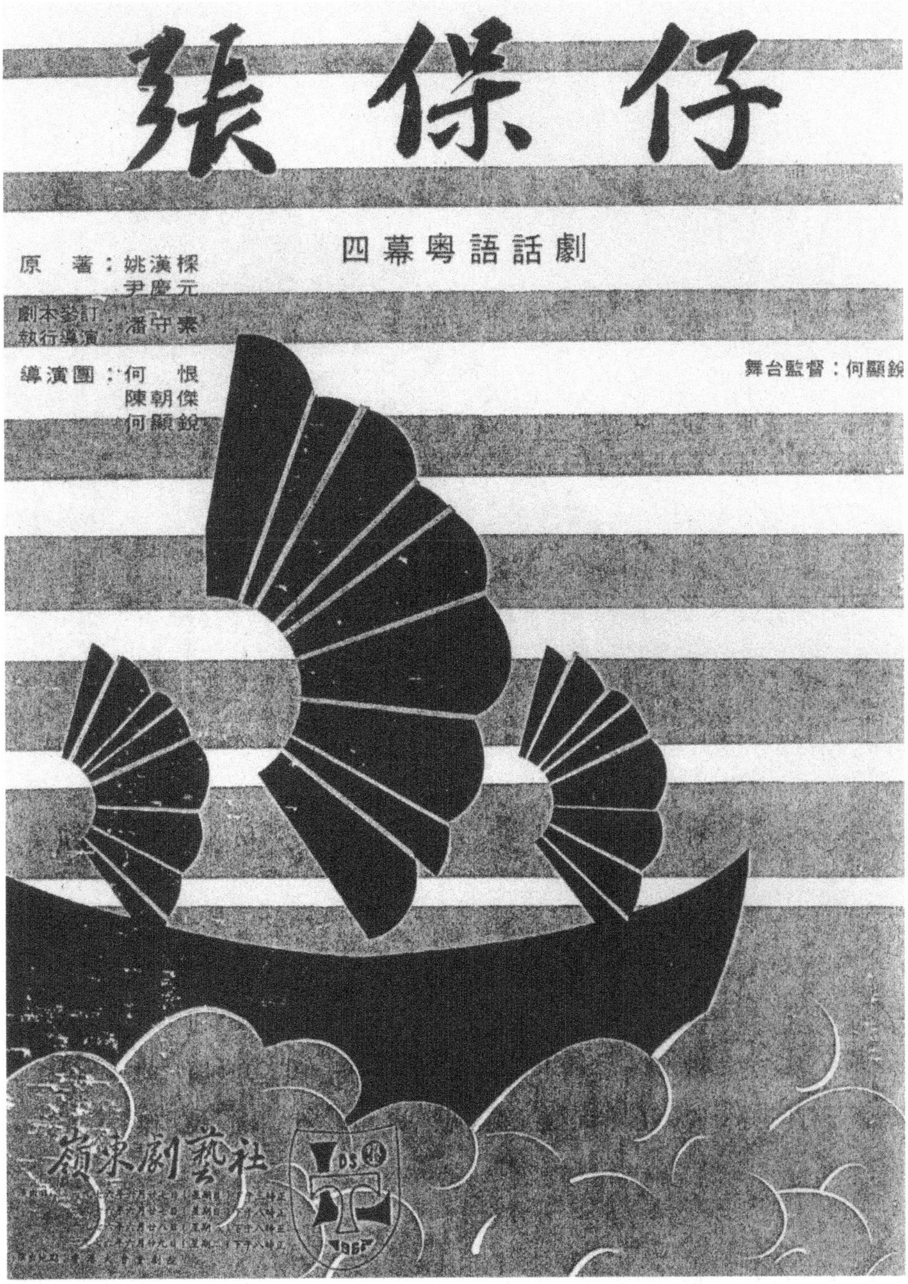

張 傑 仔

四幕粵語話劇

原　著：姚漢槎
　　　　尹慶元
劇本委訂：潘守素
執行導演：
導演團：何　恨
　　　　陳朝傑
　　　　何顯銳

舞台監督：何顯銳

新東劇藝社

Playbill of *Zhan Bao Zhai*, a play about Chang Pao, the adopted son of Cheng I Sao, written by Rao Han Liang and others and performed in Hong Kong in 1976. (Collection of Dian Murray.)

Pirates were on the northern Moroccan coast in the nineteenth century. (*Top*) Sidi Misaud on the Guelaya peninsula. The shingle bar protected the mouth of a creek where pirates could hide their boats out of reach of the British navy. (*Bottom*) A cove just north of Azanen where captured ships were beached. (C. R. Pennell.)

Azanen Beach, on the northern Moroccan coast. (*Top*) The dunes behind the beach provided shelter for the pirates and a hiding place for their boats. (*Bottom*) The curved beach at Azanen had a wide belt of sand and then rose into the dunes behind. (C. R. Pennell.)

The northern Moroccan coast. *(Above)* A rowing fisherman's boat of the pattern used in the mid-nineteenth century by pirates at Azaanen. The pirate boats were rather longer than the modern one, although they were constructed to the same pattern. They too were primarily fishing boats and only used opportunity for piracy. *(Right)* The *mihrab* or prayer niche erected by Sidi Muhammad al-Hadary, smuggler and rescuer of pirates' victims. Al-Hadary lived on the Banu Sa'id coast far beyond the reach of the mid-nineteenth century Moroccan government. While he profited mightily from his smuggling and ransoming activities he was also a man of god, and the *mihrab* was placed on top of one of his good works: a water cistern that collected rainfall for the benefit of the community. (C. R. Pennell.)

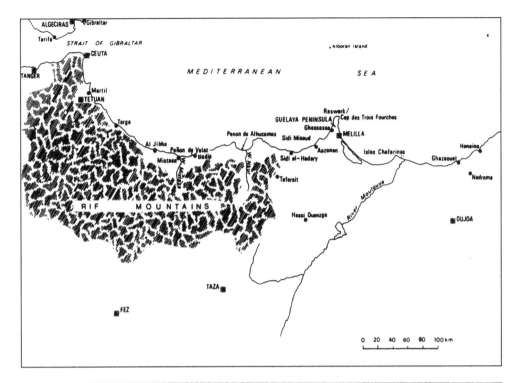

(Top) A map of the Rif coast and Strait of Gibraltar. (C. R. Pennell.) *(Bottom)* Anne Bonny and Mary Read. From the 2d edition of Johnson's *General History (A General history of the robberies and murders of the most notorious pyrates. A general history of the pyrates: from their first rise and settlement in the Island of Providence, to the present time: with the remarkable actions and adventures of the two female pyrates Mary Read and Anne Bonny* (London, 1724). (Reproduced with the permission of the British Library. 9555aaa1.)

Ann Mills with one of the spoils of war, c. 1740. From James Caulfield, *Portraits, Memoirs, and Characters, of Remarkable Persons, from the Revolution in 1688 to the end of the reign of George II., etc.* (London, 1819). (Reproduced with the permission of the British Library. 562 d12.)

Pirates as the spirit of liberty. Frontispiece of the Dutch edition of Johnson's *General History (Historie der Engelsche zee-roovers, beginnende met de geschiedenisse van Capiteyn Avery, en zyne makkers. A° 1692)* (Amsterdam, 1725). (Reproduced with the permission of the British Library. C121b24.)

Mary Read. From the Dutch edition of Johnson's *General History (Historie der Engelsche zee-roovers, beginnende met de geschiedenisse van Capiteyn Avery, en zyne
makkers. A° 1692)* (Amsterdam, 1725). (Reproduced with the permission of the
British Library. C121b24.)

Anne Bonny. From the Dutch edition of Johnson's *General History (Historie der Engelsche zee-roovers, beginnende met de geschiedenisse van Capiteyn Avery, en zyne makkers. A° 1692)* (Amsterdam, 1725). (Reproduced with the permission of the British Library. C121b24.)

The hanging of pirate captain Stede Bonnet in Charleston, South Carolina, in 1719. Seamen looked on from the crow's nest of ships and anchor in Charleston's harbor. From the Dutch edition of Johnson's *General History (Historie der Engelsche zee-roovers, beginnende met de geschiedenisse van Capiteyn Avery, en zyne makkers. A° 1692)* (Amsterdam, 1725). (Reproduced with the permission of the British Library. C121b24.

were Europeans caught in a web of institutionalized dynastic, national, religious, and racial hatreds. This multiculturalism sprang not from idealistic sentiments of the "brotherhood of man," but from a pragmatic spirit of revolt against common oppressors. While disempowered groups are typically disunited and at odds with each other, joining a pirate crew was an empowering act which could lead to the partial dissolution of social differences.

Prior to the French Revolution, rejection of monarchical authority meant rejection of national allegiance. Samuel Bellamy claimed a leadership as legitimate as that of any king: "I am a free Prince, and I have as much authority to make War on the whole World, as he who has a hundred Sail of Ships at Sea, and an Army of 100,000 men in the Field and this my Conscience tells me."[7] Captain Dirk Chivers and his compatriots "acknowledged no Countrymen; [they said] they had sold their Country and were sure to be hanged if taken, and they would take no quarter, but would do all the mischief they could."[8] The only nation many pirates claimed was the deck below their feet, and, if asked from whence they hailed, a likely reply was "From the Seas!"[9] As late as 1785, a mulatto and three white shipmates seized a schooner vowing to "perform on a Cruce in Defense of our Selves & Against all other Nation and Nations."

Nor were conflicting sectarian beliefs a serious obstacle to unity. Many pirates saw organized religion as a tool of social control and oppression wielded by the state. Bellamy railed at "snivelling Puppies, who allow Superiors to kick them about Deck at Pleasure; and pin their Faith upon a Pimp of a Parson; a Squab who neither practices nor believes what he puts upon the chuckle-headed Fools he Preaches to."[10] Profoundly alienated by the alliance of squire and parson, at least some spurned salvation out of a defiance born of rage and despair.[11]

The skull and crossbones flag not only served to strike fear in prospective victims,[12] but was also a rallying point of solidarity against traditional authority. As judicially defined outlaws, pirates were denied full due process of law. Outlawry was a medieval punishment which officially sanctioned the assault, robbery, and even murder of outlaws.[13] "Jolly Roger" was therefore defiantly flown to demonstrate "that those who had turned pirates were, being dead in law, serving under the Banner of King Death."[14] This was not, however, mere nihilism. From the twelfth century to the twentieth, the skull and crossbones has been a symbol of resurrection and rebirth.[15] Together with certain ritualistic and initiatory features of pirate society, this choice of banner implies that turning pirate may have been seen as a transformation or "rebirth," from slave to freeman.[16] Many crews, including Bellamy's, preferred unattached men whose old values could readily be replaced by loyalty to their new "Brethren."[17]

Rejection of divisiveness spawned by Crown and Church, together with the cosmopolitan flavor of the Atlantic trade,[18] ensured that most pirate crews were international in composition. In this instance, the long-standing pejorative characterization of pirates as "motley crews" does have strong basis in fact. The crew of *The Whydah Galley*, for example, included not only English, Irish, Scottish, Welsh, and British colonials but also Frenchmen, Dutchmen, Spaniards, Swedes, Native Americans, African-Americans, and Africans. Not even sharing a common language, they were united in a common enterprise transcending considerations of nationality and religion.[19] The most startling example of the lengths to which such tolerance could extend can be found in a speech allegedly delivered by a French pirate "Misson the Good" aboard a captured slaver. While probably apocryphal, it is nonetheless an extraordinary comment for the early eighteenth century.

> That no Man had Power of the Liberty of another. . . . That for his own part he had not exempted his Neck from the galling Yoke of slavery, and asserted his own Liberty, in order to enslave others. That however these Men were distinguished from the Europeans by their Colour, Customs, or Religious Rites, they were the Work of the same Omnipotent Being, and endued with equal Reason: Wherefore he desired they might be treated like Free men (for he would banish even the name of Slavery from among them).[20]

Few pirates matched Misson in either eloquence or idealism. The treatment of captive Africans fresh from coastal barracoons was unpredictable. After a slave ship had been robbed, her human cargo was sometimes left in chains. In other instances, captives were freed to take what vengeance they chose on their former captors.[21] They were occasionally set at liberty on shore.[22] Sometimes they joined the pirate crew—as did the Africans freed by Misson. Twenty-five blacks liberated from an unidentified "Guinea Ship" likewise joined the *Whydah* pirates.[23] Some captives were impressed into service.[24] On rare occasions they were sold to unscrupulous colonial merchants,[25] or became targets for piratical rage.[26]

Blacks acquainted with European language, culture, and/or seamanship routinely joined pirate crews as freemen. Such "Creoles" and other "Europeanized" blacks had varied backgrounds.[27] Ironically, some were slave ship crewmen. During the late seventeenth and early eighteenth centuries, slave traders acquired African *gromettos* ("servants") to help manage their human cargo. While some were freemen who worked for wages, others were slaves.[28] Whether slave or free, black able-bodied seamen were especially valuable pirate recruits. Perhaps the preeminent recruiting ground for pirates in the early eighteenth century was the Bahama Islands whose population included large numbers of seafaring mulattos and runaway slaves.[29] Black seamen, both slave and free, joined Stede Bonnet's crew, and the crew of John Lewis included at least forty black able-bodied seamen of English colonial origin out of a total of eighty men.[30] Francis Spriggs's cook was a black freeman.[31] Among the *Whydah* pirates hanged in Boston was a mulatto born in Amsterdam named Hendrick Quintor who had sailed aboard a Spanish brig before turning pirate.

It is likely that most pirates of African descent were former colonial slaves. In August 1699 a sloop with thirty runaway slaves from St. Thomas turned pirate and captured several vessels.[32] Most of the blacks in Roberts's crew were identified as French "Creole negroes," possibly liberated during a raid on Marie-Galante in 1721.[33] Judging from their names, the blacks in Blackbeard's crew were freemen born in British colonies.[34] Having once experienced bondage, such recruits would presumably ferociously resist reapprehension. Indeed, a group of black pirates from Roberts's crew nearly succeeded in launching an uprising against their Royal Navy captors.[35]

High ideals notwithstanding, short-handed pirate crews did not scruple at conscription.[36] Taken by pirates, a free mulatto was informed that he was "like a Negro, and they made slaves of all that Colour, if I did not join."[37] Such impressment was, however, color-blind. A *white* sailor, who likewise refused to sign articles with the same crew, was confronted by a black pirate who "damned me, and asked me why I did not go to the pump and work among the rest, and told me that was my Business and that I should be used as a Negroe." Captain Stede Bonnet overheard the exchange, and seconded the black's orders.[38]

Freedom within a pirate crew was therefore clearly conditioned on little more than the courage to seize it by volunteering. Captain Bellamy's comment to a mariner unwilling to join is instructive

> you are a sneaking Puppy, and so are all those who will submit to be governed by Laws which rich Men have made for their own Security, for what the cowardly Whelps have not the Courage otherwise to defend what they get by their Knavery; but damn ye altogether: Damn them for a Pack of crafty Rascals, and you, who serve them, for a parcel of hen-hearted Numskuls.[39]

Or as Roberts put it:

> In an honest Service, there is thin Commons, low Wages, and hard Labour: in this, Plenty and satiety, Pleasure and Ease, Liberty and Power; and who would not ballance Creditor on this Side, when all the Hazard that is run for it, at worst, is only a sour Look or two at choking. No, a merry Life and a short one, shall be my Motto.[40]

Both were speaking, of course, as *white* sailors. Confronted by far worse prospects within eighteenth-century colonialism, it is not surprising that some blacks enthusiastically embraced "visions of invincibility, with dreams of easy money and the idleness such freedom promised, and with the promise of a life unfettered by the racial and social ideology of the plantation system."[41]

Although statistics are sparse, at least a thousand pirates were active between 1715 and 1726.[42] The examples in Table 1 suggest that perhaps 25 to 30 percent of them were black.

According to the articles of Roberts's crew, "Foreigners" were not to be impressed into service.[43] Neither race nor nationality are mentioned in the articles of any other crew. Blacks received shares of booty[44] and enjoyed other perquisites of crew membership, including the right to vote. Rewards and incentives appear to have been based on an individual's ability to function effectively within the pirate crew rather than on skin color.

Some argue that blacks played only a servile role among pirates and that their de facto status was considerably lower than their de jure status.[45] There is much evidence to the contrary. Prior to the full development of the plantation system in the mid-eighteenth century, race was simply one criterion of the social order.[46] Concepts such as nationality, race, ethnicity, and creed were not as static, immutable, and/or insurmountable in the early modern period as they would become later. On the eighteenth-century maritime frontier, merit at least occasionally became a more important marker.

Blacks are accordingly found as leaders of predominantly white crews. Diego de los Reyes commanded a ship operating with the Dutch pirates and privateers in the 1630s and 1640s.[47] Ipseiodawas and John Mapoo, commanders in Henry Morgan's 1668 expedition against Portobello, were probably *zambos* of the Mosquito tribe.[48] Diego Grillo, a runaway slave from Havana, commanded a ship in Morgan's expedition against Panama, and later defeated three separate warships sent to take him.[49] Leading over a thousand men in one raid, Laurens de Graff was the buccaneer commander most feared by the Spanish during the 1680s.[50] Francisco Farnando of Jamaica retired after taking over 250,000 pieces of eight in a single robbery.[51] Nicholas de Concepcion raided Chesapeake Bay and the Delaware Capes in 1720.[52] In 1731, Juan Andres, alias "Andresote," was reported to be the leader of an insurgent group of runaway slaves and Indians on the coast of Venezuela whose robberies and murders were carried out on both land and sea. After two years of fighting, "Andresote" was presumed dead—only to resume his "malefactions" from the sanctuary of Curacao.[53]

Hendrick van der Heul, a one-time quartermaster of the infamous Captain Kidd, was black.[54] Another pirate quartermaster, Abraham Samuel, was a former slave from Martinique who retired from piracy to rule his own kingdom in Madagascar.[55] "Caesar" was a black officer entrusted by Blackbeard to ignite the ship's powder magazine in the event of defeat, and at least one histo-

TABLE 1
The Size of Some Pirate Crews

Captain	Year	Crew	White	Black	% Black	Source
Anstis	1723	60	40	20	33	Smith 1723
Bellamy	1717	180	<153	>27	>15	Turbett 1717
Charpes	1713	68	48	20	29	Gerhard 1990: 217
Cooper	1726	19	15	4	20	*BG* 21 March 1726
Davis		250	<210	>39	>16	Bradley 1989: 143
Edmonson	1726	10	6	4	40	Smith 1744/1967: 10–12
England (est. one)	1718	180	130	<50	<28	Bois 1718
England (est. two)	1719	380	300	80	21	Hill 1920, "ES," 57–59
Franco	1691	89	39	50	56	Bradley 1989: 168
Hamann	1717	25	1	24	96	Candler 1717
Hamlin	1682	36	16	22	61	Rogozinski 1995: 29
Harris	1723	48	42	6	13	Dow 1923: 292
La Bouche	1719	64			50	Johnson, *GH*: 173–74
Lewis		80	40	40	50	Johnson, *GH*: 595
Lowther	1724	23	16	9	39	Hart 1724
Philips	1724	20	17	3	15	Johnson, *GH*: 349–350
Roberts (est. one)	1721	368	280	88	24	Mortensen 1721
Roberts (est. two)	1722	267	197	70	26	Johnson, *GH*: 285
Shipton	1725	13	9	4	31	Johnson, *GH*: 357
Thatch (est. one)	1717	100	40	60	60	*Bonnet*: 46
Thatch (est. two)	1718	14	9	5	36	Lee 1974: 136
Unnamed	1721	50	1	<49	<98	CSPCS 32: 463iii
Williams	1717	40	<25	>15	>38	BNL: 24 July 1717

(Unspecified numbers of blacks were recorded among other pirate crews. No crew was described as all-white.)
SOURCES: Smith 1723: PRO HCA 1–18/35, "Deposition of Joseph Smith and John Webley," 1723; Turbett 1717: PRO, CO 5/1318, 16ii, "Information of Andrew Turbett," Virginia, 17 April 1717; Gerhard 1990: Peter Gerhard, *Pirates of the Pacific, 1575–1742* (Lincoln: University of Nebraska Press, 1990); *B.G.*: *Boston Gazette*; Bradley: Peter T. Bradley, *The Lure of Peru: Maritime Intrusion into the South Sea, 1598–1701* (Basingstoke: Macmillan, 1989). Smith 1744/1967: William Smith, *A New Voyage to Guinea: Describing the Customs, Manners, Soil, Climate, Habits, Buildings, Education . . . Habitations, Diversions, Marriages, and Whatever Else is Memorable among the Inhabitants* (London: J. Nourse, 1744; reprint, London: Frank Cass, 1967); Bois 1718: PRO CO 152/12 no. 136ii "Deposition of John Bois, 29 February 1718 [os]"; Hill, ES: Hill, "Episodes of Piracy," 1920; Candler 1717:"Captain Candler to Council of Trade and Plantations, 12 May 1717, CSPCS 29: 639i; Rogozinski: Rogozinski, *Pirates*; Dow: Dow and Edmonds, *The Pirates*; Johnson, *GH*: Johnson, *General History*; Hart, 1724: CSPCS 34: 102, "Governor Hart to Council of Trade and Plantations," 25 March 1724; Mortensen 1721: PRO CO 152/153 no.282, Deposition of Christian Mortensen 18 May 1721"; *Bonnet*: *Tryals of Major Stede Bonnet*; Lee: Lee, *Blackbeard*; BNL: *Boston News-Letter*.

rian believes that Blackbeard himself may have been a "Tawny" mulatto.[56] In 1721, the crew of the *Zant*, led by a "free Negro," plotted mutiny and piracy.[57] A leader aboard the *Good Fortune* was a mulatto known as "Old South."[58] A 1728 raid on Gardiner's Island by French and Spanish pirates was piloted by an African American formerly from Rhode Island.[59]

That no known pirate crew prohibited blacks from carrying firearms is perhaps the most telling evidence that differences in status between whites and blacks were relatively minor. Indeed, blacks were frequently recorded as active combatants.[60] On one occasion, black pirates even carried out an armed mutiny against a tyrannical captain and his cronies.[61] It would seem that the deck of a pirate ship was the most empowering place for blacks within the eighteenth-century white man's world.[62]

Linguistic evidence indicates that some white pirates may have seen *them-*

selves as runaway "slaves." As early as the first decade of the sixteenth century, runaway slaves in the Americas fled to isolated mountainous or marshy retreats.[63] They established fiercely independent free societies which resisted apprehension and occasionally went on the offensive against European encroachment.[64] These fugitives were known as *cimmarrons* ("wilderness runaways"), or simply "maroons."[65] While most were of African ancestry, they also included native Americans and Europeans. "All three racial groups were maroons as fugitives from bondage or from other forms of subjugation inherent to the slavery system. They joined in struggle against a common enemy and shared elements from their respective cultures of origin."[66] Joint raids by English, Indians, and *zambo* Mosquitos were launched from Roatan Island off the coast of Honduras on numerous occasions during 1714–1718, and especially in May 1722.[67]

Errant members of pirate crews were also "marooned" by being cast forth from the company onto a deserted island or coast.[68] Pirates were often called "marooners"[69] and a desolate coast was known as a "maroon shore."[70] The term therefore meant the radical separation, whether voluntary or involuntary, of an individual from society. "The pirate knew himself to be as surely cut off from normal human intercourse as was Crusoe on his island."[71] Some took desocialization further, and emulated the *cimmarrons'* revolt against the societies which had enslaved them. The pirate ship *Rising Sun* was also called *The Murrone [sic] Galley* by her crew.[72] Two of Sam Bellamy's vessels en route to Cuba across the Yucatan Channel in 1716 were described as "maroon periaguas."[73]

Shared feelings of marginality are a solvent which can ameliorate racial and national barriers.[74] While chattel slavery is far different from the "enslavement" of seamen under dictatorial captains, the experience of marginality itself can be more significant than the specific form of that experience. "Blacks joined white seamen in a common effort to balk the captains and merchants who abused them—although black sailors knew full well that race rarely disappeared, even among shipmates."[75] Black slaves and Irish bond-servants joined in revolt on more than one occasion during the seventeenth century.[76]

Fears that slaves might ally with pirates are evidenced by at least one governor's complaints that "the negroe men . . . are grown soe very impudent and insulting of late that we have reason to suspect their rising, soe that we can have no dependence on their assistance but to the contrary on occasion should fear their joining with the pirates."[77] The governor's fretting was warranted. Local slaves had helped French pirates sack Havana in 1538, and slave revolts had occurred when Drake's fleet approached Lima, Cartagena, and Hispaniola.[78] There are hints of alliances between maroon communities and pirate bands; especially those of Drake, Diego Grillo, and Blackbeard.[79] That pirates had ties with unsubjugated African tribes is apparent from a letter Captain Condon left at St. Mary's Island off Madagascar warning passing vessels "that they should use the Blacks kindly or he would be reveng'd of them."[80]

Other evidence relating to the status of blacks among pirates comes from court records. Traditional precedent held that servile status could absolve an individual for crimes ordered by one "in legitimate authority."[81] Servile status appears to have been presumed on the basis of skin color in instances where blacks were captured aboard pirate ships prior to 1700. Regardless of individual culpability, they were returned to their former owners, or were sold if no owner could be located.[82] Such appears to have been the fate of one of the only two survivors of the wreck of *The Whydah Galley*. John Julian, a *zambo* of the Mosquito tribe, was sold to John Quincy of Braintree in lieu of trial.[83] By contrast, if a black captured aboard a privateer could produce a certificate of manumission, he qualified for prisoner exchange, thus escaping enslavement.[84]

In response to unusually severe piratical depredations in the late 1690s, the English government responded aggressively to the threat posed by the pirates' "counterculture." Fearing they might establish "a sort of Commonwealth,"[85] a campaign of extermination was in full swing by 1699. Under heavy pressure from both government and merchant community, courts became far less lenient toward pirates.[86]

During the 1704 Boston trial of John Quelch's crew, the Queen's Advocate argued that "The Three Prisoners now at the Bar are of a different Complexion, 'tis true, but it is well known that the First and most Famous Pirates that have been in the World, were of their Colour."[87] The court found, however, that they had been forcibly carried off and had not been "active" except insofar as they had obeyed Quelch's orders. While their acquittal was based on traditional precedent, the tone of this case was ominous.

During the 1718 trial of five captured blacks from Blackbeard's crew, the Governor of Virginia asked his Council "whether there be any thing in the Circumstances of these Negroes to exempt them from undergoing the same Tryal as other Pirates." They replied:

> that the said Negroes being taken on Board a Pyrate vessell and by what appears equally concerned with the rest of the Crew in the Same Acts of Piracy ought to be Try'd in the same Manner; and if any diversity appears in their Circumstances the same may be considered on their Tryal.[88]

While all five were tried, found guilty, and executed, their testimony implicated Tobias Knight, Secretary to North Carolina Governor Eden, in various dealings with Blackbeard. Knight countered that the blacks had been improperly tried as pirates, and that their testimony was therefore inadmissible:

they are (tho cunningly couched under the names of Christians) no other than four Negro slaves which by the Laws and Customs of all America Aught not to be Examined as Evidence; neither is their Evidence of any validity against a White Person whatsoever. [89]

The Council concurred.

Although seventy blacks were as active as any among Bart Roberts's crew,[90] they were delivered to the Royal African Company in 1722 without trial.[91] This decision may have been influenced by Company employees sitting on the court. In 1724 captured black pirates were likewise sold in lieu of trial.[92]

These were, however, minority opinions. In trial after trial, blacks were placed on the same legal footing as whites.[93] They comprise an undetermined percentage of an estimated four hundred pirates executed during the decade 1716–1726. Most went silently to the gallows with little more than Hendrick Quintor's poignant comment, "Tis a Dark Time with me."[94] Others, however, retired successfully; such as "the old Negro man . . . who in his younger days had been well acquainted with many of the Buckneers, sail'd with them & knew many of their haunts."[95]

Beyond constraints of family, church, class, and state, the pirates of the seventeenth and eighteenth centuries unselfconsciously engaged in a unique social experiment—often with blacks as full-fledged participants. This experiment took the form of "social banditry" carried out in a maritime context. The result, however, was hardly noble. Like the "Beggars' Brotherhoods" of the previous century, pirates exploited others "just as they, the poor, were exploited by the upper classes . . . They were an anti-society organized against it, disbelieving in its ethics, dedicated to cheating and robbing it."[96] They were hard, brutal, and vicious men—by our standards—who lived in a hard, brutal, and vicious age as they "expropriated the expropriators." Unlike some Maroons, "The Brethren of the Coast" did not evolve into an embryonic nationhood. Lacking a geographic base, like the "Beggars' Brotherhood" of a century before, they were not a fully organized society of their own despite their conscious separation from society at large.[97]

Unable to mobilize their own full strength, as well as the potential support of other oppressed segments of the society they had rejected, the eighteenth-century pirates were, at their strongest, a tenuous collection of loosely linked, amorphous, floating commonwealths surviving only by predation on the very societies from which they had divorced themselves.[98] "Inability to disengage themselves fully from their enemy was the Achilles heel of maroon societies throughout the Americas."[99] While discipline and centralized authority helped land-based maroon societies survive, and even flourish,[100] the central feature and paramount attraction of piracy was its libertarian character. It is a profound irony that it was, in part, the pirates' own thirst for freedom which doomed them in an "aimless rebellion [which] ended by suppressing itself."[101]

NOTES

The foregoing is the subject of a larger work in progress by Kenneth J. Kinkor, Director of Research, Expedition Sea Lab and Learning Center, Provincetown, Mass.

1. Nigel Tattersfield, *The Forgotten Trade: Comprising the Log of the Daniel and Henry of 1700 and Accounts of the Slave Trade from the Minor Ports of England, 1698–1725* (London: J. Cape, 1991), xv.

2. Louis Adhemar Timothée Le Golif, *The Memoirs of A Buccaneer: Being a Wondrous and Unrepentant Account of the Prodigious Adventures and Amours of King Louis XIV's Loyal Servant Louis Adhemar Timothée Le Golif, Known for His Singular Wound As Borgnefesse, Captain of the Buccaneers, Told by Himself*, trans. Malcolm Barnes (London: Allen and Unwin, 1954), 108–114; Robert Bloch, "The Red Swimmer," in *Pirate Ghosts of the American Coast*, ed. Frank McSherry, Charles G. Wright, and Martin H. Greenburg (Little Rock, Ark.: August House, 1988), 59–60; Washington Irving, "Guest from Gibbet Island," in ibid , 145–157.

3. Christopher Hill, "Pirates," in *Liberty against the Law: Some Seventeenth Century Controversies* (London: Allen Lane, 1996), 114–122, reference here to 118.

4. Patrick Pringle, *Jolly Roger: The Story of the Great Age of Piracy* (New York: W. W. Norton, 1953); B. R. Burg, "Legitimacy and Authority: Case-Study of Pirate Commanders in the Seventeenth and Eighteenth Centuries," *American Neptune* 37, no. 1 (1977): 40–49; Marcus Rediker, "'Under the Banner of King Death': The Social World of Anglo-American Pirates 1716–1726," *William and Mary Quarterly* 38 (1981): 203–227; J. S. Bromley, "Outlaws at Sea: Equality and Fraternity among Caribbean Freebooters," in *Corsairs and Navies, 1660–1760*, ed. J. S. Bromley (Ronceverte, W.Va.: Hambledon Press, 1987); Christopher Hill, "Radical Pirates?" in *The Collected Essays of Christopher Hill* (Brighton, Sussex: Harvester Press, 1985); Robert C. Ritchie, *Captain Kidd and the War against the Pirates* (Cambridge, Mass.: Harvard University Press, 1986); Marcus Rediker, *Between the Devil and the Deep Blue Sea: Merchant Seamen, Pirates and the Anglo American Maritime Worlds 1700–1726* (Cambridge: Cambridge University Press, 1987); Jennifer Marx, *Pirates and Privateers of the Caribbean* (Malabar, Fla.: Krieger, 1992).

5. Malcolm Cowley, "The Sea Jacobins," *New Republic*, 1 February 1933: 327–329.

6. E. J. Hobsbawm, *Bandits* (London: Weidenfeld and Nicolson, 1969), 5, 17–18, 27–28.

7. Captain Charles Johnson, *A General History of the Robberies and Murders of the Most Notorious Pyrates and also their Policies, Discipline and Government from their first Rise and Settlement in the Island of Providence, in 1717, to the Present Year, 1724, with the Remarkable Actions and Adventures of the two Female Pyrates, Mary Read and Anne Bonny, to which is Prefix'd an Account of the famous Captain Avery*

and his Companions; with the Manner of his Death in England, ed. Manuel Schornhorn (London: Dent, 1972), 587.

8. Noel Stainsbury et al., ed., *Calendar of State Papers, Colonial Series. America and the West Indies, 1574–1738*, 27 vols. (London: Her Majesty's Stationery Office, 1860–1926) (henceforth *CSPCS*), 16, 115i, "Letter from Calicut November 30, 1696."

9. Donald Shomette, *Pirates on the Chesapeake: Being a True History of Pirates, Picaroons, and Raiders on Chesapeake Bay, 1610–1807* (Centreville, Md.: Tidewater Publishers, 1985), 130.

10. Johnson, *General History*, 587.

11. Christopher Hill, *The Century of Revolution 1603–1714* (New York: W. W. Norton, 1966), 77; *The Boston News-Letter*, 11 August 1718; William Snelgrave, *A New Account of Some Parts of Guinea and the Slave-Trade*, reprint of 1734 ed. (London: Frank Cass, 1971), 227; Johnson, *General History*, 217, 246.

12. Simon Smith, "Piracy in Early British America," *History Today*, May (1996): 29–37, reference here to 29.

13. *The Trials of Eight Persons Indited for Piracy &c. Of Whom Two were Acquitted, and the Rest Found Guilty. At a Justiciary Court of Admiralty Assembled and Held in Boston Within His Majesty's Province of the Massachusetts-Bay in New-England, on the 18th of October 1717. And by Several Adjournments Continued to the 30th. Pursuant to His Majesty's Commission and Instruction, Founded on the Act of Parliament Made in the 11th. & 12th of King William IIId. Intituled, An Act for the More Effectual Suppression of Piracy: With an Appendix, Containing the Substance of Their Confessions Given Before His Excellency the Governour, when They Were First Brought to Boston, and Committed to Goal.* Early American Imprint Series Microprint no. 2003 (Boston: B. Green for John Edwards, 1718), 5; Johnson, *General History*, 377–379.

14. S. Charles Hill, "Episodes of Piracy in the Eastern Sea, 1519–1851," *Indian Antiquary* 48 (1919): 56, and 49 (1920): 37–38.

15. Michael Baigent, Richard Leigh, and Henry Lincoln, *The Holy Blood and the Holy Grail* (London: Cape, 1982), 83–84.

16. Rediker, *Between the Devil*, 166, 260–261, 286–287; *Trial of Eight Persons*, 24; Johnson, *General History*, 213.

17. George Francis Dow and John Henry Edmonds, *The Pirates of the New England Coast*, reprint of 1923 ed. (New York: Argosy-Antiquarian, 1968), 227.

18. Marcus Rediker and Peter Linebaugh, "The Many-Headed Hydra: Sailors, Slaves, and the Atlantic Working-Class in the Eighteenth Century," *Journal of Historical Sociology* 3 (1990): 225–252, reference here to 226.

19. *Trial of Eight Persons*, 10.

20. Johnson, *General History*, 403–404.

21. Johnson, *General History*, 45, 70, 175–176, 356–357.

22. *Boston News-Letter*, 29 October 1717; Huntingdon Library, Blathwayt MSS., "Deposition of Richard Arnold," 1686.

23. PRO, CO 5/1318, 16ii, "Information of Andrew Turbett," Virginia, 17 April 1717.

24. Johnson, *General History,* 479.

25. "John Menzies to the Secretary of Admiralty, July 20, 1721," in J. F. Jameson, *Privateering and Piracy in the Colonial Period: Illustrative Documents* (New York: Macmillan, 1923), 318–322.

26. *The Western Journal or The British Gazetteer,* 10 October 1719; Johnson, *General History,* 235–236.

27. Ira Berlin, "From Creole to African: Atlantic Creoles and the Origins of African American Society in Mainland North America," *William and Mary Quarterly* (3d Series) 53, no. 2 (1996): 251–288, reference here to 252.

28. W. Jeffrey Bolster, *Black Jacks: African American Seamen in the Age of Sail* (Cambridge, Mass.: Harvard University Press, 1997), 50–53; William Smith, *A New Voyage to Guinea: Describing the Customs, Manners, Soil, Climate, Habits, Buildings, Education . . . Habitations, Diversions, Marriages, and Whatever Else is Memorable among the Inhabitants* (London: J. Nourse, 1744, reprint, London: Frank Cass, 1967), 91; Thomas Phillips, "Journal of Thomas Phillips," in *Collection of Voyages,* ed. Churchill (1746). Reprinted in *Slave Ships and Slaving,* ed. George Francis Dow (New York: 1927), 76.

29. Hugo Prosper Leaming, *Hidden Americans: Maroons of Virginia and the Carolinas* (New York: Garland Publishing, 1995), 129.

30. *The Tryals of Major Stede Bonnet, and Other Pirates, Viz. Robert Tucker, Edward Robinson, Neal Paterson [And Others] . . . Who Were All Condemn'd for Piracy. As Also the Tryals of Thomas Nichols, Rowland Sharp, Jonathan Clarke, and Thomas Gerrat, for Piracy, Who Were Acquitted. At the Admiralty Sessions Held at Charlestown, in the Province of South Carolina, on Tuesday the 28th of October, 1718, and by Several Adjournments Continued to Wednesday the 12th of November, Following, to Which is Prefix'd, An Account of the Taking of the Said Major Bonnet, and the Rest of the Pirates* (London: Printed for B. Cowse, 1719); Johnson, *General History,* 595.

31. Richard Hawkins, "Letter of Richard Hawkins to One of His Owners," in *The Political State of Great Britain: With the Most Material Occurrences in Europe,* ed. Abel Boyer (London: John Baker and T. Warner, 1724), 24: 153.

32. *CSPCS* 17: 880, "Journal of Captain Barker's Cruize in the Speedwell," 1699.

33. PRO CO 152/13, 282, "The Deposition of Christian Mortensen May 18, 1721"; *American Weekly Mercury,* 14 September 1721; Berlin, "Creole to African": 272; cf. Bolster, *Black Jacks,* 51.

34. Robert E. Lee, *Blackbeard the Pirate: a Reappraisal of his Life and Times* (Winston-Salem: J. F. Blair, 1974), 217; Berlin, "Creole to African,": 251–252; Leaming, *Hidden Americans,* 125.

35. Johnson, *General History,* 247.

36. Bolster, *Black Jacks,* 15.

37. *Tryals of Bonnet,* 30.

38. *Tryals of Bonnet,* 30.

39. Johnson, *General History,* 587.

40. Johnson, *General History,* 244.

41. Bolster, *Black Jacks,* 12.

42. Rediker, *Between the Devil*, 256–257.

43. *Account of the Tryal of All the Pyrates lately Taken by Captain Ogle, on Board the Swallow, Man of War on the Coast of Guinea* (London: 1723).

44. PRO CO 152/12 67iii, "Deposition of Henry Bostock," 19 December 1717; Bolster, *Black Jacks*, 12.

45. E.g., Michael Cohn and Michael K. H. Platze, *Black Men of the Sea* (New York: Dodd, Mead, 1978), 31; David Cordingly, *Life among the Pirates: The Romance and the Reality* (London: Little, Brown, 1995), 27–28; Bolster, *Black Jacks*, 15.

46. Berlin, "Creole to African," 268.

47. Thomas Gage, *The English-American: A New Survey of the West Indies, 1648* (London: G. Routledge and Sons, 1928), 349–351; Jan Rogozinski, *Pirates* (New York: Facts on File, 1995), 170.

48. Peter Earle, *The Sack of Panama: Sir Henry Morgan's Adventures on the Spanish Main* (New York: Viking Press, 1982), 65.

49. Robert S. Weddle, *Spanish Sea: The Gulf of Mexico in the North American Discovery* (College Station, Tex.: Texas A&M University Press, 1985), 385, 392; Philip Gosse, *The Pirates' Who's Who, Giving Particulars of the Lives and Deaths of the Pirates and Buccaneers* (London: Dulau and Company, 1924), 115.

50. Weddle, *Spanish Sea*, 399; C. H. Haring, *The Buccaneers in the West Indies in the XVIIth Century* (Hamden, Conn.: Archon Books, 1966), 241–243.

51. *CSPCS* 28: 158v, "Deposition of Samuel Page," 15 May 1716.

52. Shomette, *Pirates*, 232–236.

53. Wim Klooster, *Illicit Riches: Dutch Trade in the Caribbean, 1648–1795* (Leiden: Koninklijk Instituut Voor Taal-, Land- En Volkenkunde, 1998), 153–154.

54. Ralph D. Paine, *The Book of Buried Treasure: Being a True History of the Gold, Jewels, and Plate of Pirates, Galleons, etc., which are Sought for to this Day* (London: Heinemann, 1911); Jameson, *Privateering*, 222.

55. Ritchie, *Captain Kidd*, 84.

56. Johnson, *General History*, 82–83; Leaming, *Hidden Americans*, 125.

57. Rediker, *Between the Devil*, 231–232.

58. Rogozinski, *Pirates*, 29.

59. *Boston News-Letter*, 12 September 1728.

60. IOR E352 no. 17 6230, "Mr. Negus' Information about Ye Piracy committed on board Moco friggatt"; *Tryals of Bonnet*, 11–12; *Boston News-Letter*, 11 August 1718; *Trial of Eight Persons*, 9–10; "Deposition of Israel Hands March 12, 1718," in North Carolina, *The Colonial Records of North Carolina*, 10 vols. (New York: AMS Press, 1968), 2: 341; "A Most Truthful Relation of What Happened in Florida in the Month of July of this Year MDLXXX," in *Colonial Records of Spanish Florida: Letters and Reports of Governors, Deliberations of the Council of the Indies, Royal Decrees & Other Documents, Volume 2 (1577–1580)*, ed. and trans. Jeannette Thurber Connor (Deland: Florida Historical Society, 1930), 319–330, reference here to 319–323.

61. Johnson, *General History*, 605.

62. Cf. Simon Smith, "Piracy," 3.

63. Richard Price, ed., *Maroon Societies: Rebel Slave Communities in the Americas* (Baltimore: Johns Hopkins University Press, 1997), 5.

64. *CSPCS* 12: 339; Gage, *The English-American*, 208–209.

65. Price, *Maroon Societies*, xi–xii, 1–2.

66. Leaming, *Hidden Americans*, xv.

67. Personal communication from Lawrence Feldman concerning contents of Audiencia de Guatemala 299 and 300 AGI.

68. *Tryals of Bonnet*, 19.

69. Johnson, *General History*, 342.

70. Johnson, *General History*, 651.

71. J. H. Baer, "The Complicated Plot of Piracy," *Eighteenth Century: Theory and Interpretation* 23, no. 1 (1982): 3–26, reference here to 11.

72. Richard Luntley, *The Last Speech and Dying Words, of Richard Luntley, Carpenter Aboard the Eagle Snow who was Executed within the Floodmark at Leith upon the 11th January 1721, for the Crimes of Piracy and Robbert* (Edinburgh: 1721).

73. PRO CO 137/12 no. 411I, "Deposition of Joseph Eels" 3 December 1716.

74. Peter Linebaugh, *The London Hanged: Crime and Civil Society in the Eighteenth Century* (Cambridge: Cambridge University Press, 1992), 133–138.

75. Bolster, *Black Jacks*, 4–5,70–74.

76. Hill, "Radical Pirates," 169–170.

77. *CSPCS* 1718: 551, "Lt. Governor Bennett of Bermuda to the Council of Trade and Plantations."

78. Price, *Maroon Societies*, 37, 41; Leaming, *Hidden Americans*, 9.

79. Price, *Maroon Societies*, 14; Leaming, *Hidden Americans*, 124; Kenneth R. Andrews, *The Spanish Caribbean: Trade and Plunder, 1530–1630* (New Haven: Yale University Press, 1978), 138–141.

80. IOR, East India Co. Records D/97, "Deposition of Thomas Pyke at a Committee of Shipping ye 9th Nov. 1721."

81. *Trial of Eight Persons*, 22.

82. *CSPCS* 34:102, "Governor Hart to Council of Trade and Plantations," March 25, 1724"; *CSPCS* 34: 8 and 8i, "Deposition of Thome dos Santos, Manuel Pires, Sabastiano Fernandes and Diogo do Rosario, December 2, 1723."

83. *Trial of Eight Persons*, 25; "A List of Prisoners," Boston Gaol, 2 July 1717. Massachusetts Archives, Boston, Mass., Suffolk Court Files, 11664; D. A. G. Waddell, *British Honduras: A Historical and Contemporary Survey* (London: Oxford University Press for the Royal Institute of International Affairs, 1961), 10; Edward Rowe Snow, *New England Sea Tragedies* (New York: Dodd, Mead, 1960), 17.

84. *CSPCS* 32: 527, "Capt. Vernon to Mr. Burchett," 8 March 1720.

85. *Trial of Eight Persons*, 7; Cotton Mather, "The End of Piracy," in *Instructions to the Living on the Condition of the Dead [etc]* (Boston: John Allen for Nicholas Boone, 1717), 4–5.

86. Ritchie, *Captain Kidd*, 127–159, 233–235.

87. Dow and Edmonds, *Pirates*, 109–110.

88. Lee, *Blackbeard*, 136.

89. Lee, *Blackbeard*, 148–149.

90. *Account of . . . Pyrates.. Taken by Captain Ogle*, 36.

91. Johnson, *General History*, 285.

92. *CSPCS* 34: 10, "Governor Hart to Council of Trade and Plantations, March 25, 1724."

93. E.g., *American Weekly Mercury*, 17 March 1720; *Tryals of Bonnet*; *CSPCS* 33: 142, "Governor Sir Nicholas Lawes to the Council of Trade and Plantations."

94. Mather, "End of Piracy," 27.

95. Bolster, *Black Jacks*, 16.

96. Henry Kamen, *The Iron Century: Social Change in Europe, 1550–1660* (New York: Praeger, 1971), 401–402.

97. Kamen, *Iron Century*.

98. Rediker, "King Death," 226–227.

99. Price, *Maroon Societies*, 12.

100. Price, *Maroon Societies*, 18.

101. Cowley, "Sea Jacobins," 329.

Chapter 11

The Buccaneer Community

B. R. Burg

The coterminal limits of the physical and psychological boundaries of the ship, when combined with its impermeability or insulation from outside influences, created an environment for the seventeenth-century mariner that has been characterized as a total institution. This is a situation where entry or egress is severely restricted, the normally segregated activities of life—eating, sleeping, working, and recreation—are all conducted within the same spatially constricted area, each phase of the participants' lives is lived out in the immediate company of others of the institution's participants, with events being sequenced and directed from a higher authority within the institution for the attainment of a goal or goals recognized as desirable by all participants. The comprehensive effects of personality and interaction between members of any such institution are profound, but aboard buccaneering vessels the added elements of danger, frequent dietary deficiency, occasional drunkenness, the unlikelihood of ever returning to the mother country (a desire which probably affected some), the imminence of death, and the sea itself all combined to increase the "totality" of the surroundings beyond that experienced by the convicts, military men, or asylum inmates who have been studied in institutional settings.[1]

In attempting to discern possible modes of behavior by pairing pirate communities with "total institutions" such as asylums and modern shipboard communities, the same caveat that applies to prison studies and research on modern homosexual activity and pedophilia must be even more firmly propounded. There is considerable divergence, as might be expected, in the experiences of modern mariners separated by so wide an expanse of time from buccaneers. But despite the obvious technological and perceptual variations, the social structure aboard ship has changed little in many respects since the age of sail. Data garnered from men now taking their livings from the sea has considerable complementary utility in reconstructing selected features of past maritime relationships, and the correlations sometimes make the structure of buccaneer life appear more clearly from the opaqueness imposed by the passage of time. Again, trepidation and caution are watchwords in dealing with sailors in this fashion. Advances in nautical construction, varying economic expectations, increased safety, alterations in the character of work experience, improvement of physical surroundings, and the differences in outlook and attitudes occasioned by the passage of time all separate modern seamen from their seventeenth-century counterparts and prevent results of recent investigations of shipboard life from being applied uniformly and uncritically to relationships among crewmen three hundred years ago. Still, striking parallels in the responses of men to socially similar circumstances are to be found not only in comparisons of seafaring life with that in total institutions but in analyses of shipboard conditions and mariners' responses in both the seventeenth and the twentieth centuries. Sailors' difficulties in the present, in many respects, were also their difficulties in the past. The close proximity of every man to his shipmates, the complexities of evolving interpersonal relationships, and the protracted boredom on many of today's vessels were surely present aboard well-manned pirate ships and naval craft, where the necessary contingent of fighting men was far in excess of those needed for sailing and maneuvering no matter how severe the weather. Occasional difficulties and deprivations, even when the social features of deprivation were chosen rather than only endured, compounded the effect of shipboard features with potential for social disruption.

The need to ration food, alcohol, or water aboard buccaneering vessels, like smoking curfews on submarines running submerged for prolonged periods of time, exacerbated morale problems and in combination with other aspects of life aboard ship—the low turnover of pirate crewmen and the restricted amounts of usable space—often created for sailors then and now an atmosphere much like prisons, where similar conditions prevail. In both types of total institution, prisons and ships, various aspects of community produce a high level of anxiety in which antagonistic associations are formed that have directive force in the operation of the community. But in like manner, closeness, boredom, and enduring a common set of woes create situations that are primarily affective as well.[2]

The very features of shipboard life that produce this social paradox are also the features responsible for many of the situations that attract men to seafaring. Within the institutional imperatives, no matter what ratio exists between mutual hostility and interpersonal esteem, there develop stable life patterns that are, and were in the age of buccaneering, meaningful, reasonable, and normal within particular limits. According to interviews in a recent study of seafarers' attitudes, the reasons for choosing a maritime career were all of those that might be expected: the opportunity to travel, the prospect of an exciting and varied life, the chance to meet people, the possibility of advancement, and the community atmosphere aboard ship. The majority of motives given by the interviewees probably had little appeal to lads who first went to sea from English port towns in the seventeenth century, but the last mentioned attraction, the chance to participate in a community of seafarers, may have served as a particularly desirable quality for boys who were ejected early from their parents' homes, forced into vagabondage, placed as apprentices, or were put out as servants or laborers. For young men in such circumstances, whether the choice to go to sea was taken voluntarily, forced by hunger, or made at the urging of an armed press gang, seafaring may have provided the opportunity to retain for a time the adolescent dependence made difficult to perpetuate by the loss of home, parents, and familiar surroundings. Their dependence on the total institutional structure of the ship and officers created for them a home-like situation where social and physical boundaries were easily discerned and food, shelter, recreation, compensation, work, and conduct were all regulated. In a recent study aboard a nuclear submarine, an age-regressive style of juvenile gang behavior developed among the crewmen who divided themselves into units on the basis of technical skills, and similar patterns of behavior have also been observed in projective tests administered to subjects in confinement experiments. How accurately observations of present-day sailors and laboratory behavior studies replicate motives and responses of seafarers from the past is not a question that is easily answered, but the types of behavior observed by researchers in their subject populations are apparent in pirate groups as well. The desperate cohesiveness with which freebooters fought for one another and their awareness of being not only members of their own ship's community but part of a "Brethren of the Coast"—one band even carried their sense of unity to the point of adopting a group name, "The Flying Gang"—indicate that juvenile male bonding, among youths as well as their older companions, was a pervasive feature of buccaneering.[3]

The sailors who opted for lengthy voyages to distant points of England's trading patterns and the pool of men from which the bulk of pirate crews were drawn made their choice of seafaring lifestyles for a complex of reasons in which each obtained maximum gratification from living and working in an institution with low permeability. The same preference is found among sailors and officers serving on large oil tankers. Loading and off-loading procedures often keep them anchored far from shore. Their contact with persons other than their fellow crew members is at a minimum, and the periods at sea can run into months or even into years for some men who rarely leave their vessels and are considered to be suffering from what mariners call "tankeritis." In both cases, men elect to spend lengthy periods at sea because it offers a secure base for their socialization and provides the masculine security and interpersonal satisfaction unavailable ashore. For the pirate in the Caribbean, the effect of those features that made long voyages more attractive than coastal trading were amplified by serving aboard a buccaneering vessel. Limited permeability at sea was reinforced by the shiplike low permeability of the English Caribbean towns—with their limited access to women—that the buccaneers visited. There was little likelihood that pirate vessels would ever sail to England or other European ports where the crews would be paid off in the manner of merchant seamen or the sailors from men-of-war and set ashore to live in a landsman's world.

During abbreviated stays in the more complex social milieu of the landsman, if the pattern of present-day mariners is applicable at all to mariners of three centuries ago, buccaneers probably experienced uneasiness in communication and a feeling that the tavern keepers, prostitutes, and others they came in contact with in various colonial towns did not understand their way of life. A measure of the difficulty on land was undoubtedly due to poorly developed social skills resulting from extended periods aboard ship, but the dissatisfaction was also enlarged by awareness of the extortionate rates charged pirates for goods and services by merchants.[4] Pirate ships were often in and out of port on a more frequent basis than East Indiamen, and any new buccaneers they acquired were either "Brethren of the Coast," experienced merchant seamen, or novices in the business of seafaring. Socialization of the new man created little problem for the buccaneer. Pirates and merchant sailors integrated into their midst without causing more than a ripple, and prisoners, escaped servants, or convicts posed no threat to the experienced buccaneer. He was secured by his highly developed skills and the established shipboard relationships, which precluded the danger of status diminution by recently acquired replacements. By the time new personnel that survived were initiated into the ways of the sea and had mastered sufficient technical knowledge to compete with the older buccaneers, they were fully socialized and acculturated into the shipboard community. Captives who refused to join the pirates presented no difficulty. Their status as prisoners removed them from the social system that provided pirates with their identity and offered each marauder an extra tot of security in being able to exercise easy domination over other human beings.[5]

Additional impetus for rapid and permanent acculturation for men taken aboard pirate vessels was the relatively pleasant life patterns enjoyed by the crew, pleasant at least when compared with those experienced by men in the Navy or sailing aboard less desirable merchant craft. Buccaneer discipline in matters relating to day-to-day life was less rigid and less brutal, although the totality of the institution was not appreciably diminished by such liberalism. The values and non-native expectations of sailors turned freebooter retained a high degree of coherence, powerfully sanctioned as they were by the crewmen themselves. A man joining a pirate crew gained freedom from particularly galling aspects of regulation and considerable arbitrariness while at the same time retaining the institutional structure that provided for his social and psychological requirements.

Shipboard Buggery and the Nature of Prosecution

The acculturative security and tightly bonded community structure provided by ships in the seventeenth century is nowhere more apparent than in the surviving records dealing with shipboard buggery. Although the first secular statute condemning homosexual conduct in England dates from the reign of Henry VIII, over a hundred years passed before sexual relations between sailors of the Royal Navy were given official notice by high-ranking officers. It is not known if there was a single incident or series of incidents in the fleet that precipitated Admiralty cognizance of events aboard their vessels, but the propensity of King James I for male lovers may have provided the example that convinced the navy that homosexual behavior was a problem. Significantly, they did not move to restrict or eliminate it until 1627, after James was cold in his grave and Charles I, particularly prudish in matters of sex, was installed on the throne. In that year a regulation was put into effect providing that "If any Person belonging to the Fleet shall commit Buggery or Sodomy, he shall be punished with Death."[6]

Two years later, public interest in the subject was aroused when the Earl of Castlehaven was brought to trial both under the 1533 statute prohibiting homosexual practices and on several other sex-related charges. But even with the scandal created by the Earl and the new regulation requiring death for buggery and sodomy, the Admiralty prosecutions that followed were few in number. Of those actually tried, there is in every case solid evidence that more was involved than homosexual acts. Violations of shipboard community standards or interference from outside the maritime milieu seem to have determined the need for prosecutions. Robert Hewitt, brought to trial in the early 1630s, was apparently an excessive practitioner of sodomy as well as a child molester. He was accused of buggering Marmaduke Warnham, Roger Head, and a boy, George Hungerforde, all during a single voyage of the *Royall Mary*. In a similar case brought later in the decade against Robert Stone, a "saylor," there are even clearer indications that the accused was being tried not simply for violating Samuel Organ, a lad aboard his ship, but was in fact a notorious sodomite, regularly crossing the social boundaries that divided sexual and nonsexual relationships aboard ship and in all likelihood seeking partners among those already involved in permanent or semipermanent arrangements.[7]

If studies of modern seafarers give any clue to the lives of their predecessors,

the proximity of one man to another aboard ship amplified the relationships between men, intensifying sexual competitiveness when present because of the limited number of men available as partners and increasing the anxiety level aboard
the ship where the institutional "totality" prohibited easy resolution of the problem. Some quantity of the competitive viciousness generated by close quarters
and sexual competition may have been involved in the indictment of Richard
Kingston some years later where it appears that more than proscribed sex acts
brought him to the attention of the authorities. Kingston, of Magdalen College,
M.A. Oxon, and minister to His Majesty's frigate *Forsight*, was a man of some
experience as a seafaring cleric. He had served for fourteen months aboard the
Advice before joining the *Forsight*, and was commended in a deposition by the
captain of the *Advice* for doing an excellent job. Under the circumstances it
would seem unlikely that he would be indicted for sodomy, but ill luck was with
Kingston. Although his fellow crew members evidently had no complaint about
his conduct, an alleged victim of Kingston's lust, a fifteen-year-old lad named
Richard Ellery, reported the event or events when the ship returned to England.
The accused minister denied the charge, but he admitted he had whipped the boy
severely on at least one occasion. Whether the whipping was a manifestation of
homosexual sadism or punishment for some offense cannot be discerned from
the indictment, but Kingston evidently was not tried for the offense, indicating
the accusation well may have been Ellery's revenge for the flogging.[8]

Like the indictments of Hewitt, Stone, and Kingston, a 1649 incident involving the buggery of sixteen-year-old John Durrant of Stepney also had overtones
that carried it beyond an act of anal intercourse. The feature of the case that
seemed to irritate the captain who conducted the trial was not that buggery had
been committed repeatedly or that it had been done with the boy's consent. The
horror of the event was that an English lad had allowed himself to be penetrated
by a heathen, Abdul Rhyme, "Hindostan peon." Numerous witnesses testified to
having seen the two frequently involved in buggery and in mutual masturbation
on the quarterdeck as well as below. The truth of the testimony was assured by
having nine Christian witnesses swear on the Bible to the veracity of their statements. Corroborating statements were also taken from a number of Hindus, but
their word was useful only for supporting what had been attested to by Christians. It could not sustain a conviction alone, according to the trial record. In this
case, the accused mariners were convicted, and each was given forty lashes, the
wounds to be rubbed with salt and water. According to the sentence, there were
to be several later administrations of ten lashes with more salt and water, and the
sodomites were to be limited to a diet of bread and water for an unspecified period of time.[9]

Harsh as it may seem, the punishment meeted out to Abdul Rhyme and
Durrant was considerably less than the death sentence specified in the regula-

tions. But again, the rantings of the trial's presiding officer indicate that he was more agitated by acts of miscegenation that disrupted the operation of the total institution than by buggery, which was an ordinary part of the vessel's functioning. Indeed the tendency to regard interracial sex as far more serious than homosexuality was not a peculiarity of this particular captain or a feature of life aboard an individual ship. In a later satirical pamphlet, using a pirate craft for what might have been an allegorical treatment of William III and his associates, a mutineer was discredited not by accusing him of buggery but by inducing a Moor to testify that the accused had once asked to be buggered by him.[10]

In another case for which records survive, Samuel Norman, a ship captain, was accused of pulling down the breeches of his servant and inserting his "Yard or privity into his Backside" on at least three separate occasions. The alleged offenses were committed with more delicacy by Norman than those of Durrant and Rhyme. He closed the door and locked it to prevent observation by the crew, then embarked on a scenario of seduction similar in some respects to that used by prison "jockers" bringing youthful convicts into their homosexual arrangements. He first employed deviousness to induce the cabin boy to provide him with a rubdown. The ship was at anchor and Norman had been ashore horseback riding. He informed the lad after his return that his legs ached from the unfamiliar exercise and removed his breeches so that the pain could be massaged away. The fourteen-year-old was well aware of the commander's intentions and suggested another, more receptive, lad then aboard ship as a suitable partner, but Captain Norman would not be dissuaded, according to the testimony. When gentleness failed, Norman turned the boy about, bent him over, bared his posterior, and the deed was quickly done. The commander surely assumed that there would be no repercussion from his initial act and those that followed, but again, on the ship's return to England, charges were brought not by the victim or outraged crew members, but by a father incensed that his son had been used in such fashion. Norman was never brought to trial. An indictment was denied for reasons that have not survived. Still, the case bears similarities to the others in that it was not simply a matter of a buggered boy complaining but of an outsider requesting that action be taken.[11]

The use of sodomy as a political weapon was as convenient for buccaneers as for Englishmen in the homeland. During a 1680 cruise in the South Sea, a severe disagreement over whether to continue in the Pacific or return through the Straits of Magellan to sail in the vicinity of established English settlements in the Caribbean severely divided the crew of a Captain Sawkins. By the time the disagreement had reached crisis proportions, Sawkins had died, leaving the expedition without a leader. Three men evidently vied to take command:

Bartholomew Sharp, John Wading, and Edmund Cook. First Sharp was elected captain, but opposition to him remained strong and he was deposed by the supporters of Wading. Cook, too, assumed he was qualified for the post. He had sailed many years as a privateer, served as commander of a number of vessels at various times, and once led a land force of over 350 pirates in an attack on a Spanish colonial town. At this point, Cook's servant was forced or persuaded to confess "that his Master had oft times Buggered him in England. . . . That the same crime he had also perpetrated in Jamaica; and once in these Seas before Panama." Wading seized what he thought was an advantage, and tried to have Cook imprisoned for sodomy. That would have had the obvious effect of removing him as a contender for the captaincy. However, Wading soon discovered that incarcerating him for a homosexual act was too transparent a pretext, hardly a measure that would persuade seasoned buccaneers of his unfitness for leadership. Moreover, Wading's attempt to confine Cook was further weakened when the servant who had made the original accusation refused to reaffirm it as he lay dying of an unspecified malady. The only solution was to discover another odious act committed by Cook, and this was done. A paper was found in the possession of the accused sodomite listing the names of the men with whom he had sailed. It was charged by Wading, according to the testimony of privateer Basil Ringrose, that Cook planned to provide the list to Spanish prisoners aboard the ship. It was not entirely clear why Cook would give the list to the Spanish, or even if that was his intention, but when the accusation of buggery failed, another charge was needed to enable Wading to clap the hapless Cook in irons and secure his own command.[12]

A most vital factor concerning these cases is that they are not a random selection but the sum total of all such incidents for which records survive in the century between the Admiralty regulation of 1627 and the freeing of Captain Norman from Newgate Prison in 1723; there is no indication that there were other similar cases for which the records are missing. Taken as a group, they indicate that cases necessarily must involve more than ordinary buggery or sodomy for them to be considered important. They must be disruptive of shipboard totality or involve an outside factor. Robert Hewitt and Robert Stone were apparently excessive buggerers; one case involved a complaining victim of floggings; John Durrant had not only been buggered but, more seriously, he had been buggered by a heathen; another case included a complaining parent; Cook was the victim of a power struggle.

In dealing with buggery and sodomy, there appears to have been a distinction in the way it was regarded by men from different classes. With Durrant, for example, there was little attempt on the part of the participants to secure privacy for their various acts of anal intercourse or masturbation, although it is unlikely that a secret trysting place was available for crewmen in any circumstance. They engaged in homosexual acts on the quarterdeck, which was probably manned twenty-four hours a day, below decks, and between bales of cargo. The number of witnesses who testified in the inquiry demonstrates that no effort was made to hide their conduct. In their era sexual acts were not performed as furtively as is presently the custom, and indeed there is no reason to suspect that sex acts in the seventeenth century were ordinarily performed in private. This was an age when the mass of men and women lived in close proximity to farm animals—always notorious for following their sexual inclinations with or without the presence of human or same-species audiences—and for most of the world's population the private bedroom had not yet been invented. In their homes, people ate, slept, worked, and copulated in the same space, and it is only natural to assume they would conduct themselves in the same manner aboard ships at sea. In the case of Captain Norman, the trial records do contain the information that the accused closed and locked the cabin door so that he would not be observed by the crew, an indication that although buggery among the men was not always a secret practice, one in a command position with the luxury of private accommodations nonetheless would prefer to engage in sexual practices unobserved by the rabble. Yet Norman knew, it must be assumed, that there are few secrets aboard a ship, and that sodomizing a cabin boy would be known by the crew in short order.

Homosexual Association and Identification

Examining patterns of sexuality three hundred years past against a corpus of data derived from modern research contains the same potential for overextension and the drawing of unwonted conclusions inherent in pairing pirates and penitentiary inmates. But if a direct link between homosexuals past and present is dangerous, the method of approach offers some compensating qualities for illuminating the possibilities for diversity among homosexual or homosexually oriented groups. The social, intellectual, economic, and cultural variety characteristic of present-day populations engaged in homosexual activity was absent among the likes of those who became pirates, but Caribbean marauders were joined by other compelling social bonds, similar life experiences, privations endured, common economic problems, and the mastery of the same trades or techniques for survival. In this sense, they formed an interest community that went beyond sexually specified requirements, in contrast to the cliques of homosexuals frequently studied by sociologists and psychologists where there is no formal organization and only a sexual bond to unite them. Within such cliques, sex is clearly compartmentalized, and most members do not carry their homosexual associations on into their other business or leisure-time activities because of the risk of exposure and humiliation. But in seventeenth-century England, the risks were minimal, and genuine communities composed of homosexuals evolved, although they could never be self-regulating due to the dominant heterosexual culture that pervaded the land.[13]

The lack of persecution and the ease of making homosexual contacts probably eliminated the need for social centers for pirate communities similar to modern gay bars or networks of gay coffeehouses, baths, bookstores, record shops, gyms, restaurants, and other gathering places where homosexuals and those homosexually directed can not only exchange information and make sexual contacts, but where the primary function is to reaffirm the patron's worth in a generally hostile environment. Although Randolph Trumbach traces the roots of a genuine homosexual subculture back into the closing decade of the seventeenth century, the men who became pirates were, for the most part, gone from England by 1695, and those still in the homeland after that time were from levels of society far below the participants in the network of clubs, brothels, taverns, and meeting places he describes. It is not likely that there were any similarly functional institutions for males on the lowest social strata in seventeenth-century and eighteenth-century England or the West Indies. The need for such institutions was obviated by general acceptance of homosexual conduct and the opportunity for those involved to live with little fear of the authorities and no concern over the hazards of public exposure. There were of course sailors' grog shops, which were undoubtedly patronized by homosexuals and others similarly inclined, but these differed from the gay bar in that they catered not specifically to men who sought out other men as sex partners but to a clientele of sailors who happened to be homosexually oriented or genuinely homosexual.[14] The same is probably true of other establishments. With the homosexual activity among lower-class males considered to be ordinary behavior, one of the chief functions of the gay bar, the establishment of the individual's personal value through contact with other similarly oriented individuals, was not necessary.

Similarly, the problems of identification of potential sexual partners, sometimes a vexing exercise in the present day, was much less complex for the potential buccaneer. Often the visible symbols of class and occupation were sufficient for sexual classification, much as occupation might indicate possible homosexual preferences today for a hairdresser or an interior decorator. A sailor would likely be receptive to homosexual advances, but a baker, owning his own shop, with the need for a wife and children to aid him, and being a member of a class where heterosexuality was economically viable, would be an unlikely prospect. Beyond these symbols, there is no evidence from the seventeenth or eighteenth centuries to indicate that men with homosexual proclivities or preferences from the pirate-producing classes were recognizable by a system of secret signs or signals. The literature is extensive on systems for identification among modern homosexuals and men engaging in homosexual acts. The way glances are exchanged, the manner of dress, a seemingly meaningless movement, the wearing of a pinky ring, Pall Mall cigarettes ("Wherever Particular People Congregate") are understood only by the cognoscenti, while homosexual behavior obvious to the uninitiated is observable usually only in 10 to 15 percent of the homosexual or homosexually oriented population.[15] One recent study maintains that among homosexuals in prison, isolated as they are in an all-male community where homosexuality is an accepted part of daily life, recognizability rises to approximately 30 percent. But a prison environment is different in essential respects from English communities in the times of the later Stuarts and early Hanoverians, and it is distinct in essential respects from West Indian pirate communities as well.[16]

Communication and the Use of Specialized Language

The only possibility that there existed any systems to insure recognizability among homosexual pirates, beyond the indications presented by the facts of a seafaring life, was the maritime propensity for a secret language similar in some respects to the argot frequently used by members of homosexual cliques. Still, it is dangerous to place too heavy a burden of interpretative synthesis on such a factual base. Sailors, and thus pirates, have had for centuries their own speech patterns dealing with the details of seafaring. Landsmen unfamiliar with the language of the sea are pressed to remember if starboard is left or right and are lost amid references to hawsers and lifts or braces and yards. This sort of specialized nautical speech serves a function entirely different than the language of either homosexuals or homosexual pirates. It is a military language, a professional mode of expression necessary to deal with articles, practices, and procedures not encountered anywhere else, and it grew from necessity rather than to serve the purpose of concealment or identification. Modern homosexuals have their own dialogue, but as in the case of sailors, among underworld figures, in prisons, and with seafaring talk, the purpose is not to maintain secrecy but to classify and communicate common experiences. Among homosexuals, as among sailors, their private means of communication is not a language, but simply a limited set of words and expressions to communicate understanding in severely limited situations. Just as seafarer's language is extended to nonseafaring subjects only in metaphor and simile, the same is true with homosexual argot. The vocabulary that is exclusively homosexual is confined for the most part to activities that are exclusively homosexual.[17] As the terms binnacle and bowsprit have little use among men who do not make their living from the sea, so the expressions "slicklegging" or to pick up "trade" do not extend into heterosexual vocabulary.

Among pirates, the only unique portion of their vocabulary that survives, beyond seafaring terminology, is the regular use of nicknames. In this area, the practices of French and English buccaneers diverge somewhat. Nicknames relating to places of birth or residence were fairly common among the French. One of the most notorious pirate chiefs was Jean-David Nau, called l'Olonnais after his birthplace at Les Sables d'Olonnais, and pirates named in like manner were Michel le Basque and Pierre le Picard. Others carried titles that detailed their grisly physical appearance. Tete-d'Épingle and Pied de Bouc sailed with men like Bâbord-Amures, whose nose was noticeably directed toward the port side of his face. Tête-de-Mort had a nose half eaten away by an ulcer. Boisbrûlé and Gueule-de-Raie were merely ugly fellows, as one would assume was the case with Bille-en-Bois, but the character of other pirates was reflected in names such as Montbars the Exterminator or Pierre le Grand. English nicknames typically were less descriptive than those of the French. Common among them were more ordinary appellations like Black Bart, Blackbeard, Timberhead, or, in the case of one man, the simple and direct name, Bear. Both French and English nicknames sometimes carried sexual or homosexual implications. Tape-cul was so called in reference to his backside and surely Coeur d'Andouille must have occasionally detected a sly smile on the faces of those to whom he was introduced. Captain John Avery, as fierce as any who sailed in the eighteenth century, was known as Long Ben, not because of his height, and Louis Adhémar Timothée le Golif, known as Borgnefesse and who referred to his seafaring enemies as *bougres*, complained that the loss of a buttock to a caroming cannon ball made him an especially desirable partner to all manner of fellows. He of course preferred the company of his *matelot*, Pulvérin.[18]

Even though the buccaneers of Hispaniola used nicknames almost exclusively, leaving the planters who were married as the only island residents customarily employing real names, it is not likely that their propensity to select new names after arriving in the Caribbean was functionally analogous to the practice of modern homosexuals, who frequently employ assumed names or operate on a first-name-only basis to conceal their identities.[19] If this was the purpose among pirates, their concern for remaining anonymous was to conceal their piratical activities rather than their sexual preferences or practices. Being known as a sodomite among seafarers was not a socially destructive bit of information, but being identified by name as a pirate could, with a measure of bad luck, send one to the gallows at a later date. More likely the use of nicknames was a combination of the desire to make prosecution more difficult and a lower-class propensity for the practice. Especially aboard pirate vessels, the use of nicknames would have a greater opportunity to become universal since there was no need to record complete names, as was the case on merchant or naval vessels. No pay records were kept among buccaneers and neither were there formal issues of clothing or other items. Pirates simply had no need for either given names or surnames, and unlike other areas of society where both were needed, aboard buccaneering vessels the practice of using a single name was adopted for reasons unconnected with sexuality.

The use of feminine nicknames in some homosexual circles, especially the diminutive forms, in what Christopher Isherwood labeled "low camp," is part of a complex psychosocial situation that is not clearly defined or understood. While it is accepted by some, there is a hostile, almost pathological, rejection of the practice among groups who object to homosexual effeminacy. Pirates evidently would have been more in sympathy with the latter group, for although the use of assumed names was common among them, only one feminine name has survived. John Walden was called "Miss Nanney" by his cohorts, but it seems to have been conferred not because of effeminate behavior or the result of some particular sexual preference but because of his quick temper.[20]

Alcohol and Alcoholism

The excessive consumption of alcohol by pirates, when it was available in large quantities, and their predilection for debauchery, also played a part in increasing promiscuity and undermining the stability of couples. The conduct of buccaneers in port after returning from successful plundering expeditions is well chronicled, and tales of fortunes squandered, riotous excess, maniacal gaming, and lewd and drunken conduct are all substantially true. But pirate debauchery was not restricted to the rare occasions when their ships sailed into Jamaica's Port Royal and the whores and taverns of what was reputed to be the most wicked city in the Western hemisphere were available to them. It was a regular feature in the lives of successful pirates who, like human beings everywhere, required a certain leaven of festival gaiety and took the opportunity for frolic whenever it was available. At the capture of a prize, if there were wine or brandy aboard, the time was at hand for celebration. On one such occasion, Captain Charles Vane and his men sailed to a deserted island, careened their ships for cleaning and maintenance, divided the spoils of their raid, and spent several days in wild debauchery.[21] In like fashion, George Lowther and his men sailed a captured St. Christopher sloop to a small island where they cleaned their ships and amused themselves with "unheard of Debaucheries, with drinking, swearing and rioting, in which there seemed to be a kind of Emulation among them, resembling rather Devils than Men, striving who should outdo one another in new invented Oaths and Execrations."[22] Woodes Rogers described with amazement the intensity and enthusiasm of celebrating pirates. "I must add concerning these Buccaneers," he wrote, "that they liv'd without Government; so that when they met with Purchase, they immediately squander'd it away, and when they got Mony and Liquor, they drank and gam'd till they spent all; and during those Revels, there was no distinction between the Captain and Crew: for the Officers having no Commission but what the Majority gave them, they were chang'd at every Caprice, which divided them, and occasion'd frequent Quarrels and Separations, so that they cou'd do nothing considerable."[23]

Rogers did not understate his case when he noted that buccaneers were sometimes incapacitated by drunkenness. Captain John Coxon and his crew were reported on one occasion to have been too drunk to carry on negotiations with Governor John Vaughn for the release of prisoners in 1677, and some years later Coxon actually abandoned his own men after a drunken quarrel. William Dampier's crew once lost a rich galleon because they were too inebriated to fight, and accidents or disasters caused by alcohol-sodden sailors were not unusual. Not only are there records of prisoners escaping from pirates too drunk to guard them properly, but in what might have been the greatest buccaneer disaster attributable to excess consumption of liquor, a ship of twenty-six guns commanded by a Captain Bellamy ran aground off Massachusetts after the crew had consumed large quantities of Madeira. According to reports of the incident sent to London, 118 of 120 pirates aboard the ship perished in the accident.[24] Captain George Shelvocke blamed a mutiny aboard his ship on too much liquor, and there is evidence to indicate the supply of alcohol available to his sailors was sufficient to stoke considerable enthusiasm for a takeover. At one point, when an estimate was made for Shelvocke of the quantity of liquor aboard, there seemed to be enough for several years of voyaging. Either the estimate was incorrect or the capacity of the captain and his men was prodigious. Even though the spirits were diluted with water to make them last, the kegs were drained within the year. The captain himself was partially responsible for the rapid expenditure of their store. He was a regular partaker of "hipsey," a mixture of wine, brandy, and water, and his sailors later testified that he often imbibed sufficient quantities to render him unable to command his ship. When Shelvocke had consumed all their alcoholic beverages, trouble started with crewmen complaining about the dull, flat character of sobriety. A mutiny followed shortly thereafter.[25]

The large quantities of brandy, Madeira, wine, or like beverages consumed by pirates when there was opportunity are everywhere substantiated by surviving evidence. The problems created by the unregulated drinking were recognized by commanders, and in the articles of agreement subscribed to aboard Captain Kidd's ship some attempt was made to control the immoderate use of alcohol. Any man drunk during an engagement or before prisoners were made fast was to be denied his share of the loot. Even on a ship like that of Bartholomew Roberts, a much more effectively disciplined vessel than Kidd's, strong drink also created problems. The crew was frequently drunk and disorderly, "every Man being in his own Imagination, a Captain, a Prince or a King." Captain Roberts attempted to restrain the revelry of his men by proclaiming that all lights had to be out by 8:00 P.M. and all drinking must be done on deck, but it was a mild measure and had little effect.[26]

Heavy doses of alcohol were a frequent feature of pirate celebrations, and drinking, when coupled with the grim remembrance that all present at any festivity might one day end their lives on the gibbet, exerted a discernible influence on their style of humor. Like any harassed minority, buccaneers evolved their own brand of wit, which was exceedingly well-suited to their circumstances.[27] A frequent feature of their revels was an activity containing all the terrors of their lives. Several accounts survive of pirates conducting mock judicial proceedings where days were spent trying one another for robbery, piracy, "ravishing Man, Woman and Child," or whatever charge came to mind. The judge one moment was a defendant the next, but the good humor of the occasions was obviously a veneer. The trials, whether held on deserted islands or aboard ships on the high seas, all seem to have had a large measure of irony, a grim portentous quality. On one occasion, after a playful trial, a pirate was convicted, sentenced to death, and amid the laughter of his comrades, the sentence was carried out. The same style of humor was characteristic of Blackbeard, who after a prolonged drinking bout, laughed uproariously as he fired a pistol into the knee of his mate, Israel Hands, laming him for life.[28] There is no telling whether Edward Low was drunk when he captured a ship off Block Island, but with typical pirate humor, he sliced the ears from the captain's head and then supplying salt and pepper to improve the flavor, he gave his prisoner the order to eat, "which hard Injunction he comply'd with, without making a Word." Low's "bon appetit" was surely enough to ruin the digestion of any diner, but in this case the hapless prisoner might have considered himself fortunate. Roc Brasiliano, another buccaneer captain, once in a drunken frenzy began chopping off the arms and legs of bystanders.[29]

There is no reason to assume that the relationship between pirate drunkenness and homosexuality in the seventeenth century was any closer than the slight connection between the two today. The depressive effects of alcohol and the resultant facilitation of sexual transference and the lessening of psychological repression are considerations of moment in evaluating or analyzing proscribed activities, but homosexual behavior among buccaneers did not fall into that category. Nor can any inference be drawn from the oft-observed conduct of drunken males comporting among themselves with coarse familiarity, indulging in excessive sentimentality, pawing each other, and singing college songs. Although alcohol may tend to release latency in some homosexuals, the quantum effect is not large. In one study of prisoners convicted of homosexual offenses, most insisted they were not drunk at the time of their offense. But even then, the easy acceptance and general practice of homosexuality by buccaneers reduced the effects of alcohol among them, making it less significant in inducing or promoting any manner of sexual conduct than might be the case in situations involving unmarried heterosexual couples when involved in legally or ecclesiastically proscribed sexual conduct.

It is more likely that pirate drunkenness might well have been less frequent than drunkenness on the part of Britain's population in the later half of the seventeenth century. On an island where cereal grains grow everywhere, beer can be made and stored easily and in quantity by the members of any household affluent enough to own an ordinary crock or kilderkin, and both literature and public pronouncements from the reign of Henry VIII to the time of Queen Victoria contain a panoply of drunken characters and a torrent of tracts denouncing the excessive use of alcohol.[30] The poor drank beer and ale, those who could afford it poured down large quantities of Iberian wine or local brandies, and while intemperance was denounced by conforming Anglicans and in dissenting chapels with equal vigor, the admonitions had little effect. Student drunkenness was a fact of life at English universities, and in the Western hemisphere it was "observ'd that upon all the New Settlement the Spaniards make, the first thing they do is to build a Church, the first thing the Dutch do upon a new Coloney is to build them a fort, but the first thing the English doe, be it in the most remote parts of the world or amongst the most Barbarous Indians is to set up a Tavern or drinking house."[31]

Drinking to excess at every opportunity was a hallowed pirate custom, but the opportunities to do so were not as frequent as the marauders might have wished. Surviving records dealing with pirate gastronomy reveal they were chronically short of bread, butter, cheese, and meat, the items basic to a seventeenth-century Englishman's diet. These commodities, along with alcoholic beverages, were acquired from the same sources of supply, and difficulty in obtaining one implied insufficient stocks of the other. Buccaneering vessels spent little time at anchor in island ports and sometimes weeks or even months would elapse before a ship was taken that carried any large stores of provisions.[32] Occasionally they attempted to keep chickens and pigs aboard their vessels to be slaughtered when needed, and in the absence of adequate supplies of meat, there was always the possibility of improvising. Bartholomew Sharp once reminisced that in 1681 on a ship under his command there was "a little sucking Pigg . . . which we kept on Board . . . for our Christmas days Dinner, which now was grown to be a large Hogg; so we killed it for Dinner, but thinking it not enough for us all, we bought a Spaniel-Dogg of the Quarter-Master for forty pieces of Eight, and killed him; so with the Hogg and the Dogg, we made a Feast, and we had some Wine left, which made us merry."[33] At the siege of Chagre in 1670, the attacking buccaneers were reduced to beating scraps of leather between stones, dampening them to scrape off the hair, roasting them in embers, cutting them into small pieces and then gobbling down the unchewable fragments. Another pirate on a southward voyage recorded what was for him the ultimate act of culinary degradation. When supplies ran out, he and his fellow crewmen were forced to eat penguin liver to stay alive.[34]

The price paid for the dog, perhaps the highest on record for a spaniel before the twentieth century, indicates that the demand for fresh meat far exceeded the supply among buccaneers, and the same was true for other food items. There are numerous instances of pirates attacking and capturing larger vessels with more men and guns aboard because they were driven by hunger to take exceptional risks and fight with the courage of desperation. In the absence of a reliable supply of "English victuals," pirates were forced to obtain sustenance from other sources, and they frequently replenished exhausted stocks with bananas, manioc, cassava, fish, turtles, and an occasional iguana, although the last could not have been particularly desirable to men who were queasy at the prospect of dining on penguin liver. All these food items could be had by trading with natives, fishermen, and hunters, but when acquiring such supplies by trading or raiding isolated settlements on the coasts of obscure islands, the possibility of obtaining alcoholic beverages was slight. The failure of buccaneers to secure a regular supply of strong drink indicates that neither chronic alcoholism, the debilitating effects of decades of drunkenness, nor continual inebriation were a vital feature of their daily lives.[35]

Torture

An even more indelible aspect of the pirate image than their ill-deserved reputation for being regularly drunk is the commonly made association between pirates and sadism. In many works on buccaneering, the linkage appears over and again, and although at least one authority maintains the institutionalization of torture "in those early years, before the French colonizers shipped out the first cargo of women to Tortuga, . . . was a function of the way they lived together," there is no evidence that the brand of torture and cruelty they practiced correlated with buccaneer homosexuality or homosexual activities.[36] The methodical and intense infliction of pain for which pirates are known was not a figment of the imaginations of authors writing sea stories for an audience of adventure buffs. It was real and often ghoulish in the extreme, yet its causes are complex and clearly the result of conditions not directly related to sexual orientation.

The tendency to associate homosexuality and torture in a muddled cause and effect relationship is due in large measure to the willingness of many to classify homosexuality as pathological behavior. Pirates, involved as they were in both activities, provide an example, though incorrectly formulated, of a link between the two. Sadism is a facet of sexual activities involving members of both the same and opposite sexes, but violence among homosexuals is as rare as violence among heterosexuals, although it is often exaggerated in the popular mind. The equation of mental illness with selected modes of sexual expression has abated to some degree in recent years, but the personification of homosexuals and those who engage in homosexual acts as incarnations of psychosexual imbalance remains widespread.

In the seventeenth century there was apparently no tendency to associate sadism connected with homosexual manifestations with more virulent acts than those commonly connected with heterosexual activities. The sexual nature of the whippings administered to schoolboys was generally recognized by the reign of Charles II. An anonymous pamphleteer writing in 1699 complained not only of the futility of using punishment to correct academic deficiencies, but added a blast at "the immodest and filthy blows" upon the "secret parts" of youthful scholars. Thomas Shadwell touched on the same theme in his play *The Virtuoso*. An elderly man, one of Shadwell's characters, in a moment of sexual excitement asks his mistress to fetch the birch rods. He explains to the audience that he had developed a taste for the rod when a lad at Westminster School. He then enjoins his woman, "Do not spare thy pains: I love castigation mightily."[37] Similarly, in a 1671 play entitled *The Country Revel*, a rural justice comments, "If ye talke of skinnes, the best judgment to be made of the fineness of skinnes is at the whipping-post by the stripes. Ah! 'tis the best lechery to see 'em suffer correction. Your London aldermen take great lechery to see the poor wretches whipt at the court at Bridewell."[38] None of the practices mentioned were particularly gruesome by the standards of three hundred years ago, and indeed the rod was used by both homosexuals and heterosexuals in their quests for gratification.

There are, of course, surviving examples of cruelty practiced by obviously demented pirates, but individual acts seem to bear little similarity to sadistic practices familiar to Restoration play-goers or to other more ordinary instances of sadism. At the capture of Puerto Cavallo, French buccaneer commander l'Olonnais comported himself with passionate cruelty toward his

Spanish captives, hacking many to bits, licking the blood off his sword, eating the heart out of one disembowled prisoner, and threatening to do the same to others. Even more ghastly was the incident where Montbars the Exterminator, another Frenchman, opened the abdomen of a captive, took out a portion of the intestine, nailed it to a post, and then chased the prisoner with a firebrand, the intestine unraveling from his stomach as he ran and danced about frantically trying to avoid the flame. On another occasion, he beheaded every member of a captured Spanish ship save one man who was kept alive to witness the executions and then sent back to tell the governor what had transpired. Torture of this nature, the application of pain for the sake of pain, seems to have been rare, the work of men who were genuine psychopaths. There is only one surviving account of what is a likely act of pure pirate sadism. In a 1683 incident, buccaneer Captain Nicholas Vanhorn whipped a Nicholas Browne to death for what Sir Thomas Lynch described naively as no apparent reason.[39]

In harmony with naval and maritime practice everywhere in the seventeenth century, torture was an accepted practice for insuring order aboard ship. Whipping was the standard method of enforcing obedience on merchant craft, but as in the navy, where spread-eagling and keelhauling were used, there were many variations. Pirates employed all the usual methods and introduced a few of their own to deal with recalcitrant crewmen. One method used on occasion by buccaneers was called sweating. The malefactor to be punished by a sweat was stripped naked and forced to run a gauntlet of his fellow crewmen who struck him on the back, shoulders, and buttocks with sail needles. Dripping with blood, he was then thrown into a sugar cask amply stocked with cockroaches, the cask was covered with a blanket, and the man was left bleeding amid the scurrying insects to endure the West Indian heat in a covered, unventilated barrel. Pirates who had fallen afoul of their shipmates were occasionally left on islands, marooned as it was known, either to die, live alone, or be picked up by another ship. The nature of the island and its location were vital factors in determining how drastic a punishment this was. A pirate left on a tiny, sand-covered bit of land would suffer an agonizing death by thirst and dehydration, while another marooned at a more hospitable site might live in primitive comfort for years or be picked up in a short time if his island was along a frequently used shipping lane.[40]

A measure of the physical agony inflicted by buccaneers was in the nature of retaliation against similar treatment at the hands of the Spanish. The hatred of nationals of the two countries for one another was of long standing, and torture of captives was a frequent manifestation of their mutual aversion. As early as 1604, the Venetian ambassador to England wrote that two English vessels in the West Indies had been captured by Spaniards, and the crew members were relieved of their hands, feet, noses, and ears by their sword-wielding captors. They were then smeared with honey and tied to trees, allowing insects to conclude what humans had begun. Other tortures inflicted on the English by the Spanish in the West Indies were much less grim, but the practice seems to have been a part of Anglo-Spanish contact in the New World from the time of Elizabeth until over a century later when Captain Jenkins returned to London with his Spanish-severed ear in a container for all to see.[41]

The Restoration literature of flagellation, along with the fantasies it embodied and the practices it described was, like similar Victorian writings, a compromise with homosexuality and a defense against it. But there was little need for such psychological adjustments among pirates who had no need to reaffirm their sexual practices. With few exceptions, they seem to have carried out their torture systematically for the primary purposes of gaining booty or maintaining discipline among their own group. Gratuitous infliction of pain was not commonly practiced and when it was, it seemed to satisfy a need for hilarity rather than to serve as a sexual stimulant. Governor Thomas Handasyd of Jamaica reported home that on at least one occasion he knew of pirates treating prisoners well when there was no opportunity for financial gain, and in encounters with natives where prisoners could be expected to yield no plunder, torture was rarely used.[42]

The most vivid and extensive accounts of pirate torture are those dealing with cruelty practiced by the victorious expeditions Morgan led against Gibralter, Porto Bello, Maracaibo, and Panama City. Morgan seems to have had no particular interest in torture as an activity with entertainment potential, but he directed his men in relentless and systematic brutality to learn where the Spanish citizenry of the captured towns had secreted their wealth. Whippings and beatings were the usual methods used by Morgan's men, but when more extreme measures were necessary, they were employed. Buccaneers lived in an age when the infliction of pain was an art form, and if the Spanish were to be victims, they were willing to employ techniques developed by others as well as a few of their own device. Fire was a favorite instrument with Morgan, and placing burning fuses between the fingers and toes of spread-eagled captives appeared to be a fairly effective technique for causing pain. Males and females were strappadoed, hung by the thumbs, stabbed repeatedly and left to die, roasted alive over small fires, and on occasion crucified. There is at least one case where a prisoner was hoisted aloft by rope wrapped around his genitals and then the genitals sliced off. But mutilation of captives' privy parts was not common, and when it was done, it was carried out with the business-as-usual attitude that corresponded with the purpose of pirate torture. A more usual method was the rack for extracting information. Its use was familiar to most pirates, and over the centuries it had proven its effectiveness.

On occasion, however, pirates used some originality in devising their torments. A particularly maritime method of extracting information was known as woolding. To the sailor, woolding was rope wound tightly around a mast to give it added strength, but Morgan's men either discovered or learned from others that a rope wrapped around the forehead of a captive and then slowly twisted tighter and tighter produced unbearable agony along with forcing the victim's eyeballs to protrude like eggs. These tortures and others were often applied to prisoners over a period of several days to give them ample time to endure pain and reexamine their original decisions to remain silent. After Morgan's capture of Maracaibo, the torture and cruelty lasted for three weeks.[43]

The same purpose and purposefulness was the rule rather than the exception throughout the age of pirate depredations in the Caribbean. The record is full of cases like that of a Mrs. Trot who was barbarously murdered by buccaneers in an attempt to make her "confess where Col. Elding and his riches were,"[44] or the incident when the well-known Captain Edward England once threatened to sink the vessel of a captured seafarer and throw him overboard with a double-headed shot around his neck if he did not reveal the location of his money. In circumstances where captives were taken by pirates and systematic torture was not inflicted, the treatment visited on the captives was nevertheless unpleasant in the extreme. Meanness, random clubbing, and what was described as "barbarous" actions are frequent in depositions. Incidents like that which occurred when Edward England took the *Calabar Merchant* of Bristol, beat and abused the master and his crew for nine weeks, then released them, returned their ship, and provided them with twenty-one negroes as compensation for damage done are one of a kind.[45]

Yet the frequency and intensity of buccaneer brutality was a symptom of the age rather than anything that can be associated especially with piracy or homosexuality. The severity of childhood upbringing in the seventeenth century, particularly the excessive brutality of the poor toward their offspring, according to Lawrence Stone, deeply affected the personality of large numbers of adults. Imprisonment in swaddling bands during the initial months of life, the continual application of physical punishment, and ejection from the home at an early age all combined to produce adults who were cold, hostile, suspicious, distrustful, cruel, unable to form close relationships with each other except under circumstances of extreme interdependence, and liable to sudden outbursts of aggressive behavior toward one another.[46]

Severe physical punishment was only a part of home life and child-rearing practice in the seventeenth century. Men who became pirates had been raised on what seem today to be instances of inexplicably cruel practices carried out regularly by local and national authorities in England and in the West Indies. A London man charged with blasphemy in 1656, for example, was pilloried four hours, the first two in London, and then shipped from London to Westminster for the second two. His tongue was then bored with a red-hot iron and he was branded on the forehead with the letter B. Despite his treatment, the man probably considered himself lucky to have escaped with so mild a series of punishments.[47] During the Restoration, public hangings occurred on a regularly scheduled basis, severe whippings were common, jail conditions were often the equivalent of capital punishment for the poor, and branding was occasionally used. In the first decade of the eighteenth century, Celia Fiennes attested to the merciful nature of English justice by describing the punishments inflicted by the authorities as relatively mild. To prove her case, she cited felons being taken to the gallows tied to their coffins to be dispatched in a reasonably rapid manner. Important persons who fell victim to the headsman's axe could have their heads sewn back onto their bodies for burial, and only whippings and brandings were employed for minor offenses. And traitors, after all, received their just desserts, she explained. They were hanged until near expiration, then cut down while barely alive, disemboweled, the heart removed, and presiding officials took up the organ, announced that here was the heart of a traitor, and the "body . . . cutt in quarters and hung up on the top of the great gates of the City."[48]

The list of grim treatment of criminals by the authorities could be continued almost without end, and literally tens of thousands of specific cases could be adduced as examples of the brutality of the age. There would be no sweatings or woolings in the list of punishments meted out by the English system of justice, but the severity of the punishments applied to persons from petty thief to traitor was no less brutal than the tortures buccaneers visited on their captives. They represent nothing that could be labeled socially or sexually pathological within the context of their environment. The abuse of prisoners by pirates surely went beyond legally inflicted agonies, but not too far beyond them, and like the sentences prescribed by English law, pirate tortures were designed to serve a purpose rather than simply to entertain.

In other respects, the agonies inflicted by pirates could be considered mild when compared to the practices commonly employed for the discipline and training of slaves in the West Indies. Plantation owners were within their legal rights in perpetrating the most grisly forms of torture they could imagine if the victim were a troublesome black. One traveler in the Caribbean in the early eighteenth century reported a slave being nailed to the ground and burned with a firebrand from his feet toward his head. Castration of slaves was also a common practice—usually to make them more tractable rather than for punishment—but mutilation, whipping with salt rubbed into the wounds, dripping melted wax on the skin, and several other exquisite torments were the lot of the troublesome bondsman. Later in the eighteenth century, legislation was enacted on several islands preventing planters from killing, mutilating, or dismembering slaves, but this was half a century after the last pirate had disappeared from the Caribbean, and even then it was unlikely that slaves were awarded damages by the courts for injuries sustained at the hands of their masters or that planters were ever assessed the maximum penalty of twelve months in jail and fined one hundred pounds for mistreating their blacks.[49] Indeed, if there is any puzzle about the relationship between buccaneers and the tortures they meted out, it is to be found not in the fact that they used physical abuse but in the difficulty of explaining why in the vast numbers of depositions, narratives, journal accounts, newspaper reports, and other sources of information on piratical depredations there are so many that do not mention torture and so few that do. Although it is likely that some buccaneers were sadists and derived sexual pleasure from torturing captives, the limited, structured, and purposeful use of pain only to extract information and locate booty indicates that sadism was not a general characteristic of buccaneer sexuality. If it had been so, torture would have been a regular feature of piracy, practiced in more than carefully limited circumstances.

Effeminacy and the Pirate Role

Not only is sadism difficult to find among buccaneers, but effeminacy, another characteristic often associated with homosexuality and homosexual practices, seems to be absent from their communities. Aside from a few captains noted for their ornate dress, no more ornate really than that of upper-class gentlemen during the Restoration, they were garbed rather plainly in whatever was available, usually jerkin and britches of sailcloth or any other clothing they might have captured. Gold earrings, commonly worn by at least some buccaneers, were clearly a part of their fashion rather than distinctly effeminate, and on at least one occasion, a battle fought in the waning hours of daylight, the reflection of the last remaining rays of the sun on the earrings enabled the pirates to identify each other in the thick of combat.[50] Incidents of pirates sashaying or parading in costume always carry with them the enthusiasm of a successful fight or the capture of a ship carrying elaborate clothing. Captain John Evans wrote in 1728 of his experiences as a captive aboard a pirate ship, and at one point he related that after rummaging through his cabin, immediately after he was captured, "the Fellows . . . met with a Leather Powder Bag and Puff, with which they had powder'd themselves from Head to Foot, walk'd the Decks with their Hats under their Arms, minced their Oaths, and affected all the Airs of a Beau, with an Aukwardness [that] would have forced a Smile from a Cynick."[51] Père Labat, the pirate priest, relates a similar story of pirates having captured a hoard of rich clothing being a "comical sight as they strutted about the island in feathered hats, wigs, silk stockings, ribbons and other garments."[52] But this was obviously playfulness and celebration rather than a longing for effeminate trappings, and indeed the powder bag and puff were masculine rather than feminine accoutrements three hundred years ago.

The only recorded incident of pirates bedecking themselves for a nonfestive occasion was in the case of Dennis Macarty and Thomas Morris, both of whom appeared unusually ornamented. Macarty wore long blue ribbons at his neck, wrists, knees, and cap, while Morris appeared in much the same style, but with red ribbons rather than the blue. The occasion, however, was the hanging of the two men along with several others for piracy, and to interpret their behavior on this occasion as effeminate could hardly be sustained.[53]

The lack of effeminate pirates or effeminate behavior among them on any known occasion does not diminish the intensity or frequency of pirate homosexual contact or orientation. Even in modern Western society where sexual relationships are assumed to be male-female encounters, the larger number of homosexuals reject effeminacy not only because it is a threat to their own masculinity but there seems to be a preference for feminine-appearing homosexuals only among a limited proportion of homophiles. In the brief and furtive encounters characteristic of many homosexual experiences, there is no gender consciousness, and neither should any be expected. The effeminate gay cannot be assumed to hold universal attraction to men for whom women as sexual partners have little appeal. In fact, feminine identification among male homosexuals, while often the most conspicuous manifestation of homosexuality to the heterosexual world, is demonstrably rare. Most often it is the result of a maturational environment where masculine identification was difficult or impossible to establish, hardly the case for a wandering lad or apprentice boy in the seventeenth or eighteenth centuries.[54] Research by psychologists, sociologists, and even works of knowledgeable homosexual fiction reject the effeminate gay as anywhere near typical. The ordinary homosexual is a rather ordinary man, adopting neither a feminine style nor the manner of swaggering, leather-clad motorcyclists or hulking weight-lifters. To be sure, the homosexual hustler is often hypermasculine, exhibiting the badge of his saleable sexuality much as a female prostitute exhibits herself. But the need for the male image to sell the product indicates the direction of most homosexual preference. In one survey of sexual practices in the military it was found that effeminacy among homosexual psychopaths was exceedingly high, almost 50 percent of those surveyed. But significantly, in the same study among those examined and determined to be free from psychopathological symptoms, homosexuals with effeminate characteristics fell to 2 percent of the sample.[55] Among pirates in cases where indications of psychosexual pathology are absent, there is no reason to assume that the rate of effeminacy would be particularly high. On the few occasions where pirates comment on effeminate behavior it is condemned, although not with a viciousness that indicated overcompensation. Effeminate characteristics, in fact, were usually ascribed to the hated Spanish, and lumped in with other unpirately qualities such as cowardice and passivity. "But we may confidently presume that these American Spanyards, are an idle, cowardly, and effiminate people, not exercised, nor brought up, in Warlike discipline," observed one Englishman.[56] Another commentator, with close ties to French pirates, characterized Brazilian slaves pejoratively as indolent and effeminate, and added a gratuitous comment that the monks he observed were even worse. They were not only ignorant of Latin, but in their excesses they pursued women and strove "even to out-vie the Sodomites in their Debaucheries."[57]

But the matter of effeminacy in the age of piracy, whether connected with homophile sexuality or simply as a sartorial aberration, was an oddity rather than grotesque or mortally sinful. If seafarers had chosen or been inclined to divide or to constitute their groupings into male and female moieties with a relatively full range of identifiable sexual characteristics, they could have done so with considerably less difficulty than would have been possible in the nineteenth or twentieth centuries. While it may have been impossible in the Royal Navy or aboard merchant vessels, among pirates there would literally have been no impediment to such practice. But in fact effeminate behavior was no part of pirate society. Masculinity was not diminished by homosexuality among buccaneers, as is the case in social circumstances where an emotional commitment has been made to the normality of heterosexual activity. Pirates who preferred homosexuality as well as those who partook in it as the only sexual outlet available practiced their proclivity for men without the social or psychological necessity for creating the appearance of heterosexual engagement.

Buccaneers cultivated the masculine attributes of physical toughness, courage in combat, endurance, and comradeship, but these virtues were valued in every member of the community from matelot and carpenter's boy all the way up to captain. No pirate crewman was exempt from battle or received special protection due to weakness or lack of the will or desire to fight. Pirates exalted instead the virtues of physical strength, bravery, endurance, and military skill. On occasions when they boasted of their exploits, toughness, hostility, and fierceness were emphasized in every case. Nowhere did buccaneers make any pretensions of effeminacy, and even those rovers known to fancy fashionable attire took the part of the lord rather than the fool. There is nothing remarkable in their behavior. Buccaneers following ordinary human patterns internalized the social roles with which they were familiar and those they were required to assume by circumstance. The exaggerated female "role" did not become associated with homosexual behavior in England until the closing years of the seventeenth century, but if it had emerged earlier, it remains unlikely it would have been assumed by Caribbean buccaneers. In situations where the effeminate homosexual role is a recognized feature of society, it appears to have some effect on the distribution of homosexual conduct, but such conduct is not widely practiced by men involved in homosexual behavior. West Indian pirates had no need to assume a cast of effeminacy even if it had been available. Their own roles required the very opposite style of conduct. The necessary qualities for continued existence were stamina, courage, and a cruelly competitive spirit, and sodomitical pirates, like men everywhere, cultivated attributes necessary for survival.[58]

Sexual relations between pirates were an ordinary activity, condemned by no one among them and denigrated only by those classes with whom they had little contact and less familiarity. Their homosexual contact was in no way a unique thing, made more tantalizing for them by the knowledge that they participated in behavior condemned socially, ecclesiastically, and by civil statute. Church, government, and English society were far removed from their daily lives and exerted little influence. Nor were there among them a particular class of sex objects, especially effeminate pirates whose duty it was to provide sexual services for the remainder of the company. There is no evidence to indicate that pirates regarded sexual activity as something necessarily conducted between human beings who differed from one another in attitude, conduct, or personality. From them, it was an activity engaged in by men; there was no attempt to ape the practices of heterosexual society. No special vocabulary was required for identification purposes or to perpetuate secrecy for this ordinary part of their life.

It was only in dealing with women, a rare and exotic feature of their lives, that sexual difficulties arose. In this respect there were two general types of problems that relate to the pirates' own sexual orientation. Among the complete homosexuals, of course, female contact was probably avoided completely, but among other pirates there were those whose alienation from the heterosexual world was only partial, sufficient to enable them to attempt marriage and fail or at best to sustain contacts only with those females who could not pose a threat to their masculinity or to their social being. Their women had of necessity to be drawn from groups that could be dominated: those adjudged racially inferior, captives, or prostitutes. Their heterosexual skills were insufficiently developed for them to succeed with women on an equal basis. A pirate forced into a situation of equality with a female would undoubtedly have been as uncomfortable as would have been the case had he been miraculously transported from the deck of his ship to Whitehall Palace and set down to dinner with the king.

A gigantic chasm of three hundred years separates the present from the seventeenth century and to postulate truths on the nature of human actions and interactions over three hundred years when such truths are based on severely limited amounts of evidence is clearly impossible. Even the intemperate or the foolish who were not intimidated by the passage of so great a length of time would hesitate to conclude that the society evolved by buccaneers living independently of socially imposed constraints on their sexuality indicates in some way that if only heterosexuals could suppress their hostility and accept homosexuals as full-fledged members of the human community then, perhaps, with the dissipation of the opprobrium directed against them, homosexuals would be transformed into equal participants in modern society. This may be so, but adequate evidence to substantiate it is still not available. What can be drawn from a study of those features of pirate society that make it truly distinctive is not that homosexual and heterosexual can function comfortably together, but that homosexual communities can function virtually independent of heterosexual society. Aside from the production of children, homosexuals alone can fulfill satisfactorily all human needs, wants, and desires, all the while supporting and sustaining a human community remarkable by the very fact that it is unremarkable. The almost universal homosexual involvement among pirates meant that homosexual practices were neither disturbed, perverted, exotic, nor uniquely desirable among them, and the mechanisms for defending and perpetuating such practices, those things that set the modern homosexual apart from heterosexual society, were never necessary. The male engaging in sexual activity with another male aboard a pirate ship in the West Indies three centuries past was simply an ordinary member of his community, completely socialized and acculturated. The appearance and institutions of his society were substantial reflections of the heterosexual England that produced him, and the functional accommodations made to adjust for homosexuality were minor. The lives of the pirates were ordinary within the context of their chronological period and their economic requirements, and instances of antisocial, depraved, or pathological behavior were not noticeably more common than in concomitant heterosexual society.

NOTES

1. Erving Goffman, *Asylums: Essays on the Social Situation of Mental Patients and Other Inmates* (New York: Doubleday, 1961), xiii, 5–6; V. Aubert and O. Arner, "On the Social Structure of the Ship," *Acta Sociologica* 3 (1958): 200–219, reference here

to 200–201; Warren H. Hopwood, "Some Problems Associated with the Selection and Training of Deck and Engineer Cadets in the British Merchant Navy," in *Seafarer and Community*, ed. Peter H. Fricke (London: Croom Helm, 1973), 97–116, reference here to 102; Jan Horbulewicz, "The Parameters of Psychological Autonomy of Industrial Trawler Crews," in Fricke, *Seafarer and Community*, 67–84, reference here to 68.

2. Peter H. Fricke, "Seafarer and Community," in Fricke, *Seafarer and Community*, 1–7; Peter C. Buffum, *Homosexuality in Prisons* (Washington, D.C.: National Institute of Law Enforcement and Criminal Justice, 1972), 7; David Sonnenschein, "The Ethnography of Male Homosexual Relations," *Journal of Sex Research* (May 1968): 73; United Kingdom, Parliament, "Committee of Inquiry into Shipping [Rochdale Committee]," London. Cmd. 4337. 1970 (henceforward [Rochdale Committee]); Aubert and Arner, "Social Structure," 211; T. L. Wilmon and T. G. Rich, "Report on the General Health and Morale of the Officers and Crew during a 30-Day Simulated War Patrol Aboard a Snorkel Submarine," *Report No. 3 on BuMed Research Project NM 002 009, "Effect of Snorkelling on Submarine Personnel"* (New London, Conn.: Medical Research Laboratory, n.d.) Report 140a, U.S. Naval Submarine Base, 2–4; Benjaman B. Weybrew, "Psychological Problems of Prolonged Marine Submergence," in *Unusual Environments and Human Behavior: Physiological and Psychological Problems of Man in Space*, ed. Neal M. Burns, Randall M. Chambers, and Edwin Hendler (Glencoe, Ill.: Free Press, 1963), 87–125, reference here to 107–108.

3. Goffman, *Asylums*, ix–x; Wilmon and Rich, "Report," 3; [Rochdale Committee] (Cmd. 4337); Hopwood, "Some Problems," 103; Peter H. Fricke, "Family and Community: The Environment of the Ship's Officer," in Fricke, *Seafarer and Community*, 132–150, reference here to 147; J. H. Earls, "Human Adjustment to an Exotic Environment: The Nuclear Submarine," *Archives of General Psychiatry* 20 (1969): 117–123, reference here to 121; Aubert and Arner, "Social Structure," 205; G. E. Ruff, E. Z. Levy, and V. H. Thaler, "Studies of Isolation and Confinement," *Aerospace Medicine* 30 (1959): 599–604, reference here to 601; CSPCS, 29: 141; 31: 10; A. O. Exquemelin, *The Buccaneers of America*, trans. Alexis Brown (Harmondsworth: Penguin Books, 1969), 70–73; C. H. Haring, *The Buccaneers in the West Indies in the XVIIth Century* (Hamden, Conn.: Archon Books, 1966), 69; Jean Baptiste Labat, *The Memoirs of Père Labat, 1693–1738*, trans. John Eaden (London: Constable, 1931), 36–37.

4. CSPCS, 5: 622, 633, 7: 7, 49–51; 11: 395. In a study of seafarers' attitudes commissioned by the Rochdale Committee (Cmd. 4337, 1970), 24 percent of the group questioned gave evidence of discomfort when among landsmen. Officers and men aboard oil tankers, where parallels between the crew and buccaneers are more exact in that the level of impermeability is especially great in both situations, reported a higher rate of discomfiture ashore than men serving on conventional merchant vessels. The subgroup claiming the greatest difficulties getting along with the non-nautical population were the deck officers in the survey, the segment of the maritime population most likely to have been rigorously and systematically socialized into shipboard life at an earlier age than other seamen. Most joined ships directly from school or nautical college and only one out of five had previous nonmaritime employment experience, in

contrast to 75 percent of the engineering officers who had worked on land before going to sea. The effects of the total institution in this situation were evidently more profound on those with longer and more intensive socialization experiences. See Bryan Nolan, "A Possible Perspective on Deprivation," in Fricke, *Seafarer and Community,* 85–96, reference here to 94–95; and also Joseba Zulaika, *Terranova: The Ethos and Luck of Deep-Sea Fishermen* (Philadelphia: Institute for the Study of Human Issues, 1981), for acculturation problems of married Spanish fishermen on voyages with frequent visits to ports.

5. Fricke, "Family and Community," 33; Hopwood, "Some Problems," 103; Nolan, "A Possible Perspective," 89–90, 94–95.

6. *The Laws, Ordinances, and Institutions of the Admiralty of Great Britain, Civil and Military. Comprehending, I. Such Antient Naval Laws and Customs as are Still in Use. II. An Abstract of the Statutes in Force Relating to Maritime Affairs and Commerce. III. The Marine Treaties At Large. IV. A Critical Account of Naval Affairs and Commerce, From the Reign of Alfred the Great. V. The Present State of the Navy, and of the Officers, Offices, Ships, &c. Thereof. Interspers'd with Dissertations, Notes and Comments, for the Use of the Officers of the Navy, Masters of Ships, Mariners, Merchants, Insurers, and the Trading Part of the Nation in General. With A Preface, Giving A More Particular Account of the Nature, Use and Design of this Work,* 2 vols. (London: Printed for A. Millar, 1746), 1:70.

7. P.R.O., H.C.A. 1/5, 52, 53, 121, and an unnumbered sheet. Hewitt's case is cited by Evelyn Berckman, *Victims of Piracy: The Admiralty Court, 1575–1678* (London: H. Hamilton, 1979), 51–52. Berckman also cites the case of a sailor aboard the *Surety* in 1608 who was acquitted of buggery despite his confession, a further indication that seventeenth-century Englishmen were not outraged over homosexual acts. For Stone's case, see H.C.A. 1/17, 164, 171; H.C.A. 1/32, 10; H.C.A. 1/48, 234; H.C.A. 1/50, 87.

8. P.R.O., H.C.A. 1/9, 37–38, 41; H.C.A. 13/142, 15–16.

9. P.R.O., H.C.A. 1/64, 17.

20. *The Piratical Seizure of the Van-Herring,* 2 vols. (London: T. Davies, 1681), 2:3.

11. P.R.O., H.C.A. 1/17, 162, 184; H.C.A. 1/30, 151–152, 170; H.C.A. 1/55, 21; Buffum, *Homosexuality in Prisons,* 17.

12. William Dampier, *A New Voyage Round the World* (London: Argonaut Press, 1927), 38, 54, 74; John Cox, "John Cox His Travills over the Land into the So. Seas from thence Round the South parte of America to Barbados and Antegoe," Sloane MSS. 49, folio 8; Bartholomew Sharp, "A Journal Kept by Capt. Bartholomew Sharp of Passages in Going over Land to the South Seas from the Island called the Golden Island in April 1680," British Library, Sloane Mss 64A, 21, 61; Alexander O. Exquemelin, *Bucaniers of America. The Second Volume. Containing The Dangerous Voyage and Bold Attempts of Captain Bartholomew Sharp and others; performed upon the Coasts of the South Sea, for the space of two years, &c. From the Original Journal of the said Voyage. Written By Mr. Basil Ringrose, Gent. Who was all along present at those Transactions* (London: William Crooke, 1685), 2, 4, 121, 137.

13. M. Lenzoff and W. A. Westley, "The Homosexual Community," in *Sexual Deviance,* ed. John H. Gagnon and William Simon (New York: Harper and Row, 1967),

167–183, reference here to 171–172; Evelyn Hooker, "The Homosexual Community," in ibid., 184–196, reference here to 185; Evelyn Hooker, "Male Homosexuals and Their Worlds," in *Sexual Inversion: The Multiple Roots of Homosexuality*, ed. Judd Marmor (New York: Basic Books, 1965), 83–107, reference here to 93–94.

14. CSPCS, 29: 94–99. See also Nancy Achilles, "The Development of the Homosexual Bar as an Institution," in Gagnon and Simon, *Sexual Deviance*, 228–244, reference here to 228–244; Thomas J. Noel, "Gay Bars and the Emergence of the Denver Homosexual Community," *Social Science Journal* 15 (1978): 59–74; and Randolph Trumbach, "London's Sodomites: Homosexual Behaviour and Western Culture," *Journal of Social History* 11 (1977): 1–33.

15. Paul H. Gebhard, *Sex Offenders: An Analysis of Types* (New York: Harper and Row, 1965), 642; John Gerassi, *The Boys of Boise: Furor, Vice, and Folly in an American City* (New York: Macmillan, 1966), 42; Donald Webster Cory, *The Homosexual in America: A Subjective Approach* (New York: Greenberg, 1951), 80, 117; Hooker, "Homosexual Community," 175.

16. Gebhard, *Sex Offenders*, 63. By the end of the seventeenth century, a distinct homosexual subculture had evidently developed in London with stress on effeminacy, transvestism, enactment of childbirth, and marriage rituals. Several clubs were formed, and by the first half of the eighteenth century, the exposé of a number of homosexual coteries had created serious scandals. The rudimentary subculture, with its nicknames and recognized cruising areas, was distinct from lower-class and seafarers' homosexuality. It was clearly an upper- and upper-middle-class business and was a reaction against heterosexual society rather than an alternate form of sexual expression. Mary McIntosh, "The Homosexual Role," *Social Problems* 16, no. 2 (1968): 182–192, reference here to 187–188; see also Trumbach, "London's Sodomites," 15, 17, 23.

17. M. M. Lewis, *Language in Society* (New York: Social Science Publishing, 1948), 141; Gordon Westwood, *Society and the Homosexual* (London: Gollancz, 1952), 126–217; Gresham M. Sykes, *The Society of Captives: A Study of a Maximum Security Prison* (Princeton: Princeton University Press, 1958), 85.

18. Exquemelin, *Buccaneers of America*, 67, 86, 93, 114, 178; Philip Gosse, *The Pirates' Who's Who, Giving Particulars of the Lives & Deaths of the Pirates & Buccaneers* (London: Dulau and Company, 1924), 153, et passim; Sir Hans Sloane, *A Voyage to the Islands Madera, Barbados, Nieves, S. Christophers and Jamaica, with the Natural History of the Herbs and Trees, Four-footed Beasts, Fishes, Birds, Insects, Reptiles, &c. of the Last of Those Islands; to Which is Prefix'd an Introduction, Wherein is an Account of the Inhabitants, Air, Waters, Diseases, Trade, &c. of That Place, with Some Relations Concerning the Neighbouring Continent, and Islands of America. Illustrated with Figures of the Things Described, Which Have Not Been Heretofore Engraved; in Large Copper-plates As Big As the Life*, 2 vols. (London: Printed by B. M. for the author, 1707–25), 1:lxxxvii; Louis Adhémar Timothée Le Golif, *The Memoirs of A Buccaneer: Being a Wondrous and Unrepentant Account of the Prodigious Adventures and Amours of King Louis XIV's Loyal Servant Louis Adhémar Timothée Le Golif, Known for His Singular Wound As Borgnefesse, Captain of the Buccaneers, Told by Himself*, trans. Malcolm Barnes (London: Allen and

Unwin, 1954), 88–89, 98–100, 102, 114–115, 166, 168, 192, 201. In seventeenth-century usage, the term "bougre" referred to a practitioner of sodomy. It was not used to denominate a "blackguard" as was its meaning in the eighteenth century and after. See Peter N. Moogk, "'Thieving Buggers' and 'Stupid Shits': Insults and Popular Culture in New France," *William and Mary Quarterly* 36 (1979): 524–547, reference here to 539.

19. Haring, *Buccaneers*, 69.

20. Hooker, "Homosexual Community," 181–182; Gosse, *Who's Who*, 313; Stanley Richards, *Black Bart* (Llandybie, Carmarthenshire: C. Davies, 1966), 74.

21. Exquemelin, *Buccaneers of America*, 81–82; Captain Charles Johnson, *A General History of the Robberies and Murders of the Most Notorious Pyrates and also their Policies, Discipline and Government from their first Rise and Settlement in the Island of Providence, in 1717, to the Present Year, 1724, with the Remarkable Actions and Adventures of the two Female Pyrates, Mary Read and Anne Bonny, to which is Prefix'd an Account of the famous Captain Avery and his Companions; with the Manner of his Death in England*, ed. Manuel Schornhorn (London: Dent, 1972), 135.

22. Ibid., 312.

23. Woodes Rogers, *A Cruising Voyage Round the World: First to the South Seas, Thence to the East Indies and Homewards by the Cape of Good Hope* (London: 1713), xvii.

24. Peter Kemp and Christopher Lloyd, *The Brethren of the Coast: The British and French Buccaneers in the South Seas* (London: Heinemann, 1960),154; John Cox, "John Cox His Travills," folio 42; CSPCS, 9: 121; 10: 606; 29: 360.

25. George Shelvocke, *A Privateer's Voyage Round the World*, reprint of 1726 ed. (London: Jonathan Cape, 1930), 30, 40; William Betagh, *A Voyage Round the World: Being an Account of a Remarkable Enterprize, Begun in the Year 1719, Chiefly to Cruise on the Spaniards in the Great South Ocean ... by William Betagh, Captain of Marines in that Expedition* (London: Printed for T. Combes, J. Lacy, and J. Clarke, 1728), 22–25, 155, 186.

26. CSPCS, 9: 430; 17: 12–13; 18: 199; 27: 332–335; 29: 211–213; Johnson, *General History*, 211, 222, 224.

27. Richard Hauser, *The Homosexual Society* (London: Bodley Head, 1965), 33.

28. Johnson, *General History*, 292–294.

29. Ibid., 84, 334.

30. Karl Abraham, "The Psychological Relations between Sexuality and Alcoholism," in *Selected Papers of Karl Abraham* (London: Hogarth Press and the Institute of Psycho-Analysis, 1949), 80–90, reference here to 87; Gebhard, *Sex Offenders*, 292, 353.

31. "Thomas Walduck's Letters," *Journals of the Barbados Museum and Historical Society* 15 (1947–48), 35.

32. Exquemelin, *Buccaneers of America*, 190.

33. Sharp, "Journal," 108–110; Bartholomew Sharp, *The Voyages and Adventures of Captain Bartholomew Sharp* (London: 1684), 108–109.

34. Exquemelin, *Buccaneers of America*, 188; Richard Simpson, "Richard Simpson's

Voyage to the Straits of Magellan and the South Sea in 1689," British Library Sloane MSS 86 or 672, folio 21, 38.

35. Although alcoholism or the excessive consumption of alcohol is frequently associated with homosexual behavior by many in modern America, there seems to be little basis for linking the two. See Marcel T. Saghir and Eli Robins, *Male and Female Homosexuality: A Comprehensive Investigation* (Baltimore: Williams and Wilkins, 1973), 119–120.

36. Jack Beeching, Introduction to Exquemelin, *Buccaneers of America*, 11.

37. Lawrence Stone, *The Family, Sex and Marriage in England 1500–1800* (New York: Harper and Row, 1977), 439–440.

38. John Aubrey, *Brief Lives, Chiefly of Contemporaries Set Down by John Aubrey, between the Years 1669 & 1696*, 2 vols. (Oxford: Clarendon Press, 1898), 1: 395.

39. Exquemelin, *Buccaneers of America*, 91, 106–107; CSPCS, 11: 396.

40. Betagh, *Voyage*, 26; Shelvocke, *Privateer's Voyage*, 32; Johnson, *General History*, 75, 352–355; CSPCS, 29: 213.

41. Haring, *Buccaneers*, 54; CSPCS, 11: 364; 27: 144–149.

42. Stone, *Family, Sex and Marriage*, 439–440; Steven Marcus, *The Other Victorians: A Study of Sexuality and Pornography in Mid-Nineteenth Century England* (New York: Basic Books, 1964), 260; CSPCS, 24: 486.

43. Exquemelin, *Buccaneers of America*, 11, 99, 101, 130–137, 138, 147, 150–151, 200. See also CSPCS, 5: 50–51.

44. CSPCS, 24: 531–532.

45. Ibid., 30: 263–264, 410; 32: 272, 319.

46. Stone, *Family*, 81, 101–102, 194–195, 470–478.

47. John Latimer, *The Annals of Bristol in the Seventeenth Century* (Bristol: William George's Sons, 1900), 270; John Evelyn, *Diary, Now First Printed in Full from the Manuscripts Belonging to Mr. John Evelyn*, 6 vols. (Oxford: Clarendon Press, 1955), 4: 140–141.

48. Celia Fiennes, *The Journeys of Celia Fiennes* (New York: Chanticleer Press, 1949), 310–312.

49. Sloane, *Voyage*, lvii; *Code Noir of Jamaica* (London: 1789), 4.

50. Le Golif, *Memoirs*, 46; Neville Williams, *Captains Outrageous* (London: Barrie and Rockliff, 1961), 152.

51. Johnson, *General History*, 69–70.

52. Labat, *Memoirs*, 239–240.

53. Johnson, *General History*, 659–660.

54. Martin Hoffman, *The Gay World: Male Homosexuality and the Social Creation of Evil* (New York: Basic Books, 1968), 87; Donald Webster Cory and John LeRoy, *The Homosexual and His Society: A View from Within* (New York: Citadel Press, 1963), 77–78.

55. Hooker, "Homosexual Community," 182–183; Gore Vidal, *The City and the Pillar* (New York: Grosset and Dunlap, 1948), 106. An excellent collection of short works that demonstrates this point is Stephen Wright, ed., *Different: An Anthology of Homosexual Short Stories* (New York: Bantam, 1974); L. H. Loeser, "The Sexual Psy-

chopath in Military Service," *American Journal of Psychiatry* 102 (1945): 92–101, reference here to 95.

56. "Mercurius Americanus, A Brief journall or a Succinct and True Relation of the Most Remarkable Passages Observed in That Voyage Undertaken by Captaine William Jackson to the Westerne Indies or Continent of America," Sloane MS. 793 or 894, British Museum, London, folio 23; William Jackson, *The Voyages of Captain William Jackson, 1642–1645*, ed. Vincent Harlow, *Camden Miscellany*, vol. 13 (London: Camden Society, 1923). 30.

57. François Froger, *A Relation of a Voyage Made in the Years 1695, 1696, 1697, on the Coasts of Africa, Streights of Magellan, Brasil, Cayenna, and the Antilles, by a Squadron of French Men of War, Under the Command of M. De Gennes by the Sieur Froger ... ; Illustrated with Divers Strange Figures, Drawn to the Life* (London: 1698), 56.

58. McIntosh, "Homosexual Role," 192; Trumbach, "London's Sodomites."

Chapter 12

The Practice of Homosexuality among the Pirates of Late Eighteenth- and Early Nineteenth-Century China

Dian Murray

My involvement with this topic began more than a decade ago when, as a graduate student doing dissertation research on Chinese piracy in the early nineteenth century, I found myself coming across repeated incidences of pirate homosexuality. Consequently I tried to understand what meaning these actions had for the pirates who participated in them; and to date, my quest continues, for I am not sure what the practice of homosexuality meant to Chinese pirates.

The existing literature on homosexuality, largely written by psychologists and sociologists and often focused on contemporary Western society, provides little of use in apprehending the phenomenon within either a historical context or an East Asian setting. The book *Passions of the Cut Sleeve: The Male Homosexual Tradition in China* by Bret Hinsch[1] devotes 23 of its 232 pages to a discussion of male homosexuality among the elite primarily as it was depicted in literature during the Qing dynasty. There is no information on the practice of homosexuality among nonelite communities from historical sources.

The topic of homosexuality among Western pirate communities has, however, been mentioned in passing by Robert C. Ritchie in his book *Captain Kidd and the War against the Pirates*,[2] and there is one full-length book on the subject, *Sodomy and the Perception of Evil: English Sea Rovers in the Seventeenth-Century Caribbean* by Richard Burg. However, this treatise has proved inadequate on two grounds: first, the endeavor to explain buccaneer homosexuality by projecting onto the past theoretical insights from the twentieth century as a basis to determine the *raison d'être* of seventeenth-century homosexuality makes for unsatisfactory history. Second, the very different situations of buccaneers in the Caribbean and pirates in the South China Sea during the seventeenth and nineteenth centuries, have made it impossible to explain homosexuality among Chinese pirates on the basis of Caribbean pirates. Yet my objections notwithstanding, Burg's book provides a useful point of departure, for the analytical categories he has outlined may be used to launch a discussion of what homosexuality may have meant to the pirates of the South China Sea and to illustrate how sharply the conditions of the buccaneer community differed from those of Chinese pirate communities.

In contrast with the buccaneers for whom Burg contends that homosexuality provided the only form of nonsolitary sexual activity available,[3] the pirates of the South China Sea did not form a community whose only sexual outlet was male. Even at sea they often could and did have other sexual outlets. The pirates of South China were not men who had gone to sea to avoid the presence of women, and in some respects at least, piracy among Chinese seafarers could be regarded as a kind of family affair. Unlike in the West where women were persona non grata aboard craft of all types, Chinese vessels abounded with them. In lieu of fixed residences onshore, women and children lived permanently along with the pirates amidst the cramped quarters afloat. Throughout South China the handling of sampans had traditionally been the work of women, and this seems at least at times to have been the case among the pirates as well. On board ship the women worked as hard as the men. Women with unbound feet frequently held rank within the confederation and commanded entire junks themselves.[4] During the heat of battle, they often fought beside their husbands.[5] In the words of contemporary observer Philip Maughan, first lieutenant in the H.C. *Bombay Marine,* "It was surprising the number of women who lived with these people."[6] According to another, each vessel ordinarily had eight or ten women who "were destined to please all of their society indiscriminately and to do the work of their sex."[7]

Yet despite the appearance of women on board ship, there were strict rules (at least in theory) governing their presence. It was, for example, unlawful for a woman to be on board unless she was married to a pirate or being held captive, and offenses against either were to be punished severely. If a pirate committed rape or adultery, the participating offenders were put to death.[8] The men were beheaded and the women cast overboard with a weight attached to their legs.[9]

J. Turner, British captive of the pirates during 1807, has indicated that it was customary for the pirates to take their most beautiful captives as either concubines or wives, return the ugliest to shore, and ransom the rest. At the same time he has also added that having once chosen a wife from among the captives, a pirate was obliged to "be constant to her" with "no promiscuous intercourse being allowed amongst them."[10] Despite the female presence aboard ship, Turner has also commented that "the greater part of the crew are satisfied without women,"[11] and that the pirates "committed almost publicly crimes against nature."[12] Among other things, this condition may have been attributable to a kind of instinctive homosexual preference for men or to the fact that the majority of the pirates were single unmarried men in the prime of life (in many cases individuals were either too young or too poor to have started families of their own) to whom were therefore denied the privileges of women afloat.[13]

But there is little evidence to support the thesis that Chinese pirates of the early nineteenth century were either hostile to women or that the capture of women created emotionally difficult situations for them, as was argued by Burg with regard to the Caribbean pirates.[14] In fact one of the characteristics that most distinguished Chinese pirates from all others is the fact that between 1807 and 1810, when their confederation consisted of 60,000 men divided into six fleets, the pirates' overall commander-in-chief was a woman: Cheng I Sao, widow of original confederation founder Cheng I.[15]

If one grants that Chinese pirates may not have constituted a particularly idiosyncratic group of emotionally traumatized or sexually unstable men, then what role may homosexuality have played among them and why was it so frequently mentioned in the documents? For some, it seems, homosexuality, especially voluntary homosexuality, may have served to satisfy the genuine sexual desire of pirates who were either homosexual by nature or who, for the time being at least, may have had no other sexual recourse. Second, in instances where violence, assault, or same-sex rape occurred in times of combat or battle as in the instances cited above, the same kinds of dynamics of aggression and hostility that are often played out in heterosexual rape may have been at work in the pirate communities as well.

But the evidence also seems to indicate a dynamic of another sort, for homosexual relationships including rape, appear in some instances at least to have functioned as a kind of initiation rite for new gang members and as the means through which some of the patron-client relationships and male bonding, so essential for the solidification of the confederation, occurred. For example, in the case cited in the appendix, each act of sodomy perpetrated aboard Ya-tsung's vessel was initiated by either the pirate leader himself or a high-ranking member of his crew who was in one way or another distinguished from the rank and file.

A more telling example of the ways in which future leaders may have been groomed for their positions through homosexual liaisons (and in which pirate leaders themselves were often bisexual) is afforded by the encounter between confederation leader Cheng I and his neophyte captive Chang Pao. Chang Pao, the fifteen-year-old son of a Tanka fisherman, came to piracy in 1801, after having been captured by Cheng I. An unusually capable and handsome youth, he soon attracted the attention of his abductor and became his catamite. Later Cheng I and his wife Cheng I Sao also adopted him as their son and promoted him to be the captain of a junk.[16] For five years Chang Pao sailed in this capacity with his adopted father and learned the techniques of piracy from him. But after Chang I's sudden death in 1807, his wife in her new position as confederation leader quickly named Chang Pao to command the most powerful Red Flag fleet and initiated with him a sexual relationship of her own. The two became paramours and several years later, husband and wife.[17]

The practice whereby underworld leaders abducted teenagers into their gangs and then adopted them as sons was fairly widespread among Chinese pirates, bandits, and secret society members alike and in such instances there was sometimes a very thin line between adoption and the sexual abuse of promising youths by their substitute fathers. Given the tentativeness of the data, it is difficult to determine to what degree pirate leaders forcibly used homosexuality as a rite of passage and as a means of initiating a novice into a gang or to what degree homosexuality was a voluntary activity freely engaged in by the mutual desire of the two participants. However, the bisexual nature of many pirate leaders and the ease with which they seem to have moved between men, women, and young boys as sexual partners serves to differentiate them sharply from the Caribbean pirates about whom Burg has written:

> The most visible characteristic of pirate pedophiles is that in every case those men with preference for boys were not integrated members of their crews. . . . This is particularly true of the one class of pirates who most frequently sought out young companions, the captains. Command isolation is a feature of any ship, and may be necessary for the exercise of authority at sea, but in the 17th century, the need of the commander to be separate from his crew probably encouraged pedophilia among some captains, whether they commanded merchant and naval vessels or buccaneering craft. The long periods of solitude, the responsibilities of command, the inability to interact socially or sexually with members of the crew, and the presence of a youthful personal servant all contributed toward making pederasty the only available sexual outlet for the commander other than solitary masturbation, dreams, or fantasies.[18]

Clearly, that condition did not prevail among Chinese pirate crews. While the tendency toward pedophilia may have been greatest among Chinese captains, the captains also tended, more than any others, to be wed and to have aboard ship more wives than anyone else. For Richard Glasspoole, an Englishman held captive by the pirates for several weeks, reported that the captain often shared his quarters in the poop with five or six wives.[19]

There is, however, at least one additional way in which homosexuality may have been utilized by Chinese pirate communities of the nineteenth century: as a means of dodging the law. The confessions from which the evidence on homosexuality among Chinese pirates derives were extracted during testimony before government officials in a context where, according to Ch'ing law, homosexuality was a crime punishable by one hundred blows of the heavy bamboo (but in actuality only forty blows) and three years of penal servitude (t'u), while piracy was a capital offense for which the punishment was beheading. Thus, during a trial, it would have been decidedly more advantageous for a defendant to have claimed that he had been forcibly raped and retained against his will in a pirate gang than to have confessed to having joined such an organization voluntarily. Thus it is conceivable that pirates may have confessed to homosexual activities they did not commit in order to escape the death penalty for the piracy they did commit. To what extent such considerations are actually reflected in the statistics cited above, however, is not clear, but the data do indicate that for each of the fifty men who admitted to sexual assault by their pirate superiors, the punishment was penal servitude and not decapitation.

In this essay, I have suggested that the homosexuality engaged in by Chinese pirates of the early nineteenth century may have been engendered by a variety of causes. First, the needs of those who were either homosexual or bisexual by nature or those to whom other avenues of heterosexual activity were temporarily denied, to satisfy their desires. Second, the needs of others to give vent to feelings of hostility and violence during combat. Third, the needs of pirate leaders to forge bonds of solidarity within the confederation and to create strong patron-client relationships that would enhance the functioning of their operation. And fourth, the desire of those who were apprehended to receive sentences less severe under the law than those for piracy.

Yet these analyses are based on speculation, and it is impossible to determine which, if any, prevailed at any given point. Thus, unfortunately the subject of homosexuality among Chinese pirates remains almost as tentative at the end of this essay as it did at the outset. To aid readers in their own analysis of the phenomenon, I have included in an appendix a more extended discussion and translation of the relevant source materials.

Appendix

The bulk of the evidence that describes the prevalence of homosexuality among the Chinese pirate community is archival and has been drawn from the palace memorial collection of the National Palace Museum in Taipei, Taiwan. Palace memorials were secret communications written by high government officials to the emperor informing him of what was going on within their particular administrative jurisdictions. Of most relevance to piracy are the memorials written by Provisional Governors or Governors-General, who upon completing the interrogation of apprehended pirates, presented the emperor with a summary of each group's activities as well as the individual testimony itself. Although most of the pirates' individual depositions are no longer extant, the governors' summaries are, and the National Palace Museum contains a total of fifty-six memorials that deal exclusively with pirate cases in Kwangtung Province between 1796 and 1801. Of these, twenty-two, or 39 percent, actually mention instances of homosexual activity, mostly in the form of coercion; that involved at least fifty-one couples or 102 individuals.[20]

Despite the significance of this information, one should not derive the impression that most, or even large numbers of pirates were gay, for that simply was not the case. Sixty-one percent of the cases do not mention the phenomenon at all, and despite the fact that the twenty-two cases referred to above do indeed mention convictions for 51 of the 102 individuals mentioned, they also discuss the convictions, on totally unrelated grounds, of another 579 pirates whose sexual activities went unremarked.[21]

Finally, even the "hard" evidence itself is ambiguous. By way of illustration, what follows is a partial translation of one memorial which is typical of the evidence of pirate homosexuality contained in these documents.

In a memorial of CC1/7/5, the Governor-General of Kwangtung, Chu Kuei, reported on the apprehension, trial, and handling of pirates:

> I ordered the offenders brought to Canton . . . and with the *ssu-tao* (provincial officials) investigated [and learned that leader/offender] Ch'en Ya-sheng's home is in Ho-p'u County. He fished in Chiang-p'ing [a fishing market and pirate headquarters on the border between China and Vietnam but then located in Vietnam] with the city's "long-haired" [Vietnamese] resident, Ya-tsung with whom he was also well-acquainted. In December 1795 [Cl 60/11] because the fishing was no good, Ch'en Ya-sheng joined up with Ya-tsung who had one large *ts'eng-ch'uan,* two small "fast boats," and a crew of fifty-four. Ya-tsung appointed Ch'en Ya-sheng as the head of one of the fast boats and allocated to him some men. On January 14 Ya-tsung set out, and on February 5, in the ocean of Kuei-shan County, robbed a fishing boat and captured Ts'ai Hsieh-fou whom he forced to commit sodomy.
>
> On February 21 he robbed a *t'o-feng* (passenger) junk and captured Hsu Ya-tsan who was imprisoned in and forced to sweep the hold. On February 25, in the ocean off Wu Shan-t'ou of Kuei-shan County, he robbed a black-masted boat and captured Li Fa-ch'ing whom crew member [and petty officer] Ssu Lan forced to commit sodomy. The next day, still at the same place, they attacked another fishing vessel and captured and imprisoned Wang-ch'u and Shih Ya-shuang. Wang was ordered to wash dishes and cook while helmsman Ya-man forced Shih Ya-shuang to commit sodomy.

On March 3, in the ocean off Hai-feng County, the pirates robbed a fishing junk, and captured Hsu-ch'iung whom crew member Ssu T'ien forced to commit sodomy. On March 11 in a bay in Hsin-an County, they robbed another *t'o-feng* vessel, captured and imprisoned Tan Se-chin and Tan Ya-pang and forced them to gather firewood. On March 18 in the ocean of Hsin-ning, they attacked another vessel from which they captured Wang Ya-Gou and on April 10 in the waters of Vietnam, they attacked still another fishing vessel. On April 15, they had intended to sail to Chiang-p'ing to sell their booty, but when they reached the "black water" of the "Barbarian ocean" they encountered the Second Captain (*shou-pei*) of the Ying-chou battalion who arrested them. Ya-tsung used a red flag to tell Ch'en Ya-sheng to come to his big junk to help him resist the troops, who had crossed to his boat and eventually killed Ya-tsung and more than ten men of his gang. Ch'en Ya-sheng and seven others who jumped into the water were also captured alive.[22]

NOTES

1. Bret Hinsch, *Passions of the Cut Sleeve: The Male Homosexual Tradition in China* (Berkeley: University of California Press, 1990). Herein the author has remarked particularly upon the widespread nature of homosexuality in China and of the ways in which the Qing dynasty tried to limit and regulate it by law—especially male rape, which was punishable under the legal codes of the Qing dynasty. He also discusses transgenerational homosexuality as well as that between partners of equal age, class, and status. See 139–161.

2. Robert C. Ritchie, *Captain Kidd and the War against the Pirates* (Cambridge, Mass.: Harvard University Press, 1986), 123–124.

3. "They were men who eschewed service in the seafaring trades closer to home and for the most part had rejected situations where heterosexual contact was more easily available . . . all had chosen to sail on lengthy voyages, among members of a totally male society where other men were the only sexual contacts available." B. R. Burg, *Sodomy and the Pirate Tradition: English Sea Rovers in the Seventeenth-Century Caribbean* (New York: New York University Press, 1995), 67–68, 111.

4. Richard Glasspoole, "Substance of Mr. Glasspoole's Relation, Upon His Return to England, Respecting the Ladrones," in *Further Statement of the Ladrones on the Coast of China; Intended as a Contribution to the Accounts Published by Mr Dalrymple* (London: Land, Darling, and Co., 1812), 41.

5. Yüan Yung-lun, *Ching-hai fen-chi* (Record of the pacification of the pirates) 2 *chuan* (Canton: 1830), 1:10b (hereafter CHFC).

6. Philip Maughan, "An Account of the Ladrones who infested the Coast of China," in *Further Statement of the Ladrones on the Coast of China; Intended as a Contribution to the Accounts Published by Mr Dalrymple* (London: Land, Darling, and Co., 1812), 26.

7. Carloman Louis François Félix Renouard de Sainte-Croix, *Voyage commercial*

et politique aux Indes Orientales, aux îles Philippines, à la Chine, avec notions sur la Cochinchine et le Tonquin, pendant les années 1803–1804 (Paris: 1810), 3:58.

8. CHFC 1:5a–6b.

9. Maughan, "Account," 29.

10. J. Turner, "Account of the Captivity of J. Turner, Chief Mate of the Ship Tay, amongst the Ladrones; Accompanied by some Observations Respecting those Pirates," in *Further Statement of the Ladrones on the Coast of China; Intended as a Contribution to the Accounts Published by Mr Dalrymple* (London: Land, Darling, and Co., 1812), 71.

11. Ibid., 71.

12. Turner, as quoted by Sainte-Croix in *Voyage commercial*, 3:57.

13. For more details on pirate backgrounds, see Dian H. Murray, *Pirates of the South China Coast, 1790–1810* (Stanford: Stanford University Press, 1987), 161–164.

14. Burg, *Sodomy*, 111–120.

15. For more information, see Murray, *Pirates*, 71–73.

16. CHFC 1.5a; *Kuang-tung hai fang hui-lan* (Essentials of sea defense in Kuang-tung), *42 chuan*, Lu K'un and Ch'eng Hung-ch'ih compilers, n.d., 42:26B; Hsiao Wan-om (Hsiao Yun-han), "Research in the History of the Pirates on the China Sea, 1140–1950," unpublished manuscript in Chinese (1976), fol. 28.

17. Hu Chieh-yü (Woo Kit-yu), "Hsi Ying-P'an yü Chang Pao-tsai huo-luan chih p'ing-ting' (Hsi Ying P'an [West Camp] and the end of the ravages of the pirate Chang Pao-tsai)," in *I-pa-ssu-erh nien i-ch'ien chih Hsiang-kang chi ch'i-tui wai-chiao-t'ung* [Hong Kong and its external communication before 1842], ed. Lo Hsiang-lin (1959), 151–170, reference here to 152; CHFC, 1:5a–b; Hsiao Wan-om, "Research," fol. 28; Chu Ch'eng-wan, "Chi-ssu p'ing-k'ou (Suppressing the pirates in 1809)," in *Nan-hai hsien chih (Gazetteer of Nan-hai District) 26 chüan* (Taipei: 1971). This is a reprint of a work originally published in 1872, reference here to 14:20b.

18. Burg, *Sodomy*, 124–125.

19. Richard Glasspoole, "A Brief Narrative of My Captivity and Treatment Amongst the Ladrones," supplement to Yüan Yung-lun, *History of the Pirates who Infested the China Sea from 1807–1810* (London: Oriental Translation Fund, 1831), trans. Karl Friedrich Neumann, 128.

20. For examples of memorials containing incidences of homosexuality, see: Kung-chung tang (Palace Memorial Archive), National Palace Museum, Taiwan KCT 000066, CC1/1/21; KCT 000137, CC1/2/9; KCT 000827, CC1/6/25; KCT 000857, CC1/7/5; KCT 001047, CC1/8/19; KCT 001091, CC1/8/30; KCT 001092, CC1/8/30; KCT 001392, CC1/11/1; KCT 001448, CC1/11/10; KCT 001496, CC1/11/18; KCT 002481, CC2/5/6; KCT 002531, CC2/5/29; KCT 002637 CC2/6/17; KCT 002723, CC2/6*/7; KCT 002845, CC2/7/6; KCT 003347, CC2/11/2; KCT 003459, CC2/12/1; KCT 003728, CC3/2/19; KCT 003749, CC3/2/29; KCT 004578, CC4/5/10; KCT 004725, CC5/1/11; KCT 005050, CC5/2/15. The dates of the memorials used in these citations refer to the years of the Emperor Chia-ch'ing's reign (he ascended the throne in 1796) and to the phase of the moon. Thus, for example, CC1/2/5 should be read as the fifth day of the second lunar month of the first year of the reign of the Chia-ch'ing Emperor. The asterisked month, 6*, is an intercalary month.

21. On the basis of the twenty-two memorials cited, 7 pirates were sentenced to lingering death; 3 were sent to the capital prior to execution; 326 were sentenced to decapitation for engaging in piracy; 243 were banished to Muslim areas as slaves for having been captured by pirates and forced to serve them by receiving booty (although these individuals did not engage in piracy of their own volition); 50 were convicted of sodomy; 60 died either in combat or jail; 125 were released; and 14 escaped.

22. KCT 000857, CC1/7/5.

Chapter 13

Cheng I Sao in Fact and Fiction

Dian Murray

A sigh sounds and a sough replies,
Mulan must be at the window weaving.
You can't tell the sounds of the loom
From the sighs of the girl.
Ask her whom she's longing for
Ask her whom she's thinking of
She's longing for no one at all,
She's thinking of no one special:
"Last night I saw the draft list
The Khan's mustering a great army;
The armies' rosters ran many rolls,
Roll after roll held my father's name!
And Father has no grown-up son,
And I've no elder brother!
So I offered to buy a saddle and horse
And campaign from now on for Father."

In the eastern market she bought a steed,
At the western a saddle and cloth;
In the southern market she bought a bridle,
At the northern a long whip;
At sunrise she bade her parents farewell,
At sunset she camped by the Yellow River;
She couldn't hear her parents calling her,

Dawn she took leave of the Yellow River,
Evening she was atop the Black Mountains;
She couldn't hear her parents calling her,
She heard only the Tartar horse on Swallow
    Mountain/whinny and blow
Hastening thousands of miles to decisive battles,
Crossing mountains and passes as if flying!
The northern air carries the sentry's drum,
A wintry sun glints off her coat of mail.

After a hundred battles the generals are dead,
Ten years now, and the brave soldiers are returning!
Returning to audience with the Son of Heaven,
The Son of Heaven, sitting in his Luminous Hall.
Their merits quickly moved them up the ranks,
And rewards, more than a hundred thousand cash!
Then the Khan asked what Mulan desired:
"I have no use for a minister's post,
Yost lend me a famous fleet footed camel
To send me back to my village."

"When my parents heard I was coming,
They helped each other to the edge of town.
When my big sister heard I was coming,
She stood at the door, putting on her face.
When my little brother heard I was coming,
He ground his knife in a flash and went for a pig
    and a sheep.

"I opened myself the east chamber door,
And sat myself down on the west chamber bed;
Took off my wartime cloaks,
And draped myself in my robes of old.
At the window I put up my cloudy black tresses,
Before the mirror I powdered my face,
Came out the door to see my camp mates,
They'd traveled together for many a year
Without knowing Mulan was a girl!"

"The hare draws in his feet to sit,
His mate has eyes that gleam,
But when the two run side by side,
How much alike they seem!"

For an Iowa farm girl, landlocked by flat, verdant fields of corn, the mental voyage to China's coast provided an escape to places of imagined romance where sinister villains lurked in every cove. The power of this and countless other flamboyant visions, conjured up from the realm of the subconscious, probably led me into the world of Sinology in 1970. Chinese history intrigued me because of its challenges. It was a difficult world to enter: I had to understand three thousand years of history and learn a daunting language well enough to deal with its written legacy. In the end, traveling, living, and researching in the country itself caused any lingerings of exoticism to yield before fascinating new chapters in the human struggle to survive. And I chose the topic of piracy for my doctorate in 1975 because I wanted an intrinsically interesting subject that would not be a conversation stopper.[1]

Piracy in China, as in the West, is one of the oldest professions. Records dating back to the fourth century B.C. suggest a continuous tradition of petty piracy: a small-scale, income-supplementing activity that could be practiced out of a neighborhood cove using the equipment at hand. Its size, intensity, and ebb and flow were often determined by external circumstances, and by the political and social events of the world around the sea. The piracy of the most famous woman pirate of all, Cheng I Sao, took place during a rebellion in what is now Vietnam. The leaders' need for a privateer force gave employment to Chinese pirates who answered their call. Later, when Vietnamese patronage was no longer an option, leadership from within the pirate ranks enabled an essentially military organization to be transformed into a big business. The vehicle was a confederation composed of six (and at times seven) well-ordered and regulated fleets consisting of between 40,000 and 70,000 individuals who at their height were under the leadership of Cheng I Sao.

My colleagues and friends, imbued with stereotypes of Confucian China, are always surprised to learn that the leader of this confederation was a woman. Confucian philosophy dictated that throughout their lives women would remain subservient to their fathers, husbands, and sons. Confucian politics barred them from public office by prohibiting their participation in what was the world's earliest civil service examination system. Social and economic customs confined them to their homes, limited their public employment possibilities, and forced them to hobble about on bound feet. However, the joke among certain scholars has become, "Whose Confucianism was it anyway?" Were Confucian scholar Chu Hsi and his contemporaries painting a picture of Chinese society as it really operated, or were they presenting a vision of how society should operate that accorded more with their own mental dictates than with the ongoing realities of daily life?

While neo-Confucianism may have shaped elite views of properly submissive and chaste women, popular culture was rife with contrasting images of strong-willed, quick-witted individuals who in times of crisis could take charge or engage in diatribe of unforgettable magnitude. Even today, who can fail to admire the inner strength of the women depicted in such recent films as *Raise the Red Lantern, Farewell My Concubine,* and the mothers in *The Joy Luck Club?*

For centuries Chinese storytellers have been in awe of the spiritual prowess of the women of popular fiction. These figures were often regarded as dangerous seductresses in the form of fox fairies or other spirits. In times of stress (such as on the eve of the triennial civil service examinations) they were said to beguile vulnerable men and lead them astray. It was this same awe of the unseen powers of women that caused rebels and defenders alike during the Wang Lun uprising of 1774, to repel their enemies by sending prostitutes up on the city walls to take off their underclothing, loosen their hair, urinate, and bleed over the side of the wall to destroy the power of the enemy.[2]

Today, though still in its infancy, the study of women in imperial China is a rapidly expanding field. Although there is much we will never be able to discover about how women of the eighteenth and nineteenth centuries lived and worked, our knowledge is increasing. As it does, we cannot help but be impressed by the variety of lifestyles and activities that is emerging. Chinese women no longer fit into a single mold.

This is especially true of the South China maritime environment from which the pirates hailed. The coastal provinces of Kwangtung and Fukien boasted a rich mixture of non-Han (non-Chinese) ethnic groups whose social customs were not always in accord with the Han mainstream (Hakka women, for instance, did not bind their feet). Within the maritime world, there were entire communities whose members lived their whole lives on board ship without ever setting foot on land. Moreover, throughout most of South China, the major communication arteries were rivers and much commerce was conducted from the water. Even the brothels, known euphemistically as "flower boats," were to be found offshore. In the cramped conditions aboard vessels that housed entire families, women often did as much work as men. Most of the propelling and sculling of the small lighters used for so much of the transport throughout the South China Sea was regarded as women's work, and since most commerce was coastal and did not necessitate long voyages to distant waters, there was no concept of the maritime world as an exclusively male preserve.

The presence of women aboard pirate ships in China should therefore come as less of a surprise than in the West. Indeed, the evidence suggests that women participated in pirate communities as something other than cooks and bottle washers; that they sometimes held rank and commanded ships; and that in certain instances they took part in combat (just as, I might add, their counterparts did ashore). What is unusual about the case discussed here is not that it features "women pirates" per se, but rather the extent to which one particular woman, Cheng I Sao, assumed and executed leadership. Also unusual is the way Cheng I Sao, perhaps playing on male fear of her "mysterious potency," forced government officials to come to terms with her in effecting a settlement. In these instances, she demonstrated skill, cunning, and public presence not often associated with Chinese women.

To what extent the episode I describe here is unique, I do not know. Fanny

Loviot, a Californian who was captured by Chinese pirates in 1854, reported that:

> The pirates of the Chinese seas make their junks their homes, and carry their wives and children with them on every expedition. The women assist in working the ships, and are chiefly employed in the lading and unlading.[3]

So it appears that women and children continued to live and work aboard pirate ships well into the nineteenth century. What is unclear is whether Cheng I Sao's level of command was ever attained by any other woman. Her closest rival might possibly have been Lai Choi San (Mountain of Wealth), alleged to have been the commander of twelve junks in the vicinity of Macao during the 1920s. So far as I am aware, the only account of her activities stems from the American journalist Aleko Lilius and his rather dubious *I Sailed with Chinese Pirates* (London, 1930), which account I have not yet been able to corroborate elsewhere.

The study of pirates in China, like that of women, is in its infancy. How much further we can go beyond the mere chronicling of names, events, and dates will depend on the availability of sources. Detailed information on women and their lives is difficult to come by under any circumstances, but even more so in the case of pirates and other groups for whom written records were anathema. What pirate, even if she or he were literate, would want to keep written accounts of activities which, if the records should fall into government hands, would automatically convict them? This means it may never be possible to fill in the gaps and answer the questions even this brief episode brings to light. The tendency to overwrite on the basis of insufficient evidence has, in my opinion, marred many pirate studies in the West. The subject has been romanticized and glamorized to such an extent that historical fiction has overtaken history, and much of what we think is known is more myth than truth. In China, by contrast, piracy is a subject that has not only not been glamorized but is virtually unknown. So far as I am aware, no Chinese scholar or historian has attempted to liken Cheng I Sao or any other female pirate to the mythical woman warrior described in the poem at the beginning of this chapter.

Cheng I Sao's story takes place on the South China coast, where piracy was part of the human endeavor to survive. As a gathering point for the flotsam of the earth, the coasts of Kwangtung province attracted those who could make it nowhere else in society. Their only option was to prey on the establishment in any way they could, and in doing so, the line between legal and illegal often became blurred. The gambling parlors, opium dens, and floating bordellos that dotted the coast were, in part, the products of their struggle to get by. For individual fishermen, locked into recurring cycles of debt and impoverishment, a quick heist at sea or the temporary recourse to piracy as an off-season activity could help them make a living. Once the crisis had passed, those fortunate enough to have escaped arrest would throw off their pirate mantles and slip inconspicuously back into the society from which they had come. One of the leading families was the Chengs, who had been involved in piracy since the late seventeenth century. It was into this family that Cheng I Sao, the woman destined to become the leader of the confederation and China's most famous woman pirate, married in 1801.

Not much is known about this remarkable woman, and the little I believe can be deduced from the sources and stated with certainty is to be found in the first section of this chapter. But lack of "factual" information seems not to have impeded several generations of twentieth-century pirate scholars from including an obligatory chapter on Cheng I Sao in their general surveys. For the most part, when primary sources were found wanting, these individuals seem to have resorted to "fictional" details drawn from fertile imaginations. While engaged in research processes of my own, traveling to archives in China, Taiwan, Hong Kong, England, and Macao and trying to decipher detailed reports in Chinese, Portuguese, Japanese, Vietnamese, and French, I found myself increasingly frustrated, annoyed, and finally angered by this genre of imprecise and sloppy history. But despite my dismissal of most of these works as "rubbish," they have introduced Chinese pirates to Western audiences and have colored the ways many Westerners perceive them today. When closely examined, the distortion and "fiction" that have intruded in these secondary histories are easy to spot because most of the information about the daily lives of Cheng I Sao and the pirates is derived from two English-language primary sources. Both are widely available and they were at least nominally invoked by the three historians on whose accounts I focus here.

The Bare Facts: What the Sources Allow Us to Say

Cheng I Sao (1775–1844) was a Cantonese prostitute who in 1801 married the pirate leader Cheng I and assisted him in the creation of a confederation of pirates. By 1805 this included 400 junks and between 40,000 and 60,000 pirates.[4] She was also known as Shih Hsiang-ku and Shih Yang. Two sons, Cheng Ying-shih (b. 1803) and Cheng Hsiung-shih (b. 1807), were born to them.

Sponsorship by Vietnam's Tay-son[5] rulers enabled the scale of Chinese piracy to increase between 1792 and 1802 and associations of several hundred people and several dozen junks to come into being. Tay-son support also provided pirates and privateers with opportunities for communication and cooperation in joint ventures at sea. The Chengs flourished under Tay-son patronage: Cheng I's distant cousin, Cheng Ch'i, was widely recognized as one of the pirates' most able leaders.

The turning point in the Chengs' careers came in July 1802 with the overthrow of the Tay-son and the end of Chinese piracy in Vietnam. Cheng Ch'i was killed in a desperate battle near Hanoi. On 16 July the Nguyen navy reached Son Nam and after defeating the pirates sent them fleeing to China. It was at this point that Cheng I and his wife emerged as the pirates' most important leaders. They reestablished their base back across the border in China and later unified the disparate and often quarreling gangs into a confederation of seven (later six) principal fleets distinguished by a series of colored banners.

The unexpected death of her husband in November 1807 caused Cheng I Sao to make a well-calculated bid for power that secured her position at the top of the pirate hierarchy. In this capacity, she was responsible for appointing as commander of the most powerful Red Flag fleet her "adopted" son. Chang Pao was a fisherman's son who had been captured by Cheng I. Cheng I developed a fondness for the young man, adopted him, and gave him command of a ship. The death of his mentor brought little change to the fortunes of Chang Pao. He became the paramour and ultimately the husband of Cheng I Sao, with whom he had at least one son.

As the leader of what became a formidable confederation, Cheng I Sao used the creation of Chang Pao's law code to transform the series of personal relationships that existed among the pirates into a more formal power structure. This included penal sanctions as well as elaborate provisions for sharing booty. She also controlled a financial operation that extended far beyond a few sporadic heists at sea. This was achieved by setting up a "regularized" protection racket that featured the sale of "safe passage" documents to all coastal fishing workers or shippers, the convoying of the salt fleets to Canton (Guangzhou) for the purpose of protection, and the establishment of financial offices along the coast to serve as fee-collection points.

By 1808, the pirates held the military initiative along the coast of Kwangtung and demonstrated their prowess by killing the provincial commander-in-chief of Chekiang, Li Ch'ang-keng, who had sailed into Kwangtung province on a special assignment. Within the year, the pirates had also destroyed 63 of the Kwangtung area's 135-vessel fleet, and in August 1809 they threatened to attack Canton itself. The strength of Cheng I Sao's confederation forced officials in Canton to enter into a series of negotiations with the British for the short-term use of the vessel *Mercury,* fitted out with twenty cannon and fifty American volunteers. These were followed a few months later by similar negotiations with the Portuguese for the lease of six men-of-war to sail with the imperial navy for several months in late 1809.[6]

These measures failed to bring the pirates to terms, causing the Chinese government to shift its emphasis from "extermination" to "pacification" and to offer the pirates amnesty. Cheng I Sao was quick to understand the advantages such an offer could bring her followers. She took the lead in engineering the pirates' surrender and in obtaining from the government a favorable settlement. After the failure of the pirates' first attempt at surrender, during a conference arranged by Chang Pao and the Liang-kuang Governor-General on 21 February 1810, Cheng I Sao took the initiative.

In the company of other pirate women and children, she went unarmed to the Governor-General's *yamen* (headquarters) in Canton on 18 April 1810. Her negotiations succeeded: two days later the surrender took place and the pirates were liberally rewarded. Those who came forward voluntarily were allowed to retain the proceeds of their profession and were granted places in the imperial military bureaucracy. Chang Pao was given the rank of lieutenant, allowed to retain a private fleet of twenty or thirty junks, and paid a large sum of money allegedly to establish his followers onshore.

In November 1810, Cheng I Sao accompanied Chang Pao to Fukien province where he was promoted to the position of lieutenant colonel of the Min-an regiment. There he remained until his death in 1822, after which Cheng I Sao returned to Kwangtung. In 1840, the widow filed charges against the official Wu Yao-nan on the grounds that he had embezzled 28,000 taels of silver allegedly entrusted to him by Chang Pao thirty years earlier for buying an estate. The charge was subsequently dismissed by the Liang-kuang Governor-General.[7]

After this brush with the authorities, Cheng I Sao spent her last days quietly in Canton, "leading a peaceful life so far as [was] consistent with the keeping of an infamous gambling house."[8] She died in 1844 aged sixty.[9]

The Historical Facts and Their Sources

I found much of the above biographical information in two English-language sources. First, Yuan Yun-lun (Yuen Yung-lun)'s book *Ching hai-fen chi*, which was published in Canton in 1830 and translated into English the following year by Charles Friedrich Neumann as *History of the Pirates Who Infested the China Sea from 1807 to 1810*.[10] This is an unofficial history composed by an employee of the Governor-General's *yamen* who was acquainted with several Chinese officials killed in combat against the pirates. Grief-stricken, Yuan Yun-lun felt compelled to write an "objective" account of the pirates and their activities in such a way that the lessons of their ravages and the spirit of those who died at their hands would be preserved for posterity. The book is based

on first-hand information relayed to Yuan Yun-lun by people such as Lieutenant Huang Ying-tang, who engaged the pirates directly.[11]

Another account well known in the West is A *Brief Narrative of My Captivity and Treatment amongst the Ladrones,* written by Richard Glasspoole, who
was an officer of the East India Company ship *Marquis of Ely.*[12] *(Ladrone* was
the Portuguese term for the pirates.) Glasspoole and seven British seafarers
were captured on 21 September 1809 and held by the pirates until 7 December. Glasspoole's diary of this adventure, prepared for the British East India
Company, was signed the day after his release. It describes several battles and
the movement of the pirates up the various branches of the Pearl and West
rivers to "levy contributions on the towns and villages."[13]

These two texts corroborate one another and were invaluable in helping me
to work out a daily report on the pirates' whereabouts during the most crucial
two months of their existence. More important for understanding Cheng I
Sao, these two pieces have had a surprisingly wide circulation and have
formed the basis for nearly every Western account of these pirates I have
seen.[14] What is most astonishing about many of these self-proclaimed histories
is how far from their sources they stray as a result of the ways in which their
authors have misread, misconstrued, or even added to the information contained in these texts. The result has been serious distortion in what Western
audiences have been told about Chinese pirates of the late eighteenth and early
nineteenth centuries.

Even the names of the pirates are problematic, for their spellings differ from
account to account. It is difficult to convert Chinese characters into letters like
those in the Roman alphabet, and both translations of the key book, *Ching
hai-fen chi,* were completed before "Wade-Giles" became the standard system
of transliteration in the late nineteenth century. Sometimes Cheng I Sao's name
is written as "Ching," while her husband, whose name is romanized in the
Wade-Giles system as "Cheng I," appears in many accounts as "Ching Yih."
The Wade-Giles romanization for the name of his wife, "Cheng I Sao," simply
means "Wife of Cheng I" and appears in many Western texts as "Ching yih
sao." For the most part problems of romanization, though annoying, are
fairly straightforward.

The same is not true of translators' attempts to find English equivalents for
the meanings, as opposed to the sounds, of the pirates' nicknames. On several
occasions Neumann, the translator of our key text, has either misread or mis-
translated the names of the major fleet commanders in his endeavor to capture
in English the spirit of their *noms de guerre.* For instance, the nickname for
Green squadron leader Woo Chetsing (Wu Chih-ch'ing) was "Tung haepa"
(Tung-hai Pa), translated by Neumann as "Scourge of the Eastern Sea." "Eastern Sea" or "Tung hae" (Tung-hai) was the name of Woo's native village in

Kwangtung province. But in this case the character "pa" means "uncle," "elder," or "earl," so instead of "Scourge of the Eastern Sea" Woo Chetsing's nickname would more accurately have been rendered as "Earl" or "Uncle from Eastern Sea Village."

When their origins are understood, the pirates' names lose much of their suggestive exoticism, revealing themselves instead to be in complete accord with the kinds of names widely used throughout South China. Here people tended to address one another with references that denoted their position within the family (Elder Brother, Younger Brother, First Son, or Second Son), their place of origin, or something idiosyncratic about the way they looked and acted rather than by their given names.

Fact or Fiction: Three Histories

Three secondary histories, written in English, all draw heavily on the Neumann translation of *Ching hai-fen chi* and on Glasspoole's captivity narrative. These show how, in the hands of certain authors, what began as the pirates' "history" ended up being more the pirates' "story."

Philip Gosse's now classic *History of Piracy*, written in 1932, has provided a point of departure for nearly everyone with a serious interest in piracy. Gosse begins his account of the Chengs by acknowledging that it is not until the early eighteenth century, thanks to the translation of Charles Neumann, that we "get any very minute account of the activities of Chinese pirates."[15] He continues by remarking that Neumann's *The History of the Pirates Who Infested the China Sea* "is chiefly devoted to the exploits of one pirate, and that a woman."[16] This comment is certainly an exaggeration. Neither the original *Ching hai fen chi* nor Neumann's translation is chiefly devoted to the exploits of Cheng I Sao. In fact, in the Chinese text of 102 pages, her name appears only twenty-five times. Instead, the text focuses primarily on the activities of the Red, Black, and White Flag fleets whose members sailed in the area between Macao and Canton between 1807 and 1810. Cheng I Sao's leadership is mentioned in conjunction with their operations, but the account is by no means "devoted" to her. Neither is that of Gosse. Despite the interest she has aroused, not very much is known about Cheng I Sao and even Gosse soon moves on to describe the most colorful military encounters between the imperial navy and the pirates.[17]

When it comes to facts, Gosse incorrectly describes Cheng I Sao's husband as the "admiral of all the pirate fleets" who "had become such a thorn in the flesh of the government that in 1802 the Emperor appointed him Master of the Royal Stables." According to Gosse,

The duties of that exalted post seem to have been only nominal, for shortly Admiral Ching was to be found ravaging the coasts of Annam and Cochin China, until at length the inhabitants rose and after a fierce battle on land routed the pirates and slaughtered the terrible Ching.[18]

Here Gosse has misread Neumann's translation and has also confused Cheng I Sao's husband Ching Yih (Cheng I) with his distant cousin Ching tsih (Cheng Ch'i), one of the pirates' major leaders during the time of their patronage by the Tay-son. It was Cheng Ch'i, not Cheng I, who was appointed "Master of the Stables" and the appointment was made not by the emperor of China, but by King-sheng,[19] the last Tay-son ruler and child emperor of Vietnam.

The Neumann translation then goes on to describe how King-sheng, with a force of two hundred pirate junks, retook the bay of Annam, but how tyranny in its possession caused the inhabitants to turn against him. In the battle which followed, Ching tsih was killed, King-sheng's force was vanquished, and the ruling Tay-son emperors were dethroned.[20] It was only then that Ching Yih (Cheng I), the husband of Cheng I Sao, emerged as the leader of the surviving pirates. Five years after he died (in 1807), Cheng I Sao herself assumed leadership of what had become a formidable pirate confederation. Despite Neumann's explicit descriptions of their relationship, Gosse seems to have missed the fact that two members of the Ching (Cheng) family were important pirate leaders before Cheng I Sao came on the scene and that she was married to the second, Ching Yih (Cheng I), and not the first, Ching tsih (Cheng Ch'i).

Having placed Cheng I Sao in command of the confederation and of its largest squadron, the Red Flag fleet, Gosse takes pains to portray her as "an excellent business woman," a good military strategist, and "a strict disciplinarian" who "drew up a code of rules for her crews which somewhat resembled those subscribed to by earlier European pirates."[21] To keep order on board ship, the pirates seem to have had a "code of laws" which attracted considerable attention from Western authors who mistakenly attributed the invention to Cheng I Sao. The Neumann translation, however, specifically states that this code was not created by Cheng I Sao but was set up by her lieutenant Chang Pao:

Being chief captain, Paou robbed and plundered incessantly, and daily increased his men and his vessels. He made the three following regulations:

First: If any man goes privately on shore, or what is called transgressing the bars, he shall be taken and his ears be perforated in the presence of the whole fleet; repeating the same act, he shall suffer death.

Second: Not the least thing shall be taken privately from the stolen and plundered goods. All shall be registered; and the pirate receive for himself, out of ten parts, only two; eight parts belong to the store-house, called the general fund; taking anything out of this general fund, without permission, shall be death.

Third: No person shall debauch at his pleasure captive women taken in the villages and open places, and brought on board a ship; he must first request the ship's purser for permission, and then go aside in the ship's hold. To use violence against any woman, or to wed her without permission, shall be punished with death.[22]

Though Gosse accurately followed Neumann in introducing the commanders of the various fleets as "Bird and Stone," "Scourge of the Eastern Sea," "Jewel of the Whole Crew," and "Frog's Meal," in this case his fidelity to his source only served to perpetuate the translator's errors for Western audiences.[23] That Gosse should have been more careful in the reading of his sources is clear, but aside from errors in factual reporting, he cannot be accused of fabrication or of willful distortion of historical evidence.

The same cannot be said of Joseph Gollomb's *Pirates Old and New,* published in 1928. It is a work with fewer scholarly pretensions than Gosse's, but has nevertheless been cataloged as "history" rather than as "literature." Information on Chinese pirates is found in a chapter entitled "Mrs. Ching Goes A-Pirating"; like Gosse, Gollomb has drawn his account primarily from Neumann's translation of *Ching haifen chi* and from Glasspoole's narrative of his captivity.

Gollomb's chapter contains no bibliographic references or notes. On several occasions, however, he mentions the captive Glasspoole, who is incorrectly referred to as "Homer" instead of "Richard." Neither *Ching hai-fen chi,* its author, nor its translator are mentioned by name, but repeated references are made to an unspecified "historian of China" to whom Gollomb attributes words that were never written.

He "nominates" the nearest Chinese laundryman to be our guide to the "far regions in which is set the strangest story in the annals of piracy." By doing so, Gollomb introduces an ethnic stereotyping totally absent in Gosse. For, according to Gollomb:

He [the laundryman] is our best guide if we want to see vividly the yellow pirates who will swarm through our story. . . . He will help us visualize a people among whom it is womanly to wear trousers and virile to wear skirts; and he may even help bring out the colors of the gorgeous story of Mrs. Ching, chieftain over scores of thousands of Chinese pirates with whom even an emperor had to make terms. . . . When in our story we go back only a little over a hundred years the difference between one of Mrs. Ching's pirates and the man you see busy over the laundry ironing board is largely only a matter of clothes.[24]

Gollomb's comments seem typical of widely held popular views about the Chinese in American Chinatowns during the early twentieth century. Recalling the Chinese who lived in the small New Jersey town where he grew up at the turn of the century, author Robert Lawson characterized them as "foreign," "outlandish" individuals who "ran laundries" and wrote "backwards and up-side down, with a brush." Moreover, "they kidnapped children; engaged in white slave traffic; were always the villains in movies; strange; dreaded; they might cut you up; sinister, they ate rats; smoked opium."[25]

A list of American beliefs about the Chinese compiled and published by a Chinese student in the *Literary Digest* of 12 March 1927 contained the following items:

> The favorite delicacies of the Chinese are rats and snakes.
> Chinese men wear skirts and women pants.
> A Chinese is properly a Chinaman and . . . the word "Chinee" is singular for "Chinese."
> They are a mysterious and inscrutable race and . . . they do every thing backwards.[26]

Gollomb's effort to account for the rise of piracy within the Chinese water world is every bit as dubious as his characterization of the pirates themselves. He ignores the ongoing cycles of petty piracy along the South China coast and the influence of the Tay-son Rebellion on the activities of the Cheng family. Instead, he portrays Cheng I as a pirate with a crew of twelve and a leaky rowing boat who, through his own efforts and successful captures, increased his fleet to 1,800 vessels and 70,000 men.[27]

Until recently, Chinese historians frequently placed in their accounts an imaginary dialogue which they attributed to their subjects. Their purpose was usually didactic and their goal, moral instruction. These make-believe conversations also provided their authors with opportunities to express their personal feelings about their subjects. Gollomb does not differentiate between the conversations he quotes from Neumann's translation and those he has composed himself. Moreover, he includes physical descriptions of the pirates derived more from fantasy than fact. For instance, on the basis of no discernible evidence, Ching-Yih (Cheng I) is described as a hunchback with a "huge round face, [and] folds of yellow fat almost hiding his long slant eyes," an old man who "could plot like the devil himself, fight like a fiend, and live and love as greedily as though his body were fresh and twenty."[28] Equally fantastic are his description of Cheng I Sao and his reconstruction of her first encounter with Ching-Yih (Cheng I) (throughout his account, Gollomb refers to Cheng I Sao as "Hsi Kai"):

> She was the pick of all the women brought in by the squads of pirates Ching-Yih had sent scouring through the country in search of a fit one for him. . . . Brought to him tied hand and foot, she was larger than the women of her race, gloriously

formed and, says a Chinese historian, "before the beauty of her face the eyes of men grew confused."[29]

The account continues:

> Hers was not the budlike mouth of the Chinese woman, but more the voluptuous mouth of the dancing nautch girls of India. And as she stood looking at the fat old hunchback, her teeth flashed between carmined lips in one of those splendid rages beautiful to behold, but not agreeable to experience.
>
> In the Orient woman is held as less than man, and Ching-Yih signed to the captors to untie Hsi-Kai that she might kneel before him. Her feet were not deformed by binding as Chinese custom prescribed. The moment her limbs were free she sprang at Ching-Yih and almost succeeded in tearing out his eyes.
>
> The hunchback was delighted. Here was indeed a fit mate for a great pirate chief.[30]

Equally romantic (but also historically unfounded) is Gollomb's reconstruction of how Cheng I Sao assumed leadership of the confederation after her husband died:

> A great meeting of the pirate fleet was held to elect a successor to Ching-Yih. Hsi-Kai [Cheng I Sao] arose before the assembled captains. She was dressed in the glittering garb of a male fighting chief, gold embroidered dragons writhed over gorgeous purples, blues, and reds; gay jade and green, bits of painted ivory, gold and silver shimmered and glittered in the sunlight. In her sash were some of her dead husband's swords and on her head was his familiar war helmet.
>
> "Look at me, captains!" she cried. They looked at her. "Your departed chief sat in council with me. Your most powerful fleet, the White, under my command, took more prizes than any other. Do you think I will bow to any other chief?"
>
> There she was, in their eyes a goddess of a woman with a record of leadership as proud as any man's. It is not surprising, therefore, that the captains of the fleet should rise as a single man and acclaim her their chief of chiefs.[31]

By contrast, the scene is sparsely depicted by Yuan Yun-lun and his translator Neumann:

> It happened, that on the seventeenth day of the tenth moon, in the twentieth year of Kea king [about the end of 1807], Ching yih perished in a heavy gale, and his legitimate wife Shih placed the whole crew under the sway of Paou: but so that she herself should be considered the commander of all the squadrons together, for this reason the division Ching yih was then called Ching yih saou, or the wife of Ching yih.[32]

The final scene Gollomb recreates for his readers is the initial encounter between Cheng I Sao and Chang Paou (Chang Pao), the commander of the Red fleet who became her paramour and ultimately her husband:

The two fishermen [Chang Paou and his father] were seized and brought before Hsi-Kai for execution. . . . The young man crossed powerful bronzed arms over his deep chest, and with a grin of indifference looked the woman in the face. . . . He stood head and shoulders taller and broader than any of his captors, and the insolence in his flagrantly handsome face was such that Hsi-Kai could not dismiss it unnoticed . . .

Hsi-Kai, however, who on so many other occasions was indeed the bringer of death, proved on this occasion that she was after all, a woman. From the very core of him to his finger tips he glowed with vitality, with such health as models face and body, into form of beauty and makes of the spirit so robust a thing that even death cannot make it cower.

"Paou, how well do you know the sea?" she asked.

"Aside from women there is nothing I know better."

She turned to her captains. "Sink their fishing boat," she said. "Give the old man new garments and let him eat. And as for Paou, I will attend to him!"

She attended to him with such generosity that soon Paou was wearing the uniform of a captain of Hsi-Kai's fleet . . .

He learned with amazing rapidity. . . . And at last he stood at Hsi-Kai's right hand, her chief captain, her prime minister, her lover, and her ablest fighter.[33]

Gollomb's account ignores information presented by Neumann that Chang Pao was originally captured by Cheng I and that it was in his eyes, not those of his wife, that he initially found favor:

Chang Paou was a native of Sin hwy [Hsin-hui], near the mouth of the River, and the son of a fisherman. Being fifteen years of age, he went with his father a fishing in the sea, and they were consequently taken prisoners by Ching yih, who roamed about the mouth of the river, ravaging and plundering. Ching yih saw Paou, and liked him so much, that he could not depart from him. Paou was indeed a clever fellow—he managed all business very well; being also a fine young man, he became a favourite of Ching yih and was made head-man or captain.[34]

The only eye-witness description we have of a pirate is Richard Glasspoole's report of an individual he refers to as "the chief." Glasspoole was taken to the chief's vessel where he found him "seated on deck, in a large chair, dressed in purple silk, with a black turban on." According to Glasspoole, "he appeared to be about 30 years of age, a stout commanding-looking man."[35] Elsewhere after his release, Glasspoole added to his description of this individual by stating:

The chief of the Ladrones, in his person, is a man of dignified person and manners, of sound discretion, temperate habits, and bold and successful in all his enterprises; so that he has acquired an ascendancy over the minds of his followers, which insures to him the most unbounded confidence and obedience.[36]

Nothing in Glasspoole's narrative allows us to identify this figure with certainty as Chang Pao. Yet Gollomb not only assumes this to be the case, but also informs his readers that Glasspoole met both Chang Pao and Cheng I Sao. Gollomb also implies that Glasspoole "knew of the personal relation between the pirate captain and Hsi-Kai" and "realized the delicacy of his own situation" resulting from it. "It was," according to Gollomb, "a question of which would prevail, Paou's jealousy of any man whose smile interested Hsi-Kai or his fear of what Hsi-Kai would do should 'some unfortunate accident' happen to Homer [Richard Glasspoole]." Nowhere in the Glasspoole narrative is there any account of a meeting with Cheng I Sao or even any acknowledgment of a woman being in command of the confederation.[37]

Gollomb is equally wrong in his discussion of what happened to the pirates after their surrender to the Chinese government. According to him:

> Paou was made mighty commander and by edict became a "Son of Heaven" and was allowed to wear peacock's feathers with two eyes in sign of his exalted rank. And the unconquerable Hsi-Kai, whose beauty dimmed the eyes of all beholders, went to dwell in a great palace and bore three sons and one daughter to her beloved husband, Paou.[38]

Chang Pao most assuredly did not become a "Son of Heaven": only emperors were referred to as "Sons of Heaven," and Chang Pao did not become an emperor. The privilege of wearing double-eyed peacock feathers was granted only to government officials for extraordinary service to the empire. In this instance, it was the Governor-General Pai Ling and not Chang Pao who was rewarded with the peacock feathers. Cheng I Sao appears to have had a son as a result of her relationship with Chang Pao, but the claim that she lived in a palace and had three sons and a daughter is unfounded.

In the hands of Joseph Gollomb, historical license has turned to historical fantasy of the most sexist and racist kind. But equally inexcusable is the way his text has provided the point of departure for the section on Chinese pirates in Linda Grant De Pauw's recent book *Seafaring Women*.[39] De Pauw begins her account by depicting Cheng I Sao "as the greatest pirate, male or female, in all history." Like Gollomb, she attributes the origin of her heroine's piracy to untraceable floods during the spring of 1799, which impoverished China's coastal population to the point of starvation (Gollomb cites a spring flood in 1800). In both accounts, Cheng I Sao appears in male dress wearing her husband's war helmet and bearing his swords:

> Madame Ching attended, dressed in the chief's uniform; a robe of purple, blue, and gold, embroidered with gold dragons and bound with a wide sash into which she had thrust several of her deceased husband's swords. She wore his war

helmet on her head. The significance of this costume was clear enough: she meant to assume command.[40]

Like Gosse and Gollomb, De Pauw attributes the pirates' code to Cheng I Sao and not to Chang Pao, but unlike her predecessors, she implies that these regulations were written down: "All of the ships were bound to obey Madame Ching's regulations, which she had posted aboard even the smallest ship of the fleet."[41] Like Gollomb, she concludes her account by stating that after surrendering, Cheng I Sao "went to live in the palace provided by the emperor, bore three sons and one daughter, and spent her last years in the less demanding work of a smuggler."[42]

The carelessness De Pauw exhibits in her use of "Chinese" sources obtained from Gollomb stands in marked contrast to the careful way she handles Richard Glasspoole's text. Despite not having cited Glasspoole in her bibliography, De Pauw must have had access to either a copy of the "Narrative" or to more accurate references to it. Unlike Gollomb, she correctly cites Glasspoole's name as "Richard" and correctly quotes a passage about the pirates having no fixed residence on shore.[43] She also makes no attempt to follow Gollomb in his claims that Glasspoole met either Chang Pao or Cheng I Sao or was privy to any knowledge of their relationship.[44]

What accounts for these disparities? Is there still a double standard which requires greater exactitude when dealing with some (European) materials than with others, such as Asian materials and their translations, for example?

The Chinese Historians' View

Distorted and inaccurate though many of the accounts are, Cheng I Sao and her confederation have received more attention in the West than throughout most of China. Until I began working with the memorial collections of the National Palace Museum in Taipei and later in the First Historical Archives in Beijing, China's rich archival sources regarding piracy had lain untouched. Chinese copies of *Ching hai-fen chi* were unavailable in public collections in either Taipei or Hong Kong and were only rediscovered in the British Museum in London in autumn 1976. The other firsthand account, an essay, "Chi-spu p'ing-k'ou" (Suppressing the Bandits in 1809) by Chu Ch'eng-wen, was inaccessibly buried in the *Nan-hai hsien-chih* (Gazetteer of Nan-hai District), compiled in 1872 and reprinted in Taipei in 1971.[45]

One region where the pirates were somewhat familiar, however, was Hong Kong. There in the 1950s they became the subject of two historical essays.[46] Apart from greater historical accuracy, what differentiates these Chinese articles most significantly from those in English discussed above is their focus on the male pirate Chang Pao rather than on the female pirate Cheng I Sao, whose name is scarcely mentioned. Chinese historians have simply not found Cheng I Sao very compelling.

A similar situation prevails in the realm of myth, legend, and popular culture. Probably the most famous of the Hong Kong region's alleged artifacts is a cave on Cheung Chou (Chang Chou) Island where the pirates were said to have made their headquarters and buried their treasure, clearly labeled on contemporary maps as the "Cave of Cheung Po Tsai" (Chang Pao-tsai), not of Cheng I Sao. From what little I remember of a Cantonese play *Chang Pao-tsai* by Yao Han-liang that I saw performed in Hong Kong on 28 June 1976, Cheng I Sao and another woman appeared as characters, but the hero was unmistakably the male pirate "Chang Pao." Finally, the adventure story *The Cave of Cheung Po Tsai* (Chang Pao-tsai) by F. J. F. Tingay is a classic search for buried treasure that takes place in the vicinity of Chang Pao's cave.[47] Despite the fact that some of the child protagonists are girls, the tale is without mention of a female pirate. Equally curious is the fact that no Chinese author, at least as far as I know, has attempted to portray Cheng I Sao as a woman warrior, in the well-known Chinese literary tradition introduced to modern Western audiences by Maxine Hong Kingston in her book, *The Woman Warrior: Memoirs of a Girlhood among Ghosts*.[48]

Besides *The Cave of Cheung Po Tsai*, the only other fiction about the pirates available in English with which I am familiar is a short story by Jorge Luis Borges entitled "The Widow Ching, Lady Pirate."[49] Like Gosse, Borges presents Cheng I Sao as having been married to a husband who was appointed "Master of the Royal Stables" by the emperor of China and was succeeded by his widow, who later drew up a code of laws. One place where Borges seems to have misread Gosse, however, is revealed in his writing that "It is a matter of history that the fox [Cheng I Sao] received her pardon and devoted her lingering years to the opium trade. She also left off being the widow, assuming a name which in English means 'Lustre of Instruction.'"[50] "Lustre of Instruction" is the way Neumann translates the nickname of Black Flag fleet leader K'uo Po-tai, with whom not even Gosse suggests Cheng I Sao had the slightest personal relationship.

Borges contributes several additions to pirate lore, including a fable about a dragon's protection of a fox despite the fox's ingratitude (here, Cheng I Sao is the fox who, despite thirteen years of piracy, ultimately receives her pardon from the imperial dragon). In contrast to authors who have imagined Cheng I Sao as a sensual, voluptuous beauty, Borges portrays her as a "slinking woman, with sleepy eyes and a smile full of decayed teeth," whose "blackish, oiled hair shone brighter than her eyes."[51] Like his Chinese counterparts, Borges makes no attempt to link Cheng I Sao to Fan Mu-lan and the woman warrior tradition of the Middle Kingdom. But he does position her within a Western sisterhood of female pirates that includes Mary Read and Anne Bonny, though he does not elaborate on what besides gender unites these pirates.

Life on Board

Untruths and exaggeration have colored many accounts of Cheng I Sao and her confederates. But what, if anything, could these historians have said about the quality of women pirates' lives? What information would have been accessible to them? And how might they have been able to tell fact from fiction in the accounts they read and wrote?

These are problems faced by historians every day of their professional lives. The line between "historical fact" and "historical fiction" is often difficult to draw with precision. But corroborating information from a variety of sources usually constitutes strong evidence for the determination of "historical fact." In this instance, nearly all the information about the pirates' daily lives and their interaction aboard ship is to be found in English-language sources available when each of these historians wrote their accounts.

J. Turner, chief mate of the country ship *Tay*, was captured by the Red Flag fleet in December 1806. Like Richard Glasspoole, Turner wrote an account of his captivity which was first published in the *Naval Chronicle* of 1808[52] and later in *Further Statement to the Ladrones on the Coast of China; Intended as a Contribution of the Accounts Published by Mr. Dalrymple.*[53] Philip Maughan, first lieutenant of the H.C. *Bombay Marine*, arrived in China in May 1806 and was involved in a number of military skirmishes with the pirates. He expended considerable energy talking to local residents in the hope of trying to learn more about them. His essay, "An Account of the Ladrones who infested the Coast of China," was completed in February 1812.[54] A few years after completing his original essay, "A Brief Narrative of My Captivity and Treatment Amongst the Ladrones," Richard Glasspoole added an additional memoir, "Substance of Mr. Glasspoole's Relation, Upon His Return to England, Respecting the Ladrones."[55] These accounts provide us with brief glimpses into the ways the pirates lived and conducted themselves aboard ship.

Glasspoole, Maughan, and Turner all agree that entire families made their homes on board pirate ships. However, the presence of women on these crafts was strictly regulated. Says Glasspoole, "The Ladrones have no settled residence on shore, but live constantly in their vessels"[56] which "are filled with their families, men, women and children."[57] According to Maughan, the number of women who lived with them was "surprising";[58] in many instances, according to Glasspoole, "women command their junks."[59]

Glasspoole notes that "with respect to conjugal rights they [the pirates] are religiously strict; no person is allowed to have a woman on board, unless married to her according to their laws."[60] This observation is supported by Turner, who reports:

> With respect to the women who fall into their hands, the handsomest are reserved by them for wives and concubines . . . having once made choice of a wife, they [the pirates] are obliged to be constant to her, no promiscuous intercourse being allowed amongst them. . . . A few are ransomed, and the most homely returned on shore.[61]

According to Glasspoole, on one occasion after about one hundred female captives of the pirates were ransomed, "The remainder were offered for sale amongst the Ladrones for forty dollars each" with the understanding that "the woman is considered the lawful wife of the purchaser, who would be put to death if he discarded her."[62] Turner says that captive children were generally retained and brought up as servants.[63]

Of those who were married, the rank and file pirates, according to Turner, typically had no more than one wife. The chiefs and captains frequently had three or more; the greater part of the crew "were satisfied without women."[64] Glasspoole's estimate that captains generally had five or six wives is a bit higher.[65]

By all accounts space was at a premium aboard cramped and dirty vessels. Maughan comments that "Amidst such a herd of villains, it may naturally be supposed cleanliness was but little thought of; consequently their vessels were filthy to an extreme."[66] "From the number of souls crowded in so small a space," reports Glasspoole, "it must naturally be supposed they are horridly dirty, which is evidently the case, and their vessels swarm with all kinds of vermin."[67] Once on board ship, every man, according to Glasspoole, was allowed "a small berth, about four feet square" in which to stow with his wife and family.[68] Maughan adds that "all those who chose to cohabit with females had generally a small cabin to themselves . . . (where) the number of cabins were considerable in their largest boats."[69] Turner describes his accommodations on board ship as "wretched" and relates that: "At night, the space allowed me to sleep in was never more than about eighteen inches wide, and four feet long; and if at any time I happened to extend my contracted limbs beyond their limits, I was sure to be reminded of my mistake by a blow or kick."[70]

Ladrones were dressed as lower-class Chinese. Maughan has added that "a turban, composed of dark-coloured cotton cloth, was usually worn in lieu of a hat."[71] Food was scarce. Turner describes his fare as having been the same as that of the common Chinese, "coarse red rice, with a little salt fish."[72] According to Glasspoole: "The diet of the Ladrones is rice and fish (the fishermen all paying them tribute), except within they have plundered any village, in which case they get hogs and poultry."[73] He also notes that certain species of rats were encouraged to breed and were consumed as "great delicacies." He states there were "very few creatures" they would not eat; at one point during his captivity, the pirates lived for three weeks on caterpillars boiled with rice.[74]

Glasspoole also describes the pirates as being "much addicted to gambling," and spending "all their leisure hours at cards and smoking opium."[75] On one occasion he watched as members of a fishing boat came aboard the pirate junk. They spent the remainder of the day in the chief's cabin smoking opium and playing cards.[76] On another occasion he reports that:

> whilst the Ladrone fleet was receiving a distant cannonade from the Portuguese and Chinese, the men were playing cards upon deck, and in a group so amusing themselves, one man was killed by a cannon shot; but the rest, after putting the mangled body out of the way, went on with their game, as if nothing of the kind had happened.[77]

These Western observers had some overall sense of the confederation and how it operated; according to Turner, "The whole body of Ladrone vessels that I have seen are under the command of five chiefs, who are independent of each other."[78] Glasspoole indicates that the admiral of the Red Flag fleet was supreme;[79] Turner provides a description of the confederation's subunits:

> Each vessel has a captain who directs in a general way all the operations on board, etc. . . . . The captain is generally better dressed than the common Ladrones. He also fares somewhat better, and the officers or assistants mentioned above, are some of them partakers of his meals. . . . Each division is formed into several squadrons, commanded by an inferior chief by whom the captains of the different vessels are generally appointed and from whom they receive their orders.[80]

Once in motion, the confederation seems to have been a relatively disciplined group whose members fought bravely in combat. Glasspoole reports:

> In their attacks they are intrepid, and in their defence most desperate, yielding in the latter instance to no superiority of numbers; the laws of discipline and civil government are equally enforced on board his [the chief's] junk, and any transgressions from them immediately punished, which, as their vessels are filled with their families, men, women, and children, seems almost incredible. They are taught to be fearless in danger.[81]

Maughan remarks, "I have witnessed a few instances of intrepidity exhibited by the Ladrones, which, when compared with their general pusillanimous conduct on other occasions, marks them an extraordinary people."[82]

Women in Combat

Women in combat are noted three times by Yuan Yun-lun and his translator Charles Neumann. One engagement occurred in early 1809 near Lao Wan Shan. After describing how the pirate commander advanced "courageously" and took about two hundred prisoners, Yuan Yun-lun remarks:

> There was a pirate's wife in one of the boats, holding so fast by the helm that she could scarcely be taken away. Having two cutlasses, she desperately defended herself, and wounded some soldiers; but on being wounded by a musket-ball, she fell back into the vessel and was taken prisoner.[83]

In the battle between the pirates and villagers of Kan-shih (in Nan-hai district, Kwangtung), Yuan Yun-lun recalls the heroism of a villager's wife. At one point when the villager Chou Wei tang (Chou Wei-teng) was surrounded by pirates, his "wife fought valiantly by his side" until she, too, was slain with the others.[84] As the foray continued and the pirates made their way into the village, one hundred women were hidden in the surrounding paddy fields, but:

> the pirates on hearing a child crying, went to the place and carried them away. Mei ying [Mei Ying], the wife of Ke choo yang was very beautiful, and a pirate being about to seize her by the head, she abused him exceedingly. The pirate bound her to the yard-arm; but on abusing him yet more, the pirate dragged her down and broke two of her teeth, which filled her mouth and jaws with blood. The pirate sprang up again to bind her. Ying allowed him to approach but as soon as he came near her, she laid hold of his garments with her bleeding mouth and threw both him and herself into the river where they were drowned.[85]

Cruelty was also observed by Glasspoole, who states that the pirates were "so savage in their resentments and manners, that they frequently take the hearts of their enemies and eat them with rice, considering the repast gives them fortitude and courage."[86] Turner reports having been told of a similar occurrence:

> At this place a man was put to death, with circumstances (as I was told) of peculiar horror. Being fixed upright, his bowels were cut open, and his heart was taken out, which they afterwards soaked in spirits, and ate. The dead body I saw myself. I am well assured that this shocking treatment is frequently practiced in the case of persons who, having annoyed the Ladrones in any particular manner, fall into their hands.[87]

The plight of some of the pirates' female captives is noted by Glasspoole. He saw the capture of two hundred fifty women and several children from a village surrounded by a thick wood on 1 October 1809. The women were

> sent on board different vessels. They were unable to escape with the men owing to that abominable practice of cramping their feet; several of them were not able

to move without assistance, in fact, they might all be said to totter, rather than to walk. Twenty of these poor women were sent on board the vessel I was in; they were hauled on board by the hair and treated in a most savage manner.

When the chief came on board, he questioned them respecting the circumstances of their friends, and demanded ransoms accordingly, from six thousand to six hundred dollars each. He ordered them a berth on deck, at the after part of the vessel, where they had nothing to shelter them from the weather, which at this time was very variable. . . .

Here we remained five or six days, during which time about an hundred of the women were ransomed; the remainder were offered for sale amongst the Ladrones for forty dollars each. . . . Several of them leaped over-board and drowned, themselves, rather than submit to such infamous degradation.[88]

Occasionally, however, the pirates' cruelty was tempered by compassion. During the heat of battle Glasspoole reports having received special consideration from the chief's wife, who sprinkled him with garlic water which the pirates considered "an effectual charm against shot."[89]

A Remarkable Woman

These brief details of the living conditions, dress, diet, and organization aboard the pirates' ships were etched unforgettably into the memories of the individuals who observed them. Many facts about the pirates' daily routines and personal relationships are probably lost forever, but the accounts of Glasspoole, Turner, and Maughan have at least allowed us a glimpse into the existence of women and men who, without the means to tell their own story, might have slipped into oblivion.

Had Gollomb and De Pauw paid serious attention to these reports, they might have found that their own narratives needed no embellishment. For the pirates demonstrated organizational and administrative skills that are amazing in their own right, especially when we consider that they were the products of individuals so denigrated that, as fishing people, they were forbidden from participation in the civil service examinations of the Chinese government. Between 1802 and 1810, with no official patronage or support, they created an organization strong enough to sustain, both financially and militarily, a force that outnumbered the total participants in the Spanish Armada by two to one. It is an episode so vivid and compelling that it needs little in the way of myth, legend, or literature for its enhancement.

Throughout most of the world, piracy has been a male occupation that has tended to exclude women, especially from leadership. In imperial China, Confucian attitudes militated against public roles for women. Thus we might have expected the presence of Chinese women at sea and their participation in pirate gangs to have been even more restricted. But the phenomenon of Cheng I Sao and her activities is perhaps less surprising in a Chinese context than we might expect. In the world from which these pirates sprang, women participated fully in all aspects of life at sea. Not only did they work and reside alongside their husbands on board ship, but they were also responsible for much of the sculling and handling of craft of various types. In this way, their presence on pirate ships was merely an extension of everyday practice. Moreover, by the eighteenth century the precedent for women as leaders of both religious sects and antidynastic rebellion had been firmly established.

Finally, Cheng I Sao's ascent was very much in keeping with the tradition of Chinese women rising to power through marriage. Marrying well and then assuming the mantle of power on the death of a husband was the most common avenue of female mobility in nearly every Chinese social circle. Among the elites and the socially well connected, this was the path to power taken by such "notorious" femmes fatales as empresses Wu Tze-hsien and Tzu-hsi, and concubine Yang Kuei-fei.[90] More recently it enabled the rise of Chiang Ch'ing, the fourth wife of Mao Tse-tung.

Nevertheless, Cheng I Sao wielded authority in ways that made her unusual even by Chinese standards, and throughout her career she acted in open defiance of Confucian behavioral norms. As Cheng I's wife she was anything but a docile, submissive homebody. As his widow she not only failed to remain chaste, but even broke the incest taboo when it served her purpose by marrying her adopted son. Despite such conduct, she was able to win the genuine support of her followers to the degree that they openly acclaimed her as the one person capable of holding the confederation together. As its leader, she demonstrated her ability to take command by issuing orders, planning military campaigns, and demonstrating that there were profits to be made in piracy. When the time came to dismantle the confederation, it was her negotiating skills above all that allowed her followers to cross the bridge from outlawry to officialdom. And all this was done by a woman so common that her personal identity is virtually unknown.

Yet despite her success, Cheng I Sao did not create an institutional structure capable of surviving without her. With no tradition of either bureaucratic or ideological continuity to bolster them from generation to generation, such informal personal creations of power are usually dependent on the charisma of their founders. This makes them difficult to preserve for more than a generation. Consequently, when Cheng I's wife decided to retire, no individual, either female or male, could step into the organization and operate the structures through which she had exercised power.

In looking at the themes of fact and fiction that have been discussed in this chapter, I have noted with irony that there seems to have been greater concern for "truth" and accuracy from nonhistorians than from historians. For instance, Yuan Yun-lun, the employee in the Governor-General's office whose *Ching hai-fen chi* was translated into English by Charles Neumann, felt compelled for the purposes of moral instruction to write an "objective" account of the pirates and their activities. He elaborates at some length on this goal in the preface of his book, taking pains to point out that he is providing a "true account" whose every detail has been checked for accuracy. Similarly, Lieutenant Maughan's concern for the integrity of his account emerges early in his essay when he apologizes for the quality of the information available to him: "In giving my opinion of the Ladrones, I trust every allowance will be made for the imperfect means I had of procuring information, being chiefly through the fishermen and lower classes of Chinese."[91] Such concern on the part of serious, well-intentioned amateurs deserves our sincere commendation.

As a historian, I cannot but end this chapter humbled once again by the challenges of my own profession and the responsibility of re-creating, often from very fragmentary evidence, the lives and times of those who have gone before us. These are lives whose reconstruction, it seems to me, must be undertaken with the deepest respect and care, regardless of their settings.

NOTES

1. Scattered paragraphs in the notes and conclusion of this chapter have been reprinted from Dian Murray, *Pirates of the South China Coast, 1790–1810* (Stanford: Stanford University Press, 1987) and all material used here and taken from the book is reproduced by permission of Stanford University Press.

2. Susan Naquin, *Shantung Rebellion: The Wang Lun Uprising of 1774* (Ithaca: Yale University Press, 1981), 100, 101.

3. Fanny Loviot, *A Lady's Captivity among Chinese Pirates in the Chinese Seas*, trans. Amelia B. Edwards (London: G. Routledge and Co., 1858), 78. This is shelved in the British Library under 10057 a19 26.

4. Studies of Chinese prostitution are in their infancy, but those with further interest in the topic are advised to pursue it in Gail Hershatter, "The Hierarchy of Shanghai Prostitution, 1870–1949," *Modern China* 15, no. 4 (1989): 463–98.

5. In 1771 the Tay-son Rebellion broke out in what was the southern Vietnamese or Annamese province of Binh Dinh. Its leaders were three brothers, Nguyen Van Nhac, Nguyen Van Lu, and Nguyen Van Hue, merchants engaged in the betel commerce with the hill peoples of the province. The name "Tay-son," meaning "Western Mountain," derived from their native village. By 1773 this band of leaders and their followers had managed to seize the provincial capital at Qui Nhon. From there the movement spread and the rebellion, climaxing more than a century of revolt and social unrest, became a massive upheaval that constitutes one of the major episodes of eighteenth-century South-East Asian history. Until their defeat by a scion of the Nguyen

rulers from Hue, the Tay-son were continually challenged, and it was in that context, finding themselves in need of manpower and resources, that they made their appeal to the pirates along the coast of China, who in 1792 were recruited into their service. Charles B. Maybon, *Histoire moderne du pays d'Annam (1592–1820)* (Paris: Typographie Plon-Nourrit, 1919), 289–347; Lê-thành-Khôi, *Le Viêt-nam: Histoire et civilisation* (Paris: Éditions de Minuit, 1955), 296–322. This paragraph is based on information in Murray, *South China Coast*.

6. For more information, see Murray, *South China Coast*, 133–36.

7. The two provinces of Kwangsi and Kwangtung are referred to as the Liang-kuang (the two kuangs) and thus the Liang-kuang Governor-General was the chief administrative official of these two provinces.

8. "Chinese Pirates: Ching Chelung; His Son Cheng Ching-kung; Combination of Gangs in 1806; Narratives of J. Turner and Mr. Glasspoole; Chinese and Portuguese Join Their Forces Against the Pirates: Divisions Among Them, and Their Submission to the Govermnent," *Chinese Repository* 3, no. for June 1834: 62–83, reference here to 82.

9. The sources for this biographical account of Cheng's life are: *Nan-hai hsien chih* (Gazetteer of Nan-hai District) compiled by Cheng Meng-yü, *26 chüan*, reprint of 1872 ed. (Taipei: N.p., 1971), 14:20b and 25:20b; Yuan Yun-lun, *Ching-hai fen-chi; 2 chüan* (Canton: 1830), 1:5a–b; *Kuang-tung hai fang hui-lan* (Essentials of sea defense in Kuang-tung), compiled by Lu K'un and Ch'eng Hung-ch'ih, *42 chüan*, n.d., 42:26b, 32b; "Canton Consultations. Consultations and Transactions of the Select Committee of Resident Supercargoes Appointed by the Honourable Court of Directors of the United East India Company to Manage Their Affairs in China Together with the Letters Written and Occurrences," India Office, Factory Records G/12/100–G/12/174, March 1791 to January 1811; "Memorial of Lin Tse-hsu," TK20/5/15 reproduced in Yeh Lin-feng, *Chang Pao-tsai ti ch'uan-shuo ho chen-hsieng* (Chang Pao-tsai in fiction and fact) (Hong Kong: N.p., 1970), 69; "Chinese pirates . . . ," *Chinese Repository*; Hu Chieh-yü (Woo Kit-yü), "Hsi Ying-P'an yü Chang Pao-tsai huo-luan chih p'ing-ting" (Sai Ying Pun [West Camp] and the end of the ravages of the pirate Chang Pao-tsai)," in *I-pa-ssu-erh nien i-ch'ien chih Hsiang-kang chi ch'i-tui wai-chiao-t'ung (Hong Kong and its external communication before 1842)*, ed. Lo Hsiang-lin (1959), 151–70. This account of Cheng's life is similar to one prepared for the *Biographical Dictionary of Chinese Women: Volume 1: The Qing Period 1644–1911*, ed. Lily Xiao Hong Lee and Agnes D Stefanowska (Armonk: N.Y.: M. E. Sharpe, 1998), 317–19.

10. Yung-lun Yüan, *Ching hai-fen chi: History of the Pirates Who Infested the China Sea from 1807 to 1810*, trans. Charles Friederich Neumann (London: Oriental Translation Fund, 1831). A second, less accessible translation of Yung-lun Yüan's book (*Ching hai-fen chi*) was made by John Slade under the title "A Record of the Pacification of the Seas," which appeared serially in the *Canton Register* beginning on 20 February 1838 with vol. 11, no. 8.

11. This information appears in Yüan Yung-lun, trans. Neumann, 21.

12. This account was first published in George Wilkinson, esq., *Sketches of Chinese Customs and Manners in 1811–12 Taken during a Voyage to the Cape, etc. With Some Account of the Ladrones, in a Series of Letters to a Friend* (Bath: 1814). It was

also published separately as Richard Glasspoole, *Mr. Glasspoole and the Chinese Pirates, being the Narrative of Mr. Richard Glasspoole of the ship Marquis of Ely; Describing his Captivity of Eleven Weeks and Three Days Whilst Held for Ransom by the Villainous Ladrones of the China Sea in 1809; Together with Extracts from the China Records and the Log of the Marquis of Ely; and Some Remarks on Chinese Pirates, Ancient and Modern*, ed. Owen Rutter (London: Golden Cockerel Press, 1935). The version cited here is appended to the Neumann translation of *Ching hai-fen chi* and occasionally bears his editorial comments.

13. Glasspoole, "Narrative," 107.

14. Henri Musnik, *Les femmes pirates: Aventures et légendes de la mer* (Paris: Le Masque, 1934); Joseph Gollomb, *Pirates Old and New* (New York: The Macaulay Co., 1928); "Chinese Pirates," *Chinese Repository*, 3:82; Charles Ellms, *The Pirates' Own Book, or Authentic Narratives of the Lives, Exploits, and Executions of the Most Celebrated Sea Robbers*, reprint of 1836–1837 ed. (Salem: Maritime Reasearch Society, 1924); Charles Hill, "Pirates of the China Seas," *Asia*, 1924, pp. 306–10+; and Linda Grant De Pauw, *Seafaring Women* (Boston: Houghton Mifflin, 1982).

15. Philip Gosse, *The History of Piracy* (London and New York: Longmans, Green and Tudor Publishing, 1932), 271.

16. Ibid.

17. Like Gosse's version of the story, my own endeavor to write a sustained account of Cheng I Sao also contains substantial portions of material about other topics. See Dian Murray, "One Woman's Rise to Power: Cheng I's Wife and the Pirates," in *Women in China: Current Directions in Historical Scholarship*, ed. Richard W Guisso and Stanley Johannesen (Youngstown, N.Y.: Philo Press, 1981), 147–62. Also published in *Historical Reflections/Réflexions Historiques* 8, no. 3 (1981).

18. Gosse, *History*, 271.

19. King-sheng, whose name reads as Ching-sheng in accord with Wade-Giles romanization, was the Quang-toan emperor of Vietnam.

20. Yüan Yung-lun, trans. Neumann, 5.

21. Gosse, *History*, 272–73.

22. Yüan Yung-lun, trans. Neumann, 13–14.

23. Gosse, *History*, 272.

24. Gollomb, *Pirates*, 272–73.

25. Robert Lawson, *At That Time* (New York: Viking Press, 1947), 43–45.

26. These items are quoted by Harold Isaacs, *Scratches on Our Minds: American Views of China and India* (White Plains, N.Y.: M. E. Sharpe, 1980), 118–19.

27. Gollomb, *Pirates*, 277.

28. Ibid., 275.

29. Ibid., 277.

30. Ibid., 278. The source of Gollomb's speculation may have been an anecdote recounted in the Neumann translation of how upon being captured and tied to the yard-arm, a villager named Mei Ying grabbed hold of a pirate and threw them both overboard upon her release.

31. Ibid., 279–80. Nowhere (except perhaps in Gollomb) have the pirates ever

been described as wearing war helmets and so far as we know their only headgear was cotton turbans. Philip Maughan, "An Account of the Ladrones who infested the Coast of China," in *Further Statement of the Ladrones on the Coast of China; Intended as a Contribution to the Accounts Published by Mr Dalrymple* (London: Land, Darling, and Co., 1812), 26.

32. Yüan Yung-lun, trans. Neumann, 12–13.

33. Gollomb, *Pirates*, 282–83.

34. Yüan Yung-lun, trans. Neumann, 12.

35. Glasspoole, "Narrative," 103.

36. Richard Glasspoole, "Substance of Mr. Glasspoole's Relation, Upon His Return to England, Respecting the Ladrones," in *Further Statement of the Ladrones on the Coast of China; Intended as a Contribution to the Accounts Published by Mr Dalrymple* (London: Land, Darling, and Co., 1812), 44.

37. Gollomb, *Pirates,* 280. Glasspoole's overall grasp of the pirates' organizational structure appears to have been weak, and his references in the "Narrative" to a "head admiral" give no indication that he knew this person was a woman. My guess is that during his captivity, he probably heard vague references to a "head admiral" whom he never met and assumed to be a man. However, at some point, perhaps even after his release, Glasspoole seems to have learned of a woman and in his subsequent writings makes one brief reference to her: "The chiefs of the divisions are related, and a woman is at the head of this confederacy, whose son was the principal, a very intelligent and humane man, not torturing his prisoners, as the other chiefs are greatly disposed to do. The Ladrones look up to this chief with uncommon reverence, calling him a god." "Substance of Mr. Glasspoole's Relation," 40. Even at this point Glasspoole seems to manifest confusion about the relationship between the principal male and female leaders of the pirates, believing them to be mother and son.

38. Gollomb, *Pirates,* 308–9.

39. Linda Grant De Pauw is a professor of history at George Washington University.

40. De Pauw, *Seafaring Women,* 49.

41. Ibid., 50.

42. Gollomb, *Pirates,* 308–9; De Pauw, *Seafaring Women,* 52.

43. Although De Pauw gives no citation for this quotation, the passage is from 127 of my edition of Glasspoole's "Narrative."

44. De Pauw, *Seafaring Women,* 51–52.

45. The essay is found in 14:19b–23a. Like *Ching hai-fen chi,* "Chi-ssu p'ing Kou" was written by a man who had witnessed the pirates' depredations firsthand. Chu Ch'eng-wen was a teacher in Kan-shih township who, upon hearing of the impending arrival of Chang Pao and his forces, successfully led his community in local defense measures.

46. The first, "Chang Pao-tsai shih-chi kao" (Examination of the affairs of Chang Pao-tsai) by Yeh Lin-feng, was published serially in the *Hsiang-kang hsing-tao jih-pao* (Hong Kong Islands Daily), beginning 7 August 1953. The second, "Hsi-Ying-P'an yü Chang Pao-tsai huo-luan chih p'ing-ting" (Pacification of the disturbances of Hsi-Ying-P'an and Chang Pao-tsai), was published in 1959.

47. F. J. F. Tingay, *The Cave of Cheung Po Tsai* (Kuala Lumpur: Oxford University Press, 1960).

48. Maxine Hong Kingston, *The Woman Warrior: Memoirs of a Girlhood among Ghosts* (New York: Knopf, 1976).

49. Borges' story is included in Jorge Luis Borges, *A Universal History of Infamy*, trans. Norman Thomas di Giovanni (New York: Dutton, 1972).

50. Ibid., 48.

51. Ibid., 43.

52. The account entitled "Account of the Captivity of J. Turner, Chief Mate of the Ship Tay, amongst the Ladrones; accompanied by some Observations respecting those Pirates" appears in *Naval Chronicle,* 20 (1808): 456–72. Turner was released from captivity in May 1807.

53. *Further Statement of the Ladrones,* 46–73. This is the account of Turner's captivity cited here.

54. Ibid., 7–32.

55. Ibid., 40–45.

56. Glasspoole, "Narrative," 127.

57. Glasspoole, "Substance," 44.

58. Maughan, "Account," 26.

59. Glasspoole, "Narrative," 41.

60. Ibid., 127.

61. Turner, "Account," 71.

62. Glasspoole, "Narrative," 113.

63. Turner, "Account," 71.

64. Ibid., 71. Turner's comment is corroborated by archival sources, for twenty-two palace memorials submitted by the governors and governors-general of Kwangtung between 1796 and 1800 cite fifty instances of homosexual activity among the pirates (these documents are now in the National Palace Museum, Taipei). My endeavor to understand what meaning these actions had for the pirates has been included in this collection: published under the title, "The Practice of Homosexuality among the Pirates of Late Eighteenth- and Early Nineteenth-Century China."

65. Glasspoole, "Narrative," 127.

66. Maughan, "Account," 26.

67. Glasspoole, "Narrative," 128.

68. Ibid., 128.

69. Maughan, "Account," 26.

70. Turner, "Account," 61.

71. Maughan, "Account," 26.

72. Turner, "Account," 61.

73. Glasspoole, "Substance," 43.

74. Glasspoole, "Narrative," 104–5.

75. Ibid., 128.

76. Ibid., 105.

77. Glasspoole, "Substance," 44.

78. Turner, "Account," 66.

79. Glasspoole, "Substance," 42.

80. Turner, "Account," 68.

81. Glasspoole, "Substance," 44–45.

82. Maughan, "Account," 15.

83. Yüan Yun-lung, trans. Neumann, 24.

84. Ibid., 46–47.

85. Ibid., 48.

86. Glasspoole, "Substance," 40.

87. Turner, "Account," 56.

88. Glasspoole, "Narrative," 113.

89. Ibid., 123.

90. John K. Fairbank et al., *East Asia: Tradition and Transformation* (Cambridge, Mass.: Harvard University Press, 1978), 98, 120, 480.

91. Maughan, "Account," 23.

Chapter 14

Women and Piracy in Ireland
From Gráinne O'Malley to Anne Bonny

John C. Appleby

There can be little doubt that piracy was one of the most male-dominated activities in former times. Maritime plunder was a violent, ruthless enterprise, apparently drenched in masculinity, which seemed to hold out little attraction or opportunity for the participation of women. The nature of life and work at sea, among a community of men living in cramped conditions, cheek by jowl with each other for days or weeks on end, inhibited the participation of women in maritime occupations either aboard pirate or other ships. The exigencies of shipboard life created an environment pervaded by male values. The notable profanity of many mariners, their heavy drinking, and the thinly veiled brutality and violence were part of a lifestyle which few women seemed to share or even feel comfortable with. Practical considerations alone suggested that the presence of women aboard ships could be a disturbing and disruptive element among other male crew members. And while there were no legal constraints preventing women from going to sea, folklore and popular superstition created informal barriers which were very difficult to break.[1]

But this portrait of a maritime world dominated by men, and pervaded by a masculine ethos, needs some modification. The seaborne activities of mariners, fishermen, and pirates cannot be divorced from the lives of those who remained ashore. At many points these activities continued to intersect with the lives of family and kin. The very structure of life and work within the maritime community left a deep impression on the daily lives of many women. The prolonged absence of men, engaged on voyages lasting weeks, months, or longer had complex consequences for the position of women, as well as for the family and household in general. Whether the increased burdens facing such women were offset by a greater degree of independence remains obscured by the paucity of evidence, at least for the period before 1800.

Of course women within the maritime community were more than a conventionalized "helpmeet" or a silent surrogate for an absent spouse. There is plenty of scattered evidence to indicate that at certain times and in certain places women were able to play an active role in the life of the maritime community. Some engaged in inshore fishing when men were pressed for naval service; others controlled the marketing and retail of fish brought home by their husbands, as occurred at Claddagh, near Galway, during the eighteenth century and possibly earlier. Many widows seem to have continued the commercial ventures of deceased spouses in trade, shipowning, or retailing. Where these ventures were organized in partnership with others, however, some widows may have been left in the position of a "silent partner" whose control over business decisions was rather limited. Nevertheless, there is evidence of women playing a more direct role in trade and retailing. Thus by the eighteenth century the participation of women in trade in Dublin seems to have been widely accepted. Further research among customs accounts and trade directories might reveal a similar situation in other Irish ports. In addition the role of women as alehouse keepers is now fairly well documented. Within the maritime community, where the tavern or alehouse was a vital center for the drifting population of single men who served in the merchant marine, such women could easily come to play an important part in the lives of many seamen. Mariners who were between voyages no doubt relied heavily on women tavern keepers for the provision of board and lodgings, and occasionally loans or pawnbroking facilities. Although the broad impact of this on women's position in society remains unclear, in some areas the alehouse or tavern became the focus of a subculture of crime based on prostitution, theft, or the receipt of stolen goods. Thus in the late sixteenth century complaints were voiced in Dublin against women in the city for keeping taverns and enticing apprentices and others to whoredom and theft. In addition the wives of mariners were active in organizing wage protests and demonstrations on behalf of absent husbands.[2]

Women also played an active role in the business of piracy for much of this period. In part this was a reflection of the nature of piracy in the sixteenth and early seventeenth centuries. At this time the business of plunder, in both Ireland and England, was deeply rooted within the maritime community. Mariners, fishermen, and even landsmen usually turned to piracy as a means of supplementing work and wages. Such men tended to retain close connections with communities ashore, seeking aid and assistance from women when need arose. As "aiders and abettors," indeed, many women played a varied role in the business of piracy, acting as receivers of stolen plunder or harboring pirates from the authorities. In some places piracy fed off the hidden support of women. But by the same process it could easily turn women into victims: wherever piracy flourished so did the business of prostitution. The relationship between the two is clearly revealed by the spread of prostitution into the remote coastal communities of southwest Munster in the early seventeenth century, when large numbers of English pirates were regularly visiting the coast.[3] At times when piracy became an endemic problem it could affect the lives of a large number of women in a variety of ways. The effect might only be short and superficial; but occasionally it could be deeper and more enduring.

Women from diverse backgrounds were connected with piracy during this period. Moreover, in the later sixteenth and early eighteenth centuries two women of Irish background were directly involved in piratical activity. Gráinne O'Malley, the so-called "pirate queen of Connacht," is the more celebrated of the two. Her life of piracy and plunder along the west coast of Ireland during the 1580s and 1590s has assumed legendary proportions and inspired several romantically inclined modern novels. By contrast Anne Bonny, whose career during the 1720s was subsequently recounted by Daniel Defoe, has left little trace in Irish history. Her life at sea, serving aboard a pirate ship in male disguise, along with that of Mary Read, has also found a modern echo in dramatic form.[4] Steve Gooch's play, *The Women Pirates,* for example, portrays two rebel women escaping from female stereotypes in "a small 'alternative' society of anti-colonial" rebel pirates. From this perspective Read and Bonny were not just breaking with conventional life ashore, they were also trying to construct a new way of life at sea. These later interpretations in literature or drama testify to the almost unparalleled lives of both women. A detailed survey of the lives of such isolated individuals, however, would inflate the importance of women's role in piracy and piratical activity. Instead, this chapter will examine their activities within the broader context of Irish piracy as it developed during the period from the sixteenth to the eighteenth centuries.

I

Piracy was a persistent problem in Ireland throughout the sixteenth and early seventeenth centuries. It was an activity involving all social groups, including Gaelic lords, old English merchants, and new English planters. In the west, families such as the O'Malleys and O'Flahertys of Connacht maintained a tradition of opportunistic piracy which helped supplement the local economy in various ways. Much of this activity was relatively unsophisticated in character. It usually involved short-distance raids along the coast, to nearby islands, or upon isolated and vulnerable merchant shipping. There was nothing glamorous about these ventures; they were merely part of a broader struggle to survive in a difficult, sometimes inhospitable, environment. In an area where the opportunities for profitable farming were restricted by bog and rock, piracy was but one way of reaping an alternative harvest from the wealth of the sea.

This type of localized piracy was based upon a broadly defined lordship of the sea claimed by families like the O'Malleys, which included levying tolls or selling fishing rights within certain coastal areas. Its most visible expression, still to be seen today, were the castles and tower houses built by the O'Malleys in and around Clew Bay. Castles at Rockfleet, or on the islands of Achill, Clare, and Inishbofin were powerful structures that dominated the coastal waters of the region, providing a network of safe havens and bases for the O'-Malley fleets.[5]

It was within this context that Gráinne O'Malley's career unfolded during the second half of the sixteenth century. This was a time of protracted crisis within Gaelic society in the west of Ireland, marked by rebellion and internecine conflict whose complexity defies simple analysis. Hostility toward the encroaching power of the English was overlaid by the survival of traditional rivalries amongst the Irish. The combination of these elements was to affect the activities of the O'Malleys, on land as well as at sea, in complex and sometimes contradictory ways. In the case of the latter it brought them face to face with an English concept of the law and custom of the sea whose application in Ireland clearly implied an end to the independent maritime rights and customs exercised by Gaelic lords. Indeed the tension between these two different systems ran like a thread through Gráinne O'Malley's own career.

Despite the burden of legend, much of Gráinne O'Malley's maritime activities remain shrouded in obscurity. The limited evidence, which is mainly from the perspective of hostile English administrators in Ireland, has only fed the imagination of poets and historians who have portrayed O'Malley as an Irish Amazon, a "Diana of the Atlantic," or as a candidate for nationalist sainthood.[6] None is a particularly fitting description for a woman who found herself in the rare position of acting out the traditional role of a petty leader within the O'-Malley septs, from a small power base in Clew Bay. As the daughter of a chieftain of the O'Malleys, and then as the wife successively of Donal O'Flaherty and Richard Burke, she enjoyed a position of some privilege and power within Gaelic society. Certainly, the wives of Gaelic chiefs could exercise indirect influence and power.[7] Gráinne O'Malley was in this tradition. After her marriage she retained control over her family's maritime interests. In 1575, for example, when Sir Henry Sidney marched west to deal with the rebellion of the Earl of Clanrickard's sons, she was able to offer the lord deputy the assistance of three of her galleys and two hundred fighting men. Sidney did not take up the offer; subsequently he condemned O'Malley as a "terror to all merchantmen that sailed the Atlantic."[8] In 1578 the president of Munster also complained that O'Malley was the "chief commander and director of thieves and murderers at sea" who were then spoiling the province.[9]

This type of coastal raiding was a traditional pursuit of the O'Malleys. But its scale under Gráinne O'Malley is difficult to gauge. At most it probably involved about twenty vessels; often the number may have been less than a handful.[10] Most were small vessels, bearing sails and oars, and carrying ordnance of some kind. These vessels, or galleys as the English confusingly described them, were well suited to coastal enterprise of this nature: they were fast, manoeuvrable, and easy to run ashore. But they were ill suited to long-distance piracy and would have been a poor match for a well-armed Elizabethan merchantman or naval vessel in open water. They enjoyed such local advantages in the west of Ireland, however, that the English were forced either to buy or build similar ships to deal with the growing menace of O'Malley and O'Flaherty piracy.[11]

Although O'Malley's maritime activities retained their customary character, they were increasingly affected by the changing political situation in the west. In 1589 most of Mayo burst into rebellion, partly as a reaction to the harsh rule of the English president of Connacht, Sir Richard Bingham. The extent of Gráinne O'Malley's involvement in the rebellion remains unclear. However, it must have been very difficult for her to remain aloof from a rebellion which affected most of west Connacht: according to the annals, "there was not one of note from the western point of Erris [in Mayo] . . . to the Plain of Connaught [in Roscommon], that did not unite in opposition to the governor" or president of the province. Indeed, in 1593 Bingham informed the privy council in London that O'Malley was a "notable traitoress and nurse to all rebellions in the province," and had been so for the past forty years. But the only evidence that Gráinne O'Malley played any direct role in the disturbances in the west occurs toward the end of the rebellion, in 1590, when she raided the Isle of Aran with "2 or 3 baggage boats full of knaves," apparently at the instigation of Sir Morrogh Ne Doe O'Flaherty who bitterly resented the island's grant to Sir Thomas le Strange, an English administrator and adventurer.[12]

In the aftermath of the rebellion Bingham seized the opportunity to deal with recalcitrant Gaelic elements in the west once and for all. Gráinne O'Malley was one of several Gaelic leaders whom he was determined to cow into submission. By 1592 he was in Clew Bay, clearing the islands of rebel groups. This impressive display of power forced O'Malley to try and reach some accommodation with the English regime in Ireland, even though this was probably unpopular with other members of the O'Malley septs. At the same time she apparently forsook "her former trade of maintenance by land and sea." By 1593 she was living a poor farmer's life in west Connacht, impoverished by the increasing burdens of cess.[13]

The imposition of fresh burdens such as cess only served to exacerbate the social and economic dislocation in the west which the outbreak of the Nine Years' War brought in its train. One result of this was a resurgence of piratical activity by the O'Malleys and others which easily became entangled with the war against the English. Although Gráinne O'Malley avoided taking sides in the conflict, she too was involved in this activity. In 1601, shortly before her death, she set out in a galley to plunder the lands and islands of MacSweeney Fanad and MacSweeney Ne Doe in Ulster.[14] On the way north, however, the galley was forced ashore by an English naval vessel under the command of Captain Charles Plessington. The skirmish between the two vessels was brief, but it underlined the fragility of Gaelic maritime enterprise as the naval reach of England penetrated these remote western and northern waters.

Following her death, around 1603, the exploits of Gráinne O'Malley passed into local legend in the west. Later, with the subsequent accretion of myth, she became identified as a symbol of Ireland's struggle for freedom against "all the might of England." This image of a proud, undaunted woman, a patriot who would one day return from exile, was embroidered thereafter in varying guises, in popular songs, poetry, and print; at times she became almost the embodiment of Erin and her people, part of a tradition of "self-possessed and masterful women" which inspired a later generation of radical nationalists.[15] Interesting as these subsequent interpretations are, they bear little relation to the reality of Gráinne O'Malley's life and career. She was no defiant rebel engaged in a life or death struggle with the English but a petty leader who struggled to survive in an environment which was undergoing profound transformation. And within this changing situation piracy became one of the arts of survival.

II

Alongside coastal plunder of the type organized by the O'Malleys, the waters about Ireland were also visited by increasing numbers of English pirates in search of safe bases and markets. The coastal settlements of southwest Munster were especially attractive as secure bases for long-distance raids on shipping in the Atlantic. In May 1589 Sir William Herbert complained that the province was becoming a "receptacle of Pirats" because of the hospitality and favor they received ashore in Kerry. Among those whom Herbert accused of being involved in the business of receiving pirate plunder were Sir Edward Denny, vice-president of the province, and his wife Lady Elizabeth. From their residence in Tralee the Dennys provided a safe haven for pirates which propped up an "elaborate system of piracy" with links across the Irish Sea in southwest England and Wales.[16]

This illicit trade flourished after 1604 with the increasing presence of English pirates in Ireland. During the early seventeenth century as many as twenty pirate ships were regularly visiting the coastal communities of the south and west. And many of these pirates, perhaps one thousand in number, developed close connections with the community ashore. Most of the victuallers of pirates in Baltimore at this time were either the wives or mistresses of pirates, who pretended to be engaged in the trade of fishing. In August 1610 the council of Munster complained of the number of desperate and dishonest men joining the pirates, as well as "such shameless and adulterus women as daylie repaired unto them . . . [in] divers Taverns, Alehouses, and victualling houses" in Baltimore, Inisharkin, and other places along the coast.[17] According to Captain Henry Mainwaring, a former pirate subsequently pardoned and knighted by James I, one of the reasons why pirates frequented Ireland was "the good store of English, Scottish, and Irish wenches which resort unto them." When the naval captain William Monson sailed into Broadhaven in 1614, pretending to be Mainwaring, he was entertained by a local gentleman, one Cormac, who apparently "spared not his own daughters to bid them welcome." Monson later alleged that all the people of the region "in their hearts were piratically affected"; and this clearly included women as well as men.[18]

The structure of piracy in the early seventeenth century promoted close connections ashore in Ireland, especially in the "new English" settlements of the southwest, which affected the lives of women in a variety of ways. As most of the surviving evidence is from a predominantly male perspective and is more concerned with the activities of pirates at sea, most of these women tend to remain nameless or faceless characters who make only fleeting appearances in the pirate lifecycle. It is clear, however, that the nature of the connection ranged from the formal and regular to the informal and intermittent; and this was obviously an important factor in the way in which piracy influenced the lives of women ashore.

These connections are illuminated by the depositions of pirates who were caught by Admiralty officials in Ireland and subsequently tried by the High Court of Admiralty for their offenses. During 1609 John Walter escaped ashore from the company of the pirate Captain Finche, as the ship lay moored in the River Shannon. Walter, a Gloucester man, later admitted that he had also sailed with Captain Richard Bishop, who was "admiral" of the English pirate community for a time, but claimed that on both occasions he had been pressed to serve against his will. After escaping from Finche's company Walter settled at Bandon with his wife and family.[19] Other pirates also had spouses ashore in Ireland. The wife of one pirate captain, Mistress Suxbridge, ran a lodging house near Dublin with her daughters. The wife of another pirate lived on Sir William Hull's land near Leamcon. In October 1618 Hull complained that this woman had warned her husband and his fellow pirates, who were then at Schull, of the recent arrival on the coast of the naval captain, Sir Thomas Button, "by which meanes they escapt."[20]

Informal liaisons also flourished between pirates and women ashore. Baptist Ingle, one of Captain Robert Stephenson's company who came into Whiddy Island in 1612, often went ashore "to make merry with a young woman that lay at Ballygubbin." According to some of his crewmates Ingle planned to marry the young woman, but the courtship was interrupted when he ran off with £100 stolen from one of the company's chests.[21] As in many other maritime communities, prostitution thrived in the small ports and havens visited by pirates. The comments of Captain Mainwaring and the complaints of the council of Munster indicate that the increase in prostitution and alehouses, especially in the southwest, was closely related to the problem of piracy. For a time prostitution was a significant element in the social profile of settlements like Baltimore and the nearby islands, although it remained a marginal, insecure, and often dangerous activity. On one occasion in 1609 a merchant ship, engaged in trading with pirates at Baltimore, "hoysed sayle and went away . . . with . . . two of the pyratts and some of their whores, about fyve in number" still aboard, in order to evade the local Admiralty officials. And prostitution also existed in more remote ports further north. In May 1627 the crew of a Dutch pirate ship were apparently always drunk ashore with the "Queanes" of Killybegs. Sir Basil Brooke informed the Lord Deputy that the pirates were very rich, "for such as Come on shoare are full of Spanish Silver Ducketts." Indeed, Brooke complained that this "wealth [was] too much for such hoores." Others who had "runne straunge courses" since the arrival of the pirates included James and William Hamilton, high constable and minister respectively of Killybegs. Indeed the pirates apparently "glutted" themselves with "drinking and whoreing" daily at the house of the latter.[22]

Some women no doubt benefited from their relationship with pirates, or from the pirate trade in plundered cargoes. Once ashore many pirates could be generous with their plunder. The wife of Henry Skipwith, captain of the fort at Kinsale, received gifts of silverware, linen, and canvas from Captain William Baugh, partly because Baugh hoped to marry her daughter. In 1610 John Bedlake sent a kinswoman a parcel of striped canvas and blue starch which was used to make a waistcoat.[23] Other women were involved in the business of piracy as "traders, truckers or vitelers." At Leamcon the wife of Thomas Barlowe was engaged in the retail trade of beer to pirates who visited that lonely haven. On nearby Long Island "blacke dermond" and his wife supplied victuals to pirates in exchange for goods such as wine, canvas, broadcloth, steel, and other commodities. Three women were also accused of receiving various amounts of sugar out of a Dutch rover which came into Bantry Bay during 1625 to revictual. Mrs. Ashdowne, a widow from Ballygubbin, had about 50 pounds; one "Bruer's wife of the Bridge" (i.e., Bandon) received two barrels of sucketts; and the wife of Nicholas Calfe had some sugar which she subsequently sold in Bandon.[24] While the amounts were admittedly small, it is clear that this was a commercialized traffic involving a wide range of local society, although the number of women who were able to participate in the trade was obviously limited by lack of resources or opportunity.

Women also provided support and assistance for spouses or kinsmen when need arose. The wife of Thibault Suxbridge seems to have run a safe house near Dublin to harbor friends and relatives from the authorities. In July 1612 she provided safe accommodation for a brother, Henry Orange, for six or seven nights until he could get a ship to England. Orange had recently served with Captain William Baugh but fled the pirate's company after stealing a bag of jewels and diamonds. Edmund Flinte, a Chester yeoman who shared a room with Orange, later declared that the pirate recounted his story before his sister and her daughters, revealing that the diamonds were "quilled up in the plates of his hose." Orange subsequently managed to get safely aboard a Chester-bound vessel, where he tried to sell some of the stolen jewels to a fellow passenger, Lady Cooke.[25]

In these various ways the lives of many women became enmeshed with the lives of those pirates who haunted the coasts of the southwest during the early seventeenth century. But the way in which this contact affected the day-to-day lives of women or their broader social and economic position is difficult to determine. Piracy was a dangerous and risky activity, the dangers of which must have been shared by a wider circle of family and kin. Unfortunately the emotional cost, the pain of loss, or the fear of desertion cannot be recaptured from the written record. Nor is it possible to balance lengthy male absence from home against the potential independence for women ashore. Thibault Suxbridge, for example, was at sea almost without break from 1607 to 1610, when he was killed during a bitter conflict with a French vessel at Newfoundland. Although some pirates managed to send money home to their spouses this was poor compensation for the widows or abandoned wives who struggled to survive in a difficult environment. A small number of women, especially widows or women acting with husbands, were able to benefit from the illicit pirate trade. But many more swelled the ranks of the prostitutes who inhabited the unlicensed taverns and alehouses which sprang up along the coast of southwest Munster.

Above all, there was always the danger that women would become the victims of pirate violence. Thus in May 1623 more than a dozen women "were ravished by the . . . company" of Captain John Nutt, who was cruising just outside Dungarvan harbor. Rather different in nature was the attack on Baltimore by Turkish pirates in 1631 when more than one hundred men, women, and children were carried off into slavery in Barbary. Two of the victims, Joan Brodbrooke and Ellen Hawkins, were ransomed and brought home in 1646. The attack on Baltimore came at the end of a decade of mounting depredation by the Turks in northern waters. Their main purpose seems to have been the capture of human victims to sustain the economies of their city bases in north Africa. According to a report in 1625 there were more than fifteen hundred such captives in the port of Salé, including English, Scottish, and Irish men and women. The personal consequences and costs of this wave of depredation are suggested by the issue of a license to Ellen Daniel in August 1618, authorizing her to beg for two years to support herself and five children, and accumulate sufficient funds to redeem her husband, Richard, who had been seized by pirates in 1614 and later sold into slavery.[26]

The problem of piracy in Ireland in the early seventeenth century cannot be divorced from the broader social context. In southwest Munster the areas regularly frequented by pirates, the coastal communities beyond the official plantation, attracted a shifting population of men and women, both English and Irish, who lived in a casual and improvising way. And in such areas where respect for the law was tempered by the harsh realities of survival, piracy, like smuggling later, was an activity that flourished with the connivance of the community ashore.

III

Piracy continued to be a problem in the waters about Ireland for the rest of the seventeenth century. But with the exception of the 1640s and 1650s, when there was a resurgence of privateering and piracy, it remained more of an intermittent irritant than a large-scale organized activity. As the local waters about Ireland and Britain became too dangerous because of regular naval patrols, piracy became an increasingly marginal activity which continued only on the "peripheries of empire," in the Caribbean or along the eastern seaboard of the North American colonies. Even here the state's relentless war against pirates continued, reaching a climax during the 1720s when the English Navy ruthlessly hunted down pirate ships.

Unlike their predecessors in southwest Munster in the early seventeenth century, most of the Anglo-American pirate communities in the early eighteenth century seem to have had few familial ties to land and home. Among those who did, however, was Captain John Criss from Larne who died leaving three wives surviving him. Multiple marriages such as this were probably encouraged by the common law marital arrangements that prevailed within many maritime communities. Under these arrangements women might establish a temporary relationship with a mariner, "drawing his half-pay while he was at sea and looking after him in port." When times were hard such "wives" might resort to part-time prostitution in order to survive. As Criss's case suggests, relationships of this nature were undoubtedly exploited by some members of the pirate community, although their extent and significance are impossible to gauge.[27]

The lives and experiences of many English pirate captains and companies of this period were recaptured by Captain Johnson (who is sometimes identified as Daniel Defoe) in his celebrated *History of the Pyrates*. This unprecedented collection of pirate biographies, which was adorned with a number of splendid illustrations, soon became something of a bestseller, going through four different editions within three years of its publication in 1724.[28] The book's popularity was partly due to the evocation of a world which was passing; its sympathetic portrayal of many pirates may also have struck a chord among readers fascinated by a way of life beyond the pale of respectable society.

Alongside accounts of well-known English pirate captains like Edward Teach or Bartholomew Roberts, Johnson included short life histories of Anne Bonny and Mary Read, both of whom served with Captain John Rackam until their capture in 1720. According to Johnson's account, Anne Bonny was an illegitimate child, born near Cork, who was brought up as a boy to conceal her background and identity. She subsequently emigrated to Carolina with her father and mother and married a seaman who "was not worth a Groat." After being "turned . . . out of Doors" by her father she moved to the island of Providence in search of employment. It was here that she became acquainted with Rackam, a pirate with whom she eloped. Thereafter she sailed with Rackam's company disguised in male attire, as B. Cole's engraving from the first edition of the *History* convincingly portrays. Rackam's crew also contained Mary Read, who was similarly disguised. "In all these Expeditions *Anne Bonny* bore him Company, and when any Business was to be done in their Way, no Body was more forward or couragious than she, and particularly when they were taken, she and *Mary Read*, with one more, were all the Persons that durst keep the Deck." After the capture of Rackam and his company, however, both women were imprisoned and later convicted of piracy at a court of vice-admiralty held in Jamaica on 28 November 1720. Bonny was reprieved on the grounds that she was pregnant; her career thereafter remains unknown.[29]

The careers of Bonny and Read seemed so strange that Johnson was unusually defensive about including them in the *History*. Some, he admitted, "may be tempted to think the whole Story no better than a Novel or a Romance," but, he continued, "since it is supported by many thousand Witnesses, I mean the people of *Jamaica,* who were present at their Tryals, and heard the Story of their Lives, upon the first Discovery of their Sex; the Truth of it can be no more contested, than that there were such Men in the World, as *Roberts* and *Black-beard,* who were Pyrates." The defense was perhaps needed all the more given Johnson's occasional tendency to mix fact with fiction.

Johnson's account of Bonny and Read can be supported by the printed account of their trial which was published in Jamaica in 1721. According to this account both women began their piratical careers on 1 September 1720 when they agreed to sail with Rackam "to commit acts of piracy." Both were accused of taking part in the seizure of seven fishing boats on 3 September, and in the subsequent plunder of four merchant vessels about Jamaica or Hispaniola. In all the value of these captures came to £1330. Although Read and Bonny pleaded not guilty, the evidence of the witnesses at the trial was incontrovertible. Dorothy Thomas, who was taken by Rackam's company off the north coast of Jamaica, declared

> That the Two Women, Prisoners at the Bar, were then on Board the said Sloop, and wore Mens jackets, and long Trouzers, and Handkerchiefs tied about their Heads; and that each of them had a Machet and Pistol in their Hands, and cursed and swore at the Men, to murther the Deponent; and that they should kill her, to prevent her coming against them, and the Deponent further said, That the Reason of her knowing and believing them to be Women then was, by the largeness of their Breasts.

Likewise two French witnesses, Jean Besneck and Pierre Cornelian, claimed that Bonny and Read were

> very active on Board, and willing to do any Thing; That *Ann Bonny,* one of the Prisoners at the Bar, handed Gun-powder to the Men, That when they saw any Vessel, gave Chase, or Attacked, they wore Men's Cloaths; and, at other Times, they wore Women's Cloaths; That they did not seem to be kept, or detain'd by Force, but of their own Free-Will Consent.

This testimony is particularly revealing about the use of male disguise by Read and Bonny.[30]

Yet the lives of Anne Bonny and Mary Read were only remarkable for the paths they chose to follow into piracy. During the eighteenth century a growing number of women disguised themselves as males in order to follow an unconventional career. Those women who served aboard naval vessels or in the army reflected an obsession with disguise and cross-dressing, which figured so prominently in broadsides and ballads. Anne Bonny's life at sea, in particular, seems to have followed the career of the archetypal female warrior as a "high-mettled heroine who disguises herself as a soldier or sailor and goes to war for her beloved."[31] Disguise was a form of protection and a means through which women were able to break out of the constraints of customary life; it also gave some women the opportunity to flout conventional morality, as Defoe's account of Anne Bonny makes clear.

At sea, of course, piracy remained a male-dominated activity. Anne Bonny, like Gráinne O'Malley, was a rare exception whose seaborne career was almost unmatched in the history of piracy. This undoubtedly reflects the broader lack of female involvement in violent criminal activity during this period, as well as the special circumstances of piratical enterprise.[32] On land, however, it is clear that a larger number of women were engaged in the business of piracy, especially as the recipients of stolen goods. And the lives of even more women were affected by the rhythms of piratical activity, as is indicated by the experiences of women in southwest Munster in the early seventeenth century. While the documentary sources remain sparse and fragmentary they may well repay further study, not only to provide a more rounded view of women's activities but also to create a better balanced survey of piracy in past society.

NOTES

1. There is an ever-growing literature on piracy. Philip Gosse, *The History of Piracy* (London: Longmans, Green, 1932) retains its value as a single-volume survey. Recent valuable contributions include: C. M. Senior, *A Nation of Pirates: English Piracy in Its Heyday* (Newton Abbot: David and Charles, 1976), and Marcus Rediker, *Between the Devil and the Deep Blue Sea: Merchant Seamen, Pirates and the Anglo American Maritime Worlds 1700–1726* (Cambridge: Cambridge University Press, 1987). On superstitions, see also D. Vickers, "Work and Life on the Fishing Periphery of Essex County, Massachusetts, 1630–1675," in *Seventeenth-Century New England*, ed. D. D. Hall and D. Grayson Allen (Boston: Colonial Society of Massachusetts, 1984), 83–117, reference here to 112–14; P. Thompson, with Tony Wailey and Trevor Lummis, *Living the Fishing* (London: Routledge and Kegan Paul, 1983), 167–81; Judith Fingard, *Jack in Port: Sailortowns of Eastern Canada* (Toronto: University of Toronto Press, 1982), 57–60.

2. James Hardiman, *The History of the Town and County of the Town of Galway, from the Earliest Period to the Present Time* (Galway: Connacht Tribune, 1926), 300–307; M. Oppenheim, *The Maritime History of Devon* (Exeter: University of Exeter, 1968), 26–27. For Dublin women, see Raymond Gillespie, "Women and Crime in Seventeenth Century Ireland," in *Women in Early Modern Ireland*, ed. Margaret MacCurtain and Mary O'Dowd (Edinburgh: Edinburgh University Press, 1991), 42–52, reference here to 49–51; Linda Levy Peck, *Northampton: Patronage and Policy at the Court of James I* (London: Allen and Unwin, 1982), 165–66.

3. On the general context, see Senior, *Nation of Pirates*, 53–57, and Michael Mac-Carthy-Morrogh, *The Munster Plantation: English Migration to Southern Ireland, 1583–1641* (Oxford: Clarendon Press, 1986), 215–21.

4. See, for example, Morgan Llywelyn, *Grania: She-King of the Irish Seas* (New York: Crown, 1986); Eleanor M. Fairburn, *The White Seahorse: A Novel Founded on Historical Fact, 1537–1601* (London: Heinemann, 1964); Steve Gooch, *The Women Pirates: Ann Bonney and Mary Read* (London: Pluto Press, 1978).

5. Anne Chambers, *Granuaille: The Life and Times of Grace O'Malley c. 1530–1603* (Dublin: Wolfhound, 1979), 26–30; Royal Society of Antiquaries of Ireland, *The Western Islands and the Antiquities of Galway, Athenry, Roscommon &c.,* Antiquarian Handbook Series, 2 (1897): 9; Royal Society of Antiquaries of Ireland, *Illustrated Guide to the Northern, Western, and Southern Islands, and Coast of Ireland,* Antiquarian Handbook Series, 6 (1905): 37–38, 43.

6. Roderic O'Flaherty, *A Choreographical Description of West or H-Iar Connaught: Written A.D. 1684* (Dublin: Irish Archaeological Society, 1846); Basil Fuller and Ronald Leslie-Melville, *Pirate Harbours and Their Secrets* (London: S. Paul, 1935), 189; Thomas Mason, *The Islands of Ireland: Their Scenery, People, Life and Antiquities*, 3d ed. (London: B. T. Batsford, 1950), 36. For a good example of earlier nationalist rhetoric, which argued that O'Malley encouraged early marriages and the "rearing of healthy children who would be a bulwark against the enemies of faith and fatherland," see James Francis Cassidy, *The Women of the Gael* (Boston, Mass.: Stratford Company, 1922), 97–99, 117.

7. See the articles in Margaret MacCurtain and Mary O'Dowd, eds., *Women in Early Modern Ireland* (Edinburgh: Edinburgh University Press, 1991).

8. Chambers, *Granuaile*, 56–57, 77–78, 84–86; Cassidy, *Women of the Gael*, 98; *Dictionary of National Biography*. Katherine Simms has placed O'Malley firmly in "a long tradition of masterful Irish chieftain's wives." Katherine Simms, "Women in Anglo-Norman Ireland," in *Women in Irish Society: The Historical Dimension*, ed. Margaret MacCurtain and Donncha O. Corrain (Dublin and Westport, Conn.: Arlen House and Greenwood Press, 1978), 15–25, reference here to 18.

9. Chambers, *Granuaile*, 93.

10. *Calendar of State Papers Ireland 1588–92*, pp. 333, 397 (hereafter cited as *C.S.P.I.*); A. MacDermott, "Grainne O'Malley," *Mariner's Mirror* 46 (1960): 133–41.

11. On one occasion Bingham boasted that a vessel of 30 tons would be able to deal with O'Malley and all the boats of Mayo. Chambers, *Granuaile*, 142. But the types of vessels employed by O'Malley were part of a northern tradition of shipbuilding connected with Viking "long boat" precedents. See *C.S.P.I. 1600*, 446–47; *C.S.P.I. 1600–1601*, 258–59, 421, 436–37, for descriptions of galleys and ways of dealing with them.

12. *C.S.P.I. 1588–92*, 223, 333; *C.S.P.I. 1592–96*, 141; Chambers, *Granuaile*, 98–102, 109–10, 123; Mona L. Schwind, "Nurse to All Rebellions: Grace O'Malley and Sixteenth Century Connacht," *Eire-Ireland* 13 (1978): 40–61.

13. *C.S.P.I. 1588–92*, 579; *C.S.P.I. 1592–96*, 133–36, 312.

14. Chambers, *Granuaile*, 166–67; P.R.O., S.P., 63/208 part 3/81.

15. Chambers, *Granuaile,* 169–77 and 180–99 for a collection of songs and poetry. On O'Malley, see also Hubert Thomas Knox, *The History of the County of Mayo to the Close of the Sixteenth Century* (Dublin: Judges. Figgis and Co., 1908), 186–87, 196, 245, 253–54, 278–79; and Declan Kiberd, "Irish Literature and History," in *The Oxford Illustrated History of Ireland,* ed. R. F. Foster (Oxford: Oxford University Press, 1989), 285–86. See also Ciaran Brady, "Political Women and Reform in Tudor Ireland," in *Women in Early Modern Ireland,* ed. Margaret MacCurtain and Mary O'Dowd (Edinburgh: Edinburgh University Press, 1991), 69–90, reference here to 79.

16. P.R.O., S.P. 63/144/56; David Mathew, *The Celtic Peoples and Renaissance Europe: A Study of the Celtic and Spanish Influences on Elizabethan History* (London: Sheed and Ward, 1933), chapter 15.

17. *C.S.P.I. 1608–10,* 277–78; R. Dudley Edwards, "Letter-Book of Sir Arthur Chichester 1612–1614," *Analecta Hibernica* 8 (1938), 43, 47; British Library, Cotton MS Otho E VIII, f. 368; Harley MS 697, f. 36.

18. G. E. Manwaring and W. E. Perrin, eds., *The Life and Works of Sir Henry Mainwaring,* 2 vols. (London: Navy Records Society, 1922), 2: 39–40; M. Oppenheim, ed., *The Naval Tracts of Sir William Monson,* 4 vols. (London: Navy Records Society, 1912), 3: 124–27.

19. P.R.O. H.C.A. Examinations, 13/226, unnumbered. And for a fuller discussion, see John C. Appleby, "A Nursery of Pirates: The English Pirate Community in Ireland in the Early 17th Century," *International Journal of Maritime History* 2, no. 1 (1990): 1–27.

20. P.R.O., H.C.A. 13/42, ff. 223v–4; Chatsworth House, Lismore Papers, vol. 9, f. 115. Hull had also been involved in piratical activity in the Mediterranean but had settled at Leamcon, marrying Sir Richard Boyle's widowed sister-in-law. He was also deeply involved in the pirate trade. J. C. Appleby, "Settlers and Pirates in Early Seventeenth-century Ireland: A Profile of Sir William Hull," *Studia Hibernica* 25 (1989–90): 76–104.

21. P.R.O., H.C.A. 13/42, ff. 139v–141v, 156v–158.

22. Senior, *Nation of Pirates,* 57; P.R.O., S.P. 63/244/659, b and 678, b.

23. P.R.O., H.C.A. 13/42, ff. 192–193v, 213v–2144; Lambeth Palace, Carew MS 619, ff. 119, 133.

24. P.R.O., H. C. A. 13/226, 228; Chatsworth House, Lismore Papers, Vol. 11, f. 65.

25. P.R.O., H.C.A. 13/42, ff. 223v–224.

26. Senior, *Nation of Pirates,* 38–39, 64–67. In August 1615 a pirate captain left a "negro wenche" in Bearhaven as a "gift" for a local admiralty officer. P.R.O., H.C.A. 1/48/104–4v; *C.S.P.I., 1615–20,* 209.

27. Rediker, *Between the Devil;* Robert C. Ritchie, *Captain Kidd and the War against the Pirates* (Cambridge, Mass.: Harvard University Press, 1986), for the general context. On marriages, see also John R. Gillis, *For Better, for Worse: British Marriages, 1600 to the Present* (Oxford: Oxford University Press, 1985), 201, 234; Philip Gosse, *The Pirates' Who's Who* (London: 1924), 94.

28. Captain Charles Johnson, *A General History of the Robberies and Murders of the Most Notorious Pyrates and also their Policies, Discipline and Government from*

their first Rise and Settlement in the Island of Providence, in 1717, to the Present Year, 1724, with the Remarkable Actions and Adventures of the two Female Pyrates, Mary Read and Anne Bonny, to which is Prefix'd an Account of the famous Captain Avery and his Companiions; with the Manner of his Death in England, ed. Manuel Schornhorn (London: Dent, 1972); National Maritime Museum, *Piracy and Privateering, Catalogue of the Library of the National Maritime Museum (Great Britain)*, v. 4 (London: H.M.S.O., 1972), 83–97.

29. Johnson, *General History*, 159–65.

30. Ibid., 148–65; Pat Rogers, *Robinson Crusoe* (London: Allen and Unwin, 1979), 34. For the trial account, see P.R.O., Colonial Office 137/14, ff. 9–28v.

31. Dianne Dugaw, "Balladry's Female Warriors: Women, Warfare, and Disguise in the Eighteenth Century," *Eighteenth Century Life* 9 (1985): 1–20. Most surveys of piracy usually include some reference to Anne Bonny based on Defoe's account. See also N. A. M. Rodger, *The Wooden World: An Anatomy of the Georgian Navy* (London: Collins, 1986); Gomer Williams, *History of the Liverpool Privateers and Letters of Marque, with an Account of the Liverpool Slave Trade* (London: Heinemann, 1897), 118–19. A reprint of this book was published in London by Frank Cass in 1966.

32. Olwen Hufton, "Women in History: 1. Early Modern Europe," *Past and Present* 101 (1983): 125–41, reference here to 139; J. A. Sharpe, *Crime in Early Modern England, 1550–1750* (London: Longman, 1984), 108–10.

Chapter 15

Liberty beneath the Jolly Roger
The Lives of Anne Bonny and Mary Read, Pirates

Marcus Rediker

Jamaica's men of power gathered at a Court of Admiralty in St. Jago de la Vega in late 1720 and early 1721 for a series of show trials. Governor Nicholas Lawes, members of his Executive Council, the chief justice of the Grand Court, and a throng of minor officials and ship captains confirmed the gravity of the occasion by their concentrated presence. Such officials and traders had recently complained of their "Coasts being infested by those Hell-hounds the Pirates." In this Jamaica's coasts were not alone: pirates had plagued nearly every colonial ruling class as they made their marauding attacks on mercantile property across the British empire and beyond. The great men came to see a gang of pirates "swing to the four winds" upon the gallows. They would not be disappointed.[1]

Eighteen members of Calico Jack Rackam's crew had already been convicted and sentenced to hang—three of them, including Rackam himself, afterward to dangle and decay in chains at Plumb Point, Bush Key, and Gun Key—as moral instruction to the seamen who passed their way. Once shipmates, now gallowsmates, they were meant to be "a Publick Example, and to terrify others from such-like evil Practices."[2]

Two other pirates were also convicted, brought before the judge, and "asked if either of them had any Thing to say why Sentence of Death should not pass upon them, in like manner as had been done to all the rest." These two pirates, in response, "pleaded their Bellies, being Quick with Child, and pray'd that Execution might be staid." The Court then "passed Sentence, as in Cases of Pyracy, but ordered them back, till a proper jury should be appointed to enquire into the Matter."[3] The jury inquired into the matter, discovered that they were indeed women, pregnant ones at that, and gave respite to these two particular "Hell-hounds," whose names were Anne Bonny and Mary Read.

This essay explores some of the meanings of the lives of the two women pirates, during their own times and long after. It surveys the contexts in which

Bonny and Read lived and discusses how these women made a place for themselves in the rugged, overwhelmingly male world of seafaring. It concludes by considering their many-sided and long-lasting legacy. Any historical account of the lives of Anne Bonny and Mary Read must in the end be as picaresque as its subjects, ranging far and wide across the interrelated and international histories of women, seafaring, piracy, labor, literature, drama, and art. Theirs was ultimately a story about liberty, whose history they helped to make.

Much of what is known about the lives of these extraordinary women appeared originally in *A General History of the Pyrates,* written by a Captain Charles Johnson and published in two volumes in 1724 and 1728. Captain Johnson (who may or may not have been Daniel Defoe)[4] recognized a good story when he saw one. He gave Bonny and Read leading parts in his study, boasting on the title page that the first volume contained "the remarkable Actions and Adventures of the two female Pyrates, Mary Read and Anne Bonny." *A General History* proved a huge success: it was immediately translated into Dutch, French, and German and published and republished in London, Dublin, Amsterdam, Paris, Utrecht, and elsewhere, by which means the tales of the women pirates circulated to readers around the world.[5] Their stories had doubtless already been told and retold in the holds and on the decks of ships, on the docks, and in the bars and brothels of the sailortowns of the Atlantic by the maritime men and women of whose world Bonny and Read had been a part.

As the narrative in Johnson's *General History* relates, Mary Read was born an illegitimate child outside London; her mother's husband was not her father. In order to get support from the husband's family, Mary's mother dressed her to resemble the recently deceased son she had by her husband, who had died at sea. Mary apparently liked her male identity and decided eventually to become a sailor, enlisting aboard a man-of-war, then a soldier, fighting with distinction in both infantry and cavalry units in Flanders. She fell in love with a fellow soldier, allowed him to discover her secret, and soon married him. But he proved less hardy than she, and before long he died. Mary once again picked up the soldier's gun, this time serving in the Netherlands. At war's end she sailed in a Dutch ship for the West Indies, but her fate was to be captured by pirates, whom she joined, thereafter plundering ships, fighting duels, and beginning a new romance. Her new lover one day fell afoul a pirate much more rugged than himself and was challenged to go ashore and fight a duel in the pirates' customary way, "at sword and pistol." Mary saved the situation by picking a fight with the same rugged pirate, scheduling her own duel two hours before the one to involve her lover, and promptly killing the fearsome pirate "upon the spot." Her martial skills were impressive, but still they alone were no match for the naval vessel that captured and imprisoned her and her comrades in 1720.

Anne Bonny was also born an illegitimate child (in Ireland), and she too was raised in disguise, her father pretending that she was the child of a relative entrusted to his care. Her father eventually took the lively lass with him to Charleston, South Carolina, where he became a merchant and planter. Anne grew into a woman of "fierce and couragious temper." Once, "when a young Fellow would have lain with her against her Will, she beat him so, that he lay ill of it a considerable time." Ever the rebel, Anne soon forsook her father and his wealth to marry "a young Fellow, who belong'd to the Sea, and was not worth a Groat." She ran away with him to the Caribbean, where she dressed "in Men's Cloaths" and joined a band of pirates that included Mary Read and, more importantly, Calico Jack Rackam, who was soon the object of Anne's affections. Their romance too came to a sudden end, when one day in 1720 she and her mates fell into battle with a vessel sent to capture them. When they came to close quarters, "none [of the pirates] kept the Deck except Mary Read and Anne Bonny, and one more"; the rest of the pirates scuttled down into the hold in cowardice. Exasperated and disgusted, Mary Read fired a pistol at them, "killing one, and wounding others." Later, as Calico Jack was to be hanged, Anne said that "she was sorry to see him there, but if he had fought like a Man, he need not have been hang'd like a Dog." Anne, who had "fought like a Man," was forced to plead her belly to prolong her days among the living.

Of the existence of two women pirates by the names of Anne Bonny and Mary Read there can be no doubt, for they were mentioned in a variety of historical sources, all independent of *A General History of the Pyrates*. The names first appeared in a proclamation by Woodes Rogers, governor of the Bahama Islands, who on 5 September 1720 declared Jack Rackam and his crew to be pirates and warned all authorities to treat them as "Enemies to the Crown of *Great Britain*." He named the pirates involved and noted "Two women, by name, Ann Fulford alias Bonny, & Mary Read." The second mention came in a rare pamphlet, *The Tryals of Captain John Rackam and Other Pirates*, published in Jamaica in 1721. At about the same time, Governor Lawes wrote from Jamaica to the Council of Trade and Plantations that *"the women, spinsters of Providence Island, were proved to have taken an active part in piracies, wearing men's clothes and armed etc."* Finally, newspaper reports in the *American Weekly Mercury*, the *Boston Gazette*, and the *Boston News-Letter* mentioned but did not name the two women pirates who were members of Rackam's crew.[6]

The Tryals of Captain John Rackam contains testimony from the trial and verifies crucial parts of the narratives in Johnson's *General History*, independently establishing Anne Bonny and Mary Read as fierce, swashbuckling women, genuine pirates in every sense.[7] One of the witnesses against Bonny and Read was a woman, Dorothy Thomas, who had been captured and made prisoner by Rackam's crew. She claimed that the women "wore Mens jackets, and long Trouzers, and Handkerchiefs tied about their Heads, and that each of them had a Machet[e] and Pistol in their Hands." Moreover, they at one point "cursed and swore at the Men," their fellow pirates, "to murther the Deponent." "They should kill her," they growled, "to prevent her coming against them" in court, as was indeed now happening before their very eyes. Bonny and Read were at the time dressed as men, but they did not fool Thomas: "the Reason of her knowing and believing them to be Women was, by the largeness of their Breasts."[8]

John Besnick and Peter Cornelius, likewise captives of Rackam and crew, testified that Bonny and Read "were very active on Board, and willing to do any Thing." Anne Bonny apparently worked as a powder monkey in times of engagement: she "handed gun-powder to the Men."[9] When Rackam and crew "saw any vessel, gave Chase or Attacked," Bonny and Read "wore Men's Cloaths," but "at other Times," presumably times free of military confrontation, "they wore Women's Cloaths." According to these witnesses, the women "did not seem to be kept, or detain'd by Force," but rather took part in piracy "of their own Free-Will and Consent." Thomas Dillon, a captured master of a merchant vessel, added that they "were both very profligate, cursing, and swearing much, and very ready and willing to do any Thing on board."[10]

Despite the general authenticity of the tales of Anne Bonny and Mary Read,[11] many modern readers must surely have doubted them, thinking them descriptions of the impossible. After all, women never went to sea; seafaring was a man's world and a man's world only. But recent research throws doubt upon such uncritical assumptions. Linda Grant De Pauw has shown that women went to sea in many capacities: as passengers, servants, wives, prostitutes, laundresses, cooks, and occasionally—though certainly much less often—even as sailors, serving aboard naval, merchant, whaling, privateering, and pirate vessels.[12] Dianne Dugaw has written: "Perhaps the most surprising fact about eighteenth-century female soldiers and sailors is their frequency, not only in fiction but in history as well."[13] An anonymous British writer, possibly the dramatist and poet Oliver Goldsmith, wrote in 1762 that there were so many women in the British army that they deserved their own separate battalion, perhaps not unlike the contemporaneous women warriors who fought for the African kingdom of Dahomey.[14]

So Anne Bonny and Mary Read rigged themselves out in men's clothes and carried their bold imposture into the always rough, sometimes brutal world of maritime labor. Their cross-dressing adventures were not as unusual among early modern women as previously believed, but they nonetheless directly challenged customary maritime practice, which forbade women to work as seamen aboard deep-sea vessels of any kind. The reasons for the exclusion are not yet clear, but the evidence of it is incontrovertible: the ship was a sharply gendered workplace, reserved almost exclusively for male labor. Seafaring was a line of work long thought to "make a man" of anyone who entered.[15]

One reason why women found no berth would have been the sheer physical strength and stamina required for early modern maritime labor. Employing at this time a low level of machine power, the ship depended on brute strength for many of its most crucial operations—assisting in the loading and unloading of cargo (using pulleys and tackle), setting heavy canvas sails, and operating the ship's pump to eliminate the water that oozed through the seams of always-leaky vessels. A few women, obviously, did the work and did it well, earning the abiding respect of their fellow workers. But not everyone—certainly not all men—was equal to its demands. It was simply too strenuous, leaving in its wake lameness, hernias, a grotesque array of mutilations, and often premature death.[16]

A second and perhaps more important reason for the segregation of the sexes was the apparently widespread belief that women and sexuality more generally were inimical to work and social order aboard the ship. Arthur N. Gilbert has convincingly shown that homosexual practice in the eighteenth-century British Royal Navy was punished ruthlessly because it was considered subversive of discipline and good order.[17] Minister John Flavel made the same point when he wrote of seamen to merchant John Lovering, "The *Death* of their Lusts, is the most *Probable* Means to give Life to your Trade." Flavel, like many sea masters, saw the saving of souls and the accumulation of capital as complementary parts of a single disciplinary process.[18] But some version of his view apparently commanded acceptance at all levels of the ship's hierarchy. Many sailors saw women as objects of fantasy and adoration but also as sources of bad luck or, worse, as dangerous sources of conflict, as potential breaches in the male order of seagoing solidarity. Early modern seafarers seem to have agreed among themselves that some kind of sexual repression was necessary to do the work of the ship.[19]

The assumption was strong enough to command at least some assent from pirates, who were well known for organizing their ships in ways dramatically different from the merchant shipping industry and the Royal Navy. The freebooters who sailed the Mediterranean in the early seventeenth century refused to allow women aboard the ships because their presence was "too distracting."[20] The refusal was continued into the eighteenth century. The articles drawn up by Bartholomew Roberts and his crew specified: "No Boy or Woman to be allowed amongst them." Moreover, should a woman passenger be taken as a captive, "they put a Centinel immediately over her to prevent ill Consequences from so dangerous an Instrument of Division and Quarrel."

The crew of John Phillips reasoned likewise: "If at any Time we meet with a prudent Woman, that Man that offers to meddle with her, without her Consent, shall suffer present Death." William Snelgrave, a slave trader held captive by pirates off the west coast of Africa in 1719, explained: "It is a rule amongst the Pirates, not to allow Women to be on board their Ships, when in the Harbour. And if they should Take a Prize at Sea, that has any Women on board, no one dares, on pain of death, to force them against their Inclinations. This being a good political Rule to prevent disturbances amongst them, it is strictly observed."[21]

Black Bart Roberts was more straitlaced than most pirate captains (he banned gambling among his crew, this too to reduce conflict), so it may be unwise to hold up his example as typical.[22] Another, perhaps more important doubt arises from evidence that Anne Bonny and Mary Read did not cross-dress all the time aboard the pirate ship. As John Besnick and Peter Cornelius testified in court, "when [the pirates] saw any vessel, gave Chase or Attack'd, [Bonny and Read] wore Men's Cloaths, and, at other Times, they wore Women's Cloaths." In other words, they dressed as men only during times of chase or engagement, when a show of "manpower" and strength might help to intimidate their prey and force a quick surrender. At other times, presumably during the daily running of the ship, they dressed as women.[23]

The strongest test of the attitudes of male pirates toward the female would be the actual number of women who appeared on the sea rovers' ships in the early eighteenth century; the surviving evidence suggests that there were few. Two other women pirates appeared in this era, both in Virginia, where authorities tried Mary Harley (or Harvey) and three men for piracy in 1726; they sentenced the three men to hang but released the woman.[24] Three years later they tried a gang of six pirates, including Mary Crickett (or Crichett), all of whom were ordered to the gallows. Crickett and Edmund Williams, the leader of the pirates, had been transported as felons to Virginia aboard the same ship in late 1728.[25] It is not known whether Harley and Crickett cross-dressed to become pirates, nor if they were moved to do so by tales of Anne Bonny and Mary Read. The very presence of all four women among the pirates came to light only because their vessels were captured. Thus the pirate ship may have offered more room to women than either the merchant or naval vessels of the day, but still it was little enough. And in any case it existed only because radical female action created it in the first place.[26]

Bonny and Read were able to undertake such action in part because their class experiences and personal characteristics had prepared them to do so. They both drew upon and perpetuated a deeply rooted underground tradition of female cross-dressing, pan-European in its dimensions but especially strong in early modern England, the Netherlands, and Germany. Such disguise was usually, though not exclusively, undertaken by women of the working class.[27] Like other female cross-dressers, Bonny and Read were young, single, and humble of origin; their illegitimate births were not uncommon. Moreover, Bonny and Read perfectly illustrated what historians Rudolf M. Dekker and Lotte C. van de Pol have identified as the two main reasons why some women cross-dressed in the early modern era: Read did it largely out of poverty and economic necessity, while Bonny, turning her back on her father's fortune, followed her instincts for love and adventure.[28]

Anne Bonny may have been drawn to the sea and to piracy in particular by the popular lore in her native Ireland about Grace O'Malley, a pirate queen who in the late sixteenth century marauded up and down the Emerald Isle's western coast. O'Malley was fierce of action and visage: the face of this commanding figure had been badly scarred in her youth by the talons of an eagle. Sir Henry Sydney wrote in 1577 that O'Malley was "a notorious woman in all the coasts of Ireland." Such coasts would have included the port of Cork, where O'Malley had often attacked the merchant ships that sailed to the Iberian Peninsula and where Bonny was born to a family with seafaring experience.[29]

In any event, Bonny and Read became part of a larger tradition that included such famous women as Mrs. Christian Davies, who, dressed as a man, chased her dragooned husband from Dublin to the European continent; survived numerous battles, wounds, and capture by the French; and returned to England and military honors bestowed by Queen Anne.[30] Ann Mills went to sea "about the year 1740," serving as "a common sailor onboard the Maidstone frigate" during the War of Austrian Succession. She distinguished herself in hand-to-hand combat against "a French enemy" and "cut off the head of her opponent, as a trophy of victory."[31] Perhaps the best known cross-dressing sailor of the eighteenth century was Hannah Snell, who ran away to sea in 1745 in search of a seafaring husband who had abandoned her pregnant self. Accounts of her life appeared in the *Gentlemen's Magazine*, the *Scots Magazine*, and in books long and short, in English and in Dutch.[32]

Women such as Mrs. Christian Davies, Ann Mills, and Hannah Snell were also, significantly, celebrated in popular ballads around the Atlantic world. A "semi-literate lower class" of "apprentices, servants, charwomen, farmworkers, laborers, soldiers, and sailors" sang the glories of "warrior women" at the fairs, on the wharves, around the street corners, and amid the mass gatherings at hangings.[33] Anne Bonny and Mary Read came of age in an era when female warrior ballads soared to the peak of their popularity.[34]

Dianne Dugaw has pointed out that ballads about warrior women gave a surprisingly accurate, if conventionalized, reading of lower-class (female) experience, "which as a matter of course bred physical strength, toughness, independence, fearlessness, and a capability of surviving by one's wits. The prevailing material reality of working women's lives made it possible for some women to disguise themselves and enter worlds dominated by men; the same reality then assured that such women would be familiar enough within early working-class culture to be celebrated. Bonny and Read represented not the typical, but the strongest side of popular womanhood.[35]

Their strength was a matter of body and mind, for they were well suited to maritime labor and piracy in ways both physical and temperamental. By the time she was a teenager, Read was already "growing bold and strong." Bonny was described as "robust" and of "fierce and couragious temper." In "times of Action, no Person amongst [the pirates] was more resolute, or ready to board or undertake any Thing that was hazardous" than Bonny and Read, not least because they had, by the time they sailed beneath the Jolly Roger, already endured any manner of hazard. Read's mother had been married to "a Man who used the Sea" but who was himself apparently used up by it; Anne Bonny's mother was a "Maid-Servant." As illegitimate children, both faced shifting, precarious circumstances early in life. The art of survival in a rough proletarian world included a capacity for self-defense, which both Bonny and Read had mastered.[36] Read's experience in the British infantry and cavalry helped make her a fearsome duelist among the pirates. Bonny's training was less formal but no less effective, as the would-be rapist suddenly and painfully discovered.[37]

Bonny and Read were thus well prepared to adopt the sailor's and even the pirate's cultural style, which they did with enthusiasm. They cursed and swore like any good sailor. They were, moreover, armed to the teeth, carrying their pistols and machetes like those well trained in the ways of war. They also affirmed one of the principal values and standards of conduct among both seamen and pirates, that is, an unwritten code of courage. Calico Jack Rackam got his big boost in the pirate world when his captain, Charles Vane, refused to engage a French man-of-war, which led immediately to charges of cowardice, a democratic vote of no confidence, and Rackam's promotion from quartermaster to captain. Among sailors and especially pirates, courage was a principal means of survival; cowardice was an invitation to disaster and ultimately death.[38]

Courage was traditionally seen as a masculine virtue, but Mary Read and Anne Bonny proved that women might possess it in abundance. They demonstrated it in the mutinies that launched each of them into piracy and again in the skirmish after which they were captured, when Mary Read fired a pistol into the hold at her quivering comrades. Read dreaded to hear her lover called a coward; Bonny called her own lover as much as the noose neared his neck in Port Royal. The strongest evidence of the importance of courage came in

Mary Read's class-conscious answer to a captive's question about facing an "ignominious Death" upon the gallows, when she gamely insisted that "Men of Courage"—like herself—would not fear it. She indicted the cowardly rogues ashore who used the law as an instrument of oppression; in so doing she commented indirectly on the broad, violent redefinition of property relations that was taking place in her native England at the very moment she uttered her condemnation.[39]

Read considered courage a resource, something akin to a skill that offered the poor some protection in a vicious labor market. The same idea was expressed more fully by pirate captain Samuel Bellamy, who lectured a captured captain thus:

> damn ye, you are a sneaking Puppy, and so are all those who will submit to be governed by Laws which rich Men have made for their own Security, for the cowardly Whelps have not the Courage otherwise to defend what they get by their Knavery; but damn ye altogether: Damn them for a Pack of crafty Rascals, and you, who serve them, for a Parcel of hen-hearted Numskuls. They villify us, the Scoundrels do, when there is only this Difference, they rob the Poor under the Cover of Law, forsooth, and we plunder the Rich under the Protection of our own Courage.[40]

Courage was thus the antithesis of law; the working class had to have it in order to make their way in a world of sneaking puppies, hen-hearted numbskuls, crafty rascals, and scoundrels. This was the secularized eighteenth-century voice of the radical antinomian who had taken the law into his or her own hands during the English Revolution.

An antinomian disdain for state authority was evident in another part of the class experience of Anne Bonny and Mary Read, that is, their marital and family situations. Both women engaged in what John Gillis has called the "proletarian practice of self-marriage and self-divorce." Mary Read happily wedded herself to her husband. Anne Bonny, once she had prospects for a life of some wealth and class privilege, promptly turned her back on them, married a poor sailor, and headed off to a place known to be "a Receptacle and Shelter for Pirates & loose Fellows." The property-preserving marriage practices of the middle and upper classes were not for her. Nor, apparently, was the marriage to James Bonny, for she soon tried, with the help of her new lover, Calico Jack Rackam, to arrange a popular form of divorce known as a "wife sale" in order to end an old relationship and begin a new one. Calico Jack was to give her husband "a Sum of Money, in Consideration he should resign her to the said *Rackam* by a Writing in Form, and she even spoke to some Persons to witness the said Writing." When Governor Woodes Rogers refused to validate the popular custom, threatening instead to whip and imprison Anne for such "loose Behaviour," she and Calico Jack, "finding they could not by fair Means enjoy each other's Company with Freedom, resolved to run away together, and enjoy it in Spight of all the World." Bonny and Read thus exercised marital liberty, the collective choice of which helped to generate the passage of England's Hardwicke Act of 1753, designed to restrict legal marriage to public ceremonies conducted in the church.[41]

Anne Bonny and Mary Read threw down their greatest challenge to state authority by choosing the life of the pirate, which was yet another class experience and no less, in its way, about liberty. Captain Charles Johnson recognized piracy as a "Life of Liberty" and made the matter a major theme of his book. Bonny and Read took part in a utopian experiment beyond the reach of the traditional powers of family, state, and capital, one that was carried out by working men and at least a few women. They added another dimension altogether to the subversive appeal of piracy by seizing what was regarded as male liberty. In so doing they were not merely tolerated by their male compatriots, for they clearly exercised considerable leadership aboard their vessel. Although not formally elected by their fellow pirates to posts of command, they nonetheless led by example—in fighting duels, in keeping the deck in time of engagement, and in being part of the group designated to board prizes, a right always reserved to the most daring and respected members of the crew. They proved that a woman could find liberty beneath the Jolly Roger.[42]

Did Anne Bonny and Mary Read, in the end, make their mark upon the world? Did their daring make a difference? Did they leave a legacy? Dianne Dugaw has argued that the popular genre of ballads about warrior women like Bonny and Read was largely suffocated in the early nineteenth century by a new bourgeois idea of womanhood. Warrior women, when they appeared, were comical, grotesque, and absurd, since they lacked the now-essential female traits of delicacy, constraint, and frailty. The warrior woman, in culture if not in actual fact, had been tamed.[43]

But the stubborn truth remained: even though Bonny and Read did not transform the terms in which the broader societal discussion of gender took place, and even though they apparently did not see their own exploits as a call for rights and equality for all women, their very lives and subsequent popularity nonetheless represented a subversive commentary on the gender relations of their own times as well as "a powerful symbol of unconventional womanhood" for the future. The frequent reprinting of their tales in the romantic literature of the eighteenth, nineteenth, and twentieth centuries surely captured the imaginations of many girls and young women who felt imprisoned by ideologies of femininity and domesticity.[44] Julia Wheelwright has shown that nineteenth-century feminists used the examples of female soldiers and sailors "to challenge prevailing notions about women's innate physical and mental weakness." Bonny and Read, like many others, offered ample disproof of then-dominant theories of women's incapacity.[45]

Anne Bonny, Mary Read, and women like them had captured many an imagination in their own day, including those at work in the realm of literature. Bonny and Read were real-life versions of Defoe's famous heroine, Moll Flanders, with whom they had no small amount in common. All were illegitimate children, poor at birth and for years thereafter. All were what Defoe called "the offspring of debauchery and vice." Moll and Anne were born of mothers who carried them in the womb while in prison. All three found themselves on the wrong side of the law, charged with capital crimes against property, facing "the steps and the string," popular slang for the gallows. All experienced homelessness and roving transiency, including trips across the great Atlantic. All recognized the importance of disguise, the need to be able to appear in "several shapes." Moll Flanders too had cross-dressed: her governess and partner in crime "laid a new contrivance for my going abroad, and this was to dress me up in men's clothes, and so put me into a new kind of practice."[46] Moll even had a brush with pirates during her passage to Virginia, though she encountered no women on board. Had she decided to join up with those who sailed beneath the Jolly Roger, the lives of Anne Bonny and Mary Read might be read as one possible outcome to the novel, which was published the year after our heroines' adventures in any case.

Christopher Hill has written, "The early novel takes its life from motion." Writing of the seventeenth and early eighteenth centuries, he concludes that "the novel doesn't grow only out of the respectable bourgeois household. It also encompasses the picaro, the vagabond, the itinerant, the pirate—outcasts from the stable world of good householders—those who cannot or will not adapt." Peter Linebaugh has agreed, emphasizing the proletarian origins of the picaresque novel in the early modern age, especially in England where the literary form "reached an apogee in the publication of *Moll Flanders* in 1722." Thus the experiences of the teeming, often dispossessed masses in motion—people like Anne Bonny and Mary Read—were the raw materials of the imagination. Hannah Snell's contemporary biographer made the connection when he insisted that his subject was "the real *Pamella*," referring to Richardson's famous novel. The often-desperate activity of working-class women and men in the age of nascent capitalism thus helped to generate one of the world's most important and durable literary forms, the novel, which indeed is inconceivable apart from them.[47]

Anne Bonny and Mary Read also affected another major area of literary endeavor, that is, drama. It is widely known that John Gay's *The Beggar's Opera* was one of eighteenth-century England's most popular and successful plays. It is less widely known that in 1728–29 Gay wrote *Polly: An Opera, Being the Second Part of the Beggar's Opera.* The sequel's obscurity was a matter of political repression, for it was censored by none other than Prime Minister Robert Walpole, who was less than happy that he had appeared in *The Beggar's Opera* as "Bob Booty." Disliking Gay's effort to establish moral equivalence between highway robbers and the prime minister's own circle in government and considering the new play to be a still-seditious continuation of the old, Walpole had *Polly* banned. But in so doing, he may have made *Polly* even more popular. Demand for the new play was clamorous: thousands of subscriptions brought Gay a handsome sum of money, though not nearly as much as would have been his if twenty-odd pirate printers and booksellers had not produced and sold their own editions. *Polly* achieved a popular presence and visibility well before its first performance in 1777.[48]

The namesake of the play was the daughter of a Jonathan Wild-type character called Peachum. Polly came to the New World, the West Indies in particular, in search of her love, Macheath, the highwayman of *The Beggar's Opera,* who had been transported for his crimes. Macheath, Polly discovered, had turned pirate, disguised as Morano, a "Negro villain" and captain of a crew of freebooters.[49] En route to America, Polly's money was stolen, which forced her to indenture herself as a servant. She was bought by a Mrs. Trapes, who ran a house of prostitution, then sold by the madame to a wealthy sugar planter, Mr. Ducat. Polly escaped the situation by cross-dressing "in a man's habit," going to sea as a pirate in search of Macheath. She did it, she explained, "To protect me from the violences and insults to which my sex might have exposed me."[50]

The very act of writing a play that featured women pirates only a few years after Anne Bonny and Mary Read had stood trial suggests that Gay knew of and drew upon the adventures of the real women pirates. The likelihood is made even stronger by specific similarities between the play and the freebooting reality of the Caribbean earlier in the decade. Jenny Diver, a prostitute in *The Beggar's Opera* and Macheath's (Morano's) "doxy" aboard the pirate ship, may have, in the new play, been modeled on Anne Bonny. Like Anne, Jenny is the lover of the pirate captain; she also falls for another pirate who turns out to be a disguised woman, in this case the cross-dressed Polly rather than Mary Read. For her part, Polly resembles Mary Read in her modest, even "virtuous" sexual bearing.[51]

Anne Bonny and Mary Read may have influenced posterity in yet another, more indirect way, through an illustration by an unknown artist that appeared as the frontispiece of the Dutch translation of Captain Charles Johnson's *A General History of the Pyrates,* now called *Historie der Engelsche Zee-Roovers.* It featured a bare-breasted woman militant, armed with a sword and a torch, surging forward beneath the Jolly Roger, the international flag of piracy. In the background at the left hangs a gibbet with ten executed pirates adangling; at the right is a ship in flames. Trampled underfoot are an unidentifiable document, perhaps a map or a legal decree; a capsizing ship with a broken mainmast; a woman still clutching the scales of justice; and a man, possibly a soldier, who appears to have his hands bound behind his back. Hovering at the right is a mythic figure, perhaps Aeolus, Greek god of the winds, who adds his part to the tempestuous scene.[52] Bringing up the rear of the chaos is a small sea monster, a figure commonly drawn by early modern mapmakers to adorn the aquatic parts of the globe. The illustration is an allegory of piracy, the central image of which is female, armed, violent, riotous, criminal, and destructive of property—in short, the very picture of anarchy.[53]

The characteristics of the allegory of piracy were equally those of the lives of Anne Bonny and Mary Read, who were, not surprisingly, featured prominently in the *Historie der Engelsche Zee-Roovers,* not only in its pages but in separate illustrations and even on the cover page, directly opposite the frontispiece, where the book proudly advertised its account of their lives. It seems almost certain that these two real-life pirates, who lived, as their narrative claimed, by "Fire or Sword," inspired the illustrator to depict insurgent piracy in the allegorical form of a militant, marauding woman holding fire in one hand, a sword in the other.

It is instructive to compare the work to a famous painting, Eugène Delacroix's *Le 28 juillet: la Liberté guidant le peuple,* for the similarities are striking.[54] Compositionally the works are remarkably similar: a central female figure, armed, bare-breasted, and dressed in a Roman tunic, looks back as she propels herself forward—upward, over, and above a mass of bodies strewn below. The working-class identity of each woman is indicated by the bulk, muscle, and obvious strength of her physique; Parisian critics in 1831 were scandalized by the "dirty" Liberty, whom they denounced as a whore, a fishwife, a part of the "rabble."[55] Moreover, flags and conflagrations help to frame each work: the Jolly Roger and a burning ship at the right give way to the French tricolor and a burning building in almost identical locations. An armed youth, a street urchin, stands in for the windmaker.[56] Where the rotting corpses of pirates once hung now mass "the people." Two soldiers, both apparently dead, lie in the forefront.

There are differences: Liberty now has a musket with bayonet rather than a sword and torch. Still she leads but now takes her inspiration from the living rather than the dead. "The people" in arms have replaced "the people"—as a ship's crew was commonly called in the eighteenth century—who are hanging by the neck in the Dutch illustration.[57]

More importantly, Delacroix has softened and idealized both the female body and the face, replacing anger and anguish with a tranquil, if determined, solemnity. His critics notwithstanding, Delacroix has also turned a partially naked woman into a partially nude woman, exerting on the female body an aesthetic control that parallels the taming of the warrior woman in popular balladry. Liberty thus contains her contradictions: she is both a "dirty" revolutionary born of action and an otherworldly, idealized female subject combining a classical artistic inheritance with a new nineteenth-century definition of femininity.[58]

It cannot be proven definitively that Delacroix saw the earlier graphic and used it as a model. The artist discontinued his journal—where he might have noted such an influence—in 1824 and did not return to it until 1847. And in any case, both the Dutch and the French artist probably drew on classical depictions of goddesses such as Athena, Artemis, and Nike as they imagined their subjects.[59] Regardless, there is a great deal of circumstantial evidence to suggest that the allegory of piracy may have influenced Delacroix's greatest work.

First, it is well known that Delacroix drew upon the experiences of real people in his rendition of *Liberty Leading the People,* including Marie Deschamps, who during the hottest of the July days seized the musket of a recently killed citizen and fired it against the Swiss guards, and "a poor laundry-girl" known only as Anne-Charlotte D., who was said to have killed nine Swiss soldiers in avenging her brother's death.[60] These real women, like Anne Bonny and Mary Read, were bound to appeal to the romantic imagination.[61]

Second, Delacroix himself noted in his journal that he often studied engravings, woodcuts, and popular prints as he conceptualized his paintings and sought to solve compositional problems. By the time Delacroix composed his famous painting, late in 1830, at least twenty editions of *A General History of the Pyrates* had appeared, six (or more) of these in French and many containing the Dutch illustration. The majority of these editions—which, including the French, advertised the stories of Bonny and Read on their title pages—would have been available to the artist in Paris.[62]

Third, and most importantly, it can be established that piracy was on Delacroix's mind at the very moment he was painting *Liberty.* The English romantic poet Lord Byron was, according to art historian George Heard Hamilton, "an inexhaustible source of inspiration" for the painter. Delacroix engaged the work of Byron intensely during the 1820s, exhibiting three major paintings on subjects from Byron's poetry in 1827 and executing several others on the Greek civil war, in which Byron ultimately lost his life. More crucially still, Delacroix was reading Byron's poem *The Corsair*—about piracy—as he was painting *Liberty.* At the very same salon in which he exhibited his greatest painting in 1831, Delacroix also entered a watercolor based on Byron's poem.[63]

The image of piracy (1725) preceded the image of liberty (1830) by more than a century. And yet it seems that the liberty seized by Anne Bonny and Mary Read—the liberty they found so briefly, so tantalizingly, beneath the Jolly Roger—took a strange, crooked, still poorly understood path from the rough, rolling deck of a ship in the Caribbean to the polished, steady floor of an art salon in Paris. It was a case of liberty seized in action; of low culture affecting high; of New World struggles supplying and driving what once would have been seen as the genius and originality of European art and culture. It would be a fitting tribute to Anne Bonny and Mary Read if the example of these two women who seized liberty beneath the Jolly Roger in turn helped to inspire one of the most famous depictions of liberty the modern world has ever known.

NOTES

1. *Boston News-Letter,* 19–26 December 1720. On the trial, see *The Tryals of Captain John Rackam and Other Pirates* (Jamaica: 1721). I have analyzed Rackam's generation of pirates in Marcus Rediker, *Between the Devil and the Deep Blue Sea: Merchant Seamen, Pirates and the Anglo American Maritime Worlds 1700–1726* (Cambridge: Cambridge University Press, 1987), chapter 6, which is reproduced in this present collection.

2. *Tryals of Captain John Rackam,* 15.

3. Captain Charles Johnson, *A General History of the Robberies and Murders of the Most Notorious Pyrates and also their Policies, Discipline and Government from their first Rise and Settlement in the Island of Providence, in 1717, to the Present Year, 1724, with the Remarkable Actions and Adventures of the two Female Pyrates, Mary Read and Anne Bonny, to which is Prefix'd an Account of the famous Captain Avery and his Companions; with the Manner of his Death in England,* ed. Manuel Schonhorn (London: Dent, 1972), 152.

4. Literary critic John Robert Moore argued in *Defoe in the Pillory and Other Studies* (Bloomington: Indiana University Press, 1939), 129–88, that Captain Johnson was in truth none other than Daniel Defoe. His claim soon gained wide acceptance, as reflected in the republication of *A General History of the Pyrates* in 1972 with Defoe as author. Recently, however, scholars have begun to doubt the attribution. Moore has been challenged by P. N. Furbank and W. R. Owens, *The Canonisation of Daniel Defoe* (New Haven: Yale University Press, 1988), 100–121. Having worked on *A General History of the Pyrates* for more than fifteen years, I have come to the conclusion that its author had a deeper and more detailed knowledge of things maritime than Defoe could possibly have had.

5. The publishing history of A *General History of the Pyrates* can be followed in Philip Gosse, *A Bibliography of the Works of Capt. Charles Johnson* (London: Dulau, 1927).

6. See "By his Excellency Woodes Rogers, Esq; Governour of New-Providence, &c. A Proclamation," *Boston Gazette,* 10–17 October 1720; *Tryals of Captain John Rackam,* 16–19; Governor Nicholas Lawes to Council of Trade and Plantations, 12 June 1721, in CSPCS, America and the West Indies (London: HMSO, 1933), 32:335 (italics in original); *American Weekly Mercury,* 31 January–7 February 1721; *Boston Gazette,* 6–13 February 1721; and *Boston News-Letter,* 13–20 February 1721.

7. It is possible that the author of *A General History of the Pyrates* used this pamphlet, as he did others, in preparing his text. See Schonhorn's commentary in Johnson, *General History,* 670.

8. *Tryals of Captain John Rackam,* 16.

9. Linda Grant De Pauw notes that women frequently worked in artillery units during the American Revolution. See Linda Grant De Pauw, "Women in Combat: The Revolutionary War Experience," *Armed Forces and Society* 7 (1981): 209–26, reference here to 214–17.

10. *Tryals of Captain John Rackam,* 16.

11. The narratives are in almost all respects plausible. Literary convention of the day played a part in constructing the narratives, to be sure, as in the invocation of the conflict between Mars and Venus in the life of Mary Read. But it has been established by scholars that, apart from one fictional chapter (on Captain Misson), the author of *A General History of the Pyrates* was indeed a "faithful Historian," remarkably reliable in presenting historical facts. For assessments, see Philip Gosse, *The History of Piracy* (New York: Tudor, 1932), 182; Hugh F. Rankin, *The Golden Age of Piracy* (Williamsburg: Colonial Williamsburg, 1969), 161; Rediker, *Between the Devil,* 258; and B. R. Burg, *Sodomy and the Pirate Tradition: English Sea Rovers in the Seventeenth-Century Caribbean* (New York: New York University Press, 1995), 196. See also Schonhorn's introduction to *A General History of the Pyrates,* xxvii–xl.

12. Linda Grant De Pauw, *Seafaring Women* (Boston: Houghton Mifflin, 1982), 18, 71. Seafaring was only one of many lines of work formally to exclude women, for the sexual division of labor was clearly established and indeed growing in the eighteenth century, even if not yet as severe in some respects as it would become. Medieval guilds and the apprenticeship system had long ago segregated the majority of crafts by sex. See the excellent work by Bridget Hill, *Women, Work, and Sexual Politics in Eighteenth-Century England* (Oxford: Basil Blackwell, 1989), especially her comments at 49, 260.

13. Dianne Dugaw, ed., *The Female Soldier, or, The Surprising Life and Adventures of Hannah Snell,* reprint of 1750 edition, *Augustan Reprint Society,* no. 257 (Los Angeles: Williams Andrews Clark Memorial Library, University of California Los Angeles, 1989), v; Linda Grant De Pauw has pointed out that during the American Revolution, "tens of thousands of women were involved in active combat," a "few hundred" of these—like Deborah Sampson, Sally St. Clair, Margaret Corbin, and a woman known only as "Samuel Gay"—fighting in uniform with the Continental line. See De Pauw, "Women in Combat," 209.

14. "Female Warriors," originally published in the *British Magazine,* was republished as an "unacknowledged essay" in Peter Cunningham, ed., *The Works of Oliver Goldsmith* (New York: Harper and Bros., 1881), 3:316–19.

15. Historians have only recently begun to study the process by which seafaring became a masculine activity; indeed, the collection in which the present paper was first published was conceived to address this very issue. Margaret S. Creighton and Lisa Norling, eds., *Iron Men, Wooden Women: Gender and Seafaring in the Atlantic World, 1700–1920* (Baltimore: Johns Hopkins University Press, 1996). Given the limitations of current scholarship, the speculations that follow should be regarded as tentative.

16. Rudolf M. Dekker and Lotte van de Pol, *The Tradition of Female Transvestism in Early Modern Europe* (Basingstoke: Macmillan, 1989), 80, 81; Julie Wheelwright, *Amazons and Military Maids: Women Who Dressed as Men in the Pursuit of Life, Liberty, and Happiness* (London: Pandora, 1989), 51, 53, 78. Maritime employers probably felt about women sailors the way employers of indentured labor felt about the ten thousand or so women who were transported as felons to Britain's American colonies between 1718 and 1775: they considered these women to be less skilled, less capable of heavy physical labor, and more likely to lose labor time to pregnancy. See A. Roger Ekirch, *Bound for America: The Transportation of British Convicts to the Colonies, 1718–1775* (Oxford: Clarendon Press, 1987), 48–50, 89.

17. Arthur N. Gilbert, "Buggery and the British Navy 1700–1861," *Journal of Social History* 10, no. 1 (1976): 72–98, reference here to 87–88.

18. John Flavel, *A Pathetic and Serious Disswassive . . .* (Boston: 1725), 134; De Pauw, *Seafaring Women,* 162, 184–85. The women who regularly came aboard were passengers and increasingly the wives of officers, the great majority of whom were separated from the crew by chasms of gender and class. The trend of captains' wives accompanying them to sea reached a peak in the nineteenth century and declined in the twentieth.

19. The fear of female sexuality probably drew upon an older superstition about the magical, spiritual, and supernatural powers of women that arose during the terrifying early days of seafaring. Linda Grant De Pauw maintains that it is a "myth" and a shoreside invention that women were regarded as bad luck at sea, having little or nothing to do with the actual beliefs of seamen. But her argument is contradicted by too much evidence (some of which is her own) to be persuasive. See her *Seafaring Women,* 15–18.

20. C. M. Senior, *A Nation of Pirates: English Piracy in Its Heyday* (Newton Abbot: David and Charles, 1976), 39.

21. Johnson, *General History,* 212, 343; William Snelgrave, *A New Account of Some Parts of Guinea and the Slave-Trade,* reprint of 1734 ed. (London: Frank Cass, 1971), 256–57.

22. Roberts and his crew may have known—and disapproved of—Bonny and Read. Another of their articles of agreement stated: "If any Man were found seducing any of the [female] Sex, and carry'd her to Sea, disguised, he was to suffer Death." See Johnson, *General History,* 212.

23. *Tryals of Captain John Rackam,* 18.

24. "At a Court held at Williamsburg" (1727), PRO HCA 1/99, fols. 2–8. Mary's husband, Thomas, was also involved in the piracy but somehow eluded arrest. For

information on Thomas and Mary Harvey, identified as husband and wife, see Peter Wilson Coldham, *English Convicts in Colonial America* (New Orleans: Polyanthos, 1974), vol. 1, *Middlesex, 1617–1775*, 123. Mary was transported to the colonies in April 1725. Thomas was sentenced in October and transported in November of the same year. The leader of the gang, John Vidal, requested and was granted the king's mercy, receiving pardon for his capital crime in September 1727. See *Executive Journals of the Council of Colonial Virginia*, ed. H. R. McIlwaine (Richmond: Davis Bottom, 1925–) 4:149, 150.

25. "Proceedings of the Court of Admiralty [in Virginia]" (1729), PRO HCA 1/99. See also Coldham, *English Convicts,* 67 (Crichett), and 290 (Williams). No record exists to show whether the hangings actually took place.

26. By limiting the role of women aboard their ships, pirates may have made it more difficult to reproduce themselves as a community and hence easier for the state to wage its deadly assault upon them.

27. Julie Wheelwright has written: "Women who enlisted as soldiers and sailors were most often from the labouring classes where they were used to hard, physical work. They came from communities where the women were confident of their strength as they worked side by side with men in the fields" or other areas. See Wheelwright, *Amazons and Military Maids,* 42; and Dekker and van de Pol, *Female Transvestism,* 2.

28. Based on a study of 119 instances of cross-dressing found in the archives of the Dutch East India Company, Rudolf M. Dekker and Lotte C. van de Pol have concluded, "Throughout the early modern era passing oneself off as a man was a real and viable option for women who had fallen into bad times and were struggling to overcome their difficult circumstances." Dekker and van de Pol, *Female Transvestism,* 1–2 (quotation), 11, 13, 42.

29. See Anne Chambers, *Granuaille: The Life and Times of Grace O'Malley c. 1530–1603,* 3d ed. (Dublin: Wolfhound, 1988). Sydney quoted at 85. See also De Pauw, *Seafaring Women,* 24–25. Mary Read, in turn, who kept an inn at Breda, may have influenced the Netherlands' most famous female cross-dresser, Maria van Antwerpen. See Dekker and van de Pol, *Female Transvestism,* 40.

30. James Caulfield, *Portraits, Memoirs, and Characters, of Remarkable Persons, from the Revolution in 1688 to the End of the Reign of George II: Collected from the Most Authentic Accounts Extant,* 4 vols. (London: H. R. Young and T. H. Whitely, 1819–20), 2:43–51.

31. Ibid., 4:111, 112.

32. Dugaw, *The Female Soldier,* vi, 1, 5, 6, 17, 19, 22–23, 39, 41. Hannah Snell's story was often told in celebration of the British nation, emphasizing the patriotism of her military service. The stories of Bonny and Read admitted of no such emphasis, for the inescapable fact remained that they had attacked *British* ships and *British* commerce, refusing the logic of nationalism in their depredations.

33. Dianne Dugaw, *Warrior Women and Popular Balladry, 1650–1850* (Cambridge: Cambridge University Press, 1989), 20.

34. Ibid., 1, 48.

35. See ibid., 122 (quotation), 124, 131. Dugaw's conclusion about the positive

popular reaction to women warriors would appear to be at odds with that of Rudolf Dekker and Lotte C. van de Pol, but this may be a matter of different responses in England and the Netherlands. See Dekker and van de Pol, *Female Transvestism*, 97–98.

36. Bonny and Read's cross-dressing and going to sea should be seen in the broader context suggested by Peter Linebaugh: "I think that to the many acts of survival and getting by, we should add the power of seeming to be what you are not as among the characteristics of the thick, scarred, and calloused hide of the English proletariat." See Peter Linebaugh, "'All the Atlantic Mountains Shook,'" *Labour/Le Travail* 10 (1982): 99.

37. De Pauw argues in "Women in Combat" (223) that in the eighteenth century, "engaging in hand-to-hand combat was not considered unfeminine behavior."

38. *Tryals of Captain John Rackam*, 16, 18.

39. Johnson, *General History*, 151; *Tryals of Captain John Rackam*, 11; Douglas Hays et al., eds. *Albion's Fatal Tree: Crime and Society in Eighteenth-Century England* (New York: Pantheon Books, 1975); E. P. Thompson, *Whigs and Hunters: The Origin of the Black Act* (New York: Pantheon Books, 1975); Peter Linebaugh, *London Hanged: Crime and Civil Society in the Eighteenth Century* (Cambridge: Cambridge University Press, 1991).

40. Johnson, *General History*, 597.

41. John R. Gillis, *For Better, for Worse: British Marriages, 1600 to the Present* (New York: Oxford University Press, 1985), 13, 14, 18, 37, 84, 85, 99 (quotation); Anonymous letter from South Carolina, August M6, PRO CO5/382, fol. 47 (quotation). Richard Turnley, who not only refused to witness the wife sale but informed Governor Rogers, became an immediate object of revenge. With "many bitter Oaths and Imprecations," Bonny and Rackam swore that if they had been able to find him (and they went in search of him), they would "have whipp'd him to Death." See Johnson, *General History*, 623, 626. The narrative also suggests that this particular wife sale was initiated not by the husband, as was customary, but rather by Anne Bonny herself. On wife sale, see E. P. Thompson, *Customs in Common* (London: Merlin Press, 1991), chapter 7; Samuel Pyeatt Menafee, *Wives for Sale* (Oxford: Oxford University Press, 1981); and Hill, *Women, Work, and Sexual Politics*, 216.

42. Johnson, *General History*, 391. On the class dimensions of piracy, see Rediker, *Between the Devil*, chapter 6; and Marcus Rediker, "Hydrarchy and Libertalia: The Utopian Dimensions of Atlantic Piracy in the Eighteenth Century," in *Pirates and Privateers: New Perspectives on the War on Trade in the Eighteenth and Nineteenth Centuries*, ed. David J. Starkey, E. S. van Eyck van Heslinga, and J. A. deMoor (Exeter: University of Exeter Press, 1997), 29–46.

43. Dugaw, *Warrior Women*, 73, 75, 155. The warrior woman ballad declined in England just as cross-dressing declined in the Netherlands. See also Dekker and van de Pol, *Female Transvestism*, 102–3.

44. Wheelwright, *Amazons and Military Maids*, 11, 78, 159; Dugaw, *Warrior Women*, i, 3–4. On the subsequent editions of Johnson, *General History*, see Gosse, *Bibliography*.

45. Natalie Zemon Davis, "Women on Top," in Natalie Zemon Davis, *Society*

and Culture in Early Modern France: Eight Essays (Stanford, Calif.: Stanford University Press, 1975), 131, 144; Wheelwright, Amaz*ons and Military Maids,* 15, 119 (quotation).

46. Daniel Defoe, *The Fortunes and Misfortunes of the Famous Moll Flanders* (London: 1722; reprint, New York: Penguin Books, 1978), 28, 33, 208–9, 228.

47. Christopher Hill, *A Tinker and a Poor Man: John Bunyan and His Church, 1628–1688* (New York: A. Knopf, 1989), 362; Linebaugh, *London Hanged,* 119–20; Dugaw, *Female Soldier,* 40–41.

48. James R. Sutherland, "'Polly' among the Pirates," *Modern Language Review* 37 (1942): 291–303, reference here is to 291–92; Joan Hildreth Owen, "Polly and the Choice of Virtue," *Bulletin of the New York Public Library* 77 (1974): 393. Gay's play helps to prove that warrior women were a major "imaginative preoccupation of the early modern era," as suggested by Dugaw, *Warrior Women,* 1; see also her interesting interpretation of *Polly,* 191–211.

49. John Gay, *Polly: An Opera, Being the Second Part of the Beggar's Opera,* in John Fuller, ed., *John Gay, Dramatic Works,* 2 vols. (Oxford: Clarendon Press, 1983), 2:95. The name Morano may refer to the Spanish word *moreno,* meaning brown, or it may refer to *marrano,* the term used to describe Jews who converted to Catholicism rather than leave Spain in 1492. This latter meaning would further play upon the theme of disguise.

50. Gay, *Polly,* 99, 140.

51. Ibid., 129.

52. On Aeolus, see Rudolf Wittkower, *Allegory and the Migration of Symbols: The Collected Essays of Rudolf Wittkower* (New York: Thames and Hudson, 1977), 94; and Michael Grant and John Hazel, *Gods and Mortals in Classical Mythology* (Springfield, Mass.: G. and C. Merriam Co., 1973), 27–28. It is also possible that the malevolent god Typhon is the source of the winds, which would have made them "the allies of disorder, the powers of chaos." See Yves Bonnefoy, comp., *Mythologies,* 2 vols. (Chicago: University of Chicago Press, 1991), 1:510.

53. Maurice Agulhon has noted that allegorical depictions of anarchy included a dagger and a torch, which signified crimes of destruction. See Maurice Agulhon, *Marianne into Battle: Republican Imagery and Symbolism in France, 1789–1880* (Cambridge: Cambridge University Press, 1981), 13. In fashioning this particular image, the unknown artist may have drawn upon Pieter Bruegel's eerily powerful painting *Dulle Griet,* which features the wild, disorderly, sword-toting virago named "Mad Margot" striding fearlessly across the mouth of the gates of hell, impervious to the devils, demons, and creatures all around her. See Leo van Puyvelde, *Pieter Bruegel: The Dulle Griet in the Mayer van den Bergh Museum, Antwerp, The Gallery Books,* no. 10 (London: P. Lund Humphries, 1946).

54. The art-historical literature on Delacroix's *Liberty* is enormous. Some of the most important works include Lee Johnson, *The Paintings of Eugène Delacroix: A Critical Catalogue, 1816–1831,* 6 vols. (Oxford: Clarendon Press, 1981), vol. 1 (1816–31), 144–51; George Heard Hamilton, "The Iconographical Origins of Delacroix's 'Liberty Leading the People,'" in *Studies in Art and Literature for Belle da*

Costa Greene, ed. Dorothy Eugenia Miner (Princeton: Princeton University Press, 1954), 55–66; Hélène Adhémar, "La Liberté sur les barricades de Delacroix: Étudiée d'après des documents inédits," *Gazette des Beaux-Arts* 43 (1954): 83–92; N. Hadjinicolaou, "'La Liberté guidant le peuple' de Delacroix devant son premier plan," *Actes de la Recherche en Social Sciences* (June 1979): 3–26; Hélène Toussaint, *La Liberté guidant le peuple de Delacroix: Catalogue.* Dossiers du Département des Peintures 26 (Paris: Éditions de la Réunion des Musées Nationaux, 1982); T. J. Clark, *The Absolute Bourgeois: Artists and Politics in France, 1848–1851* (Princeton: Princeton University Press, 1973), 7–20, 22, 25–26, 29; and Marcia Pointon, "Liberty on the Barricades: Women, Politics, and Sexuality in Delacroix," in Marcia R. Pointon, *Naked Authority: The Body in Western Painting, 1830–1908* (Cambridge: Cambridge University Press, 1990), 59–82.

55. Marina Warner, *Monuments and Maidens: The Allegory of the Female Form* (London: Weidenfeld and Nicholson, 1985), 272.

56. The four winds under the charge of Aeolus were usually depicted as children or beardless men, which might help to explain Delacroix's choice of the youth. See J. C. Cooper, *An Illustrated Encyclopaedia of Traditional Symbols* (New York: Thames and Hudson, 1978), 192.

57. It is curious that art historians have not explored the possible maritime meanings of the symbolism in the painting, especially in light of Delacroix's proximity to the sea in his youth, where he would have seen bare-breasted women as figureheads on a variety of ships. The artist would likely have known that many sailors considered these figures to have protective supernatural powers, in particular the capacity to silence the tempests they faced at sea. See Margaret Baker, *Folklore of the Sea* (Newton Abbot: David and Charles, 1979), chapter 1; and Horace Palmer Beck, *Folklore and the Sea*, 1st ed. (Middletown, Conn.: Wesleyan University Press, 1973), 15–16.

58. Lynda Nead, *The Female Nude: Art, Obscenity, and Sexuality* (London: Routledge, 1992), 9, 47. The distinction between the naked and the nude was pressed by Kenneth Clark, *The Nude: A Study in Ideal Form* (Princeton: Princeton University Press, 1956), 3–29. When, a generation later, the new definition of femininity had taken hold, Eduard Manet would scandalize the art establishment afresh by painting women who were naked rather than nude. See T. J. Clark, "Preliminaries to a Possible Treatment of 'Olympia' in 1865," *Screen* 21 (1980): 18–41.

59. See Warner, *Monuments and Maidens,* chapters 6, 8, 12.

60. There is also the story of the "Maid of Saragossa," well known for her courage during the defense of her Spanish home against the French in 1808. For discussion of these sources, see Pointon, "Liberty on the Barricades," 64; Hamilton, "Iconographical Origins," 63–64; and Johnson, *Paintings of Delacroix*, 147. The influences discussed here do not displace or diminish the widely acknowledged importance of artists such as Gericault, Gros, and Guerin to Delacroix's painting.

61. The female image of piracy may be seen as a forerunner of a specifically radical image of liberty that emerged during the French Revolution. Lynn Hunt has pointed out that this image-armed, "bare-breasted and fierce of visage" woman as an active agent of change existed in tension with a conservative image of a woman "seated,

stolid, tranquil, and often without lance or liberty cap," as a passive reflection of stability. See Lynn Avery Hunt, *Politics, Culture, and Class in the French Revolution* (Berkeley: University of California Press, 1984), 93. On the genesis of liberty as a symbol in France, see Agulhon, *Marianne into Battle*, chapter 1. The radical image would in turn make its way into the socialist tradition: Eric Hobsbawm, "Man and Woman in Socialist Iconography," *History Workshop Journal* 6 (1978): 121–38. See also Maurice Agulhon, "On Political Allegory: A Reply to Eric Hobsbawm," *History Workshop Journal* 8 (1979): 167–73.

62. Gosse, *Bibliography*.

63. See three articles by George Heard Hamilton: "Eugène Delacroix and Lord Byron," *Gazette des Beaux-Arts* 23 (1943): 99–110; "*Hamlet* or *Childe Harold?* Delacroix and Byron," *Gazette des Beaux-Arts* 26 (1944): 365–86; and "Iconographical Origins," 63, where Hamilton notes that Byron was much on Delacroix's mind during the winter of 1830–31. *The Corsair* can be found in *The Works of Lord Byron*, ed. Ernest Hartley Coleridge (New York: Octagon Books, 1966), 3:227–96.

Chapter 16

Women among the Uskoks of Senj
Literary Images and Reality

Wendy Bracewell

In the sixteenth and seventeenth centuries the small port of Senj, perched under the mountains on the northern Adriatic coast, was one of the main strongholds of the tripartite frontier between the Hapsburg Monarchy, the Venetian Republic, and the Ottoman Empire. This was the haunt of the uskoks, border raiders nominally in the service of the Hapsburg Military Frontier. Throughout the sixteenth century they scoured the Adriatic and the Dalmatian hinterland, pillaging Ottoman and Venetian possessions for their livelihood, until brought under effective Hapsburg control after the Venetian-Hapsburg war of 1615–17. Historians have largely treated their story as a means of examining the power struggle between Venice, the Hapsburgs, and the Ottoman Porte, but the mass of documents generated by this diplomatic conflict can also be used to investigate the lives of the uskoks, even though these border raiders left little written evidence themselves.[1] Aspirations toward a more complete history, one that would also include the experiences, ideas, and values of the people of the frontier, lead inevitably to questions about the women of Senj. Sources for their lives are even more limited than those for their menfolk. Nevertheless, uskok women do appear in the margins of contemporary discussions of the uskoks. Here I would like to look at the images of women in Senj presented in contemporary polemics, and follow up some of these themes as seen through other sources. My purpose here is not only to integrate the women of Senj into the larger history of the uskoks, but also to explore some of the difficulties in assessing uskok realities through the available sources.

The contemporary literature dealing with the uskoks arose, for the most part, out of the conflict between the Hapsburgs and the Venetian Republic over the actions of the uskoks, and was written toward the end of the sixteenth century and in the early seventeenth century, reaching a climax with the pamphlet polemics that accompanied the so-called Uskok War of 1614–17.

Among the works that I wish to consider here are the best-known Venetian histories of the uskoks: the *Historia degli Uscochi* by Minuccio Minucci, Archbishop of Zadar, and the *Aggionta* and *Supplimento* to Minucci's History by Paolo Sarpi, the Venetian theologian, along with his manuscript work *Trattato di Pace et Accommodamento*.[2] Another less well-known Venetian work dealing with the uskoks is the report by Vettor Barbaro, secretary to Provveditore Generale Filippo Pasqualigo, "Relatione di Segna e di Uscocchi," written after a prolonged visit to Senj in 1601. This was not published, but circulated widely in manuscript form, providing the basis for later Venetian accounts of the uskoks.[3] The tracts written by Hapsburg supporters were usually less concerned with the activities of the uskoks, with the notable exception of an anonymous Italian work, written in response to the histories of Minucci and Sarpi. This defense of the uskoks is set in the form of a dialogue between the inquisitive Antonio and the well-informed Giovanni who had spent many years on the Croatian Littoral as a member of a Fermo merchant family, and was intimately acquainted with the affairs of Senj.[4] All these works, although they are primarily concerned with political and military matters, make some reference to the women of Senj in their discussion and analysis of the uskok phenomenon.

Venetian authors, such as Barbaro, Minucci, and Sarpi, were united in the opinion that the uskoks were essentially thieves and brigands, plundering and raiding to satisfy their own greed, intent on enriching themselves without the fatigue of honest toil and concealing their rapacity beneath the hypocritical cloak of crusade against the Turk. This combination of greed and idleness was also attributed to their womenfolk, who, if not the original cause of uskok raiding, at any rate actively encouraged it in their desire for a lazy life of luxury.

> The women never touch a needle, a spindle or any other task, instead devoting themselves to rouse their husbands with opprobrious words to go a-pillaging, living in the hope of booty until their return, and playing ball and tip-cat [*pandol*] in the public streets.[5]

And

> The women of Senj, used to wallowing in idleness and to dresses of scarlet and silk, without any knowledge of the use of distaffs and spindles, perpetually urged their husbands to go out to plunder, reproaching them with their idleness and the needs of the house.[6]

Both Barbaro and Minucci constructed their criticisms around the proverbial symbols of the diligent woman (and Barbaro places them in opposition to the ball and bat used in frivolous games). If the needle and spindle, the basis of the virtuous housewife's domestic economy, were neglected by the women of Senj, could their husbands be expected to bend their backs to mattock and shovel to supply the town's economy?

These Venetian authors explain the uskoks' success in their career of crime—in spite of constant Venetian vigilance—through the help given them by the peasantry of Dalmatia; the protection extended them by powerful Hapsburg patrons; and even, according to some authors, their mastery of supernatural forces. Kinship ties were one of the reasons that the uskoks were able to rely on the assistance and cooperation of the Dalmatian population under Venetian rule, according to both Minucci and Sarpi. However, these ties are presented not as natural bonds of interest and affection rising out of family connections, but rather as alliances forced on the families through the abduction of their daughters.

> Wherever there was a marriageable daughter of good family on the islands or the maritime territories of Dalmatia, they came unexpectedly, by night or at other more opportune times, and forced the house, abducting her and marrying her to one of them. Then they made peace, and made excuses for the act with her relatives (who had no remedy when the damage had already been done), and tried to convince them to recognize [the uskoks] as relations, and to favor their affairs with information, warnings, and other help.[7]

That such a marriage was not a love match is a secondary issue here, though we shall see that at least one of these writers did consider sentiment a necessary element lacking in uskok marriages. But the wishes and desires of an eligible daughter were not always a consideration in cementing an alliance of interests with marriage among the great families of Venice either. However, to coerce the consent of the girl's family was to turn the traditional marriage alliance on its head. To Minucci such a marriage was "contrary to human and divine law." Sarpi too presents such uskok marriages as a mockery and a perversion of the ideal of marriage.

But however twisted the foundations of these and other uskok marriages in the eyes of the early seventeenth century, some wives depicted by our Venetian authors were nevertheless tied to their criminal husbands by bonds of loyalty as strong as those of more legitimate unions. Paolo Sarpi, in particular, attempting to explain the ineffectiveness of the Hapsburg commissioners in disciplining the unruly uskoks, gives several examples of uskok wives interceding with the authorities for their husbands in prison, and buying their lives by bribing the greedy commissioners with booty.[8] Their loyalty and courage in interceding for an imprisoned husband, which in other circumstances would be praiseworthy, is here rendered suspect by the fact that these women were interceding, in Sarpi's eyes, for hardened criminals, "wicked indeed, and deserving every punishment."

These and other reasons for continued uskok immunity from retribution were not enough for some Venetian authors, whose wounded self-esteem sought a supernatural explanation for the failure of continued Venetian attempts to rid the seas of the uskok menace. Hence the constant reiteration of the accusation that the uskok women indulged in magic and witchcraft, usually used to explain the sudden storms and the *bura* of the Kvarner:

> These women claim that by setting certain fires in the caves in the valley near the city, they can suddenly rouse a stormy north-east wind whenever they like, and say that in this way they have saved the uskoks from falling into the hands of the [Venetian] fleet many times.[9]

Not all our authors subscribe to such superstitions, but they nevertheless repeat the story, casting doubt on the beliefs and practices of the women of Senj while preserving for themselves an air of detached rationality.

So far, these examples have illustrated the ways that Venetian authors used uskok women to explain specific aspects of the uskok phenomenon—the causes of uskok raiding and the reasons for its continued success. More generally, these authors used images of unwomanly women to symbolize their vision of the topsy-turvy nature of uskok society, described in much the same way as contemporaries imagined a putative criminal counterculture, as a distorted reflection of normal society.[10]

It should be noted that the articulation of this Venetian vision of Senj is not limited to the description of women, but regularly finds expression in discussions of many other aspects of uskok life—family honor, for example:

> The most honored families, and those considered of the greatest merit, are those who for the longest time have traced their origins in a continuous descent from those hanged, cut to pieces, and foully massacred in other ways in their pursuits.[11]

In the world turned upside-down of uskok Senj, where to steal was not a sin, and where living in peace was cowardice, women neglected the use of spindle and needle to take up arms and man the walls like Amazons. Vettor Barbaro depicts the Senj women as completely devoid of sentiment, so that when they hear the news of "a misadventure with the gallows or some similar sort of wretched death that their husbands often meet with," they take their share of the booty and mourn their late husband for a few hours, "but even as they cry they negotiate a new marriage, so that for the most part they celebrate the funeral rites of one husband and a wedding with another on the very same day." Among the many widows who had gone through three or four husbands, Barbaro reported "there was one, not old, who had had eleven."[12] In contrast to the ideas of some historians who have questioned the value placed on sentiment in marriage in early modern Europe, Barbaro here plays on the evident expectations of his readers that marriage should not be a purely economic arrangement, that women should be emotionally attached to their husbands, and that there should be a seemly period of mourning at the death of a spouse.

The cold-hearted women of Senj, however, unmoved by the death of a husband, were (literally) transformed into bloodthirsty harpies by the death of an enemy, such as the hated Hapsburg commissioner sent to discipline Senj, Joseph Rabatta. Minucci describes them as, "after various maledictions, licking with their tongues the blood that issued from his wounds" as his body lay in church after his murder.[13] This story was picked up by a number of historians of the uskoks, who added such embellishments as the women of Senj "bowling his head about in the mud of the street for several days, singing verses in mockery of his name."[14] These atrocities, like those of their husbands (usually associated with rituals of revenge), were used to demonstrate the uskoks' reversal of the norms of society:

> All those things which are universally detested as contrary to every humanity, are always praised by them as proper to men of valor.[15]

The image of women presented in the defense of the uskoks by Giovanni of Fermo stands in complete opposition to the viragos of the Venetian authors. This author presents the uskoks as defenders of Christendom against the Infidel, forced into raiding by poverty, want, and the short-sighted self-interest of Venice. Nevertheless, according to Giovanni, the uskoks are careful, even when pressed by necessity, to distinguish between illicit Christian goods and licit booty (the goods of Turks, Jews, and Venetian merchants compromised by collaboration with the Turk). Like the uskoks as a whole, the uskok women are forced into an awkward role by circumstances, and adapt as best they can. When these Senj women "appear on the earthworks with arms . . . handling the arquebus as well as the principal men of Senj and their husbands," it is not to reverse gender roles in defiance of divine law, but "out of necessity," because of the attacks of the Turks.[16]

Giovanni advances the defense of the Catholic faith as the main motive for the uskoks' actions, and he devotes much space to illustrations of the uskoks' piety. Among his other anecdotes is the tale of an unexpected kiss at Christmas mass in Senj. As he recounts it,

> a very beautiful gentlewoman of about 45, among the principal women of the city, came up to me and offered me her mouth, and kissed me, and in order not to be rude I kissed her, and she added "Bože vam daj dobar Božić" [God grant you a merry Christmas]. I thought she was crazy,

but his companion goes on to explain it as an ancient Christian custom, the kiss of peace, exchanged at the masses of Christmas and Easter (a pious practice, as

Giovanni notes, long since abandoned in Italy). All this kissing should not be interpreted as evidence of licentiousness.

> Because certain Italians didn't content themselves with only one kiss, and wanted to embrace the women and also add words that were inappropriate to such ceremonies, it was decided that in future the women would exchange kisses among themselves, and that the men would do likewise.

His friend Antonio adds disapprovingly that

> Italians always, or most of the time, introduce some evil usage wherever they go.[17]

Giovanni's description of Christian traditionalism and purity in Senj leads here without a blink into a discussion of the moral purity of the women of Senj (both contrasted with the corrupt practices of those Italians who criticize the uskoks' Christian motives).

Giovanni also uses the high value placed on the purity of Senj women to illustrate the moral qualities of the uskoks—again in contrast to Italian morals. Antonio raises the question, remarking insinuatingly that he knows "that the Slav women can be good companions from those that have tried them." Giovanni's response is to relate

> something that will astonish you. I have never seen such a thing elsewhere, not in Rijeka, nor in all Dalmatia, nor in Italy. It is only to be seen in Senj: in that city you will not find a single prostitute, even if you wished to pay a gold piece,

and then, lest this be too much to swallow,

> I'm speaking of the old city, but those who do exist, are foreign, from other countries.[18]

He goes on to discuss the jealousy with which the uskoks guard the honor of their women, so that should one "satisfy her whims, even one time," she would be killed by a relative. He then relates an incident that took place in his time in Rijeka, in which the pretty wife of a citizen of Senj was abducted by force and then released by her ravisher on condition that her husband accept her back. Though the husband was given a handsome bribe to sweeten his dishonor, he nevertheless slaughtered the woman and sent her body back to her abductor, promising to murder him as well.[19] Though Giovanni remarks only that this was because of "the value which they place on the honor of their women," he also implies that the uskoks are equally concerned with their own honor and that of their families, preferring to sacrifice even that which is dearest to them, rather than submit to dishonor—a principle which is mirrored in his account by their refusal to bow to political expediency and refrain from attacking the Turk in spite of the threats of the Venetians and promises of their Hapsburg masters.

All the works that I have discussed here are essentially moral fables, presenting the actions of the uskoks in terms of good and evil. All of them use images of women to stand for the larger uskok society, to symbolize the moral qualities which are attributed to the uskok phenomenon as a whole. For the Venetian authors who see the uskoks as consistently transgressing both human and divine law, the vignettes of unwomanly women among the uskoks are used rhetorically to reinforce the image of Senj's topsy-turvy world. For Giovanni of Fermo, the purity and honor of the women of Senj stand as a metaphor for the Christian purity and honor of the uskoks as a whole.

The extent to which women are used as symbols in these histories leaves us in some doubt about the ways in which women actually participated in the uskok phenomenon. Though all these writers offer the historian valuable clues to the role of women among the uskoks—their importance as reinforcements, the way they acted as vehicles for kinship alliances, the attitudes to their honor—the way in which this evidence has been selected and presented for its symbolic value makes it partial and suspect. Though these histories claim to give us the truth about uskok life, they have the effect of hiding the actual lives of uskok women (in particular) behind a veil of rhetoric. How is the historian to uncover the reality of women's lives in uskok Senj?

The loss of the city archives makes it impossible to reconstruct many aspects of the lives of Senj's women—issues that might have been illuminated by such records as parish registers, testaments, property inventories, and civil and criminal suits must remain dark. But it is possible to find references to the roles of uskok women in the reams of documents produced by the Venetian administration in Dalmatia. Because of the difficulties the uskoks caused Venice, the Dalmatian *provveditori* regularly recorded news of their activities. Their references to uskok women have a less overtly polemical purpose (though they are not devoid of rhetorical devices), and cast a slightly different light on their roles. In particular I would like to use these sources to reexamine two of the areas touched upon by our polemicists: the role of women as marriage partners, and the role they played as active participants in uskok actions.

The Venetian authors discussed above were right to emphasize the importance of kinship ties in shaping the relationship between the uskoks of Senj and the rural population of Dalmatia and the Ottoman hinterland. These ties, however, were both more extensive and stronger than Paolo Sarpi, for one, was willing to admit in his discussion of marriage by abduction. Many uskoks, particularly those who had only recently left their homes and emigrated to Senj (as many did throughout the entire period of uskok activity in the sixteenth and seventeenth centuries), remained integrated into a network of family relations that retained their meaning even after they had left their native village, influencing not only the areas that they raided, and whom they attacked, but also where and with whom they could count on finding support and shelter. Reports from officials responsible for preventing uskok raids across Venetian territory in Dalmatia constantly emphasize the aid given the uskoks by the Dalmatians "who have relatives and friends among them," thus excusing their own failures.[20] Venetian attempts at retribution occasionally make it possible to unravel these relationships. For example, an uskok attack on Makarska in 1556 was carried out with the aid of men from the island of Brač, among whom was one Vice Stipetić. When he was seized as an uskok spy, the explanation for his acts was that he had two brothers in Senj.[21]

Marriage was an important means by which the uskoks maintained and extended these family ties among the rural population. The dispatches of Venetian commanders in the Adriatic do occasionally mention uskok abductions of marriageable girls from the Dalmatian islands, as in 1597, when a band of uskoks is reported as having

> abducted by force a young girl of marriageable age from her own house . . . and forced the priest of that village (Novalja) to wed her forcibly to one of them, and took her away with them in their bark.[22]

As in this example, the emphasis in the incidents, as reported by the families of the girls, is usually on the uskok use of force. One case which is a little better documented, however, hints that forcible abduction could be a ruse in order to escape the awkwardness which a conventional courtship and wedding might bring upon the family (in much the same way that abduction (*otmica*) was used in other neighboring areas to bypass inconvenient marriage conventions).

In 1606 Justina Vuković, daughter of Vicenzo Vuković of the village of Bol on Brač, was abducted by a group of uskoks. They wanted to force the village priest to perform a wedding then and there, but he had hidden in fear, so they carried her off to Senj, accompanied by Vicenzo Margitić, her relative, who went along with Justina in order to represent her family at the wedding in Senj. This was presented by the Venetian authorities as an abduction, but the presence of a relative for the ritual purposes of the wedding hints that the truth was more complicated. It emerged that Justina and her uskok suitor had "long been in love, as he had already been asking for her hand in marriage for some time." Her father had refused a formal agreement (fearing the penalties imposed by the Venetian authorities for collaboration with the uskoks). It appears that this "abduction" provided a face-saving solution, allowing Justina to wed her lover with the quiet support of her family, but without incurring Venetian retribution.[23] (To stray a little from the chronological boundaries of this paper, the nineteenth-century Croatian writer August Šenoa opens his novel of uskok patriotism and Venetian intrigue, *Čuvaj se senjske ruke* [1875], with an uskok abduction of a bride, playing on the nineteenth-century romantic ideal of marriage as a union of sentiment against all obstacles, and contrasting the uskok way with that of the corrupt Venetian suitor, gone awooing in hope of material gain. A neat reversal of the meanings Minucci and Sarpi found in uskok abductions!)

These marriages were exceptional, documented precisely because they were out of the ordinary. Innumerable less sensational marriages also sustained the links between the uskoks and the population of the countryside. Some evidence about them can be found in the interrogations of the wives (and widows) of Senj, picked up by the Venetian authorities on their visits to relatives in Dalmatia—women like Vicenza, widow of Vicenzo Salinović of Senj, and the mother-in-law of a notorious uskok, Ivan Bosotina, who was interrogated in 1600 as she returned home to her relatives (possibly deprived of her pension as an uskok widow by the new regulations introduced by the reforming Hapsburg commissioner Joseph Rabatta), "to eke out my life as best I can."[24] Women like these mediated between the uskoks and the people of their native villages—though it should not be assumed that such communication always meant complete understanding between the two groups. When a group of uskoks raided Bol in 1599, Kamerica, the widow of one of their number, was unable to prevent the revenge murder of a man of the village. "When she began to call these uskoks by name, they wounded her too in indignation."[25] But as we shall see, women like these played an important part as go-betweens, journeying from Senj to their family homes with a freedom that their menfolk could often not risk, passing under the noses of Venetian guards to collect ransoms, carry news, and collect information.

It is perhaps worth mentioning that marriage did not serve only to integrate the uskoks into a wider Dalmatian society. It could also serve to integrate new uskoks into Senj society. Scattered references illustrate the way that marriages between uskoks and the daughters of the old Senj families helped to blur the boundaries of civil and uskok Senj, uniting all its members in a single, mutually profitable society organized for raiding.[26] Marriage to a Senj woman could also be used to bind a new recruit more closely to the uskok collective, as was done in 1607, when an Albanian Muslim was accepted into the uskoks. He was first baptized, and then to cement his new ties, he was given a Senj girl as a bride.[27] In contrast to Minucci and Sarpi, the Provveditore Generale in 1612 found it useful to emphasize the strength of such ties, noting morosely that his plans to detach a young shipbuilder (banished from Piran for smuggling salt) from the uskoks with the offer of a pardon would probably fail, because he had now married a woman of Senj.[28]

This discussion of women as uskok marriage partners has largely treated women as the passive objects of marriage strategies, circulating among the uskoks of Senj and the people of Dalmatia and the hinterland as the instruments (however imperfect) of social cohesion, fulfilling the role that Levi-Strauss has suggested brides share with goods and services and with linguistic messages: a medium of communication within a social group. But the women of Senj also participated much more actively in uskok undertakings. The best documented aspect of their involvement is financial. The women of Senj did indeed have an interest in uskok booty, but in ways that went beyond the petulant demand for fripperies ascribed to them by our Venetian authors. Women with the means to do so invested in uskok expeditions, joining syndicates of private investors who supplied the uskoks with provisions in return for proportionate shares of the booty on their return. In particular, widows of uskoks were able to use the pensions they received from the Hapsburgs in recognition of their husbands' services as capital for such investments. When Rabatta took away these pensions as part of his reorganization of Senj, it caused intense resentment (and the uskoks justified their rebellion against Rabatta in part by the hardship it had caused to such "poor women," hoping by this reference to evoke pity from the Hapsburg officials).[29]

Part of the booty taken on uskok raids was made up of captives to be ransomed. The women of Senj played an active role in the trade in ransoms, buying up the rights to prisoners and arranging their release themselves. The uskoks themselves noted in their complaint against Rabatta's misrule in Senj that

> women bought [captives], and intended to return them to Turkey as ransom for their husbands and sons, who had been captured by the Turks.[30]

Such negotiations on behalf of family and friends in foreign captivity was a common practice all along the border. Senj women seem not to have confined their speculation in ransoms solely to the redemption of husbands and sons, however. This could be a lucrative trade, as demonstrated by the price asked for the release of a Morlak girl from the Trogir hinterland, Klara Petrović. In 1558 she was redeemed from the hands of the wife of Ivan of Senj, an uskok vojvoda, for 75 ducats, a sizeable sum.[31]

It is also in connection with prisoners that we have a glimpse of the more strenuous part taken by Senj women in uskok life. Women were often responsible for guarding prisoners awaiting redemption in Senj, particularly when large uskok expeditions left the fortress otherwise undefended. In 1597 some Ottoman captives tried to seize such an opportunity to take the fortress, killing many of the women in the city,

> but this was seen by a woman who was there on guard, and she closed the doors of the citadel.

On this occasion, as on several others, the captives fled, to the loss of those who held the rights to their ransoms.[32] It was also, as mentioned above, the women who often traveled outside Senj to arrange and collect these ransoms. The advantages they had in this were summed up by a Venetian official:

> Because it is not so easy for their men to do so, the Senj women come under the cover of their female sex, and under the name of relatives in the places of Your Serenity [Venice], where they make their contracts, receiving their payments from the Turkish subjects in cash or in goods, on account of their ransoms.[33]

This type of activity—acting as go-betweens, collecting ransoms, gathering information—is the best documented aspect of women's involvement in uskok actions. Many witnesses testify to the presence of Senj women (usually the wives of important uskoks) on excursions devoted to trading in captives and buying goods in Dalmatia. As far as official evidence goes, it seems to have been more unusual for these women to take part in plundering and raiding expeditions—as our preconceptions of women's roles might lead us to expect. But there is one tantalizingly brief description of a woman leading an uskok raid—against the territory of Dubrovnik, in revenge for the murder of her husband. This was the wife of Vojvoda Juraj Daničič, who had been killed in 1571 in an encounter with the troops of the Republic of Ragusa—whether by treachery, as the uskoks claimed, or in the heat of an armed clash, as the Ragusans explained it, is still unsettled.[34] Shortly after this incident the dispatches of the Republic's representatives were filled with reports of raids undertaken in revenge for this death—raids led by Daničič's widow and their young son. There were rumors on Korcula that

> Daničič's wife has sold everything she has in the world in order to gather a great number of uskoks to send to pillage the Ragusans, and they say that she has gathered together two thousand altogether.

This, the writer thought, was an exaggeration—nevertheless, Daničič's wife and son, with several barks of uskoks, were reported to have raided Mljet and to have murdered and plundered elsewhere on the territory of the Republic.[35] Here the information on this woman ends. Although other writers (notably Giovanni of Fermo) describe Senj's revenge against the Republic of Ragusa, describing this as the beginning of Daničič's son's career as an uskok vojvoda, his wife is not mentioned again. Identified only as "Daničič's wife," we do not even know her name. Indeed, given the silence about her exploits elsewhere, it is open to question whether in fact she did take an active part in the uskok revenge against Ragusa. Could she too have been mobilized for rhetorical purposes, to impress Ragusa's subjects and allies with the ferocity and intemperate character of the uskoks?

This abruptly truncated episode illustrates the limitations of documentary evidence about the lives of the women of Senj. Both in polemical discussions and in administrative sources these women are largely anonymous, leaving behind little or no written evidence of their lives except when their acts impinged upon the interests of authors or bureaucrats, each with their own particular purposes for discussing aspects of women's experience. In the works of contemporary polemicists uskok women appear as familiar tropes—pious wives or armed viragos, depending on the stance of the writer. But in spite of their ostensibly more neutral character, routine bureaucratic documents are not innocent of using images of women for rhetorical purposes either. This insight should encourage us to look more closely at the images of women elsewhere in discussions of pirate communities, and the purposes they served. Nevertheless, these sources do give us some sense of the place of women among the uskoks: as symbols, as mediators between the uskoks and the outside world, and as members of the uskok community in their own right.

NOTES

1. C. W. Bracewell, *The Uskoks of Senj: Piracy, Banditry, and Holy War in the Sixteenth-century Adriatic* (Ithaca: Cornell University Press, 1992) is an attempt at this sort of frontier "history from below."

2. Minuccio Minucci, *Historia degli Uscochi . . . Co i progressi di quella gente sino all'anno 1602* (Venice? 1603?); Paolo Sarpi, "Aggionta all'Historia degli Uscochi di Minuccio Minucci Arcivescovo di Zara: Continuata sin'all'Anno M.D.XIII; Supplimento dell'Historia degli Uscochi di Minuccio Minucci Arcivescovo di Zara, and Trattato di Pace et Accommodamento . . . ," in *La Repubblica di Venezia, la Casa d'Austria e gli Uscocchi,* ed. G. Cozzi and L. Cozzi (Bari: Laterza e figli, 1965).

3. There are copies in the Correr Library in Venice (Cod. Cicogna 2855), and in the Historijski Arhiv, Zadar (hereafter H.A.Z.), Ostavština Šime Ljubića, 2/33.

4. This manuscript, discovered in the Medici Archives in Florence, where Giovanni was apparently employed in the 1620s, was published by F. Rački, as "Prilozi za poviest hrvatskih uskoka," *Starine JAZU* (Zagreb), 9 (1877): 172–256.

5. H.A.Z., Ostavština Šime Ljubića, 2/33, Vettor Barbaro (hereafter Barbaro), 281[v].

6. Minucci, *Historia*, 16–17.

7. Sarpi, "Aggionta," 20. See also Minucci, *Historia*, 108, for the abduction and forced marriage of a "well-born girl" from the Zadar archipelago.

8. See Sarpi, "Aggionta," 82, for the tale of Andrija Frletić's wife, and 375 for the wife of an uskok called "Gianulla" by Sarpi.

9. Barbaro, 281[v].

10. See for example the contemporary descriptions of criminals in terms of countercultures in P. Camporesi, ed., *Il Libro dei vagabondi* (Turin: G. Einaudi, 1973).

11. Barbaro, 281–281[v].

12. Barbaro, 281[v].

13. Minucci, *Historia*, 111. The story was reported soon after Rabatta's murder. K.

Horvat, *Monumenta historiam Uscocchorum illustrantia,* Monumenta spectantia historiam Slavorum meridionalium, vol. 32 (Zagreb: JAZU, 1910), 2:2–3.

14. Bibliotheca Marciana, Ms. It. VII, 877 (=8651), "Relazioni delle cose d'Uscocchi" by Girolamo Ptaston.

15. Nicolò Contarini, "Le historie venetiane," in *Il Doge Nicolò Contarini: Ricerche sul patriziato veneziano agli inizi del seicento,* ed. Gaetano Cozzi (Venice: Istituto per la collaborazione culturale, 1958), 325.

16. Rački, "Prilozi," 197.

17. Rački, "Prilozi," 236–37.

18. Rački, "Prilozi," 235.

19. Rački, "Prilozi," 235–36.

20. K. Horvat, *Monumenta Uscocchorum,*1:161.

21. Archivio di Stato, Venice (hereafter A.S.V.), Senato, Secreta, Reg. 70, August 6, 1556.

22. A.S.V., Provveditori da terra e da mar 1263: May 7, 1597.

23. The relevant documents are in A.S.V., Provveditori da terra e da mar 1265: March 21, 1606 (A. Michiel, Capitano del Golfo, Šolta); Provveditori da terra e da mar 420: March 22, 1606 (Report of A. Boldù, Rector of Brač); April 15, 1606 (interrogation of Jeronim Pervaneo of Hvar); April 15, 1606 (Report of Mattio Pacifico Cenza, Split, noting that the General of Croatia, Klesl, has promised to punish those involved "according to their merits"). J. Tomić gave a highly colored version of the story in *Iz istorije senjskih uskoka, 1604–1607* (Novi Sad: 1907), 98–99.

24. A.S.V., Provveditori da terra e da mar 923: October 31, 1600.

25. H.A.Z., Arhiv Trogira, b. 25, 11/1480 (March 15, 1599).

26. Again, this is a process that cannot be clearly followed without the parish registers for the town. However, according to an eighteenth-century genealogy of the Daničič uskok family (allegedly immigrating to Senj from Bosnia in the middle of the sixteenth century), Juraj Daničič, the second uskok vojvoda of this name, married a daughter of the old Senj nobility in the 1580s, and his brother Matija Daničič another noblewoman, Katerina Mikulanić. The Mikulanić family is also described in contemporary documents as having had family ties with Posedarski, an uskok vojvoda (and a noble of Zadar). See, for example, the documents published by M. Magdić in "Prilozi za poviest starih plemičkih obitelji senjskih," *Starine JAZU* 12 (1880): 224–29.

27. A.S.V., Provveditori da terra e da mar 1313: September 28, 1607 (Report from G. A. Quadri, a spy in Senj).

28. A.S.V., Provveditori da terra e da mar 425: January 23, 1612 (A.M. Venier, Rab).

29. See R. Lopašić, *Acta historiam confinarii militaris Croatici illustrantia,* 3 vols., Monumenta spectantia historiam Slavorum meridionalium, vols. 15, 16, 20 (Zagreb: JAZU, 1884–89), 1:300–305.

30. Lopašić, *Acta historiam,* 300–305.

31. A.S.V., Provveditore sopraintendente alla camera dei confini 243, Processus Tragurii: May 3, 1558 (Testimony of Barth. Bigonich).

32. Horvat, *Monumenta uscocchorum,* 1:156.

33. A.S.V., Secreta, Materie miste notabili, 27: 1591 (B. Contarini, Capitano in Golfo).

34. Most of the relevant documents are in the Državni Arhiv, Dubrovnik (hereafter D.A.D.), Lettere Levante, vol. XXI (1571), especially 78–80; and in the dossier compiled in their own defense by the Ragusans in Diplomata et acta 16 st., 16: 466/36 (April 14, 1572). The incident has been described by V. Foretić, *Povijest Dubrovnika,* 2 vols. (Zagreb: Nakladni zavod MH, 1980), 1: 473 ff.

35. D.A.D., Diplomata et acta 16 st., 11: 450–i/22 (August 3, 1571); 450–d/8 (August 5, 1571).

Contributors

John L. Anderson, now retired, was Senior Lecturer in Economics at La Trobe University in Melbourne, Australia. His research interests focused on economic history and maritime history and he has written several works on piracy in world history.

John C. Appleby is Senior Lecturer in History at Liverpool Hope University College in Britain. His research interests include English maritime history and colonial history from 1500 to 1700. He has edited *A Calendar of Material Relating to Ireland from the High Court of Admiralty Examinations, 1536–1641* (Dublin: Irish Manuscripts Commission, 1992) and, with Paul Dalton, *Government, Religion and Society in Northern England 1000–1700* (Thrupp, Stroud, Gloucestershire: Sutton Publishing, 1997).

Wendy Bracewell (Ph.D. Stanford) is Senior Lecturer in History at SSEES/UCL, University of London, and currently serves as Director of the Centre for South-East European Studies. She has written on early modern Balkan frontier societies, focusing especially on raiding communities, border warfare, and brigandage. She is currently collaborating on a joint project on violence and the Triplex Confinium. Her book *The Uskoks of Senj: Piracy, Banditry and Holy War in the Sixteenth-Century Adriatic* (Ithaca: Cornell University Press, 1992) has recently been translated into Croatian. In addition she has published studies of gender and nationalism in South-Eastern Europe, and on historiography and national ideology.

J. S. Bromley, who died in 1985, was Emeritus Professor of Modern History at the University of Southampton in Britain. Over a long academic life between 1950 and his death, he edited several collections, including *The Rise of Great Britain and Russia, 1688–1715/25,* volume 6 of *The New Cambridge Modern History* (Cambridge: Cambridge University Press, 1970), and *The Manning of the Royal Navy: Selected Public Pamphlets, 1693–1873, Publications of the Navy Records Society;* vol. 119 (London: Navy Records Society, 1976) along with more than forty articles, many of which were republished in J. S. Bromley, *Corsairs and Navies, 1660–1760* (London: Hambledon Press, 1987).

B. R. Burg is Professor of History at Arizona State University and a former Director of the American Studies Research Centre in Hyderabad, India. He is the author of numerous books and articles, including *Sodomy and the Pirate Tradition: English Sea Rovers in the Seventeenth-Century Caribbean* and *An American Seafarer in the Age of Sail: The Erotic Diaries of Philip C. Van Buskirk, 1851–1870.*

Kenneth J. Kinkor received his B.A. in History at Loras College in Dubuque, Iowa, in 1976, and thereafter conducted postgraduate study at the University of Iowa and Illinois State University. He has been Historian for the Whydah Project since 1986, and currently also serves as Director of the Whydah Exhibit in Provincetown, Massachusetts. The Whydah, wrecked off Cape Cod in 1717, is the only pirate shipwreck site so far authenticated. Mr. Kinkor frequently lectures and writes on topics related to the colonial maritime history of New England, as well as on the history of piracy from 1678 to 1728. He resides in Eastham, Massachusetts.

Gonçal López Nadal has doctorates in history from the Universitat Autònoma de Barcelona (1984) and Leeds University (1995). He is currently a lecturer on the history of economic institutions at the Universitat de les Illes Balears, in Palma de Mallorca, Spain, where he specializes in maritime history. His research is focused on commercial structures in the Mediterranean between the sixteenth and eighteenth centuries and particularly on corsairing and the relations between European and North African states. He is the author of *El corsarisme mallorqui a la Mediterránea occidental 1652–1698; un comerç forçat* (Barcelona: Conselleria d'Educació i Cultura de les Balears, 1986) and editor of *El Comerç Alternatiu: Corsarisme i contraban (ss.xv–xviii)* (Palma de Mallorca: Conselleria de Cultura, Educació i Esports, Govern Balear, 1990), and author of some thirty published articles.

Dian Murray is Professor of Chinese History and Associate Dean at the University of Notre Dame. She is fluent in Chinese and has traveled to both Taiwan and the People's Republic of China many times. She is the author of two books and more than twenty articles on Chinese history. Her first book, *Pirates of the South China Coast, 1790–1810,* brought to light information on a previously unknown confederation of Sino-Vietnamese pirates who sailed the South China Sea during the late eighteenth and early nineteenth centuries. This book has been translated into Chinese as *Hua Nan Hai Dao* by Liu Ping and published by the Press of the Chinese Academy of the Social Sciences. She is also the author of numerous articles.

C. R. Pennell is al-Tajir Lecturer in Middle Eastern History at the University of Melbourne. He did his Ph.D. at Leeds, Britain on the Rif War in Morocco in the 1920s. He has taught in Libya, Turkey, Singapore, and Kenya. He is author of *A Country with a Government and a Flag: The Rif War in Morocco, 1921–1926* (Wisbech: MENAS Press, 1986), *Piracy and Diplomacy in Seventeenth Century North Africa: The Journals of Thomas Baker, English Consul in Tripoli, 1677–1685* (London and Madison: Associated University Presses, 1989), and *Morocco since 1830* (London: Hurst and New York: New York University Press, 2000).

Anne Pérotin-Dumon has a doctorate in history from the Sorbonne (Paris I) in France. She has worked in universities in the United States, France, Spain, and Latin America. She is now teaching at the Instituto de Historia of the Pontificia Universidad Católica in Santiago, Chile. She researches the 16th- to 18th-century Caribbean and is author of *La ville aux Iles, la ville dans l'île Basse-Terre et Pointe-à-Pitre Guadeloupe, 1650–1820* (Paris: Karthala, 2000) and *Être patriote sous les tropiques: La Guadeloupe, la colonialisation, et la révolution (1789–1794)* (Basse-Terre: Societé d'histoire de la Guadeloupe, 1985). She is also author of an electronic book, *El género en historia*.

Marcus Rediker teaches history at the University of Pittsburgh. He is author of the award-winning book, *Between the Devil and the Deep Blue Sea: Merchant Seamen, Pirates, and the Anglo American Maritime World, 1700–1750* (Cambridge: Cambridge University Press, 1987). His new book, coauthored with Peter Linebaugh and entitled *The Many-Headed Hydra: Adventures of the Atlantic Proletariat*, will be published by Beacon Press in 2000.

David J. Starkey is Wilson Family lecturer in Maritime History at the University of Hull in Britain. His doctorate, from the University of Exeter, was published as *British Privateering Enterprise in the Eighteenth Century* (Exeter: University of Exeter Press, 1990). He also edited, with E. S. van Eyck van Heslinga and J. A. de Moor, *Pirates and Privateers: New Perspectives on the War on Trade in the Eighteenth and Nineteenth Centuries* (Exeter: University of Exeter Press, 1997) and has written extensively on privateering and piracy.

Permissions

C. R. Pennell, "Brought to Book—Reading about Pirates" appeared in part as "Who Needs Pirate Heroes?" in *Northern Mariner/Le Marin du Nord* 8, no. 2 (1998): 61–79.

Anne Pérotin-Dumon, "The Pirate and the Emperor: Power and Law on the Seas, 1450–1850," first appeared in *The Political Economy of Merchant Empires*, ed. James D. Tracy (Cambridge: Cambridge University Press, 1991).

C. R. Pennell, "The Geography of Piracy: Northern Morocco in the Mid-Nineteenth Century," first appeared in *Journal of Historical Geography* 20, no. 3 (1994): 272–282.

David J. Starkey, "The Origins and Regulation of Eighteenth-Century British Privateering," first appeared in *Pressgangs and Privateers*, ed. Tony Barrow (Whitley Bay: Bewick Press, 1993), 40–51.

John L. Anderson, "Piracy and World History: An Economic Perspective on Maritime Predation," first appeared in *Journal of World History* 6, no. 2 (1995): 175–199.

David J. Starkey, "Pirates and Markets," first appeared in *The Market for Seamen in the Age of Sail*, ed. Lewis R. Fischer (St. John's, Newfoundland: International Maritime Economic History Association, 1994), 59–80.

Gonçal López Nadal, "Corsairing as a Commercial System: The Edges of Legitimate Trade," first appeared as "El corsarismo en las estructuras mercantiles: las fronteras del convencionalismo," in *El Comerç Alternatiu: Corsarisme i contraban*, ed. Gonçal López Nadal (Palma de Mallorca: Conselleria de Cultura, Educació i Esports, Govern Balear, 1990), 267–276. It was translated for this edition by C. R. Pennell.

Marcus Rediker, "The Seaman as Pirate: Plunder and Social Banditry at Sea," first appeared in its present form as a chapter in *Between the Devil and the Deep Blue Sea: Merchant Seamen, Pirates and the Anglo American Maritime World 1700–1750* (Cambridge: Cambridge University Press, 1987).

J. S. Bromley, "Outlaws at Sea, 1660–1720: Liberty, Equality, and Fraternity among the Caribbean Freebooters," first appeared in *History from Below: Studies in Popular Protest and Popular Ideology in Honour of George Rudé*, ed. Frederick Krantz (Montreal: Concordia University, 1986). This collection was republished in 1988 by Basil Blackwell in Oxford and New York and the article was reprinted in J. S. Bromley, *Corsairs and Navies, 1660–1760* (London: Hambledon Press, 1987), 1–21.

Kenneth J. Kinkor, "Black Men under the Black Flag" has not previously been published.

B. R. Burg, "The Buccaneer Community," first appeared as chapter 5 of his book *Sodomy and the Pirate Tradition: English Sea Rovers in the Seventeenth-Century Caribbean* (New York: New York University Press, 1983). The second edition was published in 1995.

Dian Murray, "The Practice of Homosexuality among the Pirates of Late Eighteenth- and Early Nineteenth-Century China," first appeared in *International Journal of Maritime History* 4, no. 1 (1992): 121–130, and her "Cheng I Sao in Fact and Fiction," in *Bold in Her Breeches: Women Pirates across the Ages*, ed. Jo Stanley (London: HarperCollins, 1995), 203–239.

John C. Appleby,"Women and Piracy in Ireland: From Gráinne O'Malley to Anne Bonny," first appeared in *Women in Early Modern Ireland*, ed. Margaret MacCurtain and Mary O'Dowd (Edinburgh and New York: Edinburgh University Press and Columbia University Press, 1991).

Marcus Rediker, "Liberty beneath the Jolly Roger: The Lives of Anne Bonny and Mary Read, Pirates," in *Iron Men, Wooden Women: Gender and Seafaring in the Atlantic World, 1700–1920*, ed. Margaret S. Creighton and Lisa Norling (Baltimore: Johns Hopkins University Press, 1996).

Wendy Bracewell, "Women among the Uskoks: Literary Images and Reality," first appeared in *MOST* (Zagreb), 2 (1988): 44–51.

Index

Lightning Source UK Ltd.
Milton Keynes UK
UKOW05f1849161117
312874UK00012B/400/P